INTRODUCTION TO THE PHILOSOPHY OF HISTORY

Introduction to the Philosophy of History

AN ESSAY ON THE LIMITS OF HISTORICAL OBJECTIVITY

RAYMOND ARON

Translated by George J. Irwin

BEACON PRESS
BOSTON

First published in France in 1938 under the title
Introduction à la philosophie de l'histoire
Revised edition 1948

First published in the United States in 1961 by Beacon Press
by arrangement with George Weidenfeld and Nicolson Ltd
First published as a Beacon Paperback in 1962

Printed in the United States of America

CONTENTS

Section IV
HISTORY AND TRUTH

INTRODUCTION

THE TITLE of this book runs the risk of misleading the reader who might identify the philosophy of history with the great systems of the beginning of the nineteenth century, so discredited today. As for the subtitle, it marks the point of departure rather than the goal of our study, and it too is ambiguous. It may, then, be well to point out briefly the object and plan of our study.

At the very beginning let it be understood that the word 'objectivity' is not to be taken in its common sense. We disregard the individual preferences of the historian; we are considering, as it were, an ideal historian. Objectivity does not mean impartiality, but universality. At a certain stage of our experimental knowledge, a physical law compels universal recognition. Can the same validity, at a certain stage of scholarship, be attributed to an historical reconstruction?

We exclude from our investigation anything approaching the proof of facts or the criticism of texts. We assume the strictly scientific character of these preliminary steps. Expressed in simpler terms, our study deals only with synthesis (choice, interpretation, the organization of the material). We also disregard the artistic setting, the problems of expression. We assume that the account is reduced to a series of connected judgments. We are aware of the extent to which such a device varies from reality, but we, nonetheless, believe it is legitimate; tacitly accepted by nearly all who have dealt with methodology, it is indispensable as soon as one poses the question of truth in history or the social sciences.

It is true that the necessity of such a question may be challenged. It will be objected that, deriving from an academic context, it is foreign to authentic history, and may well distort its nature.

Let it be noted to begin with that we do not propose to measure historical knowledge by an *a priori* criterion. We do not try to reduce it to a type of knowledge proclaimed in advance as the only truly scientific one. Quite otherwise, we follow the natural movement which proceeds from knowledge of self to that of the collective development. We use a descriptive, or, if one prefers, a phenomenological method. We never separate knowledge from reality, since, in any case, man's consciousness of the past is one of the essential characteristics of history itself.

As for the exact question of the *limits of objectivity*: it merges with the *critical* or *transcendental* question. But instead of the Kantian formula: 'Under what conditions is historical knowledge possible?' we shall ask: 'Is a universally valid science of history possible? To what extent?' Lacking a science of history whose existence would be universally accepted, we substitute the search for *limits* for that of *bases*. (We have discussed elsewhere this question of a critique by some German authors of *theories of history*.)

But, it will be objected, the danger of being arbitrary will not be obviated. Is transcendental analysis adaptable to the structure of the historical object? It is indeed doubtful, and we shall try to show that, as it has been practised by the Southwest German school, this type of analysis does not permit the resolution of the problems of the philosophy of history. But the question as stated, despite its traditional form, aims at the central point of a theory of history. It implies no prejudice, nor postulate, and expresses the doubt which inevitably overcomes the individual who reflects upon his position as a historical being wishing to become a historian.

Scientific truth is separate from the consciousness which expressed it because, within a certain limit, it is eternally valid. Is this true for a historical reconstruction? Does not the historian express both himself and his time in his vision of the past? Is it the man of one epoch or a transcendental ego that is the subject of this science? Is the latter separable from all philosophy? Is it not bound up with the historical present and condemned to change with it? In other words, we are wondering whether the science of history, like the natural sciences, develops according to a rhythm of accumulation and progress, or whether on the contrary each society rewrites its history because it chooses for itself and re-creates its own past.

Our study develops simultaneously on three planes, which we call, to simplify matters, *epistemological, transcendental,* and *philosophical.* We shall not examine special methods. We shall try to establish the truth of the most general propositions from which a methodology would be developed (in fact, methods so vary according to countries and individuals, that another book would be needed to advance from principles to their applications). Nevertheless, the plan of this book and most of its divisions, are the result of a theory of knowledge. The second and third sections deal with the two basic processes of historical thought, *understanding,* and *causal explanation*; the fourth is an attempted synthesis, aiming at an understanding of the whole—at a *global reconstruction.*

We make no distinction between epistemology and criticism because both consider the activity of knowledge, a description of reality and the knowledge of it which we possess. And yet certain divisions secondary from the point of view of methodology: for example, those concerning the *construction of the fact, the understanding of ideas, the dissolution of the object*, are decisive with regard to transcendental analysis. Moreover (and this is essential), the connection between Sections II and III changes, depending on whether one assumes the epistemological or the critical point of view: epistemologically the two sections are co-ordinate, having as common themes, understanding (primary and spontaneous process), and causality, a more elaborate form of interpretation; critically, though, Section II follows the establishment of fields; Section III supposes them established and considers the organization of the necessary relations. The former lies, partially at least, within the scope of the task of science, demonstrating the postulates and hypotheses of which scholars are scarcely aware.

A philosophical inquiry which is the *raison d'être* of the book always underlies the description of knowledge and transcendental analysis. In Section I, we define human, as opposed to natural, history, and stress the prime fact that history for man is not something external, but the essence of his being. All the subsequent discussions are governed by the assertion that not only does man exist in history, but he bears within him the history he explores. Thus viewed, the book is dominated by the two paragraphs which open Section II and by those which close Section IV. I discover myself, I among others, and in the objective spirit I recognize the object of history as the arena of my action, spiritual history as the content of my consciousness, history as a whole as my nature. I merge myself with my development, as humanity merges with its history.

Our work, then, moves simultaneously from elementary methods of knowledge to global understanding; from establishment of categories to the organization of experience in terms of causality, and to the total account; from knowledge of self to knowledge of the past, and back to self. The theory of knowledge involves a theory of reality, leads to a certain way of philosophical thinking; pondering the historian, the philosopher reflects upon himself, observes his own historicity, even though he does not abandon the effort to transcend it.

Depending on whether the one or the other of these planes is considered, the idea of the *limits of objectivity* assumes a different value. Viewed epistemologically, we seek to distinguish the strictly objective procedures, those subject only to the rules of logic and of probability, from the subjective ones expressing an individuality or an epoch. The distinction is decisive against positivism because it makes it possible to establish the borderlines of universally valid knowledge and to preserve, beyond science, the rights, not of belief, but of philosophy. Section III, for example, demonstrates the impossibility of a purely causal historical or social science because fragmentary determinism demands a synthesis. Moreover, limited by science or immanent in it, philosophical or voluntary decisions play a part in the construction of limits, the selection of facts, and in the interpretation of the whole. Scientific knowledge remains inseparable from living man and his history.

The rights of philosophy and the historicity of knowledge show up more clearly still when viewed transcendentally. The history of a spiritual universe, art, science, philosophy, exists only for the individual who posits both the reality and the progressive unity of that universe. History implies synthetic *a priori* judgments. This last expression is partially inexact, for we do not observe on the one hand tangible matter, and on the other the subject, but an individual mind in a tradition, struggling to judge the historical movement of which he is a part. *A priori* synthetic judgment, the validity of which is not dependent on experience, comes, in fact, from reality and responds to it. The structure of a history of philosophy demands a philosophy which in its turn is historically constructed.

On the upper level, our book leads to a *historical philosophy* opposed to scientific rationalism as well as to positivism. The consideration discussed in the last Section is defined by the fact that it rejects committed thought, not by the fact that it is governed by scientific activity. This historical philosophy would make possible the understanding of actual consciousness, of the passions and conflicts which stir man, and of the historical ideas of which only an abstract transformation is given by the ideas of the moralists. Since it is a national or class philosophy, it would, in any case, be a political as well as a scientific philosophy, for the whole man is at once the philosopher and the subject matter of the philosophy.

Such a philosophy would have to rise above the opposition between the philosophies of moralists or novelists which give expression to a private existence, and those of theorists or scholars which seem foreign to the preoccupations of life. The philosophical attitude is, of course, individual, as is any attitude concerning life, and in this sense the philosopher is only one individual among others. But in so far as he considers attitudes he distinguishes the truth in them, shows the logical demands of each of them, and the significance of each in history. If this consideration were to arrive at a determination of man's true destiny it would suggest a true interpretation of the past. This would be neither a total nor an imperative truth, for philosophical truth always follows the event, and historical decision engages the individual. In this ever-renewed progression from life to consciousness, from consciousness to free thinking, and from thought to willing, philosophy is developed.

This historical philosophy is also in a sense a philosophy of history, but only if one defines history not as a panoramic vision of man's whole existence, but as an interpretation of present or past as linked to a philosophical concept of existence, or as a philosophical conception which recognises itself as inseparable from the epoch which it interprets and from the future which it foresees. In other words, the philosophy of history is an essential part of philosophy; it is at once both the introduction to it and its conclusion. It is the introduction, because one must understand history in order to think in terms of human destiny, at any or every time; and the conclusion because there is no understanding of development without a doctrine of man. If one conceived of philosophy according to the schema of the deductive theories, such a double nature would be contradictory, but it becomes intelligible in the context of the dialectic of life and mind which ends in self-realization of the being who places himself in history and measures himself by truth.

himself: a totality of impressive reality, the philosophical truth always follows the event, and like [illegible] emerges the individual. In the awareness and [illegible] upon life in its manifold form, consciousness to the thinking, and from thinking to willing, all these have developed.

This historical philosophy is thus in essence a philosophy of history, but only if one defines history not as a pragmatic account of man's whole existence, but as an interpretation of present experience, indeed as a philosophical concept of existence, or as a philosophical concept [illegible] which recognizes itself as inseparable from the spirit which is the creator and formative force [illegible], in other words, the philosophy of history is an essential part of philosophy; it is at once [illegible] the introduction to it and its conclusion. It is the introduction because one must understand history in order to think in terms of human destiny, in the present time, but it is conclusion because there is no understanding of development without a conscious grasp of time conceived of philosophically according to the schema of the dialectic process. Such a [illegible] world [illegible], but rather [illegible] of the dialectic of life and mind which ends in the realization of the being who places himself in history and understands himself through it.

SECTION I

THE PAST AND THE CONCEPTS OF HISTORY

INTRODUCTION

HISTORY, in the narrow sense, is the science of the human past. In the wider sense, it studies the development of the earth, of the heavens and of species, as well as of civilization. On the other hand, in the concrete sense, the term 'history' designates a certain reality; in the formal sense, the knowledge of that reality. This double ambiguity will be the theme of our first section.

One is tempted to keep to the wider meaning of the word: we would understand by history any investigation of beings or of things which no longer exist, an inquiry forced to proceed by indirect means because, by hypothesis, we should be seeking that which has disappeared. But we must ask to what extent history taken in this wide sense is truly *one*. Is the unity of human and natural histories subjective? Is it based upon the same orientation of curiosity, upon a similitude of methods? Is it materialistic? And does it reflect the continuity of an evolution which, starting with the primordial nebula, would end in the period called historical, microscopic and cosmic achievement? All history emphasizes the past, but is the past the object of a unique science?

We shall take as a point of departure the doctrine of Cournot which in its entirety deals with both natural and human history (Chapter I). We shall next try to show the methodological (Chapter II) and the real opposition (Chapter III) between the different histories.

Thus we shall arrive at a limitation of the scope of our study. The originality of the historical dimension within the human order excludes the confusion of the sciences and the assimilation of the natural kingdoms.

I. THEORY AND HISTORY
(Order and Chance)

IN THE following pages we assume a familiarity with Cournot's philosophy in order to confine ourselves to a few critical remarks. The concept of history, even in this philosophy, is really multiple and complex, and an analysis of Cournot's examples is enough to convince us of it. We shall show how the metaphysical concept of order allows an apparent evasion of the distinctions which are inevitable when a system of *development* and a system of *achievement of an evolution* are confronted.

* * * *

Cournot distinguishes two categories of sciences, theoretical and historical. On the one hand, we organize the system of laws according to which phenomena are connected, on the other we go back from the present state of the universe to the conditions which have preceded it and we try to reconstitute the change.

This opposition, at first sight, is clear and we can give it a prime significance, setting aside Cournot's fundamental concept, order. Indeed, let us suppose that a stone falls: either we regard the event as susceptible of repetition in order to determine the laws of falling bodies (either on the earth's surface or elsewhere); or, on the contrary, we interest ourselves in the peculiarities of *this* fall: the stone fell from a certain cliff, a certain movement caused it, etc. The closer we get to the concrete event, to this particular fall, exactly described, the less will the incident be separable from the spatio-temporal whole to which it belongs, the less legitimate it will be to discern singularity (qualitative) and uniqueness (temporal). For the unique characteristics of the event are explained only by all the circumstances which conditioned it. Let us agree to call the universe offered to our perception real: for each instant of our consciousness there is a corresponding state of the universe and the succession of these states constitutes a history, of which the cosmological sciences attempt, from a greater or less distance in time and space, to give an account.

This first definition is, from any standpoint, insufficient. Past reality does not represent the goal of the structure of science; it does not suggest the idea of a finished discipline. In addition, this definition does not agree with Cournot's thought, for he does not oppose one line of research to another, nor sense data to laws; what he separates is two different sectors of the universe, nature and cosmos. Not every succession of events is historical; also it cannot be explained wholly by laws. The historical fact is essentially irreducible to order: *chance is the foundation of history.*

The definition of chance proposed by Cournot is familiar: the concurrence of two independent series or of a system and an accident. That a tile should be loosened from a roof by a high wind is understandable in accordance with known laws; that a person should pass beneath the roof going about his business is also understandable; that the tile fall upon the individual is a coincidence both necessary and irrational. Necessary, because it results from the determinism which rules the series, irrational, since even for a divine mind it obeys no law. In the same way, let us suppose that the solar system be struck by a foreign body; here again there would be a historical fact which we, unable to calculate or to foresee, must simply observe. Thus, history is concerned with events essentially defined by their spatio-temporal localization; the theoretical sciences, on the contrary, establish laws, derived from reality and valid for isolated wholes. We arrive thus at another concept of history: no longer the *concrete universe in its development,* but the *events* which will be called accidents, chances or coincidences, which occur rather than exist, and which definitely defy reason.

Is the concept of history adequately defined by chance? Indeed it is not. A succession of fortuitous events (the series of drawings in a game of lotto) does not constitute a history. Let us consider, on the contrary, astronomy or biology; time's special significance is to permit the realization of *systems.* The history of astronomy assumes as its task the reconstruction of the formation in the past of the organized *system* which we observe today. In the same way the living order has been progressively formed; it is a mixture of intelligible necessities, fixed once and for all, and of accidents whose results are still effective. History is characterized less by coincidences than by the orientation of a development.

These three concepts may be seen in a dialectic progression. In order to explain *actual development,* it must be analysed into causal relations, which are inevitably abstract. Referred to continuing reality, these relations create data of coincidence which are, so to speak, the obverse of a theoretical science. Hence, in order to bring together these scattered events, we have the concept of evolution which preserves and transcends the two notions of actual development and of chance.

* * * *

Implicitly contained in Cournot's texts, these notions are never clearly isolated because in accordance with his probabilism, he refuses to separate subjective and objective: theoretical laws must correspond to the principles of an eternal order. Hence the constant shifting from relative distinctions to absolute and transcendent oppositions.

Let us consider the two categories of theoretical and cosmological sciences. As long as we oppose two directions in scientific procedure, the science of the laws of life on the one hand, and a description of the living forms and of their development on the other, no problem arises. But for Cournot it is always a question of arriving at the radical separation of the living order and the historical data. We must then consider order, not as the result of scientific explanation, that is, inevitably provisional and based on observation and abstraction, but as the primary concept. Thenceforth, entirely free, the philosopher decrees that a certain general fact (the number of teeth or vertebrae in a given species), in spite of its generality, belongs not to order, but to history. This is a metaphysical judgment, for the living order becomes a source of discrimination, and it is held, by reason of its intrinsic harmony, to be anterior and superior to actual life, which is only an imperfect reproduction of it.

Is it a question of physical science? Cournot succeeds no better in detaching the theoretical from the historical. The law of gravitation is seen as one of the fundamental laws of the world, valid without respect to time, because it involves no cosmological datum; whereas the law of falling bodies at the earth's surface would imply certain data subject to modification (centrifugal force). But such a distinction remains provisional. We are never sure of having grasped one of the principles of the physical order. And, in any case, even these principles are bound up with reality, since observation is necessary to bring them to light, and experiment in order to verify them. Here again we see not so much a transition to the absolute as a reversal of the legitimate sequence. The scholar moves from fact to law; Cournot begins by postulating an order (inaccessible in its totality).

One may say that Cournot defines the historical datum positively as the datum that evades calculation. Certain events have left no trace, sometimes we cannot go back from the final state to preceding states because the same final state may result from differing anterior states. Finally, accidents, such as the meeting of a meteor and the earth, are unforeseeable and, after the event, knowable only by observation. Cournot outlines a distinction between physical and biological or human science on the basis of the possibility of prediction and retrospective explanation. In the case of a physical reality the future is strictly determined by present condition, to such an extent, that it is often better known to us than the past. However, a living being imposes historical inquiry because its future reaction depends on its past, inscribed, as it were, in the organism. Anticipation is as contingent as is reconstruction.

But it seems that the possibility or impossibility of calculation varies with our legitimate knowledge. Now, Cournot claims that historical data are in themselves absolutely inaccessible to science. For the formula 'incalculable for us,' we must substitute, then, the formula 'incalculable in itself'. But if every coincidence has as its origin the necessary unfolding of diverse series, how can it be said that the fact of chance *in itself* evades all calculation? Is there not here a contradiction between determinism and ontological unpredictability?

Will it be said that the coincidence, subject to no law, is nonetheless incomparable to the foreseeable fact, conforming to a rule? Of course, there exists no law which governs the series of numbers at roulette, and in this sense chance would be a reality, even for God. But would not the Infinite Mind possess concrete circumstances from which each spin of the wheel results, a total knowledge which would make any computation of averages needless for Him? We may of course consider such recognition of the particular unworthy of Divinity and invoke the idea of order. For a rational system is absolutely opposed to a succession of fortuitous instances or to isolated accidents.

So, the importance of the opposition between cause and reason is immediately understood. If the number six results at a given turn of the wheel, it is the result of multiple causes, of concrete antecedents of the event. But if we observe that out of a great number of turns the numbers on one side of the table come up more frequently than the others, we seek the reasons for the fact: irregularity of the numbers or tilting of the table, etc. The antecedent is real, the cause is an idea taken from our organic experience. But the reason is the explanation which satisfies the mind. This opposition is acceptable and clear as long as it is applied only to particular cases (in the example chosen, the reason is also a sense datum, although it accounts for multiple events). Defined solely by the satisfaction given to the needs of our intelligence, reason remains a relative concept as long as we do not consecrate it by a metaphysical, or even theological, mandate, as long as the reason for things is not projected into the mind of the Creator.

Actually Cournot explicitly states that the idea of order is fundamental and primary, and that it has the singular capacity to criticize itself. Philosophical probability would make legitimate the transition from the subjective to the objective: ideas would correspond to the structure of reality, for it would be absurd (an unbelievable chance would have to be admitted) for it to be otherwise. Unfortunately, order is a vague concept, just as consistent with physical laws as to the living harmony. Order is not so much a means as an end: Cournot not only takes it for granted—he omits any analysis and elucidation of its forms and various values. Instead of observing it as it is, human and changing, he sets it up as absolute, and thus slips from individual reason to universal reason.

Cournot moves from the observation of laws to postulation of a theory, from partial systems to an integral order. He fails to see the ambiguity of this order which being immanent in things and in mind, and variable according to the field of discourse, presupposes a basis of theological belief. It is impossible for history to have more unity than the term to which it is supposed to be contrasted.

* * * *

Even in Cournot's doctrine, there remains a fundamental difference between the histories of nature and human history. The cosmological, physical or biological sciences exist only in an order of which history is the negation. As a matter of fact, these disciplines are either descriptions of the data or reconstructions of the past. In the first case, they may be self-sufficient, but they amount to a simple introduction to theoretical inquiries. They are autonomous in so far as past development, thanks to the order towards which it tends, represents an evolution, as well as a series of chances: for example, the history of the heavens which retraces the formation of the solar system, the history of species which explains the realization or the progressive transformation of the living order, both of them oriented towards a condition of stability.

Order is primary here, at least for the scholar. But in the human realm, it is the development which is of first importance because order is, as it were, only the internal structure of development. In one case the problem is to reconcile the primary definition of history as an arena of accidents with the finality suggested by the direction of the historical movement. In the other, however, it is a question of rising above the particular facts, of which neither the connection nor the logic is at first discernible.

We shall set aside the first problem. Cournot's formulae on the subject of initial states are vague,[1] because as a philosopher he wishes to ignore the Providence in which he believes and which perhaps his concept of order implies. On the other hand, the principles of historical etiology, characteristic of human history alone, are interesting.

In fact Cournot limits himself to formulating, in would-be strict terms, and by use of his favourite concepts, the ordinary and traditional idea: beyond chance—individual passions, voluntary decisions,

[1] He himself points out diverse hypotheses: perhaps they are fortuitous, perhaps on the contrary they are already oriented toward the end which they are preparing; perhaps it is a question of mutual reactions.

natural catastrophes, wars, etc.—we would discern an order which would make intelligible the chaos which at first is presented to the historian. Whoever looks down from above on a landscape sees, in their broad outlines, the courses of the rivers and the lines of high relief. Thus, by rising above details, the philosopher would succeed in bringing out the reasons for the over-all movement. After many wars and revolutions, political conditions in Europe have finally assumed approximately the aspect resulting from the inevitable geographical conditions, division of resources, etc. The influx of gold gave Spain a temporary hegemony, but the necessity which assigns her a rôle of secondary importance in Europe finally triumphed. This method of reasoning is the more easily accepted in that it is spontaneously and legitimately utilized by all who seek the origin of a particular event. Contrasted with the accidents—assassination at Sarajevo, Austrian ultimatum—which explain the exact moment when war began, are the underlying causes (domestic difficulties in the Austro-Hungarian Empire, German imperialism, French thirst for revenge, the Anglo-German rivalry) which account for the very possibility of a European war. It is implicitly assumed that accidents disappear, that long term movements govern movements of short duration. That in certain cases the accidents finally compensate for each other will be easily granted, but we should be unwarranted in considering such counter-balancing as general or inevitable. If the date of an event is attributable to chance, how are we to limit the consequences of that chance? By what right can it be said that in 1908 or in 1911 the outcome of the struggle would have been the same? Are not the consequences of the fact that the Greeks triumphed over the Persians prolonged to our times if it is true that the Greeks, under submission to Persia, would not have known the free development of a culture in which we still live today? Cournot himself admits that the consequences of certain facts, far from disappearing, continue indefinitely (distinction of races).

If Cournot, in the end, believes in this counterbalancing, it is because otherwise historical etiology would have to be despaired of,[2] and because his whole formal philosophy of history is dominated by a material interpretation: the period of history itself is destined to come to an end. Between the organic solidarity of primitive tribes and the rational order of future societies, history properly so-called, that of wars, of Empires, of individual initiatives, forms only a necessary but brief transition. As in the case of natural histories, he recognizes the

[2] Theoretically, he recognizes the opposite possibility, that is that time extends the effects of chance. *Essai sur les Fondements de nos connaissances*, §311.

total system with reference to which accidents are defined, the terminus towards which the evolution moves. Thus, once again an entirely relative distinction (for, depending on the level at which we place ourselves, the same fact may be either the underlying cause and reason or the apparent cause) is carried to the absolute.

Cournot liked to compare history with games in order to show the common source of the two systems of logic: the theory of chance. Contrasted with baccarat, whose games succeed each other without evidencing any order, a chess match already offers a multiplicity of events connected both by the order of intentions and the chance of coincidence. This is a suggestive comparison, but Cournot has granted himself, at little cost, the equivalent of the plan followed by each player. He granted himself the right to observe the development as though it were at its end. Thus he succeeded in evading the master difficulty of a historical logic: how can we apprehend the global movement as long as it is incomplete? The historian does not soar above the historical landscape: he is on the same level as the development he is trying to retrace.

Cournot, then, offers us more problems than solutions.[3] Supposing that the same concepts are found in all historical disciplines, it still remains for us to make clear their meaning and relationships within each system. Theoretical system, vital organization, master lines of evolution, these terms have in common only the label '*order*' which Cournot applies to them. Beyond these verbal analogies we must seek the unity of methods or of realities.

II. NATURAL HISTORIES

IN ORDER to show the diversity of the historical disciplines, we shall discuss first the most interesting example: biology. Historical research is indeed an integral part of the science of life, since any systematic classification of living beings is linked with the theories of the origin of the species. Besides, the importance of transformism in the history of ideas is well known. The dramas of the human and biological past have mutually supported and confirmed each other. In both were found the diversity of individuals and the similarity of types, continuity and

[3] These remarks would be even more true if the theory of human history were being considered. The history of ideas and etiology are in juxtaposition. It is difficult to perceive the synthesis of continuous human progress which characterizes the course of civilization and of the law of growth and decline which governs the things of life (even in empires and peoples). In truth, it is a question perhaps less of insufficiencies than of a profound concept of the plurality of historical movements, *without system because the so-called composing elements are too heterogenous to make possible any result. Matérialisme, vitalisme, rationalisme,* Paris, 1923, p. 170.

change; in both the historical and comparative methods were simultaneously applied.

Of course, the enthusiasm of the last century was followed by the crisis of today. But the latter, despite appearances, is for us a favourable circumstance, for the object of our study is to specify the proper nature of historical research. Now, the current difficulties are due to a dissociation between the various procedures by which we go from the present into the past. The progress of knowledge compels separation of the procedures which Lamarck and Darwin did not even dream of distinguishing, because their provisional results are contradictory.

* * * *

The transformist interpretations of the past century, although they did contribute to the spread of historical understanding, were, it may be said, as unhistorical as possible. They reduced the idea of history to its most meagre content. Lamarckism, for example, used, in order to explain the evolution of the species, hypotheses confirmed by present day experience. The creation of organs as demanded by necessity, the adaptation of the living organism to environment would be neither historical nor contemporary facts, but phenomena essential to all life, which we have the right, based on present observation, to project into the past. There would be no solution of continuity between the theoretical science and the historical reconstruction. The evolution ought to continue, to such an extent that critics today talk of a vicious circle of Lamarckism: why should we not witness the creation of new species? Why have certain primitive species, instead of disappearing into superior forms, become stabilized? Determined by timeless laws, the succession of true forms was developing into an intelligible evolution. Chance intervened only in order to account for detail; in its broad aspects, the history of life was obeying a logic available to today's scholars.

In another form the same confusion is found in Darwinism. The principles of explanation available for the past are empirically established: variability of living organisms, struggle for life, natural selection, resulting in the directional accumulation of mutations. Evolution would continue, with only the necessary passing of time preventing our perception of its manifestations. Thus we find in Darwin's books the same incessant transition from theoretical study (laws of heredity) to historical reconstruction: the comparison of species, separated either geographically or by intervention of breeders, presents to him the very image of the process realized by nature in the course of time.

Two discoveries have made this confusion impossible: the difference of nature between fluctuation and mutation, and the criticism of the *natural providences* naïvely invoked by the founders of transformism. Lamarck considered the inheritance of acquired somatic characteristics proved. Darwin granted himself an infinitesimal genetic variation (and he likewise believed in the inheritance of acquired characteristics, so that the problem of variation did not disturb him much). Now, the majority of biologists today do not admit the inheritance of acquired characteristics. And they all consider genetic variation as erroneous: the descendants of a pure lineage are strictly identical, and only the influence of environment differentiates them. Under these conditions one is obliged to oppose to the normal facts of heredity—the transmission of characteristics—the theory of evolution, which calls for genetic variation. Without doubt variations which are immediately hereditary are observed, but it is still necessary to ask in which cases these mutations give rise to new species.

At the same time, biologists no longer recognize any force comparable with necessity or natural selection which has the virtue of explaining what is not understood. Darwin could be content with infinitesimal variations because, in a manner of speaking, natural selection then took over the whole burden. But a minute difference, even favouring a living organism, is not enough to insure its survival. It is not always the best adapted which lives and founds a line. Moreover, the accumulation of infinitesimal variation becomes incomprehensible. A rudimentary organ has no utility. The organization of genetic groups remains a mystery. Selection, insisted on by biologists, has lost all creative power. It eliminates, but invents nothing; it chooses, but often haphazardly. No one today believes either that need is sufficient to cause the appearance of an organ or that environment determines adaptation. The biologist has available, to explain evolution, mutations which are frequent but of small magnitude, and a quite negative natural selection.

Thus we must admit the basic distinctions between the *establishment of historical facts* and the *explanation of changes*. The paleontologist, by means of documents (fossils) reconstructs successive forms of life, but the *fact of succession* does not logically impose the *hypothesis of descent*, and this hypothesis itself does not solve the problem of the *mechanism of evolution*.

* * * *

Let us examine briefly the various proofs of evolution. They interest us because they are, in reality, various modes of inference from the present to the past. They belong in entirely distinct categories: first, paleontological data, then anatomical observations, and finally the data of parasitism or geographical distribution.

The paleontological data would be of decisive importance because they are equivalent to direct proofs, not implying the intervention of probable rationalizations or of doctrinal preferences. They show the traces, preserved by nature, of events we wish to reconstruct. Earth strata are a sort of spatial image of the passage of time. The remains of living organisms are thus dated by their very position. The diversity of fauna and flora is observed at various epochs of the earth's past; the appearance of species is noted, their diffusion, and often, also their disappearance.

Unfortunately these data are fragmentary and incomplete. We have no documentary evidence of early primitive times. To quote a biologist, the earliest phases of evolution will always escape us, those times 'in whose course life must have appeared and the broad lines of evolution, those which determined the constitution and physiognomy of the principal groups and their main subdivisions, must have become clear'.[4] If this lack of knowledge is beyond remedy we shall never have direct proof that the 'broad lines of evolution' are historical. On this point the fixation theory can then be refuted only by philosophical arguments, or by the discovery of mechanisms capable of explaining complete structural transformations.

In still another direction paleontological data might prove evolution: intermediate forms would be an irrefutable evidence. But contemporary discussion has become more complex. Intermediary forms are so rare that some biologists invoke their absence as an argument against evolution. On the other hand, the transformists refuse to conclude that the present gaps in our knowledge imply any real flaws.

In spite of these incapacities, paleontological documents have nonetheless furnished information on the general trend, on the rhythm of the development of species, on the relatively late appearance of the vegetables and animals considered superior. In particular, the over-simple picture of a continuous and regular movement has been subject to revision. Certain stable forms have not varied since time immemorial; each group has its period of expansion, then of decline. Everywhere, today, we are struck by interrupted sequences.

Arguments based on the present structure of organisms are quite different. In this case the student observes, not documents, but actual life. The famous law, that ontogeny mirrors phylogeny, gave physiologists the impression that the past of life was still entirely present, as though accumulated, in the higher beings in the first stages of their

[4] Caullery, *Le Problème de l'Evolution,* Paris ,1931, p. 34.

individual development. Embryogeny, *transitory comparative anatomy*, made possible the foreshortened survey of the successive periods of evolution. This law has been so much modified that it has been in effect abandoned. Embryogeny is no longer held to be a *recapitulation of the past*, but *generative of the future*. The immediate result is that the inference from past to present is complicated. Embryonic forms are no longer the witnesses, but at most the signs of history. Between the signs and the thing signified are intercalated probable reasoning and philosophical claims.

Of course, within each large group we succeed in going back, 'thanks to embryogeny, to a basic form from which are derived, by diversification, all the forms met with today'.[5] Even more, the similarity of embryonic stages would authorize approximation of the types of organization distinguished by Cuvier, and thus there would be conceived the unity of descent of the whole animal kingdom. We are not qualified to discuss the scientific value of this argument. We can simply observe that evolution is a possible, but not a necessary, explanation of the similarity of the primary embryonic stages (the fixationists would give a different account). This explanation imposes itself by reason of a limited knowledge on the one hand, and of our philosophy on the other. As M. Caullery writes: 'the future is already virtually present in the egg . . . the most clearly adaptive tendencies . . . are realized automatically and completely, previous to any actual use of them.'[6] If the past is not the mechanical and fortuitous cause of this complex and co-ordinated arrangement, how can finality or providence be evaded? This dilemma shows also the exact nature of the inference. History *must* be the accidental origin of apparent finalities.

The third category of arguments is taken from fragmentary cases of evolution in parasites or within a limited geographical area. The parasite would enable us to know 'special secondary evolutions, based on definite groups, evolutions whose beginnings we clearly and authentically perceive and whose final development we precisely observe'.[7] The specific character of the flora and fauna of islands, in particular the comparison of them with those of the continents of which the islands were formerly a part, would show in the same way the progressive changes in living organisms under the influence of their conditions of life. These two arguments directly prove isolated cases of evolution; they operate in favour of the doctrine of evolution as a general way of conceiving of the development of life; they do not

[5] Caullery, op. cit., p. 110.
[6] Ibid., p. 249.
[7] Ibid., p. 164.

prove that the great classifications of organisms are derived from each other.

Thus the proofs for evolution as a whole are not direct; the direct proofs lead only to isolated instances. Now, at the same time, the laws of heredity, particularly genetics, suggest that living matter is astonishingly stable. Hence we observe today among scholars a curious reaction against transformism and, in philosophy, a state of confusion, or, as it is called, of crisis.

The confusion comes first from the multiple meanings of the words evolution and transformism. We understand by that either the fact that living beings are changed in relation to their conditions of life, or that all species are descended from one or from a small number of primitive species, or else a certain image of the development of species (for example, the regular and continuous progress, by accumulation, of infinitesimal variations) or, finally, a certain way of explaining this transformation (mechanisms indicated by Lamarck and Darwin). We have had to abandon or revise the mechanisms of evolution accepted in the last century, to modify the picture which had been formed of the history of the species. The fact of the solidarity of living beings among themselves and with their environment is definitely achieved, but how can the hypothesis of descent be expressed? One philosophy concludes with a definition as vague as the following: 'There are laws of birth.'[8] And biologists usually are content with affirming this descent without making it specific because they do not know its workings.

This ignorance would more easily be accepted if evolution and adaptation were not connected problems. Darwin and the positivists used history to account for order, without abandoning determinism. Transformism made useless, at least, special acts of creation. Now, what is the meaning of history for the biologists?

As far as the apparent nature of final causes is concerned, the usefulness of organs or functions is no longer postulated as evident at the beginning. As long as an all-powerful selection was available, the liking for natural harmonies was easily reconciled with the positivist outlook. Today, research begins with an opposite inspiration; it tries to show that the so-called final causes are illusions on the part of the observer, that the functioning of the organism is far from being perfect, that other arrangements would have been better. Unable to find the desired explanation in history, they would like to pass over the problem in silence. Pre-adaptation, for example, eliminates the mystery of the accord between the individual and the environment. Chance,

[8] Le Roy, *L'Exigence idéaliste et le fait de l'Evolution*, Paris, 1927, p. 101.

the elimination of the non-adapted and adaptation by coincidence, is substituted for Darwinian selection. History becomes a series of events and no longer an intelligible succession.

In the same way, apropos of the mechanism of evolution, the doctrine of chance develops. Geneticists recognize no other factors of transformation than mutations. Living forms would be reducible to collections of living atoms, of genes. Genes and germinal mutations would present an immense number of possible combinations, which history, as in a game, would sort out. It would be enough to add a confession of ignorance in so far as orthogeneses are concerned. As for transformations of types, one would imagine other unknown accidents, sudden catastrophes, which would have brought in their wake great convulsions of living matter.

Most biologists do not consider this solution satisfactory. Neither the reciprocal adaptation of the parts of an organ, nor the statistical adaptation of individuals to the environment would be explicable by means of the play of fortuitous coincidences. A positivist like M. Caullery proclaims the insufficiency of integral mutationism. The rôle of mystery is made less, but there still remain complex forms which could not be accounted for by mutations accumulated by blind selection. And to understand the passage from one type of organization to another, one must suppose cytoplasmic variations and perhaps also an environmental influence which would complete and organize the mutations. The difference between present and past would prevent our observation today of these hypothetical phenomena. So, history, originally indispensable to a positivist explanation of the nature of final causes, is next called in to prove the unintelligibility of evolution. A contradictory double necessity, but a contradiction, doubtless, inevitable.

In effect, lacking an internal or external factor, providential or natural, which directs the historical movement, we end with verbal formulae which simply express what we should like to know, physico-chemical determinism, interaction between organism and environment, or lastly, the idea of history unalloyed. For the catastrophes imagined by the mutationists roughly mean this: events must have occurred, coincidences must have happened, which produced the forms of life which we wish to explain, but of which we can only observe the existence.

Can metaphysics fill in the gaps left by science? There is no doubt that Bergson's creative evolution would make the diversity of species intelligible. But in spite of its attractiveness, scholars have not rallied to the Bergsonian theory because it is limited to a statement in metaphysical terms of the data of the problem. Natural selection would have been an explanation because, conformable with determinism, it corresponded to observable and observed phenomena. Creative evolution or the vital force are and will ever remain, demonstrated or belied by the facts, because they express exactly our ignorance and our curiosity.

Mutationism, conscious or not of its insufficiency, completed or not by residues of Lamarckism, Bergsonian metaphysics, fixation with evolution inside types of organism, providentialism, such today would be the most typical answers among which we do not have to choose. It is especially important for us to show in history, the *asylum of our ignorance*. History furnishes answers to all questions as long as it is conducted by a naturally intelligent force. In truth, history itself demands explanation. Evolution appears evident to the positivists if the only other interpretation is that of separate creations. But do we gain much by asserting evolution as a fact, when we are ignorant of the *laws of birth*, whose existence we proclaim by such an assertion?

* * * *

The foregoing analyses have not only allowed us to recognize and specify the various concepts of history, they have also suggested a distinction between two ways of reconstructing the past, one based on the present and laws, the other by means of documents. Ontogenesis is a sign of the development of the species, fossils are their remains. To compare and contrast human and natural history, we can take into account the following opposition: what is the inductive progression from the present to the past? To what extent do we understand the past in the light of the present?

History begins when we become interested in individual realities (we mean, not indivisible objects, but simply qualified things, distinct from other phenomena of the same species). There is a history of the earth and a history of the heavens, but not of physical phenomena.

It seems however that history begins with physics, without any direction of human curiosity upon objects. Certain laws immediately suggest an inference from what is to what has been. For example, the law of degradation of energy is used by certain physicists to attribute to the universe an oriented evolution, to restore to the relative time of relativity the essential character of elapsed time, that is irreversibility. Of course the application to the whole of the Universe of a law valid for isolated systems is not accepted by all scholars; but even if we assume this application is admitted, the explanatory bearing of the hypothesis would be little. For, if the law is interpreted in the light of the atomic theory by means of the transition from a less probable to a more probable distribution, it would be necessary to assume a most improbable distribution at the beginning of history. Thus the mystery is shifted, but not cleared up. On the other hand, if we apply this law only to isolated systems, it imposes the idea of an irreversible transformation of a given fragment of matter, but unless we are interested in these fragments themselves in their concrete singularity, we shall not push the historical inquiry further.

In the same way, the knowledge of laws according to which uranium changes into lead would make it possible to establish the age of different geological formations. One would start with the content of uranium ore and apply the directly verified formula (at the end of 3,000 million years one gram of uranium gives 0.646 of uranium and 0.306 of lead).[9] Thus, geologic past could be dated, and indirectly, life's past. This is legitimate inference, even though it reaches into a past anterior to the appearance of the first consciousness. But, since we are obliged to assume an irreversible temporal unfolding, we think in terms neither of an evolution nor of a combination of events and order, nor even of a series of states. This duration is considered historical only because the direction of its flow is fixed.

With the history of the heavens and of the earth, we approach true history. Of course we never reach an event exactly localized in time or space (besides, we are not interested in unique events). On the other hand, we interpret an astronomical or terrestrial development only in the light of our legitimate knowledge. In spite of these reservations the idea of history is already richer, for the scholar interests himself in individualized objects whose past he tries to reconstruct. This reconstruction is the outcome of inductions whose present state constitutes the beginning. In the most favourable instance, that of geological periods, the present reality is the spatial projection of the development. In the case of the various histories of the heavens, hypothesis makes it possible to understand the formation of the observed system and leads back to an induction of the probability of causes. We seek to explain the present distribution of the stars by imagining a certain foregoing distribution which makes the former at least probable. The history of the earth, at the same time, uses these various methods: to make intelligible the present arrangement of continents and oceans, for example, we construct a different arrangement which would normally have produced the present map and which we date by means of knowledge gained of the structure of the earth at different epochs. In addition, certain historical phenomena (erosion, changes of coastlines, etc.) continue to unfold before our eyes; finally, accidents (sink-

[9] Caullery, op. cit., p. 28.

ings or risings of terrain) have left traces making them accessible to retrospective observation.

The history of the species, we have seen, *partakes of* both natural and human history. It explains a geographical distribution of the species or a contemporary organization (for example, embryonic) by hypotheses of natural causes. Moreover, it preserves not only the consequences of events or their traces, but documents, that is, past life preserved and transmitted to us. Of course a fossil is not a document in the same sense as are the pyramids. In one case we have a human monument which refers us to its creator, in the former the remains of a living organism whose form is, as it were, carved out in matter. The comparison is no less legitimate in spite of these differences. Thanks to fossils the biologist reconstructs *directly* certain once living species. But he understands their sequence only in the manner of astronomers, that is, by means of laws. The crisis in transformism results just from the diversity of these two inferences, logically and in fact autonomous. In the history of nature, the hypotheses may change, they may be contradictory; a crisis comparable to the one in transformism is not conceivable, because, to use Cournot's expression, these forms of history are entirely dependent on theory.

The formal originality of human history would easily be deduced from the foregoing reflections. The historian is interested in individuals, and not, like the biologist, in the examples of a species, in exactly localized events, and not only in astronomical, geological, or geographic phenomena, which have been repeated or have lasted, and which are significant only in their general aspects. The historian is capable of understanding directly, and not by means of laws, a sequence of facts. To understand one of Caesar's decisions, it is enough to attribute an intention to him, as we do to the gestures or the words of people around us. Now, human activity leaves traces of the fact that it produces monuments. To reanimate the human past we have no need of science, but only of documents and our own experience.

In short, the human past extends into the present in an entirely different manner from the past of nature. The latter is not preserved in the present in its intrinsic pastness; we explain present forms by a hypothetical history; for example, the similarity of the early and embryonic stages in the whole animal kingdom by common descent. These early stages are today an integral part of an individual, contemporary development. The conservation of fossils is not at all of the same order as the permanence of embryonic forms. And the preservation of fossils is in its turn not of the same order as the transmission of human monuments. In nature, documents exist only by chance. On the contrary, man, by his very nature, creates documents, since he extends his physical activity by tools and since all his creations immediately reveal the action of a mind.

* * * *

The differences just pointed out will, I think, be accepted without difficulty. But it will be objected that they do not answer the crucial questions. We have shown the variety of the inferences which proceed from present to past. We have pointed out the significances of history, now creative and now destructive, accidental source of order or irrational cause of disorder, necessary to solve the question of apparent finality or to account for fragmentary disorder. But we have left unanswered the essential problem: can one really speak of a history of nature? Can a continuity between cosmic and human development be demonstrated? Or, if this continuity is to be broken, at what point? Logical distinctions, however useful they may be, leave the philosophical questions untouched. Can we evade them or give them an answer?

III. NATURAL HISTORY AND HUMAN HISTORY

OF COURSE these problems, if all their implications are considered, go beyond the limits of our inquiry. Our limited goal is still to answer the question: is it possible, is it necessary, to define the history of man in terms of the general concept of history? Now, we have shown that the latter, according to Cournot's doctrine, derived its apparent unity from a metaphysics leading to Providence. Next, we showed the methodological differences between human and natural history, but there still remains the *argumentum baculinum* suggested by common sense: the history of man is the continuation of the history of species, social changes follow from the unfolding of life. Is not the continuity between cosmic development and the human past thus evident? And does not this continuity impose a single theory of history, which would go back to earliest times anterior to the formation of our planet, to return in the end to the present?

* * * *

Von Gottl-Ottilienfeld,[10] who speculated on this problem, tried to refute this asserted continuity. He invokes first of all the absolute heterogeneity of the sciences of life and the natural sciences. The

[10] Cf. *Wirtschaft als Leben*, Jena, 1925 (and especially *die Grenzen der Geschichte*, 1903—which is a part of the collection) and *Wirtschaft und Wissenschaft*, Jena, 1931 chap. IV).

former reconstruct the total experience of rational beings, the latter set up, on a basis of strict logic in agreement with all the objective data, a system of abstract relations. Even if these relations are applied to a development (as in the case of geology or biology), they retain their fictive character. The durations of time geology deals with are incommensurate with the real time whose passing is experienced by consciousness; they are only a transposition of spatial relations. The two categories of science, incapable of meeting each other, speak different languages, aim at different goals, obey incomparable rules. The *logical truth* of natural history could not contradict the *ontological truth* of human history.

There doubtless would be many reservations to be made about this absolute opposition of reconstitution and construction, of ontological and logical truth. Of course, history and certain intellectual sciences aim at the *ensemble of experience,* but this ensemble, in its totality (Allzusammenhang), is inaccessible: history, too, constructs. As for the opposition between the two times, cosmic and human, it might perhaps be acceptable, if it were offered as a simple description. Established as a metaphysics, it becomes paradoxical. Granted that cosmic time is the result of a total objectivation; it does not by that fact become unreal. Moreover, time measured by the transmutation of bodies is in some way connected with an ageing of things. It retains the characteristics of irreversibility, of regular and directed flow which defines the duration of consciousness. Nothing forbids maintaining a continuity of succession between the scientific time of astronomy and biology and the human time of history.

Such a conclusion is valid on one condition: we must attribute reality to the constructions of science. It is legitimate and necessary to note the differences between the language of history and that of physics, but how can one be qualified as true and the other as fictive unless the propositions of all sciences are considered fictive? Just as physical space is abstracted from perceived space, so abstract time derives from experienced duration. In one sense these two sorts of space and time remain definitely separate, but measured time signifies a true past and makes it possible to date the appearance of life. We put *homo sapiens* in his place in the evolution of life, which is itself set into the geological development. Can it be denied that consciousness is in fact, for us, linked with a certain vital organization? The history of consciousness begins at a certain time, it comes after a long period which the mind today succeeds in knowing, but which has been experienced by no consciousness (at least human). Is there in this, for any idealist doctrine, a paradox and a scandal? Instead of being primary, consciousness would seem in this view to be a late and subordinate phenomenon. Thus, *ideal necessity* and the *fact of evolution* have been opposed, and the two terms reconciled in a metaphysical view. At the beginning there would be Thought, although human thought appears only at the end of the process. For the latter as a whole would be the manifestation of a creative impulse, of spiritual essence, which in man would attain lucidity.

Another idealist doctrine, in order to evade this solution, at once both facile and vague, recalls that historical science is the product of the mind. There is no past except for and by means of consciousness. The history of Egypt is first of all that of Egyptology, the reality is not ready made, previous to our investigation; it merges with the knowledge we gain of it. But is it possible, without metaphysics, to uphold this last formula when it is a question of our fellow men, who have lived as we are living, irreducible, as we are, to reflection or to science? And if we postulate the reality of human history, at what moment shall we stop, since we go back from history to pre-history, and from the latter to animal evolution?

We need neither the myth of total and original thought nor an absolute idealism. We have recognized the fact of succession: human history came after the history of species. But succession does not yet signify continuity. Certainly, when there is available a spiritual impulse capable of creation, of sudden innovation, the heterogeneity of the entities brought together in an evolutionary series matters little. The continuity is then as easy to affirm as it is difficult to prove and impossible to refute. For positivist science, true continuity would imply the reduction of the superior to the inferior, or at least the explanation of the former by the latter. Now the mechanism of the evolution of the species remains a mystery, nor do we understand any better the rise of life nascent from non-life. Nor do we understand any better the birth of man or of intelligence. Under these conditions, even if the fact of succession be admitted, the historical vision neither imposes nor implies any philosophical consequence. Every one has the right to interpret the past whose traces we collect and whose phases we establish.

Continuity is illusory in still another sense. If the biologist seeks intermediary stages numerous enough to fill the gaps between heterogeneous forms, most of the time he succeeds only partly in doing away with the jumps, in uniting by means of multiple transitions one species with another, one type of organization with another, one fauna with another. The discontinuity is even more striking if we link the history of mankind with the development of the universe.

One may object that these two arguments are founded on the present insufficiency of our knowledge. But could not one already cite certain evolutive series which, by the succession of forms, present the picture of regular and directed progress? Moreover, may not the mechanism of the evolution be known tomorrow? In the absence of proofs, is not the fact of succession sufficient to create a favourable presumption, so that the oneness of the types of history would remain the most likely hypothesis? It is not enough, indeed, to invoke our ignorance which always stands the chance of being temporary; we must analyse, *via* the ideas, the essences themselves.

* * * *

Let us go back to the question asked at the beginning: does there exist a history of nature? We have pointed out that the historical inquiry is entered upon as soon as we become interested enough in a fragment of the reality to make it a starting point for an explanatory regression. We try to reconstruct the states through which the earth or the heavens have passed before assuming the forms observed today. If the question bears upon nature as a whole, we have no way of choosing philosophically between the various answers. The primary datum is the sensory diversity offered to our perception. Behind this variegated and changing surface, are we to imagine a world of atoms, indifferent to duration? Are the bodies which seem to us stable only accidental systems due to combinations of atoms, among the infinitely possible combinations? In that case, historical changes would be apparent, and the permanence of the elementary parts would correspond to the authentic reality. Or, on the contrary, is the whole universe like a disaggregating nebula, an energy in degradation, atoms being transmuted, a body increasing in volume? Is it subject to an alternating rhythm of expansion and contraction or to an irreversible evolution? How can the philosopher decide between these various hypotheses? Once the mechanism of historical reconstitution in the natural sciences is analysed, once the uncertainty inherent in the generalization of partial laws is exposed, we can only observe the uncertainty or the contradictions in the results, and leave the history of the universe to the development of scientific theories.

This conclusion is, however, not satisfactory. For, more or less consciously, we give another meaning to the question of whether nature has a history. The statement that man has a history is not limited to the observation that there exists a scientific discipline or that human societies change and succeed each other. Such an assertion goes further; it implies a certain way of conceiving the preservation of the past within the present, and suggests that history is inseparable from man's very essence. Let us admit that the species evolved from each other; the monkey remained a monkey after giving birth to man. For an animal species, history is to come into existence, to spread, then to disappear. If, due to germinal mutations or influenced by the environment, a new group is formed, that is an event. But the individuals will remain no less natural and unhistorical, for those who have remained the same, like those changing, will have learned nothing from each other, created nothing for each other.

Man, however, has a history, because he develops throughout time, builds structures which survive him, collects the monuments of the past. History-reality and history-science have true existence beginning the moment men pass on to each other their common gains, and progress by means of that inheritance. For the survey of experience or thought introduces the double possibility of unconsciously reliving the past or of recognizing it in order to accept or reject it. Henceforth, free to choose, mankind has a history because it is in search of a destiny.

It may be said that, between the conscious survey of the past and ephemeral matter existing entirely in a vanishing present, we have forgotten the kingdom of life. Does not life offer this same preservation of the past, this accumulation of experience? Let it be said at the very first that life, as observed today, is crystallized. Generations of living creatures follow each other without differentiation (it matters little that chance of heredity or the actions of breeders may change certain individuals). In the course of individual lives the past is preserved as habits or conditioned reflexes. But—and nothing illustrates better the special quality of the historical order—these individual gains disappear totally. To establish the comparison, we must view the history of the species. A mutation would be comparable with a historical event, the succession of species with that of societies, the animal kingdom as a whole with the totality of human development. The subject of evolution is life, as here it is mankind.

Certainly, between the things we think are momentary, and the mind inseparable from its history, intermediate complexes are conceived. All matter is in a certain sense plastic and retains traces of the influences to which it has been subject. There would be occasion to analyse the various ways in which a reality keeps the impress of its past: reversible and irreversible physical changes, irreversibility of vital phenomena, the impossibility of a living entity rebecoming what it has been, the future state of cells and the fatal ageing of complex beings, etc. In any case the law of biogenetics, as we have seen, does not justify the statement that life's past remains present in living beings.

The essential point was for us to show the irreducibly specific character of human history. Now, this is confirmed by all the attempts to deny it. The human species has a history while *the* species (plural) would have only one in common, hence the statement: Evolution, arrested in the animal world, continues in humanity. It is singular that biological evolution leaves the living entity in its individuality, in its heredity, approximately similar to itself. One may doubtless make comparisons between the spread of reptiles in the past and that of men today, but the primary originality does not lie in the conquest of the planet, for humanity did not need to spread out over the earth to have a history. It was enough for it to create tools and monuments and to transform itself by its creations. Only man has a history because his history is a part of his nature, or rather it is his nature.

Even if, according to a certain metaphysics, man were defined as an animal who makes tools, this originality would have been implicitly recognized. For the act by which man has determined the conditions of his existence by creating his means of production, a primary act of history, demands of the actor as well as of his companions a sort of intelligence. And that is why it can be said, without this definition leading to a spiritualism opposed to materialism, that human history implies a spiritual bond among individuals. History is always history of spirit, even when it is the history of the forces of production.

* * * *

If this opposition, between history essential to man and fortuitous history, exterior to things and living beings, is well founded, the denial of continuity between cosmic and human development assumes a quite different significance. It is no longer a question of a provisory rupture, of a lacuna in science: it is a matter of recognizing the limits beyond which our objective science could not go.

In fact, scientists have gradually constructed a physical universe which they project into a hypothetical past, into which they fit the history of the species. Legitimate though these interpretations may be, even if seen as complete and coherent, they would not reduce the human past to an accident of matter, they would not destroy the peculiar value of human history, for consciousness will never be explained in terms of the unconscious, nor reason in terms of unreason.

The impossibility of deducing consciousness is obvious, for the deduction itself implies consciousness. The first term of the deduction already assumes its claimed conclusion. Of course some will see in that a simple submission of our intelligence and will unhesitatingly say that biology retraces the genesis of consciousness. But that is an illusion with respect to the significance of the scientific results.

We have admitted the fact of succession; we do not doubt that man appeared at a certain date. And man's appearance coincides in time with the appearance of consciousness. But, supposing that the mechanism of this appearance were discovered, the formation of mind would still lack explanation. Biology, by methodological principle, does not recognize consciousness in itself, or else it recognizes it as one thing among others, as a form of behaviour or as a collection of signs. It disregards then, and would be unable to unravel, what consciousness is in and for itself. We do not claim that man has always existed, but that the spiritual order transcends realities explored by the natural sciences.

In the same way intelligence, the capacity to understand a situation as unique or to organize means to an end, does not result from a simple development of sentient consciousness or from a blind instinct. Intelligence could arise from non-intelligence only by a sudden upheaval.

An illusion masks these solutions of continuity. One imagines one is filling up the gap between matter and life, life and consciousness, adherent consciousness and intelligence, by imagining between one stage and the next a progressive transition—as though time were of itself creative and sufficient to bring together essentially heterogeneous realities. The multiplicity of intermediary forms would not yet imply the assimilation of genera.

We shall study in human history this retrospective illusion. If the search for origins has assumed such importance in religion or ethics, it is because it seemed to offer a means of reducing the specificity of the religious and moral fact. It is forgotten that the perspective, directed toward the present, always converges on the higher term. It is man who seeks his ancestors in the animal kingdom, the adult being that tells of his childhood, evolved societies which explore primitive groups, positivists who locate superstitions and theologies in history. The continuity of the account covers the opposition of the essential parts. And yet, if the historian neglects the intrinsic meaning of morality and of religion, he will reconstruct a development in vain, for he will have explained nothing.

* * * *

Thus, we shall maintain, concerning the relation between the Universe and mankind, both the fact of succession and the heterogeneity of the primary groups. Positive science will never discover what, by principle, it has decided to ignore. Thus, the exploration of the outer world is only one aspect of human history. The latter, then, will always remain autonomous. In addition, the history of the spirit is, for man, a natural history.

IV. TIME AND THE CONCEPTS OF HISTORY

IN THE preceding pages we have outlined three concepts of history. The first two were explicitly outlined at the very beginning: one linked with the notion of chance, implies discontinuity in the causal fabric; the other, connected with the idea of evolution, implies on the contrary a global and oriented movement. In addition we have set human history, defined by the preservation and conscious survey of the past, in opposition to all natural history.

We should like to show that the first two concepts are valid for all forms of history, but that they assume different values depending on whether they apply to nature or to humanity. They give an idea of the reality of time, but only the conscious survey of the past makes it possible to define true *historicity*.

* * * *

History, according to the first two definitions together, requires that scattered changes combine into a directed movement without the movement's concealing the coincidences either of the system and exterior data or, within the system, between relatively independent facts. To deny history is to conceal one or the other of these complementary aspects. Either the changes do not compose into a totality, or else the latter does not change irreversibly. The cycles of rise and fall would correspond to the last hypothesis, the laws of uniformity to the first. Any atomic view of nature leaves room only for local events, for elementary fluctuations, connected with each other, but with no other tie than the chance of their coincidence.

We said above that it is the province of science to determine whether, in these differing senses, nature was historical or not, in what domain it was so. We also showed that it is enough to confine oneself to a concrete object—a planet, a solar system—to construct a partial history. Finally, life offers to an eminent degree characteristics bringing it close to the historical order: the ageing of the living being, the evolution of the species, show both the accumulation of experiences, the renewal of forms and the global progress towards an end of some sort or other.

Is it possible, without scientific discussion, to go further? Is it possible that these variable appearances may hide a changeless eternity? Is it possible that life and history fit into a stable reality, fixed once and for all, or reducible to a multiplicity of elements of which only the combinations would be unstable? This amounts to asking whether time is an illusion, or whether, on the contrary, the reality of time does not imply that of history. As a matter of fact, we are going to try to prove that the same characteristics that permitted us to discern histories make possible the definition of actual time.

The latter is usually pictured as partaking of the nature of experienced duration. At the beginning, we attributed to the development of the concrete universe the continuous series of states observed in ourselves. Even the abstract idea reserves this privilege. One imagines an unending chain whose links would pass one by one through existence, to plunge immediately into nothingness. The past, a container opened onto the future into which it would always penetrate, would gather together what has been and consequently no longer is. The chain moves on unendingly, and there is no turning back. But, separated from the things which are in it, time becomes only an empty concept, a word. In fact, spatial time, too, is linked with changing realities; we measure it by motions. Neither the plurality of times nor the relativity of simultaneities, then, is unintelligible and absurd.

These paradoxes have little effect upon the historian. Absolute simultaneity is that of actual experiences; now, the historian sees himself as reconstituting a series of such experiences in and for which the impression is not distinguished from the object (the impression is itself the object of the science). So the impossibility of separating time from multiple systems and of arriving by scientific measurements at one, absolute time of a total system seems unimportant. The famous rocket traveller would return older than his contemporaries who had remained on earth if the rapidity of biological changes varies with the speed of motion, but he would not, on his return, view in reverse the succession of events.

Only the irreversibility, not the uniqueness and regularity, of the course of time, interests the historian. Now, it seems that we inevitably conceive the universe as temporally oriented at the same time as determined: indeed, we consider two different conditions successive only by connecting them with a causal relationship. The rule of determinism constitutes the order of duration. Could the chain, being reeled up, lead back to the beginning? In order to answer the question, let us ask what representations of a reversible series are possible. One must assume groups of actions and reactions such that the cycles are exactly reproduced, with the last term bringing back the initial state of things. An ideal mechanism would escape from development: that is to say, that an actual mechanism is transformed by the fact of the multiple influences to which it is exposed.[11] Time shares in the irreversibility of discontinuous determinism and all determinism, projected into nature, is inevitably lacunary, composed of series and of relatively isolated aggregates—which implies fortuitous coincidences, with prolonged consequences. Of course that is a certain representation of reality, obtained by giving an objective value to a certain perceptive or scientific experience. But the latter seems scarcely capable of being contradicted, for any positive knowledge, being essentially analytical and partial, isolates a fragment of the world. Besides, if certain laws seem, from a certain point of view, to suppress history, they also imply a discontinuous causal web which excludes the exact repetition of a state of the whole universe. In any case, on our scale, if we consider the relative and provisory unities represented by things and beings, we observe a real multiplicity which entails both the opposition of chances and evolutions and the irreversibility of development.

* * * *

So far, we have been content to take the word event as synonomous with coincidence or accident. We confused it with the concrete fact in its spatio-temporal context or with coinciding series. We must now carry the analysis further, for these two definitions already apply to a construction of the mind.

The event is the most primitive *given*: that which is not being but happening, that which passes through existence at the imperceptible boundary separating two instants: this stone fell, that individual uttered a cry, I went to such and such a place. The pure event is instantaneous and fugitive. It vanishes in the instant of accomplishment (in the double sense of the word). It is the content of a perception, but not of a stable perception which would consecrate a lasting present. Fundamentally, it exists only for a consciousness: either it is the act of consciousness in its immediacy or else it is the intentional object of such an act.

A flash of comprehension, or the comprehension of an instant, it cannot be grasped or perceived; it lies within all knowledge. At most it is possible for memory to resurrect it, for a narrator to recall it. It matters little whether it concerns a natural or a human event; we tell of a landslide, an explosion, as well as a course of behaviour. In fact, the reconstitution still belongs in every way to a history made by and for man. Within such a history, a material phenomenon has a place,

[11] Cf. R. Ruyer, *Le Sens du temps*, in *Recherches philosophiques*, 1935–36.

because it has been part of individual or collective life, the matter of the account.

In so far as an event is natural, an event, to be preserved, must be put in its place within a determined series. Thanks to established regularities, perhaps also by taking into consideration the separation into parts of spontaneous perception, we obtain series and systems. At all levels, in ordinary life as in the world of science, we know accidents or coincidences which, inevitably created by the separation of things or laws, by the isolation of individuals or aggregates, transpose and make intelligible the event which cannot be grasped.

However, the human event can be preserved without being expressed in causal terms because it is, being human, understandable. Rainfall, a natural event, will become a historical fact: at a certain moment, condensation of water vapour brought on precipitation, the condensation itself being the result of cooling due to certain masses of air, etc. On the other hand, my reaction to this event, however momentary and fleeting it may be supposed, is understandable in its fleeting development to the extent that it is reasonable. The behaviour of a madman is not intelligible to others: like the natural event, it would require the construction of a determined series. The act of a mind is, as an act, understandable only to the actor; in so far as it is reasonable, it is understandable to everyone. In the same way, any line of conduct, animal or human, which, as the observer sees it, presents a combination of means and ends, is understandable, but the interpretation is valid only if the combination, consciously or not, existed at the beginning of the action.

It may be objected that in the notion of the event we have mixed two ideas: the idea of the passing of time and that of instantaneity. According to this, natural or conscious phenomena are not necessarily events. On the contrary, conscious phenomena always stand out against a static background. Certain languages contrast continuing and terminated actions, the verbal changes distinguishing both the relation between future and past, and the more complex relation between the beginning, the continuation, and the completion.

The end in relation to which the event is defined allows many meanings; either it merges with the causal context, sequence, or system, which we call *evolution* if it is involved in an oriented development, an *order* if it it seems temporarily or definitely stable, or it corresponds with that which lasts in contrast with what is passing.

These three hypotheses are as valid for nature as for humanity. In both we distinguish progressive change of form and mutation, the condition of a system and sudden changes (equilibrium and crises), long-lived individuals and those whose life is short, the fact opposed to things. But with the human order these oppositions take on a richer meaning.

Provisorily we shall limit ourselves to connecting the opposition to the diversity of the kingdoms which compose human history. A living being, from one moment to another, is continually changing, but with conscious will there intervenes the possibility of conversion and break. Habits, manner of being and character are fixed: the call of grace, the light of truth, the radical decision, all imply a sort of denial of fixity. The antithesis between duration and the instant is also connected with the antinomy of life and mind, central to each individual and to the whole species.

Thus, we perceive once more the specificity of human history. Innumerable natural histories are observed, provided that isolated objects are treated. But, as we reach out toward wider contexts, or towards first principles, it is in vain that we look for the evolution that would assemble the fragments or orient the global movement. But the living accumulate experiences without recognizing them or passing them on. All men, like animals, move toward nothingness. But this time, on the upper level, infinite horizons are opened. It is by rising to the totality that the essence of human development is discovered. Only the human race is engaged in an adventure whose goal is not death, but self-realization.

* * * *

Formal concepts, then, apply to all orders of development just as they characterize the most general history, the one which is linked with the irreversibility of time's course. But we do not see in them, when mankind is concerned, the same value as did Cournot. The phase which he called historical was characterized by the rôle played by accidents. He was prepared to despair of the etiology of history unless he arrived at the conclusion that the final state would somehow or other be produced. Events were to permeate, retard, or accelerate, but not to divert, the evolution.

As we see it, the concept of history is not essentially tied in with the hypothesis of a total order. The important thing is the consciousness of the past and the desire to understand oneself as a product of it. The distinction between men and peoples who are authentically historical and those who are not, is not to be deduced from either the rhythm of change or from the originality of the institutions. To live historically is to preserve, to relive, and to pass judgment on the life of one's ancestors (and other societies). In this sense we understand Hegel's expression: Only those societies are really alive which elaborate a science of their development.

The preceding pages make it possible to outline and establish the origin of our inquiry. Since human history is essentially distinct, we shall consider no other. Since knowledge of the past is one aspect of historical reality, we shall not separate reflection on science and description of the historical process. Theory, like language, must not dissociate subject and object.

In another book we examined the main attempts at a *theory of historical knowledge*, and we arrived at negative results. Here is no critique existing prior to philosophy or independent of it. In the work of Rickert, as in Weber's, when all is said and done, the specific characteristics of reality control the individuality of scholarship. Rickert starts with the transcendental ego, but he surreptitiously reintroduces the qualities of the object which he had excluded. Starting with an abstract and formal definition of value (all that interests us), he rediscovers the value content of a spiritual assertion. He recognizes that meanings, defined with reference to values, are immediately given. The opposition established by Xénopol between *facts of coexistence* and *facts of succession* would be equally insufficient. Ambiguous for the same reason as is the opposition between order and history, it demands the bringing together of studies as diverse as the history of the heavens, that of the species, and of societies.

Furthermore, there exists no science of history whose validity would impose acceptance as indisputably as did the Newtonian physics in the case of Kant. The critique of historical reason must then be, as Simmel thought, more descriptive than constructive, more phenomenological than logical. It does not have to deduce a universality admitted by postulate, but to recognize attainable objectivity.

This dual result can easily be explained: the subject is not a transcendental ego, but a historical being. It is vain, then, to ask whether the historian's curiosity or the structure of history is to be considered in the first place, since they refer to each other. For a classification of the sciences there will perhaps be hesitation between various antitheses: nature-society, nature-spirit, nature-history; the choice, unless it is based on a metaphysics, will inevitably be pragmatic. For our study it is proper to analyse the knowledge which man, in history, acquires of himself and of evolution. It is a study of the consciousness of history, which is the beginning of philosophy as well as of methodology, since the same question dominates both: how does the individual succeed in understanding the human totality?

SECTION II

HUMAN DEVELOPMENT AND HISTORICAL UNDERSTANDING

GENERAL INTRODUCTION

Understanding and Meaning

FROM now on we take the word history in the narrow sense just given, in both its objective and subjective sense (it is impossible really to avoid this double meaning, which could be called well-founded, since knowledge is inseparable from the historical process). The science of the human past enjoys a unique privilege: it has to do with beings who have thought and whose life and conduct it wishes to rethink. Now there is good reason to distinguish between *understanding,* which attempts to show a relation immanent in reality, and the *explanation* of the inorganic or organic world. We understand Kepler's laws, but we explain nature. Man understands himself and he understands what he has created.

Such, in short, is the basic distinction that we would propose between the two types of knowledge. However, we shall not have to use it; only the difference between *understanding* (grasp of an intelligibility objectively given) and *causality* (establishment of causal rules according to the regularity of series) will be important.

In this introduction we should like to note the other definitions which have been offered of the concept of understanding (translated from the German *Verstehen*), in order to specify the one upon which we shall settle, and, in so far as possible, to dispel ambiguities.

Considered as a new psychology, the theory of *Verstehen* may be attributed to Dilthey, Jaspers, Freud or even Spranger. As one studies one or another of these writers, the essential idea varies.

Dilthey had expressed the opposition which became academic in Germany: 'we explain nature and we understand man.' Structure is indwelling to psychic phenomena; all we have to do is to bring it out. On the other hand, we reconstruct physical phenomena by beginning with the elements, whose composition comes from the psychic context. Reality has a total character in one case, an atomic one in the other.

Jaspers' conception has an entirely different origin. In order to systematize the quite different results of psychology and psychopathology, he proposed to separate understanding (comprehensive relations) entirely from causality (causal relations). That the weak may hate the strong, the unfortunate may envy the rich, that the ill-favoured individual should care little for higher values, we understand quite clearly, immediately, without reference to a rule or law. On the contrary, we note that according to the law of sequence, syphilis brings on general paralysis, but we do not understand it.

We have also seen in Freudianism an application of the comprehension method, because psychoanalysis interprets the unconscious rationality of behaviours apparently mechanical or fortuitous, a rationality depending, it is true, on irrational complexes, but which is nevertheless, like all expressive thought, directly intelligible to the psychologist.

Spranger, finally, refers to *understanding* also, but here it is a question of a *spiritual* psychology, so to speak, which bears not so much on the facts of consciousness, as on the objective mind in which the individual consciences participate. Thus, he tries to explore the different worlds of values and of ideas in which men live.

This last method hardly belongs to psychology; it leads us to the other origin of the theory of understanding. In Dilthey, especially towards the end of his life, understanding denotes the act by which we pass from the sign to the thing signified, from the expression to the consciousness which has expressed itself, a decisive step, a requisite of science and of human relationships, since each of us, shut up in himself, reveals himself to others only by his works (in the widest sense of the word).

In the general way, understanding designates the forms (or one of the forms) of the knowledge of others. A definition of it is sought in order to lay the foundation of the logic of the social sciences, or, as they say in German, of the humane sciences.[12] This diversity of intentions is, of course, bound to multiply uncertainties and confusions, all the more so since each of these concepts offers difficulties. How define the structure of which Dilthey speaks? Does it include all of psychic life or do there exist outside it unintelligible and, as it were natural, series of facts? How characterize the comprehensive relations of which Jaspers talks? How far do they extend? Is it the action of the body on the soul (or the opposite) which is properly incomprehensible? If we do not understand the general syphilis-paralysis relation, is it because we do not know the mechanism of transmission or the law from which this proposition would be deduced, or because it is essentially incomprehensible? Are we not thus brought to the opposition

[12] Translator's note: *Geisteswissenschaften.*

of mediate-immediate understanding, or again to the opposition of construction and discovery?

If, on the other hand, we consider the knowledge of others, other questions will occur. Do we grasp directly the experience of others? Or is it by association of mind, the inevitable means of communication between individuals? Do we succeed in sharing states of mind or do we merely reconstitute them, etc.? It would be easy, but useless, to draw out this list of questions. For the moment, we must settle arbitrarily on a definition, not solve problems.

We might reserve the word *understanding* for one of the forms of knowledge of others (we shall come back to this point), but we prefer to take the wider meaning. Understanding is the knowledge we acquire of human life and works, as long as the latter remain intelligible without the elaboration of causal regularities. But, it will be asked, how characterize this intelligibility? Dilthey insisted on the relation of the part with the whole, Jaspers on that of means and end (rational action was, for him, the type of understandable behaviour), others on the relation of sign to thing signified or of expression with feeling. How are we to choose, or, which amounts to the same, how define the concept of *meaning*, correlative of understanding (which is always grasp of meaning)?

We shall also take the word in its broadest meaning: any ideal content, any object of an intentionality, will be for us a meaning. Neither the end, nor the value, nor the totality merge with the meaning, a concept superordinate to all contexts and all connections in which the mind recognizes itself. We speak of understanding when *knowledge shows a meaning which, immanent to the reality, has been or could have been thought by those who lived or realized it.*

A theory of understanding would be beyond the limits of this book, since it should serve as an introduction to the moral sciences and, partly at least, to psychology as well as to history. Also, it is hard to isolate the study of historical understanding, the closest and at the same time the most complex form.

The world of the historian is the world of daily life in its immediate totality. The realms carved out and set aside by the sciences are again brought together into the naïve consciousness. This naïveté in no way implies simpleness. All partial understandings come into history, since the object is the development in and by which spiritual worlds come into being. Science has a bearing both on these worlds and on the development which is their origin, perhaps their unity.

Without taking in the whole problem, we shall go back, in the *first part,* to the source of all understanding and meaning, namely experience and reflection. In the following two *parts*, we shall outline a logic of understanding, stressing two problems decisive for our inquiry: starting with the *plurality of systems of interpretation*, we shall look for the possibility of a static understanding, one universally valid; then we shall study the reconstitution of historical movements. In short, we shall trace the search for truth along the two lines of the fragment and of the whole—for the totality is not distinguished, by definition, from the evolution of history itself.

First Part

FROM THE INDIVIDUAL TO HISTORY

INTRODUCTION

WE HAVE just stated the central theme of this *part*: to describe how consciousness understands itself, so as to specify the relations of experience and meaning, of resurrection and reconstruction, of participation and knowing. At the same time we shall try to put historical knowledge in its place among the diverse aspects of man's own knowledge of himself.

It will be neither impossible nor artificial to attain this double objective. Indeed, in order to estimate the deviation between what is experienced and what is thought, it is normal to analyse successively the reflection of a solitary consciousness concerning itself and the grasp of a psychological state by an outside observer. Moreover, to make clear the intention of the historian as well as the structure of the object, historical knowledge must be considered in the extension of the knowledge of self and of others. The historian is to some extent both a spectator and an actor; he seeks in the past both himself and another than himself. Finally, the objective mind, present in me, creates the common bond which makes it possible for me to communicate with others; it determines the collective reality the development of which interests the historian. It is, then, as a conclusion of these three studies directed towards this end and limited by it (Chapters I to III), that the import and character of historical knowledge will appear (Chapter IV).

I. KNOWLEDGE OF SELF

EACH of us is for himself at once both the nearest and the most mysterious of beings. The intentions of my conduct, my habits, my character, the *other* knows perhaps better than do I. And yet everyone rebels when anyone affirms even the possibility of such a superiority of the spectator over the actor (at least unless the superiority is reduced to that of the impartial observer over the interested party). For, to begin with, we do not *know* ourselves—we *are* ourselves. Of our state of mind we have at all moments a consciousness which it is for us to explore and elucidate. The mind's reflection concerning itself is infinitely repeated and bears witness to a sovereign power. However, we do not need reflection: what we are is revealed to us at each moment by a global intuition made up of multiple sensations. We *are* for ourselves this 'incomparable monster, preferred above all'[13] and not this intellectual image—a collection of dispositions or of acts—which others have constructed and which they cast back at us like an illusory reflection of our nature.

Knowledge of self is both the most incontestable and the most difficult type of knowledge, because it imposes upon us the fact of the primary solidarity of subject and object. Hence it results that, through an endless dialectic, all knowledge of self is part of its object which it inevitably transforms, for the one who knows himself is already no more what he was before he became conscious of himself.

Finally, the end pursued by knowledge of self is, in spite of appearances, vague. Is to know oneself to become the historian of one's past, the psychologist of one's character, the psychoanalyst of one's unconscious? Is it, on the contrary, to discover one's possibilities, choose one's volitions, coincide with one's ideal?

The following discussions propose to exhaust none of the problems pointed out. They should merely put in their places the various forms assumed by knowledge of self, thus specifying the relations of thought and experience, of self and others, and place the effort of retrospection and of history in the movement by which the living individual learns to know himself by knowing man's world.

* * * *

Knowledge of self is first of all momentary, like its object; it goes with each fragment of our living span. Not that we are always detached from ourselves. In action, everyone is a part of society, in such a way that no room is left for reflective duplication. Nevertheless, even when we are absorbed, we do not entirely lose ourselves in the reality; we anticipate at least the possibility of again coming to an understanding of ourselves. For if the fact of consciousness is a psychological datum, if consciousness is both consciousness of something and at the same time of itself, the act of consciousness which takes itself as an object is to be understood only by the necessities of life itself. Therefore,

[13] A. Malraux, *La Condition Humaine*, Paris, 1933, p. 66.

efficacy is asked of it rather than truth. When I try to distinguish the movements that I make, I want to rectify, not to know them. Momentary consciousness of oneself is an example of control. It makes little difference, then, whether it is absolutely contemporaneous with its object or whether it is an immediate retention of it. It matters little whether it is limited to pure contemplation or reaches out towards an anticipated or desired future, which enriches the present. This consciousness of self is a solitary knowledge the origin of which is biological and the proof of which is practical.

And yet, knowledge of self is the common source of both scientific and social knowledge of man by himself. Indeed, we can freely direct this sort of reflection. According to our liking, our attention may be concentrated, detached, may choose, may isolate. Introspection, serving psychology, would be reflection which, instead of concentrating on a certain peculiar aspect of our experience, would contemplate the psychic processes as a whole. Phenomenology would be the use of this reflection with a view to a total exploration of man and the world, for, in the *transcendental ego*, separated by the 'ἐποχή' from all other existence, the essences remain present. And the universe as a whole could be grasped at the root of its formation.

Consequently our theme seems to broaden beyond measure: is not self knowledge, according to Socrates, Saint Augustine, or Husserl, the programme for all philosophy? It is then proper to specify that here we are interested only in the knowledge which I acquire of myself. Knowledge of the transcendental ego should be examined only to the extent that it appears as the condition for each person's knowledge of his own individuality.

Would it be possible to stop short at the momentary consciousness of self? Could we not say that absolute sincerity would in the long run be the ever-renewed coincidence of the individual with himself, the absolute respect for naïve impressions? Is not authentic knowledge of self the creation and support of the illusion that one is a stranger to oneself, and that one discovers oneself without changing? Its literary attraction, notwithstanding this ideally passive sincerity, is unacceptable. It is unrealizable because, claiming to respect them, it mutilates and deforms the facts of human life. Such a sincerity would be as unstable as its object. How would it distinguish between the superficial and the fundamental, between wandering thoughts and rooted impulses? It could not distinguish between the feelings actually experienced and those one imagines one has had. Thus, it would hold all experience sacred and construct the self, under pretext of not constructing. For, willingly or not, we determine ourselves, at least partly, by the idea we form of ourselves. If certain ethics were obeyed, one would create oneself by that obedience, but instead of creating oneself as a *unity*, perpetual renewals would be imposed—or at least accepted because development would be the supreme value.

The unity of the individual was possible, was perhaps a source of strength, before consciousness brought on division and, as a result, doubt. But we do not go back beyond this acquisition of consciousness—either in the case of the individual, or for the species. The individual who rejects lucidity, is as far removed from true naïveté as a people which rejects history is from primitive simplicity.

Then too, we never attain this coincidence. Moral knowledge of self is not so much a recognition of experience contemporary with the inner course of time, as a *post eventum* assent to the memory of what one has been. To conceive of passive sincerity as an ideal, two things must be admitted: first, the possibility of retrospectively knowing oneself with mirrorlike fidelity, and second, the duty and capacity to make this knowledge ineffectual, in such a way that life continues to evolve according to its law, indifferent to collective prejudices and rational imperatives. But how can one's past self be revealed without taking into account its conscious preferences, and influencing, by that very fact, its future?

To describe the knowledge we have of a moment of our former life, we must disregard pure memory (Bergson) or, in any case, involuntary memory (Proust). If by good fortune a fragment of the past in all its fullness were conveyed to our present consciousness, this miracle of resurrection would make knowledge, in the proper sense, useless. We should again *be* the same self that we had been. We shall also leave out of account the immediate recall which prolongs the moment just spent and extends into the present impression. We are looking at the typical instance. As my own historian, am I doomed, as I am for other people's pasts, to *think out* my own experience?

In 1930, I decided to study Marxism in order to submit my political opinions to philosophical review. Now I feel incapable of recovering the psychological atmosphere of that period in my life: doubt about the function of philosophy, a desire to find an object of reflection not too far removed from personal, actual, preoccupations, etc. But all these signs are abstract; they express in conceptual terms a state of mind which I recall, remember. My thought is fixed on a past experience, but the state of consciousness '*memory of the decision*' is different from the state '*decision*'. Even if my thinking were the same today as it was seven years ago: need to review Marxism—even if the *inten-*

tional object of my present consciousness were identical with the one at which my consciousness was then directed, there would still be an impassable gap between the two states, considered in their concrete reality: the multiplicity of impressions, the aura of feeling which gives each moment of life a unique colouring—these have forever disappeared. In this respect life is inaccessible to thought and each of us is alone with himself, shut up within the solitude of the moments of his own life.

Let us admit that our whole past is there, buried in the depths of the unconscious, and that it depends on us to call forth all our ghosts—the moments of our lives remain no less incomparable. Of course there are nearer memories, charged with emotions, which bring back the atmosphere of times past. I cannot recall certain childhood adventures without a sense of shame bringing back to me, alongside the experiencing of feelings strange to me now, the feeling of my identity, or at least my continuity. And yet, even in such a case, it is not the child's shame I again live through, all the impressions which today accompany that shame, the sentences I pass on it, are other than the original experience. I am living in a different state, only one bit of which is like the resurrection of a former self forever vanished. Nor could I succeed better in thinking again as I did at twenty, or at least I should have to set out on a voyage of discovery, almost as though it concerned someone else. Often, to discover the former self, I must interpret his expressions, his deeds. We are rather insensitive to this development of our minds, because we have stored up the best of our experiences; our past understanding interests us—except for introspective curiosity—only in so far as it would be deserving of our present interest.

Whether it is a question of feeling, thought, or action, the review of the past is subject to the same limitations. Perhaps we limit ourselves to knowing that we have felt a certain emotion, aimed at a given goal, made such and such a decision. In that case, the past state is viewed by virtue of the present, known by it; but this intellectual knowing could without an essential difference apply to a moment of an alien consciousness. Or, we strive retrospectively to experience former feelings, to rethink old ideas. And we succeed to some extent, but there is still a gap: we know that a recalled feeling, again expressed, does not belong to our present experience. An idea, if we try to rethink it, seems already old to us. Our state of consciousness is different because of the very fact that it is pervaded by the memories it is supposed to reproduce. We try, not to relive the moment of decision, or to know that we have made a given decision, we seek to know the decision—that is, to make it intelligible. Between abstract knowing and complete coincidence, retrospective knowledge is organized.

* * * *

We have simplified the discussion by assuming two separate states of consciousness. In reality it is only retrospective contemplation which differentiates them; consciousness endures, and continuity is not made up of states of consciousness in juxtaposition. To specify the deviation between the experienced past and our present knowledge of it, we must describe the reconstruction of the inner duration by the present self.

Let us go back to our former example: to know the former decision, is to rediscover the goal or goals which motivated the action and later seemed to justify it. We shall call the representations upon which the mind dwelled *before* the decision, and which we *subsequently* evoke, *motifs*. But we do not wish to know only the plans of which our actions are the more or less complete realization. We wish to explain our behaviour *psychologically*. Of course, the *motif* often serves as an explanation, and I could say that I decided to study Marxism to justify my political preferences; the more distant goal appearing as an explanation of the more immediate one. But this relation of means to end is only a pseudo-explanation; it is a question of two *motifs* successively or simultaneously conceived. On the other hand, if, starting with the cited *motif*, I retrace the states of consciousness in order to follow the formation of this *motif* itself, my investigation is quite different. Not that *motifs* are not psychological realities, but they are *intentional objects* of states of consciousness; they are not connected by a psychological determinism; they obey intelligible laws (review of Marxism, sociological research, the logic of politics, are all linked by a mind seeking a theme of philosophical reflection). In fact, the distaste for thought separate from life, the fear of going into over-lengthy scientific studies, may today appear to me as *mobiles*[14] (that is, psychological antecedents).

Neither the succession of *motifs*, nor that of *mobiles* exactly reproduces the experienced duration. Today I discover *motifs* where there was an uninterrupted development, a sometimes incoherent succession of thoughts always mixed with feelings. The retrospective recall of an argument is not assimilable to the anticipated examination of a possible consequence any more than reflection on the *motifs* is confused with meditation on the reasons. The different moments of

[14] We borrow the distinction between *motifs* and *mobiles* from Schütz (A.) *Der Sinnhafte Aufbau der sozialen Welt*. Vienna, Springer, 1931.

deliberation are connected according to the living rhythm of a consciousness successively directed at multiple projects, expected pleasures or half-seen inconveniences. The definite project is as it were the natural conclusion of this process. Unable to trace in all its details the inner approach to the action, we rationalize the duration, divide it into moments, and substitute for the unfolding of a state of consciousness an intelligible order.

In so far as *mobiles* are concerned, we have a commonplace theme of moralists and philosophers, the impossibility for any individual to fathom himself completely. In even the most disinterested act the moralist sees a subtle element of self-love. Of course the ulterior motive, assumed after the event, is not necessarily real merely because of the fact that it is possible; but what judge can decide? On this point the wisdom of nations refuses to trust interested parties. And there is no need of a pessimistic theology to recognize that each of us is for himself an inexhaustible mystery. In certain cases the spectator or actor may well have the irresistible intuition that he perceives the true *mobile*, but this feeling, whether sudden or the result of patient analysis, is incommunicable.

Moreover, supposing that the *mobile* of an act is apparent, the search still remains indefinite. Deep-rooted impulses tend to escape our consciousness, and our most voluntary choices may be an indirect consequence of desires we refuse to admit. Again, any psychological explanation sends us inevitably back to the past, since every personality (Freud has sufficiently proved it) is first of all a history. Thus, a psychological explanation is essentially indeterminate because the exploration of *mobiles* and the regression toward the beginnings are equally unending.

The uncertainty of *motifs* is not exactly comparable to that of *mobiles*. The former comes not from a lack of knowledge, but from an embarrassment of choice. We have no trouble discovering the plan or plans as conceived before the action (save in exceptional cases where our act surprises ourselves and our whole inquiry bears upon the *mobiles*). But as soon as there are several plans, how should one choose? In practice, this choice is usually one of self-interest: we seek a retrospective justification, excuse the consequences of the act by recalling the intention, or the fault by invoking the circumstances. If I retrace a situation, how do I assign to various thoughts their places and values without taking into account the causal influence, transcendent to the intelligible relations? In the history of a life, the religious anxieties of youth will have differing meanings, depending on subsequent development. If I, an unbeliever, consider them in retrospect as accidents of puberty, they deserve at most, in memory and in the account, a passing mention. Following a conversion, old anxieties, beyond scepticism, would take on the value of a sign or proof. The uncertainty of *motifs* is, then, fixed by the perspective of the observer: each, according to the idea he has of himself, chooses his past, even the author of *Si le grain ne meurt*, for the will for sincerity here coincides with a certain moral will: to show the necessary and legitimate triumph of temperament over inculcated moral principles and family and social prejudices.

This element of subjectivity in the account will be readily admitted. Let us assume a will for objectivity, let us admit that confession is not an attempt at justification; the one who tells his story *is* still, at least partly, the person he has been. His idea of his past is dependent on the manner in which that past determines his present. Our present is the sequel to our past, but, in our consciousness, our past depends on our present. This conclusion perhaps has a general import: there is no contemporary knowledge of psychic facts, and if all retrospective knowledge is tied in with the intention of the spectator, how could it claim a universal validity unless it expresses the truth or the totality of a history, that of an individual or that of a group?

Indeed, in different degrees of depth or of wholeness, psychological explanation is capable of partial truth. Even leaving aside the intuition of the *mobile*, even neglecting the total exploration of the unconscious, everyone can explain his acts in a way valid for others to the extent that he finds in them an example of psychological mechanism. Now this interpretation by means of general relations could be the deed of the autobiographer himself. Far from immediately knowing himself, everyone, in order to establish the causes of his acts, is constrained to proceed by means of a body of knowledge.

* * * *

Knowing oneself is not to know a fragment of one's past, or one's intellectual acquirements, or one's feelings; it is knowing the whole and the unity of the unique individual that one is. And this is why the foregoing analyses might seem rather unsatisfactory. If we cannot relive what we have experienced, the two states are equally parts of a whole which it is possible for us to grasp.

Doubtless we can know our *selves*, if by that is meant the totality o our reactions, of our sentimental preferences or of our systems of value. But this knowledge attains neither the whole, nor the unityf or at least our self is a constructed unity, situated in infinity, like t h unity of all objects. We perceive a series of inclinations which are ours:

the self would be the fictive source of them. The more we extend our inquiry, the closer we get to the totality without ever reaching it.

Is this to say that we are merely a bundle of feelings, of ideas? The impossibility of attaining the unity and the totality does not have such a significance: the object self can be organized and unified. Furthermore, we are capable of perceiving this order in our nature. Psychological generalities and classification of types help us to discover our characters. But this knowledge is gradual, incomplete and inadequate, because it is, in the strict sense of the word, exterior.

It matters little whether it makes use of perceivable facts or of inner data, whether it is based on public acts or secret information. The externality of which we speak has nothing to do with the nature of the information, but with the character of the knowledge. As soon as man tries to know himself he becomes, for himself, an object, and consequently inaccessible in his entirety.

But, it may be said, our unity is not constructed. It is immediately given in the certainty of our continuity and permanence. Are we not rather *I,* than *myself*? Of course, but it is important to distinguish between an entirely affective consciousness of oneself and the reflective doubling which gives us only an empty *I.*

We are conscious of our identity in time. We feel that we are always the same indecipherable and evident being, of whom we are eternally the only observer. But it is impossible for us to express or even suggest the impressions assuring the stability of this feeling. The explanation of the fact matters little. We do not mean to say that only the organic or bodily sensations are incommunicable and constant; we merely describe and state a fact: the unique colour of experience, the clinging of the mind to life, make consciousness of self incomparable with any other knowledge and prevent its incorporation as a form of knowledge.

As for the *I,* it is always present at each moment of the inner duration; it is only the conceptual expression of a feature peculiar to human consciousness. To be conscious is also to be aware that one is conscious, and so on *ad infinitum.* But how set up this form or this abstraction as an authentic self? I should, in this case, fill out the *I,* choose among my thoughts and feelings those which seem to me best to define my true nature. A metaphysics of the individual would perhaps make possible the attribution to this constructed self of the dignity of an essential self. God would understand the ultimate intention of my whole existence, despite errors or weaknesses. Lacking this metaphysical system, this pseudo-self is merely a part of my past life, a part of my ideas or of my inclinations which, thanks to the power of reflection, I separate from other elements which I say are impure or alien because they are not in agreement with other parts of myself (for example: value judgments). The confusion of the subject-self which is indeterminate and which is present at each moment of consciousness and the selected fragments of our objective self creates the illusion that the essence of the individual is attained in oneself.

But is not this illusion justified if everyone is essentially what he wishes to be? It is not granted to us to know ourselves completely, as long as we seek the inaccessible goal of exhausting the exploration of an incomplete being. The self, a sum of our ways of life, always escapes us partially because it is not yet fixed. It continues to live and change. But we are always capable of possessing ourselves because we can determine ourselves. And, as a matter of fact, any grasp of consciousness is efficacious: our judgment of our past behaviour is part of ourself and influences our future. Knowledge of self does not aim at an ideal of pure contemplation: to know oneself is to define what one wants to be and to strive to attain one's concept of oneself.

No doubt a description failing to recognize the indisputable fact and power of reflection in life would be false. But it may not be said that the will is all-powerful under the pretext that its limits cannot be fixed in advance. Besides, to oppose a naked will to a self which is the result of heredity and environment is to simplify the data considerably. The will does not come into being *ex nihilo*, it emerges gradually from the process of experience which it is capable of influencing because it is the expression of it as well as its judge.

This double restriction does not invalidate the preceding remarks. All self-knowledge, as of a past or an individual, implies a certain idea of oneself. And this idea is animated by certain assertions of value. Even those who claim to discover themselves passively, choose themselves. But this will exerted upon self is not intelligible, except in the continuity of a life not so much suffered as recognized. In other words, knowledge of self develops according to a dialectic: between an ever incomplete discovery and a never triumphant decision, the individual defines himself by a double effort at lucidity and creation. Always menaced by Pharisaism or resignation, he can relax neither of the two tensions. In order to make his nature synonymous with his desire, he never ceases to observe himself as an inexhaustible nature, nor to confirm the choice by which he is unceasingly defining himself.

Our power over ourselves is partial: one is not free not to tremble, not to desire, any more than one is free to love. But perhaps we do succeed in disposing of ourselves. To do or not to do, to say yes or no; it is not wrongly that the traditional examples of liberty are of this type. Even if one is afraid, one can not retreat. Liberty can be experienced only in action. Knowledge of self, then, is open to the future, since it awaits the future's accomplishment and the proof of its own truth.

* * * *

We can now understand and organize the different types of knowledge of self. First, that of the psychologists and moralists, who think above all of a certain form of lucidity: to recognize one's faults, not to overestimate one's virtues, to discern the *mobiles* of one's actions, even if they are rather unflattering, etc. In these prescriptions, the concern with virtue is merged with the desire to know. The moralist hesitates between psychoanalysis and sermon. *After the event*, nothing can put an end to the psychological inquiry. No obstacle is insurmountable for the subtlety of La Rochefoucauld or of Freud. Perhaps, scientifically applied, *analysis* would make it possible to reach the true explanation which would make our behaviour intelligible, without engaging us in an endless dialectic. But the individual finds no end to the tracking down of his evil thoughts; he is never sure that he is not the plaything of his complexes. One does not succeed in knowing oneself as long as one accepts oneself.

Thus, there becomes apparent the legitimacy of the other extreme form of knowledge of self, that of the philosophers who admit more or less explicitly that *one is what one wants to be*. The psychoanalyst spies out the moments of relaxation when repressed desires express themselves: Alain absolutely rejects this 'monkey psychology'. Neither the lapses, nor the dreams, nor the hovering images belong to us, there is no thought in these phenomena which are more physical than psychic. Our true self emerges at the top, in the judgment.

The contrast is clear: the psychologist, looking back, analyses, not actions, but states of consciousness. Involuntary signs interest him more than deliberate decisions. Spontaneously, he explains *from below*, heroic courage by overcompensation, religious fervour by sublimation. The philosopher on the other hand rejects fatality of character, he invites individuals to look ever ahead and, in sincerity, he sees the mark of liberty.

This is a real contrast—which it would be easy to pursue in detail. Both doctrines seem to us to leave out of account a part of reality. We are *at one and the same time* these *drives* which the psychologist has revealed and this *decision* to which the philosopher appeals. Good intention defines a person no more truly than do his evil deeds, but his evil thoughts are no more characteristic of him than his good behaviour. The psychologist will distinguish rightly between the pose and inner feelings. But conscious preferences shown by pose are a part of the individual just as much as the feeling which only science brings to light.

Each of these doctrines, strictly interpreted, leads to absurdity. Under the pretext of will, the philosopher ends by not knowing his very self and making a virtue of his lack of lucidity, to such an extent that in all simplicity he imagines himself free at the very instant when he yields to passions which he would reject with horror if he recognized them. But psychology alone draws the individual into an indefinite quest, and one in which the uncertainties are increased as one progresses. Observation of self ends in a partial knowledge which in the end one must stop and judge.

We must always be recreating our self by connecting past and present.[15] Thus are joined, in an ever renewed dialectic, retrospective knowledge and choice, acceptance of the given and the effort to transcend. One discovers oneself through action as well as by introspection.

II. KNOWLEDGE OF OTHERS

KNOWLEDGE of others constitutes a chapter of philosophy as well as of psychology. Any type of idealism must, beginning with *a* self, discover the *selves*: a necessary, and perhaps difficult process, since it claims to grasp first *thought in general*, and then perceives only *thoughts*. Moreover, in a doctrine such as Husserl's the recognition of the *alter ego* has a decisive bearing. Objective reality is distinguished from imagined or feigned reality only by the agreed upon testimony of the monads. This recognition is, then, the equivalent in the *Cartesian meditations* of the proofs of extended substance and of the outer world, in Descartes' 5th and 6th meditations. The comparison even points to the fundamental divergence of the two methods. By 'ἐποχή', we have not rejected all assertions of existence, but we have put them in parentheses. The transcendent ego whose exploration is undertaken by phenomenology contains within it all the meanings amid which natural life unfolds. Hence the necessity not to invoke, as does Descartes, divine truthfulness in order to prove bodily reality, but to reintroduce, by means of the plurality of the *egos*, a criterion making possible the distinction between fictive and real.

This, of course, is not the primary reason for the interest that the German philosophers took in the subject of *knowledge of others*. They tried to demonstrate the originality of the humane studies (*Geistes-*

[15] Psychological knowledge, moreover, is only one of the forms of retrospective knowledge. We purposely simplify the analysis.

wissenschaften): now, this originality has to do with the nature of the object, namely, men, the development of societies and of the mind. The way in which anyone perceives or divines what is going on in another consciousness is the origin and the explanation of this specific logic. In his sociology, Simmel puts the question in Kantian terms: 'On what conditions is society possible?' And he answers by indicating, among other conditions, the knowledge that individuals at all times have of each other. But this communication between personalities is a condition of historical knowledge as well as of social life.

Moreover, the psychologists inevitably ran into the same problem. How does the child gradually build up his personality? What part does the influence of others play in the process? Does he understand immediately *expressions* of others? Phenomena such as imitation, the understanding of emotions, led the student back to this basic study. Finally, in order to define psychology, to compare it with other forms of the knowledge of mankind, or to contrast it with them, it was most necessary to analyse everyday experience as well as theoretical science, beginning with their common source, the relations of the monads to each other.

The following analyses are neither at the level of transcendental phenomenology, nor at that of empirical psychology. We put aside questions of origin, the discovery of the *alter ego* by the self of philosophical meditation, the discovery of others by the child who knows himself only as the world of humans becomes apparent to him. Other personalities are given, their existence is certain: how, and to what extent do we succeed in understanding the experiences undergone by others?

* * * *

First let us examine the knowledge of others which, comparable to self knowledge, would be contemporaneous and momentary. Just as I am conscious of all the impressions the succession of which constitute my duration, so do I immediately grasp the feeling of this *other* whom I see with face twisted, with frowning brows, etc. Or again, I interpret exactly the gesture of the ticket collector who, in the tram, holds out his hand to me. Further, I have at least the illusion of sharing the ardour of those who march by with me to the sound of the *Marseillaise* or the *Internationale*. And I suffer momentarily with the exiles who tell me of their trials. These examples would suggest the following distinctions: There would be at least *three forms of immediate knowledge of others*. One consists of grasping the state of mind from the expression, another is anonymous, limited to the interpretation of a (typical) gesture or of words, intelligible in themselves, without going back to an individualized consciousness. These impersonal relations with all who exist for us only through their functions, fill a part of our daily lives because they are a necessity of any sort of life in common, a characteristic of our rationalized civilization. Finally, pure knowledge transcends—and sometimes precedes—sharing or at least affective communion, sympathy in the original sense of the word. Let us put aside for the time being anonymous or active knowledge, and sympathy, and try to analyse the way we grasp the state of mind from the expression.

We know immediately that this person clenching his fists is angry, we divine in the glance directed at us a plea, and in this plea an alien soul revealing itself to our own.

Traditional theory here introduced an argument by analogy. We know, from personal experiences, what gestures accompany anger. Seeing these gestures made by another, we attribute to him, by analogy, the corresponding feelings. This theory has long since been shown to be inadmissible. We are inwardly conscious of our emotions, but we are usually almost completely unaware of the way we show them; they are perceptible only to others. And the assumed similarity of others' expressions and mine is quite gratuitous: or at least the assimilation would have as a condition and a consequence the generalization of the cases; we should see only states defined in abstract terms, instead of particular situations, unique expressions. Strictly speaking, we should project into the consciousness of others *our* anger, whereas in reality we get an idea of *another's* anger, qualitatively different from our anger and from *typical* anger. Psychologically, considered as an explanation of origin, this theory collides with the fact that the child recognizes living individuals before things, understands others' feelings, even when he is scarcely conscious of his own body, knows that people exist while he is still talking of himself in the third person. As an explanation of the present mechanism, this theory lapses into the absurdity of complicating what is simple, of artificially reconstructing a spontaneous inference. Neither in the history of the individual, nor in that of the species, does man need to understand himself to know his fellow men.

Human expressions are immediately given as a language spoken by living bodies. Just as we read, not words, but meanings, just as we see, not scattered and incoherent qualities, but objects, so we see anger, and not knitted brows. The adherence of the sign to what is signified is even closer here. For bodies are concrete totalities, of which, it seems, each part in a way expresses the whole. Even less than we divide a sentence into syllables, do we separate a global attitude into a plurality of gestures and movements. In any event, the interpretation of one element is possible only with constant reference to the whole. Moreover, the state of mind is not separable from its expression, because the consciousness is not, objectively, separable from the body. It is, in a way, present in the face; it is, as it were, its *intention.*[16] The immediate intelligibility of the human physiognomy represents and confirms the total unity of the individual.

Despite this quality of immediateness, the instant knowledge of others is certainly knowledge, not a participation. I recognize the anger—I do not live it. I do not experience the same condition; I grasp directly the condition experienced by the other. We talk of intuition because neither reasoning, nor construction, intervenes, and because the understanding of the singular overflows, in its perceptible richness, the conceptual formulae. One might even use the term perception: we perceive another's consciousness, but that is to say that *this consciousness has for the observer become an object.* It is essentially different for him from what it is for the subject (unless the latter, becoming a spectator of himself, gives up the privileges which are those of life, but not of knowledge). The fact remains that if the self is primarily defined by living experience or by coincidence with the will, the alien consciousness will never be authentically given. Psychological reality, if made objective, is deprived of one of its dimensions.

Moreover this knowledge remains exterior to its object which it in no way exhausts. It is not limited to judgment: I know that this person is angry; in the glance I exchange with a passer-by, it is not a general nature or a typical feeling to which I apply myself; I have in view the condition of the *other* in his particularity; but neither the totality of the person, nor the history of the emotion he is experiencing are apparent to me. The understanding of the unique is uncertain, like the interpretation of a sentence the words of which have a fixed sense, yet the whole has an original significance.

But, in order to understand the *nuance* of an experience, must I not know the individual essence? Is it not present in every moment of existence? Does not every creature, isolated, remain unintelligible, inaccessible?

Actually we do have, at first meeting, a global impression of other individuals. Just as our consciousness preserves for us, throughout time, a certain affective identity, so each individual, as seen by others, is characterized by a certain manner which makes him himself and unlike any other, even though he has gone from Fascist to Communist or from criminal to virtuous citizen. But to this intuition, which is both

[16] In the strict sense of the word (intentionality).

insistent and vague, it is difficult to give logical form. It presents a guarantee of veracity only when thoroughly examined and corrected. This intuition of the whole combines with the immediate understanding of the expression and gives us the illusion that we arrive at the essence of the individual. Actually, both of them, being partial and ambiguous, need to be developed, to be made finer and more certain by means of practice and by the attainment of a body of knowledge.

The foregoing analysis will perhaps be deemed artificial, since it isolates the interpretation of the expression of others, which, as a matter of fact, never occurs alone. Does there not always exist, between spectator and object, a minimum of community based either on affective communication (of which the crowd constitutes an example), or on intellectual communication by means of language, or, finally, on active collaboration in which forms of behaviour are brought into mutual agreement or similarly adapted to the situation?

It goes without saying that we do not have to study all the elementary forms of human relations; they interest us only in so far as they determine the knowledge which individual consciousnesses acquire of each other. For the psychologist, affective communication is undoubtedly an object of various and complex studies. From the reaction of the child to the feelings of others up to the transfer of emotions by the power of the orator or the hypnotist, including the mechanical contagion of laughter or of tears, there would be observed numberless variations of the same phenomenon, a sort of echo between man and man.

For every one of us others are the sources of most of our troubles and our joys. Their judgments affect us directly without reference to our interest, without any unconsciously selfish calculation. The approval or friendship of others is the goal we seek. In the same way, the irrational sensitiveness to the presence of others precedes our knowledge, anticipates our affections, and controls them.

Sympathy in the strict sense is, then, only a particular form of this living communication, basically a rather rare one. The suffering of others may seem odious to us (because it obtrudes upon us) or ridiculous (seeming unjustified). If we respond to the other's feeling, we do so rarely with an analogous or similar feeling. I am never indifferent to what is felt by a person whom I like, but if I must be sad because he is sad, if I must share, I still must know the motive for my sadness or pity, which assumes a knowledge of others, but does not explain it. In any event, we do not experience what others are experiencing or have experienced. The chagrin we feel at the relation of misfortunes alien to our own experience is qualitatively different from the experiences which it does not reproduce, to which it responds, but does not correspond.

May it be said that it is given to several of us to feel the same affection, to have the same idea in common? That partisan crowds, like learned societies, bear witness to this assimilation of minds and souls? Let us distinguish two extreme limits in which all concrete instances share in varying proportions. In patriotic or revolutionary exaltation individuals are possessed by the same passions, communal life predominates and invades individual life. But the merging of the individuality into the flood of collective emotions proves first of all the power of the collectivity. A single feeling, coming from without, totally fills all consciousnesses. This accord is due not so much to the identity of *intentionalities* (even emotional ones) as to a mechanical or biological contagion. But one can conceive of a communion in which men's inner consciousness would be concerned, a communion entirely based on the identity of *intentionalities*. But the same idea, as conceived by several people, may have for each one a different coloration. Neither the affective aura, nor the sense perception remains the same from one presentation to another. It matters little here that the individual may receive his concepts, his judgments of fact and value, his preferences, from the group. The fact still remains that individual personalities, if we consider them in their concrete totality, without dissociating them by virtue of metaphysical criteria, are eternally separate from each other.

Of course the individuals forget this separation in the warmth of fellowship or of love. But they overcome it above all by means of intellectual communication, which itself is dependent on language. The word is, at times, like a gesture or a facial movement, the means of expression, and for others the sign, of real experience; at times, also, it is intended to cause in others an action or a feeling, it is connected with the situation or the experienced contact. But as these signs become voluntary rather than spontaneous, symbolic and not natural, they assume a new function—they *represent* the meanings, the intentional objects. All complex human relations imply this understanding of others by way of signs expressing thoughts. Whatever complications these intermediary steps may bring in, even though the words and the writings may serve individuals to conceal as much as to reveal, to create and transfigure their lives as much as to express them, it is here that we find the origin of really historical exchanges. The mind survives only by concentrating on a subject.

Active collaboration does not necessarily imply this intellectual communication. Unconscious and natural signs, or even gestures, are enough when the situation is understood by all. Pedestrians, drivers of vehicles, adversaries in games, silently adapt themselves to each other. In human collectivities, especially in ours, understanding in action often partakes of impersonal understanding. Social systems resemble the crystallization of ideas: they constitute a language intelligible to all. Individuals fathom each other because they are all members first of a group, heirs of a function, and only afterwards, separate consciences.

All these phenomena, always merging, suggest that to know others is not always to know another than oneself. Knowledge of others, aside from intuitive perception, tends toward communion by the similarity or identity of intentions. But these phenomena also confirm the fact that, properly speaking, there is no fusion of individual states of consciousness.

* * * *

The contemporary knowledge of an act by its doer is direct and, it seems, total. To use the common expression: *one knows what one is doing*. Actually, as we have seen, this knowledge is limited to the plans which preceded the act, the memory of which remains with us. As soon as it becomes a question of explaining, that is *after the fact,* we must reconstruct either the intelligible succession of *motifs* or the psychological linking of *mobiles.* The observer also avails himself of an immediate knowledge. When we see someone strike wood with an axe, *we know what he is doing,* since we attribute to him a *motif* (the one that seems obvious: this person is cutting firewood). The difference between doer and observer here is above all a matter of the data each has available. The first knows *from inside,* he remembers the ideas he conceived, the feelings he had before acting. The spectator, on the other hand, first observes the movements. Normally, he projects into the consciousness of the *other* the intentions corresponding to the actual movements. This opposition, though commonplace, is of considerable importance. For there is a deep conflict between the actor who assimilates his unknown self with his authentic self, and the others who judge him by his behaviour and deeds. The root of this conflict, which is a moral rather than a psychological one, of course, lies in the fact that we know men's actions better than we do their thoughts—except when one is dealing with oneself.

The retrospective explanation of the conduct of others is comparable with the retrospective explanation of one's own behaviour. In particular, the distinction of the *motifs* and *mobiles,* already outlined, assumes clearer meaning. If we suppose the noble savage, dear to the eighteenth century, to be back among us, confronted with the Stock Exchange, or on a train, it is not to the psychologist that he would apply for an understanding of what takes place. Physics would help him to interpret the behaviour of the engine driver, the rules of railroad management, the behaviour of the station-master, the technique of financial exchange that of the brokers. In daily life we possess the knowledge which makes intelligible the actions of those about us. But the labour of the historian, another outsider, often consists in rediscovering those systems which govern the lives of individuals, and are not reducible to any psychology.

Whether concerned with self or others, the search for *mobiles* does not differ in nature. At most there will be noticed a tendency to look more outside the individual, to bring into the case circumstances rather than dispositions, the past rather than present choice, upbringing rather than character. The inner nature is observed, not explained, and so there is the temptation to diminish its importance. In addition, we objectify the other person in order to observe him; so we deprive him of the capacity for decision which we ourselves claim.

A still more important difference comes from the fact that the uncertainty and the intrinsic plurality of *motifs* is indistinguishable here from the ambiguity of documents. Unless we consider only the act, we are surely obliged to have recourse to the testimony of the interested party, a testimony doubly suspect. What is the *motif*? Is the *other* willing to tell us or deceive us, to justify or humble himself? Again, even assuming complete good faith, the fact remains that the doer's interpretation enjoys no privilege, that is, it is neither infallible nor immediate. Knowledge of others is usually subjected to the critique of knowledge of self. But there results no essential superiority of the latter: the observer or the psychologist makes use of other information, particularly of all the involuntary signs by which individuals so often betray themselves (in the double sense of the word). The spectator is freer, more detached, and will see *mobiles* which the author of the act—because of censorship or blindness—insists on ignoring, *motifs* of which he is unaware because they are either unconscious or obvious.

Indeed, if we decided to limit ourselves to the goals explicitly conceived, the end would quickly be reached, but it is impossible to stop there. In order to understand the decision of a businessman, the organization and situation of the firm must be known. The historian's interpretation does not coincide and does not try to coincide with the deliberations of the actor.

The search for *motifs* thus gradually widens until it includes the environment itself. The antecedents lead us back to origins, without an absolute beginning ever appearing. Thorough examination of *mobiles* is, as we know, by nature indefinite. Could not unity of character, perhaps, set a limit for our inquiry? Perhaps personality over and above the double rational and psychological explanation, represents a relatively autonomous whole by means of and in which, when all is said and done, the entire career, as well as the smallest act, would take on its exact meaning? Do we succeed in comprehending this totality of life and person?

* * * *

The unity of the person, as pointed out above, is perhaps given to a global intuition, but that intuition, not to be expressed in words, does not yield a true knowledge. The most one could say is: 'This person is capable of this and that' (and the chances of error in such judgments are many). Although this impression, usually immediate, plays a decisive part in human relations, it is less a knowledge than an illusion of one. As soon as the observer tries to be specific, tries to express the essence of the individual, he must dissect it in order to reconstruct it. This dual necessity is imposed for a single act, *a fortiori* for a personality considered in totality. Consequently such an interpretation implies, not merely as does the elementary interpretation, an indefinite retrogression, but also essential uncertainties.

Even if we assume a determined point of view (the psychology of the character, an account of the development or interpretation of the productions), we do not avoid the plurality of reconstructions. Whatever the system may be, a principle of unity must be selected, and this choice could not be valid universally. Of course biographers today are careful to respect life's complexity, to show their heroes' weaknesses or inconsistencies. However, they never stop with a mere juxtaposition of acts or impulses, they always compose personalities or lives. More or less consciously, they arrange accomplishments and adventures, shadows and lights, virtues and faults, according to a certain controlling idea, rarely apparent, but all the more effective. Moral judgment, or at least the appreciation of values, inspires this selection—and legitimately so; why should not everyone be defined by what is best in him? As a result, the diversity of images reflects not so much the ambiguity or freedom of interpretation as it does the conflict of emotions.

In autobiography this difficulty scarcely occurs because the pose assumed concerning oneself determines one's concept of oneself, the view of one's history. The arrangement of the facts results immediately from the assertions by means of which one expresses and commits oneself. The biographer's selection would be the equivalent of the choice which, in each individual, connects the past, which has become conscious, with a future, which is the object of desire.

Besides, this decision is not gratuitous or arbitrary; it, too, expresses a human experience, the relation of two beings, the conflict or accord between two temperaments. No one is entirely revealed to a single observer. We know perfectly well that all our friends do not have the same picture of us. They see us differently because we show a different aspect of ourselves; each of them sees us differently and we are these different individuals at once. In order to rise above this multiplicity one would have to grasp the common source of all these poses. But if the intuition of the essence is a myth, there remains a hesitation between diverse hypotheses, on the one hand, and on the other a decision similar to that arising naturally from living contact. The biographer, like the intimate friend, discovers a part of a man who is inaccessible in his totality.

This plurality of images, varying with the observer, will no doubt be admitted as evident *de facto,* but paradoxical *de jure.* How can it be denied that there exists a reality, and consequently a true idea of each person? And yet, we should like to uphold this paradox. We know the essential character of an individual no more than we understand the ultimate intention of an act. The only construct that can be called universally valid according to a given theory is the psychologist's: it conforms with both the facts and with the established generalities. Beyond this interpretation, essentially limited, no truth is even conceivable. God alone could weigh the value of all our deeds, put contradictory episodes in their places, unify character and behaviour. The idea of this absolute truth must vanish along with theology. It is not a question of denying the capability of the mind, but of discarding a fiction in order to describe the conflict of perspectives and the dispute between the self and others. The knowledge of others is neither more nor less privileged than is self-knowledge; it moves towards a goal situated at infinity, but, in contrast with the positive sciences, it is always open to question. Just as every individual transfigures his own past, so does the painter transfigure his model, and the biographer his hero.

* * * *

Knowledge of self and of others is in one sense complementary, in another contradictory or to put it better, dialectically opposed.

In the first place, without even going back to origins, it is clear that each of us develops his own idea of himself in contact with others. I am for myself different from the ideas which others have of me. Spontaneously I claim to know the final reason, the common origin of all these contradictory pictures. But this knowledge, assuming its accuracy, is neither indifferent nor superior to others' judgments. Either by assent or reaction we define ourselves by measuring ourselves by these ghosts. We wish to be the one imagined by others or, on the other hand, we evade arbitrary description.

On the other hand, the interpretation we give of our behaviour and character implies a certain psychological knowledge. As much as, and more than, from scientific writings, we glean our learning from the experience of life and men, accumulated throughout our own lives. One must, then, observe others to discover oneself. We see objectively in others what we should have continued to refuse seeing in ourselves. But, on the other hand, the behaviour of others would still be alien to us, even though subject to laws, if we were not able by an effort of sympathy, to put ourselves in their place, to guess at a consciousness similar to that which is immediately revealed in ourselves—and only in ourselves. In ourselves the intuition is concrete; it must contemplate others to be lucid.

But if my knowledge of myself is linked with what others know of me, or with what I know of others, there is a real opposition between the perspective of the observer and that of the actor, between the construction of each one through and for himself and the construction of an individual through and for an observer. We can approximate the effective identity with the understanding of the individual style of an individual, but the fact remains that one *lives* one's own experiences, and that one knows the experiences of others *objectified*. Of course, as my own spectator, I make of my character or past an object in order to explore it from outside, but I am still capable of coinciding with my own duration or volition. These two concurrences, one by means of which we define life, the other in which the creation of the personality is completed, denote the irreducibly specific quality of knowledge of self.

Of course I am addressing *alter egos*; the *thou* form is an absolute subject like my own *me*. In this sense I am conscious of the particularity of my knowledge, and the communication between individuals transcends that particularity. It is not important for us to analyse this communication and the different types of dialogues between the *I* and the *thou* (since we are seeking the origin only of the science of history). It should suffice that we have shown both the fundamental similarity and the disparity, the reciprocal qualities and the contrast, between the two forms of knowledge. Life experience is shut in upon itself, decision constitutive of the individual for himself, is inaccessible to others, but I discover my character and my past as I do those of others. Solitude is actual as are the interrelations; social and spiritual communion enriches the interrelations without, perhaps, rescuing the individuals from solitude.

III. OBJECTIVE MIND AND COLLECTIVE REALITY

So far, we have simplified the analysis by supposing, first, an isolated individual, then by bringing two individuals face to face, outside of any social or spiritual community—a convenient abstraction, but one which distorts the situation. The moment one speaks of a system of signs, or even simply of voluntary signs, the existence of a society is implied. In order that the meaning of signs may be known by the listener, as it is by the speaker, an explicity or tacit agreement is necessary, a common belief. In fact, communications between men develop within collectivities which penetrate and govern elementary relationships.

We do not have to study the various forms and aspects of collective life; that would be the object of an introduction to sociology. In this work we need merely show how this dimension of reality changes the object in history and, as a result, the historian's intention.

* * * *

In studying knowledge of others we distinguished various types of exchange between individuals: intellectual communication, active collaboration, affective understanding. Starting with these three concepts, we shall try to show three ways of looking at social fact, three of its aspects.

We have taken as an example of intellectual communication, a conversation. Such communication warrants a consciousness to think the same object that another has in mind, without becoming other than itself. Of course the identity of the object is never total because of the shift between the meaning of a word, fixed by usage, and the meaning given it in certain circumstances by a certain person. Moreover, concretely, the *noema* is never separable from the *noesis*, and the latter in turn, from the life experience. In spite of these reservations, the example gives the type of association at which the historian aims, which unites men within a group. Is not the supreme goal of an interpretation (of a text or a work of art) *total fidelity*—to rethink the creator's thought? And yet the presence in each mind of the same language reveals the immanence in each of them of both spiritual and objective realities.

Besides, a dialogue is a simple case of a *social relation.* The words of one party are understood by the other. The second person's answer will have as its *mobile* the question, and the answer was the questioner's *motif.* Without going into detail, we see the possibility of a study based on *social behaviours,* like those of Von Wiese and Max Weber, or by defining the relationship in terms of *propinquity* or *distance,* or by characterizing *motifs* and *mobiles* of social acts and relationships.

Affective communication, also, though not representing an autonomous aspect of collective life, reminds us of another prime datum—the feelings which individuals within a group have for each other, the impulses which cause them to act socially, to conform to rules or customs, the emotions by which their belonging to society is revealed to them and is expressed and maintained.

Let us add that the sociologists try to grasp the relative autonomy and exact meaning of the different totalities, from the anonymous and passing power of crowds up to that of the nation, a power ideal rather than real, imperceptible and yet so authoritatively effective. Finally, the objectivation of catchwords into laws, of affections or ideas into celebrations, customs, institutions, makes it possible to contrast the inner life of communities and the outer manifestations which express and at the same time confirm it.

These sketchy indications suffice; they recall to mind, first the alternative (traditional in sociology), of methods dealing with the *elements* and with the *totality,* then the various points of view from which the *primitive forms of sociability* are defined. It may be vain to seek a *trúe* classification, given the plurality of modes of consideration and the infinite diversity of societies. One fact is for us fundamental: the common feeling created in each individual by the priority of the objective mind over the individual mind is the historically and concretely primary datum. Men arrive at consciousness by assimilating, unconsciously, a certain way of thinking, judging and feeling which belongs to an epoch and which characterizes a nation or a class. Before becoming detached and isolated, minds were opened to the outer world; they are similar before being different, so to speak. In so far as they are social, they spontaneously share manifestations and convictions. Biological individuality is given; the human personality of the individual is constructed, based on a common foundation.

We shall put aside the various types of social relations and sentiments, the various degrees of association, the description of partial and of complex structures. We shall apply ourselves only to the change the historical object undergoes because it is not made up only of psychic events, but of *objective mind*, institutions and systems which control the infinite plurality of individual actions.

* * * *

Whether it is a question of daily life or of the most vitally important decisions, everyone naturally obeys historically varying customs. The way we dress or eat, as well as marriage rites and family organization are, with a wide margin of initiative reserved in each case, fixed by the collectivity; it matters little whether it is a question of laws, a matter of tradition, or of dress.

It seems then that in one sense individuals, similar to each other, can more easily know each other. They speak the same language in the broadest sense of the term, they make the same gestures, use the same words. But a society is never entirely contemporaneous with itself. Mores, legal and religious rules, all constitute a living past, since they are passed on to those who, from generation to generation, are responsible for upholding them. Consequently we act without understanding the institutions which cause our actions (at least their primitive meaning escapes us). Thus is explained Durkheim's advice to treat social facts as things. These facts are inherent in each of us, established by voluntary behaviours, often crystallized by habit or imposed by scarcely conscious ideas or convictions. But these behaviours, from the act of greeting to the formalities of citizenship, we adopt spontaneously, knowing their usefulness or their function *for us*; they bring us into accord with others and with the social imperatives, but we do not know their origins and history.

We need not mention even the inheritances which oblige us to repeat and reproduce the lives of the dead; of present customs we rarely have exact and complete knowledge. Social facts overflow the immediate limits of consciousness and are fixed in rites which assume imperative form, sometimes indifferent, but more often sacred or at least proper, and tyrannous to rebels and nonconformists. Any contact of societies or civilizations leads first to the shock of contradictory manifestations, from which mutual lack of understanding comes. The difference between the expressive gestures by which profane or religious feelings are conveyed is enough to create a sort of estrangement. The prayer of the Mohammedan tempts the Christian's laughter.

However transcendent their strangeness or power, social facts of the institutional type retain their privileged status as psychic events; they are comprehensible, they are not comparable with natural phenomena which would have to be classified according to regularities or reconstructed, but with human actions or works which must be interpretated like a literary or philosophical text. Beyond words we find states of mind, in the records we find thought and affections, in collective life, we find a culture.

The comparison is all the more valid since in fact the *objective mind,* a totality of ideas, beliefs and mores of an epoch or a group, comes to us at least partly *objectified.* Let us give the name *objectified mind* (to use Mr. N. Hartmann's expression) to what Dilthey called objective mind, that is, all natural objects on which the mind has left its stamp: printed books, carved stones, painted canvas. Let us reserve the expression *objective mind* for what we often call *collective representations,* that is, for all the ways of thinking and acting which are characteristic of a society, judicial, philosophical, religious, etc. Man lives amid the remains of a past which again gives a sort of presence to those who no longer exist. He lives in a community both social and spiritual, within each individual, since it is shown by the partial assimilation of personalities, exterior to all since no one is the origin of the common practices, since no one has chosen the state of knowledge and the hierarchy of values which he has accepted and adopted.

* * * *

The mind, objectified or objective, is at the same time more accessible and ambiguous than the psychic event.

A monument can be considered either as a document or as a spiritual reality, virtual so to speak, offered to all of us. As a document the Mona Lisa would show a certain way of thinking or creating, a man's soul at a moment or in a period. As a work of art, the painting appears as beauty crystallized which *is*, time notwithstanding, for centuries, without other need than understanding and love to recover its original freshness.

Thus a dual knowledge of the past would be possible, the one bearing directly on mind as recorded in matter, the other on the consciousness of an individual or group made accessible by means of these *objectifications.* This alternative is not connected merely with the situation of the historian, but also with the essential structure of reality. If the historian proposed to relive the *other's* experience, the work of art would represent an obstacle as well as a means: he must progress by way of intentional contents which, having become autonomous, hide rather than express the life from which they emanate. But the work of art is, just as is the consciousness, an object of history. History withdraws from life, or more exactly, clings to *historical life,* characterized by the dual movement of abstraction and revival.

The objective mind shares this ambiguity. The transcendent quality of the work is connected with two things: on the one hand, the creation is, as it were, never conscious, and the creator's intention is less important than the result, on record for everyone; on the other hand, according to Simmel's formula '*Wendung zur Idee*,' the propositions of a science or of a philosophy, even if they were originally at the service of a practical goal, are organized in a universe no longer obeying any other than its own law. The objective mind, to which everyone naturally conforms, includes fragments of these universes, as well as collective prejudices or arbitrary convictions. The plurality of *systems of interpretation* which we shall study later is valid for social facts as well as for monuments.

But, whether collective or incorporeal, the object of history is, as it were, externalized. Institutions are accessible from without, one is not limited to the uncertain testimony of the interested party or of the spectator. The fact itself, being perceptible, is subject to examination or recorded in texts. Of course these texts are at times mysterious, as are ceremonies or practices; they may have not *one* but *several* meanings, depending on individuals or epochs, for forms often outlive beliefs. Nevertheless, the inquiry starts with the documents and is directed towards an end which at least avoids the irreducible obscurity of living experience.

As a result, reality is *disindividualized, rationalized,* at times even *systematized.* Individual events disappear for one interested only in common certainties or in the logic (always incomplete) of collective behaviours. Furthermore, the personality, integrated with an institution, fades into anonymity, the ideal public official is one who entirely forgets his human preferences. The goals pursued by social activities are more visible because they are less personal, more regular and more rational. In historical movements it is true that individuals, cut adrift from their habits, become subject again to the most varying impulses, to the call of prophets, to the suggestions of propaganda rather than to the calculations of self-interest. In spite of all, the historian first of all studies typical situations in which the individuals were subservient, and the individuals, subject to a party or church, again abandon their own personalities. Militant or faithful, their action depends more on the circumstances, on the organization, than on the inner will of each.

Finally, bodies of laws, constitutions, form largely coherent wholes. Historical reality in this case seems to have the unity of intellectual works. It is true that laws, as they are expressed in codes, represent only one element of the law of life: without even considering sanctioned violations, the law as applied is not confused with what is written. But, on the other hand, certain behaviours themselves compose an organic whole because of the mere fact of the mutual dependence of choices made by each individual and by the group (in economic life, for example). Here again, the historian needs less to create than to demonstrate an inherent rationality.

One can now see how inexact is the argument which maintains that historical data, fragmentary and chaotic, are mere dust. The historian searching the archives at first assembles collections of facts, but, as soon as he comes to compose even a simple narrative he is no longer confronted with chaos. He observes neither isolated individuals, nor detached events: the former fit into groups, the latter are inseparable from a condition of the collectivity or of the institutions. The intelligibility of *motifs* (and at times of *mobiles*) is gradually communicated to the collective and unconscious achievements, society and history.

* * * *

In the above description we have tried to avoid two classical antinomies, that of the individual and society, and the one between collective representations and authentic thought. We shall still have many occasions to return to these problems. For the moment we should like merely to say why we have neglected them.

History, according to a classical formula, is the spontaneous memory of societies. The past which is of interest is first that of the group; historical curiosity seems to be connected with the feeling each individual has of belonging to a whole which transcends him. This is certainly true for primitive forms of history, but in so far as individuals have become conscious of themselves, the historian is no longer limited to exalting by memory, to justifying by legend, or to consecrating by an ideal example, a collectivity or a power. He undertakes his inquiry as he approaches present problems, following the variations of social reality and personal judgment. Monumental history has the same dignity as social history because the effort of self-construction is on the same level as political will.

Even this opposition is still artificial, because it supposes society and the individual external and, as it were, foreign to each other. Now society is present in the individual even while he thinks he is solely responsible for himself. One can break family or professional ties, but one still retains the language, the system of concepts or of values which are essentially ours, since we succeed in defining ourselves, even if only negatively, only by using this common fund.

In fact, the opposition depends on political ideology. There are times of peace when men (most of them) recognize each other in their environment. There are other times during which social relations are taken as a tyranny of fate, of things, or of a minority. Revolt against a society is in fact one of the springs of the historical process. Also, in the order of ends, the communal ideal and the individual ideal represent the two terms of a fundamental alternative. Either the individual realizes himself in and through social life whose obligations he conscientiously accepts, or, on the contrary, he wishes the collectivity to leave each individual as broad an independence as possible, and reduces the state, the symbol and executive of the general will, to an administrative function.

It may perhaps be objected that we have not separated in objective mind what belongs to a historical group in its particular aspect, and what goes beyond the frontiers of groups, and is valid universally. Of course we appreciate the gap between the spirit of a regiment or a school, the spirit of an epoch or a nation, and, finally the state of what is known at a given moment, but at first glance we see no solution of continuity. The objective mind is multiple, incoherent, without definite unity or certain limits. Also, no activity is in fact closed in upon itself, no rite is not subject to some influence. Customs, or gods, are passed on, skills are often invested with sacred values. Even the pure sciences have, as a condition and as creators, men who are inextricably bound up with certain social relations. Consequently, it is by the analysis of spiritual universes, of activities in their essential meanings, that one can fix the characteristics and independence of various histories.

In and through individuals common representations become clear, in and through them are realized the communities which precede and transcend them. The description justifies no metaphysic, either of *national souls* or of a *collective consciousness*, but it confirms the existence of a reality both transcendent to and within men, social and spiritual, total and multiple.

IV. HISTORICAL KNOWLEDGE

IN THIS chapter we should like to define historical knowledge on the basis of the three preceding studies. We shall arrive at this definition by two different routes.

So far, we have retained all the forms assumed by the science or the understanding of human events. It is now important to take account of the fact that the object in history belongs to the past, that it is in the process of development, and that it partakes of the nature of collective and spiritual reality at once both inherent in and transcendent to conscious personalities. Between the raw duration and pure reason, within the limits of generalities but above and beyond the juxtaposed elements, we discern the original direction of the historical inquiry.

Moreover, this inquiry is derived from knowledge of self and of others. It tries to overcome the partiality and the reciprocity of spectator and actor, the dialectic of the self and the other. Thus there emerges, when all is said and done, the special intention of historical knowledge which, inseparable from human life, confronts the present with the past, what each individual is with what he has been, the subject with other individuals; a knowledge which is a reflection, the moment of a dialectic beginning with life and returning to it.

* * * *

Even in the case of knowledge of self, we have noticed the typical break between living experience and retrospection, which never is resurrection, and is always conceptual reconstruction. In this sense knowledge of self and of others, both contemporary and restrospective, would be of the same genus. In this genus, historical knowledge would represent the lowest species; the gap between knowledge and its object attains extreme dimensions.

Individuals, as they become more distant from us, are lost in abstraction. The *other*, being present, reminds us always of his capacity for change; absent, he is imprisoned in the image we have made of him. The personality of the historical character is definitely fixed in his behaviour and achievements. Nothing can wrest him from the rigidity of what has been and will always have been. Again, if in our friends we distinguish between what they are and what they do, the distinction disappears as men merge into the past. This is an apparent injustice, but it is possible that the ideal of resurrection is not so much inaccessible as it is alien to history.

Quality and quantity of information vary. Lacking documents, most of the attempted psychoanalyses of historical characters are at best attractive and without any possible verification. The inner being becomes more and more elusive, even if the behaviour remains intelligible. The easiest rational interpretation, always a likely one, tends to reject the interpretation by *mobiles* (especially irrational *mobiles*). This is all the more true, since men of the past are interesting in the first place because of their historical activity, with which they tend to merge, so that they are, so to speak, disindividualized.

In the same way the element of sympathy preceding, accompanying, or following a knowledge of human events, varies. Knowledge of self, of others (when it is experienced, direct) unfolds in an atmosphere of intimacy. We have, with our contemporaries, enough ideas and affections in common to understand, usually, how one can have the experiences which the documents—actions or works—suggest to us. As the common expression has it, we put ourselves in their places.

Historical knowledge is often lacking in this sharing of consciousness. Only psychological diversities would be of a sort absolutely to separate contemporaries. Between individuals belonging to different epochs, to other civilizations, communication remains strictly intellectual. We reconstruct the system of thought, the system of values, we explain them both by the circumstances, but rarely do we succeed in giving back life to the man who expressed himself in that world, or at best the success is the reward of long familiarity, the privilege of art or of the great historian.

Does this mean that historical knowledge is always inadequate? It all depends, really, on the purpose assigned to it. It rediscovers neither the fleeting impressions, nor the rare feelings, nor the affective totality which make up the climate of life. The impression conveyed only by actual presence, the details, frivolous yet meaningful, the style of the individual, which makes people dear or repulsive to us—all that gradually sinks into oblivion. Fundamentally, the historian discovers personalities only through ideas, the ideas of the works which he tries to rethink, ideas which come from us and which he substitutes for the actual experiences in order to make them more intelligible. An irremediable loss? That which affects us most is not necessarily that which merits survival.

So far we have discussed history as a projection of biography and autobiography. Now, we can say that biography is not a type of history, or at least that biography and history start in different directions. The biographer is interested in the private man, the historian above all in the public man. The individual becomes history only by the influence he exerts on the collective development, by his contribution to the spiritual development. The biographer would like to ressuscitate the irreplaceable individual, that is, each of us in himself and for those near him. Doubtless there are historical biographies: the private and public man, the individual and the historical person would have to appear equally in their inseparable unity. And yet even in such a case, the opposition stands at least partially. A biography gets a grasp of the epoch at the same time as of a man, but it is directed at the man; the historian, after all, visualizes the epoch beyond the man. The purposes remain contrary while the objects tend to merge.

As a result, the perspective is reversed: history is no longer the backward species, the poorest and driest discipline; it becomes, on the contrary, the full realization of an inclination which was apparent beginning with the knowledge of self, the achievement of the attempt to think life, by showing and reconstructing the rationality inherent in it, even when that rationality was often unperceived by the very beings who lived it. Science, unable to coincide with the duration, nevertheless fulfills its calling, since it again grasps the movement of life towards spirit, of individuals towards a collective destiny.

In fact, neither this intellectualization of the duration nor this spiritualization of the object are enough to define history. They allow a distinction between historical knowledge and psychology, living experience and retrospection. But all knowledge of events is retrospective. Strictly, we observe events at the moment they occur, it is only afterward that we explain them, organize them intelligibly. Human consciousness appears, so to speak, only to the memory or to the spectator. Living experience is as though absorbed into itself. It is transformed, dissolved as soon as it is expressed or known.

All retrospective knowledge, then, is not historical. Broadly, three tendencies would appear. Either one aims at generalities of an especially psychological order (psychological laws, theories of psychoses, character types), in which case events are made use of but not considered in their temporal localization; it may be added also that by means of scientific abstraction a fact is substituted for the event. Or, the tendency is towards totalities transcendent to the duration (essential ego, true humanity). Or, finally, the attempt is to reconstitute a development. Only this goal is characteristic of history (even though for fear of losing himself in an endlessly gradual progress, the historian, in his desire to reach fixed points, is always ascending to generalities or totalities transcendent to the development). At a certain moment in time an individual reflects about his adventure, a collectivity about its past, mankind about its evolution: thus are born autobiography, special history, universal history. History is the *retrospective grasp of a human development, that is, it is at once both social and spiritual.*

* * * *

We have observed a sort of dialectic between knowledge of self and of others. I know my impressions or my motives, and the acts of others. We define ourselves in our own eyes by the best of ourselves (what we think we are or should like to be) and we judge others by their conduct and, so to speak, by their success. Our idea of ourselves is incomplete, we do honour to ourselves (except in cases where we blame an ungovernable temperament to excuse our faults). On the other hand, we tend to imprison others in a formula both vague and imperative, often the more absolute the vaguer it is.

Is it possible, and if so how, to overcome this dialectic? In practice, we observe that there are multiple images of each individual and of each form of behaviour, that each image corresponds to *one* spectator's point of view, the diversity of points of view being as irreducible as the opposition of subject and observer. But to the extent that history rises above psychology, or at least subordinates the psychology to the work or to the event, it evades the two opposite partialities of actor and spectator; it is closer to the latter than to the former, without being subservient to the outlook of either. The act retained by the historian is not the act which a certain spectator, situated at a spot or at a particular moment, observed, but the act as it is historically defined by its place in a situation or a development, by its effects on the collectivity. In the same way, the work in which the individual is expressed and with which he merges, eludes the psychological alternative and the prejudice of the interested party as well as of the indifferent one, the prejudice of the admirer and of the enemy.

So, perhaps, the privileges of retrospection compensate for the bondage to which it is subject. The historian, as distinguished from the contemporary, knows the whole of the individual life. What might have become of the individual he definitely does not know. But he knows completely what he did do. Now, a fate remains uncertain as long as it is incomplete, since at every moment a man decides and, so to speak, chooses himself anew. Even for the man alone, conversion on the last day changes the meaning of the previous life.

When it is a question of ideas, the historian perceives their consequences, he judges the teacher by his disciple, the ancient doctrine according to the modern science. What the creator could not guess at, the historian, thanks to perspective, sees immediately. In this sense the present lights up the past: modern psychology renews understanding of the most ancient mythologies, microphysics the Kantian conception of the object or the ancient philosophies of the atom. Thus, the historian excels not merely the spectator, but also the actor, since he has available documents which are by definition inaccessible to those who spontaneously, unconsciously, lived history.

Here again, then, the historian overcomes the elementary uncertainties, not so much by changing from an amateur into a scientist, as by changing objectives. The plurality of perspectives upon an event persists as long as we remain at the level of the individuals, as long as we claim coincidence with the imperceptible movement of the consciousness. The foregoing analysis suggests a possible dual truth, that of the fact having become objective, and that of the development which by its progress, creates the truth of the past.

* * * *

We pointed out above that the very goal of self-knowledge seems indeterminate. Is to know oneself to perceive that of which any man is or ought to be capable? Is it, on the contrary, to determine one's singularity? A worship of originality, or of humanity? Apparently, we were neglecting this question. In fact, all our discussion was leading back to it.

At the elementary level, the dialectic of self and of others appears again; it directs, it seems, both inquiries towards particularity. But this opposition is illusory, for in oneself one already perceives the other than self, the one one no longer is or might have been and, in others, one recognizes oneself.

But it is necessary to distinguish two types of communities, one psychological, the other historical. I surely must observe in myself a way of acting or feeling at least analogous to what I see on the outside, otherwise I should narrate facts without understanding them. But this identity of human impulses, whatever be the level of formalism or of abstract impoverishment to which I must rise to reach it, suffices only the moralists, the narrators who judge the infinite variety of adventures and individuals by the simplicity of final tendencies. History would remain only a collection of cases for the psychologist. Between my thought, my will, and those of others, the similarity of psychological mechanisms would not suffice to create a union. If I understand my fellow citizens or my contemporaries it is because we have in us the same objective mind, we use the same language, have acquired the same values, share the same certainties.

From this community there follows a double consequence. Historical knowledge is *part,* it is a *means,* of the knowledge of self. I discover the past of my collectivity partly in myself; when I interest myself in it, I am not obeying a simple curiosity, I am not seeking memories or images, I am trying to find out how my collectivity became what it is, how it made me what I am. Again, if I am, first and above all, such as my intimates and my milieu have formed me, if I spontaneously do not distinguish between the ideas I have received and *my* ideas, I am condemned to explore the world of mankind in order to show what perhaps makes me unique, what, in any case, is mine essentially because I have sanctioned it by my choice.

Certainly if to know myself is to become distinctly conscious of the unique nuance of a given experienced episode or of my unvarying self,

I need perhaps to shut up within myself, to absorb myself in my impressions. And again, even to bring to light the qualitative originality, a sort of confrontation, at least implicit, is imposed. As soon as I aspire to know, I must emerge from myself. I grasp the impulses causing me to act only by other men's experience. First of all, knowledge of self as a singular person follows inevitably on the discovery and exploration of other persons. Each individual defines himself by contrast, an epoch with its past, a culture or a nation with another, a person with his time or his milieu. At all levels knowledge of self is last; it marks the achievement of knowledge of others.

Thus at least we arrive at a statement of the decisive question. This rising above the singularities is not equivalent to an explanation of the facts by a law, or of individuals by types. Either history ends in an incoherent plurality in which one finds oneself by comparison and choice, or else it assigns to humanity a vocation which subordinates the various missions of men and of groups to a final unity, the unity of an abstract imperative or of a collective task.

*   *   *   *

The historical being is neither the one who endures and accumulates experiences, nor the one who remembers; history implies the awakening of consciousness by which the past is recognized as such, at the moment when consciousness gives it back a sort of presentness. That is why we have sought the origin of historical knowledge not in memory, nor in experienced time, but in *reflection,* which makes each man his own spectator, in *observation,* which takes as its object the experience of others.

We could have analysed the gap between experience and retrospection by the example of memory, for recollection is not preserved and fixed between impression and evocation, like a material atom in the depths of the unconscious. It partakes of my life, it changes with it. Only certain exceptional moments perhaps elude this evolution and, stamped in us forever, manage to come back. In any case, these involuntary recalls, always fragmentary and supratemporal as it were, do not suffice to assure the continuity of our ego, nor to protect consciousness from duration.

Memory is allied with the primitive forms of history because it furnishes its materials. Early accounts string together events which the narrator remembers in order to recall or reveal them to others. But they depart from experience in the same way as does knowledge: the narrator does not reproduce, either for others or for himself, what he saw or experienced; he has the illusion of seeing or feeling again; in fact, basing himself on the traces which the past has left in him he reconstitutes, he expresses in verbal forms the facts and deeds he witnessed. His testimony offers certain guarantees of truth or at least of authenticity (it would be easy to enumerate the irreplaceable advantages of contemporary chroniclers), but in spite of everything he is limited by the limited view of the spectator or/and the actor. Neither has *lived* the historical reality if the latter is not at the level of the individual. Neither one relives it or brings it back to life.

Memories are not only documents for knowledge, but are also a condition of it, in so far as, without continuity, the individual would not enter into history, not even his own. Thanks to immediate retention, successive moments come together; thanks to the amassing of acquired knowledge I *am* my past, the sum of my experiences; thanks to the relative permanence of my affections I can coincide with my distant impressions and remain the same for those around me. The creature who evolves is one who becomes richer by conserving but who in order to progress must also forget. History makes its appearance with consciousness of this destiny, with the detachment which breaks the unity of simple duration. Instead of adhering to the pattern of development and giving himself over to its inner dynamism, the individual seeks to know himself by standing outside himself. By reflection he makes historical the evolving process which is merely one with his existence. History belongs, not to the order of life, but to the spirit.

CONCLUSION

IN THE preceding description we have touched on almost all the problems we shall meet in the remainder of our study. This anticipation is inevitable, since the whole philosophy of history comes from what is fundamentally given, the individual in a developing collectivity, who reflects upon himself, upon his past, upon his own reflection. In this conclusion, we shall only show two kinds of results, those concerning the nature of understanding on the one hand, and on the other the original reasons for the relativism threatening the science of the human past.

If we go back to the analysis of knowledge of others, we may hesitate between two definitions. Either we shall call understanding the intuitive grasp of a state of consciousness in an expression, of a total being in the physiognomy or the body, or we shall reserve the word for the more elaborate forms of knowledge, the grasp of *motifs*, of *mobiles*, or of a personality. Without other justification (since it is a question of a nominal definition), we shall keep to the second term: understanding, for us, will be the reconstruction of the consciousness of others or of the works which are products of their conscious personalities. (Thus we immediately distinguish understanding, or sympathy, and affective participation.)

There are two objections, it seems, to this definition. The understanding of self progresses through memories; it is easily seen that it may be confused with a reconstruction. But in the case of others it requires the use of signs; the interpretation of signs themselves, or the inference from signs themselves to the thing signified, adds a new dimension to the phenomenon, and another uncertainty arises: do we understand the consciousness of others, their works in themselves, or the relationship between the former and the latter? Again, to the extent that we substitute constructed connections for life experience, does the inherence of intelligibility in the reality, which we said was a characteristic of understanding, still stand?

The plurality of understandings is a datum of observation. Men communicate, using systems of signs, they create monuments; a certain sort of understanding, then, contemplates a meaning which has become objective, the ideal content of words or of a text. Since the meaning of a writing, or more generally of a work of art, exists only by means of an act of creation, one gets back to the consciousness of the writer or of the artist. This procedure is another form of understanding, of particular importance for the historian. Moreover, in both cases, understanding strives to retrieve the *intention* of another mind: the goal of the attempt would, then, be an integral correspondence, a particular knowledge, and not a generality.

In the case of involuntary, non-conventional signs (gestures, mimicry, facial expressions) it is true that we attain a closeness not perceived by the party concerned. The angry man is not thinking of the significance of clenched fists; he is not trying to communicate or to express himself. But this is of more interest to the psychologist than to the historian. We shall put aside the science of expressive symptoms, of abortive actions, calligraphy, physiognomy, etc. Let us note merely that this immediate inference is not characteristic of understanding, that it is not even limited to human phenomena, since any effect is a sign of its cause (the smoke from the railway train) for the one who recognizes the connection. Really, a sign belongs to understanding only if it *represents* an idea or at least shows an *intention*.

In the same way, the reconstruction of a duration does not contradict the principle of immanence. The psychoanalyst's interpretations, in most cases, reveal to patients who were ignorant of them the reasons for their actions. But the rationality of the resentful reaction is no less intrinsic to the behaviour whose prime mover, as it were, it was. The immanence of intelligibility is defined with reference to life and not to the moment of consciousness. This is a basic distinction if, as we shall see better in *Part II*, the object of history is to understand life by showing a system of knowledge and of values, without becoming subservient to ideologies, that is, to the ideas men made, or tried to make of themselves.

The relationships between phenomena set up by science compel acceptance by all who want the truth. Are comprehensive relations universally valid in the same way? Or is understanding part and parcel of the interpreter's personality? The first three chapters of this *Part* each suggest a question.

The historian belongs to the development he studies. He comes after the events, but within the same changing process. The science of history is a form of a community's consciousness of itself, an element of life in common, as knowledge of self is one aspect of personal consciousness, one of the factors of individual fate. Is it not at the same time a function of the present situation, which by definition changes with time, and of the will which inspires the scholar, who is unable to abstract himself from himself and from the object of his study.

But on the other hand, a contrary difficulty, the historian tries to penetrate the consciousness of others. He is, with reference to the historical being, *the other*. Psychologist, strategist, or philosopher, he observes from without. He cannot *become* his hero as the latter was in himself, nor see the battle as does the general who saw it or lived through it, nor understand a doctrine as did its creator.

Finally, whether it is a matter of interpreting an act or a work, we must reconstruct conceptually. Now, we always have the choice between multiple systems, since the idea is both inherent in and transcendent to life: all monuments exist by and for themselves in a spiritual world; judicial and economic logic is intrinsic to the social reality and superior to individual consciousness.

These three problems, in practice, are scarcely separable. The externality of the observer is apparent in the selection of a system as it is in the interpretation within a given system. The historicity of the historian is expressed in the *point of view* of the spectator as well as in the *perspective* of the development. Nevertheless, these distinctions enable us to organize our study: we shall first study the historian as external to his object, then the historian within the history whose movement he retraces. We might again say: first the observer of others, then the historian of his own past.

Second Part

INTELLECTUAL UNIVERSES
AND THE
PLURALITY OF SYSTEMS OF INTERPRETATION

INTRODUCTION

LET US take as a starting point one of the conclusions reached in the preceding *Part*. The human event, as it occurs in consciousness, is inaccessible. Later, we reconstruct what was lived. What are the uncertainties and ambiguities of this reconstruction? To what extent is it separable from the situation and intention of the historian? To what extent susceptible to a universal validity?

We pointed out in Chapter III of the preceding *Part* the objectification of consciousness in works of the mind and social wholes. There results from it a *plurality of systems of interpretation*, which will be the first subject of our study.

But, assuming this plurality to be irreducible, the question will arise whether, within a certain system, an interpretation may be said to be true. This truth will be sought either in the direction of the element, or in a more or less extensive totality. Besides, truth is menaced either by the dissolution of the object (an imperceptible atom, an ambiguous totality), or by the intervention of the observer in the reconstruction. The same problems might again be expressed as follows: the universality of understanding would be condemned either by the structure of historical reality, always incomplete and rich in new meanings, or by the activity of the historian who, involved in historical evolution, remains external to the past.

We shall discuss first the plurality of systems of interpretation and the impossibility of a scientific simplification (Chapter I), then partial interpretation, that of ideas (Chapter II), of psychological events (Chapter III) and of facts (Chapter IV), always keeping in mind the various questions: the possibility of a true understanding, fragmentary or total, the relativity or universality of understanding, the distinction between and the inevitable collaboration of the systems.

1. THE PLURALITY OF SYSTEMS OF INTERPRETATION

WE INDICATED in Chapter III of the preceding *Part* the origins of the problem we wish to examine.

To communicate, men make use of systems of signs which they

receive from outside. Thus, a word has a meaning objectively fixed (by convention, usage, etc.), but the sense given it by *this* certain person, using it at *such* a moment, always differs more or less from the common meaning. In current conversation, to fill the gap between what the *other* means and what he says, one is obliged to grasp the silent language of gestures and bodies, to share the tacit accord which specifies for intimates the value of each term. When the interlocutors are separated by centuries, the very interpretation of the language implies a reconstruction of the systems used by the epoch or by a given person, without one's ever being certain of grasping the particular impression which was expressed in a way perhaps obvious to contemporaries.

With the desire to *create,* and no longer to *communicate,* the gap between the living experience and the monument increases. One would vainly seek the beauty of a painting outside the material which serves as a vehicle for an aesthetic value once and for all offered for everyone. Between the consciousness and the becoming conscious, between the clear intention and the creation, there is a break perhaps for the individual himself, and always for others.

From now on we shall assume the point of view of the interpreter in order to show the plurality of systems of interpretation, connected with the situation of the historian and with the structure of the real.

* * * *

Let us take as an example the understanding of the writings of J.-J. Rousseau. Let us put aside the work of philology, the comparison and criticism of texts, the collation of different editions, etc. Let us pay no attention, either, to the study of certain facts relative to the works like the number of editions or printings, the circulation of the book, public acclaim, etc. Whatever the importance of that sociological study may be, the labour of the historian does not end there. Whether it is a question of *La Nouvelle Héloïse* or of *Le Contrât Social,* the historian also wishes to show the ideological or artistic content of the works. Not to repeat what the author said, not to summarize it, but to elucidate and rethink.

It is easy to formulate abstractly the ideas Rousseau more or less directly expressed in his novel. But to expose the conscious intentions of a writer is still not understanding a work. The meaning of a novel is never merged with that of the moral, political or religious conceptions which the author imagined he was illustrating or defending. In the same way, the *Contrât Social* would not be understood if the historian had merely shown Rousseau's political preferences, recalled the possible borrowings from predecessors or contemporaries, or even analysed the attitude of Rousseau, at once both a citizen of Geneva and a man of the people rebelling against the salons. The meaning of a political philosophy, on condition that it admits that *such a philosophy has a right to exist,* is beyond biographical incidents or social and literary influences; it demands, to be understood, an effort of sympathy.

Let us make very clear the importance we attribute to these remarks. There might be a question about the task which the historian *must* impose upon himself. The study of borrowings and sources is not enough. The technique of history or of criticism would be brought back into question: how can aesthetic values be expressed in another language without distorting them? With the same psychological ideas, with the same experiences, Proust might have written, instead of *A la Recherche du Temps Perdu,* a commonplace and boring scientific treatise.

But this is not the direction in which our analyses are aimed. This technique, and the means of expression at its disposal, is of little importance. We suppose that the historian claims to know and we are asking how he succeeds in doing so. Now, any knowledge which left out of account the indwelling order and unity of a monument, would distort its object, for a work, or a creation, is intelligible only by reference to its authentic end. Between observation of facts, explanation by causes on one hand, and aesthetic appreciation on the other, comes the understanding which should logically be independent of both and precede both. Lacking this, the historian mutilates or is ignorant of the spiritual reality of the past.

In the discussion just above, it seems that we have again found the classical distinction between the interpretation from within and the objective interpretations. But our purpose was not merely to recall this distinction, for as we see it, it represents only a privileged example of the *plurality of systems of interpretation* because of the fact that it contrasts two extreme systems.

We showed, in the preceding *Part,* that any interpretation is a reconstruction. Even if, in the end, we contemplate the consciousness of beings who have disappeared, we proceed by means of intelligible relations. Now we note the plurality of relations which can be used.

Suppose it is understanding Rousseau as a whole, that is, showing the unity of his different works: we try to imagine the citizen of Geneva, the utopian who dreams of a just political system and of a reformed pedagogy, and at the same time, the solitary thinker, etc. The inconsistency or consistency of the ideas would matter less than the affective coherence of the different themes. Indeed, if we study the *Contrât Social* in itself or in the evolution of political theory, the interpretation should be not inconsistent in the strict sense: is civil religion reconcilable with the pantheism of the letters to Monsieur de Malesherbes, with the cult of liberty? Depending on the goal he pursues, the historian establishes different connections between the components; he uses different concepts: but *it is the historian himself who assigns himself this goal.*

Have we gained anything by observing the relationship of the interpreter to the historical monument, and no longer the process by which life may transcend itself? There is no doubt that the shift was still possible, but not necessary, as long as attention was fixed on the phenomenon of creation. But the plurality of interpretations is obvious as soon as we look at the labour of the historian. For as many interpretations arise as there are systems, that is, vaguely, as there are *psychological conceptions and individual systems of logic.* Even more, we can say that *the theory precedes the history,* if we understand by theory both the determination of a certain system and the value given to a certain type of interpretation.

* * * *

In order to confirm, less the exactness than the importance of the foregoing analyses (one might indeed consider them useless, they are so commonplace), let us examine certain forms of external interpretation, for example the varieties of method called materialistic. It seems that we may distinguish four of them: causal explanation, psychological explanation, explanation by concepts such as expression, reflex, and finally historical explanation. Let us consider them in order.

Most often, we speak of *determining* or *conditioning.* Let us exclude those cases which we shall meet further on when we shall study the notion of historical causality. Even now, it is clear that the causal explanation always assumes an understanding from within. Before seeking the causes of an idea, it is still necessary to know what it signifies, that is, really, *what it is.* Will it be said that, on the contrary, we learn it from external circumstances? Such an objection assumes as admitted the very theory in question, namely that the true significance of ideas emerges from study of the environment and influences. And further, even in this case, the distinction between and order of the two procedures remain valid, but social understanding is accepted as conclusive, by reason of a philosophical theory.

Besides, the causal inquiry sanctions no appreciation. The truth or value of a production of the mind is not measured by the circumstances of discovery or creation. Moreover, there is a choice of but one of two alternatives: if all ideas have social causes, we must consent to a radical separation of judgment of value and establishment of sources. Otherwise we should come to the point of disqualifying all ideas (those of the historian included). If on the contrary, certain ideas have no social causes, it follows that the materialistic interpretation is neither the only one, nor is it entitled to preference, and consequently it leaves room for understanding from within.

Although the causal explanation is commonly taken to be the explanation *par excellence*, it is rarely met with. It is, in fact, difficult to find regular patterns of connection between facts and ideas. Most of the time, the historian uses terms like *reflex*, *superstructure*, or psychological concepts such as *justification*, *dissimulation*, *sublimation*, *escape*, etc. The liberal economy serves to *justify* capitalism, the so-called economic harmony *dissimulates* the actual situation, religion serves to *sublimate* poverty, transcendent imaginations *escape* from the world in which each one lives out his unique existence.

It is clear that such an explanation is partial. It allows no conclusion concerning truth or falsity, or even simply the meaning of ideas. It is still one among others, scientifically valid on condition that one is conscious of its limits.

No more do social effects or the falsity of an idea allow an assertion relative to source. The capitalist's interest in the theory of the inevitability of financial crises does not imply that the theory is false. And, assuming that it is false, it does not follow that those who support it are hypocritical or cynical. At most we have the right to conclude that the error implies a reason of the psychological order, if the mind, as a mind, is not mistaken.

It will be objected that the historian does not study, on the one hand, ideas, and on the other, men. He does not admit that this duality is irreducible. On the contrary, he tends towards unity, because ideas for him are the *expression* of human attitudes or of social situations. Suppose we take the example, just used, of the liberal economy. The historian will not set up the intentions of bourgeois economists versus the logic of science, for the concepts used, the reasoning and investigating procedures, the whole apparatus of thought, express a class will as much as they do the desire to sanction private property and free competition. Such a method might be justified by propositions which would at least be probable: every person's thinking is the image of his ways of life; the different activities of a group or of an individual are not independent of each other; they bear the mark of the same inspiration; they correspond to an intuition or to a peculiar style.

Here again it is a question of an available procedure, the legitimacy of which, among others, is not in doubt; but it is important to point out its implicit assumptions and limits. The make-up of totalities of ideas (liberal philosophy, for example), of social totalities (a certain class), the bringing into relationship of these totalities—all these procedures imply a certain orientation of curiosity. The moment one brings together into the unity of a single context various creations of the mind: religion, science, philosophy, etc., the system of interpretation chosen necessarily remains within specific logical limits, and one tends towards a sort of sublimated psychology. But such a history could not exclude or disqualify the history of pure ideas, nor that of men in action.

Finally, a formula such as 'the historical significance of such and such a doctrine has been . . .' belongs to another category. It represents the historian's last recourse: if Cartesian mechanism has the factory system, neither as its cause nor consequence, if it expresses neither the psychology nor the biological attitude of factory man, there remains a temporal coincidence suggestive of historical judgment. Henceforth the historian, freed from any obligation of proof, freely organizes the historical evolutions in and by which facts and works take on their exact meaning. It is enough to ask the question: is retrospection, which is perhaps truer than contemporary vision, definitive? Or, is it not doubly relative—to the historian's theory and to his perspective? It implies, then, and cannot demonstrate, the truth of the philosophy on which it depends.

* * * *

The foregoing analyses permit, it seems, three conclusions:

1. Far from replacing it, explanation presupposes understanding.
2. The plurality of interpretations is an incontestable fact, which the historian must accept. Certain interpretations, under whatever conditions, remain independent.
3. Only a theory, legitimately anterior to the historical inquiry, makes it possible to fix the value of each interpretation, the possibilities of objective explanations, and the nature of intrinsic understanding.

This last conclusion will perhaps appear paradoxical and at the same time trite. Paradoxical, for after all, is it not for fact rather than reasoning to show us whether, and to what extent, ideas are explained by economic and social circumstances? Trite, for who has ever hoped that the study of Athenian society would reveal Plato's final thought in the *Parmenides*? Let us try to justify the paradox, and sanction the banality.

Of course it is by empirical research that the causes of ideas are discovered. And philosophy, logically anterior, is more or less suggested and rectified by this research. But one reaches, mostly, the results desired: an intellectual movement always implies, directly or indirectly, economic and social conditions. The assured success of the method does not prove that the *authentic* meaning of the ideas is the one that flows from such and such a historical circumstance.

Another objection would aim at the bearing of these conclusions. Would not the essential thing be to determine which interpretations are autonomous (whatever be the admitted theory)? Without even outlining a theory (and each universe must have one), some elements of an answer can be indicated.

The understanding of a work with reference to its purpose is always transcendent to the establishment of the psychological or social causes or circumstances. The historian explains perhaps entirely, by historical phenomena (economic, political, psychological), the technique or even the artistic form, the diffusion and decline of a genre; he accounts for the fact that at a certain date men had a certain idea of beauty, but not for the fact that a certain work is beautiful or that a given art is, or appears to us to be, of a quality superior to some other. Aesthetic understanding (of technique, of form, of structure, of expression) is, as such, irreducible, like the appreciation of values, of which, moreover, it represents an indispensable condition.

However, this intrinsic understanding, depending on the fields of study and the *theories*, will stand as conclusive or on the contrary as special and in a way secondary. The truth of a scientific proposition is, under any conditions, independent of its source, an independence which, universally valid, has not the same import for the social sciences as for the natural sciences. If the objective propositions in sociology and history are always inserted into contexts which are themselves connected with extra-scientific volitions, the subjectivity of those contexts (explicable objectively) will matter more, perhaps, than the universality of judgments which state facts and causal relationships. In addition, the transformations of reality condemn knowledge in many ways to a development which cannot be compared with the progress in physics.

These two arguments apply to the case of philosophy, which in its totality always seems to express an existence and not a pure thought, to have in view an incomplete and changing object, man himself. The subjective interpretation, the one which would be concerned with the systematic account, runs the risk of neglecting the deeper significance, either because the historical significance outweighs the ultimate significance, and the human value the value of truth, or because the stages of philosophical inquiry, being dependent on particular epochs or ways of life follow each other without being systematized into a definite body of knowledge.

So, at one moment intrinsic understanding deteriorates into a technical interpretation, and at another it rises to the interpretation of mind, of quality, or of permanent meaning. The function of *theory* is not only to show the possibilities and the limits of sociological explanations—it must, above all, by determining the essence of the activity and of the work, fix the proper importance of each interpretation.

This general study, then, is a simple introduction. It would call for *theories* in the double sense just indicated. It nonetheless suffices to condemn the dogmatism which forgets the plurality of legitimate interpretations or claims to base the exclusive truth or superiority of one of them on empiricism. *Sociologism* would, in the end, doubly contradict our experience, since it tends to deny the freedom of interpreter and creator alike, and to confirm one of these two denials by the other. In fact, the historian must make his way through the diversity of works in order to come to the unity, both evident and perhaps intangible, of human life.

II. THE UNDERSTANDING OF IDEAS

IN ANOTHER book we ran into the problem we wish to discuss in this chapter. Simmel contrasted psychological understanding (and the subjective meaning) with objective understanding (*Sachverstehen*): one understands the words, or the speaker. On a higher level, one understands the monument, or life. This distinction would be all the more important since, logically, the subjective sense would be unique, while, even logically, one would recognize as many *objective meanings* as there were interpretations not contradicting each other or the texts. As for Weber, he admitted the plurality of historical interpretations, but tried to lessen the consequences of it. History would bear only on the meaning as lived. Every event, even spiritual, would in the last analysis be of a psychological nature, and history would forbid itself any appreciation, either moral or aesthetic, and would attain a universally valid truth. One would establish the causes of a work of art provided that no attention be paid to its beauty. The order of values is transcendent to the historical experience, even though the latter represents the retrospective organization of human development in and by which values are realized.

We shall first discuss these two theories, Weber's in order to justify the autonomy of the understanding of ideas as such, and Simmel's so as to avoid the disorder with which it threatens the interpreter who turns aside from meaning as experienced. We shall then try to show why the understanding of ideas, while never definitive, remains susceptible of revision as long as history continues and men change.

* * * *

In fact, Weber's practice does not conform with the logical principles he expresses. Like all jurists, he recognizes the *spirit of a body of laws* (the spirit of Roman law), an ideal whole the elements of which were more or less confusedly the life experience of individuals, but which in its unity and coherence transcends the reality. The historian, then, takes at least the first step which Weber in theory condemns, the one which ends by showing the logic which is inherent in behaviours.

There may be the objection that the *meaning as lived* still remains the *atom* of the historical world. Assuming that a historian of laws is studying a fact divided into small portions, he will indeed consider what took place in the consciousness of a person performing an act regarded as lawful by society. Of course, the whole question is one of knowing whether psychological data are *general subject matter* or *immediate object,* a decisive distinction at which Weber balked.

In Weber's view only causal relations were an integral part of the science. Ideal types, though instruments necessary for dividing up a field of investigation and for selecting the data or establishing the rules of the determinism, were only *means* and never the *goal* of knowledge. But, assuming, even provisionally, that all propositions of understanding are at the same time causal, this solution retains an abstract, and, so to speak, a fictive character.

In fact, the final result is that the effective labour of the scholar is excluded from the science: in the chapter on the sociology of laws in *Wirtschaft und Gesellschaft,* the necessary connections which theoretically would constitute the whole of the science are rare.

Moreover, the historian is not in search of a pre-existing meaning. He, no more than the jurist, reproduces an interpretation which would already have been present in another consciousness. If one considers a wide enough group of social relations, the plurality of experienced meanings compromises the simplicity which was attributed to reality; whether it is a question of a lawyer or a layman, a judge or an advocate, the same obligation is differently experienced, and all these individuals are equally parts of the reality. The understanding of each one of them requires an intelligible organization of ordinary life, *a fortiori* the understanding of the incoherent whole which they make up. Instead of the antithesis historical-object versus subject-of-the-science, we come back to the true situation: the attempt of an individual in history to rethink the experience of other individuals.

Perhaps in order to answer this difficulty, Weber tried to define law *from the outside,* without accepting any one of the definitions of it which might have been given by the judge, the advocate, or the plaintiff. The reality of a rule of law is equivalent to the chance that a given action (which violates the rule) may bring on a certain reaction by other persons. But there are two possibilities, only one acceptable: Either we observe only the succession of *perceptible* facts, and the historian is then ignorant of not only the idea, but also of the consciousness, in which case he fails in the rudiments of understanding, neglects the meaning that laws had for men (an obligation is not generally felt as is a certain possibility of enforcement); or, we consider the original judicial experience and, because we cannot reproduce the chaos of experienced relationships, we rise above them so as to understand them. Historians and jurists elaborate intelligible systems which include a law or a whole body of laws, an individual or a historical group, which obey their own particular logic, and not the laws of psychology or the regularities of determinism. These systems are different depending on whether they are dogmatic or historical (in this case they must correspond in some way to the perceptible or psychic events), but they always represent the end of an attempt at rationalization.

To maintain the absolute opposition between means and ends of positive knowledge, Weber was obliged not only to reduce science to a matter of causal connections, he also had to admit the fundamental irrationality of the given and the impossibility of discovering in it any intrinsic truth or intelligibility. Rational relationships, for the historian, would be simple mental habits (hence, facts) and ideal types to be used to discover causes (that is, instruments). But on this basis there would be only a history or a sociology of errors. Science would study not so much the rise of the Gothic, based on the new technique of vaulting, as the psychological or social causes of that original style; not so much the formation of Aristotelianism resulting from a consideration of the Platonic theory of ideas, as the personal intentions or the external causes which determined the system. We do not question the relative values of these two interpretations. One fact is certain: most historians consider both of them explanations. He who shows the progress from Cartesian pluralism of substances to Spinozistic unity, or the Marxian transposition of Hegelian alienation, ends with a proposition the validity of which undoubtedly implies agreement with the texts, but *which is accepted as explanatory exactly in so far as it is philosophically true, or, at least, rational.*

Thus the principle of the doctrine we are discussing would again be questioned. Faithful to the absolute separation of fact and values, to the postulate of a univocal reality, Weber would have demanded what at bottom is paradoxical—that the historian disregard, in past beings, the will for value or truth, without which the historian himself would not exist and the artist or the contemporary student would become unintelligible. This is an impossible ambition, for the historian passes as naturally from man to ideas as from ideas to man.

If we accepted Weber's conception, the *Critique of Pure Reason* and the delirious hallucinations of a paranoiac should be put on the same level. It is enough to imagine its application to see the illusion. The historian of philosophy is moved by the wish to recover the coherent unity of a thought, to explore ideas at first seemingly contradictory or unacceptable. The value attributed to monuments is not without importance. Not only because it is the masterpieces that are considered (the argument would only confirm the arbitrary character of selection); the attempt to understand is otherwise. The historian of Kant submits to rules, assumes duties unknown to the sociologist who by studying mediocre authors concerns himself with collective representations. The historian is aiming at the authentic sense; hence the problem is as follows: how define the sense towards which the interpreter, by his exploratory effort, tends?

The absolute separation of means and end, of understanding and causality, is not only artificial—in the end it compromises the very objectivity it claims to assure, for all science partakes of the subjectivity attributed to understanding as soon as the latter is either independent of or even inseparable from causality (not anterior to it).[17]

If we have in view the understanding of a literary or philosophical work, can we at the least maintain the conception of the meaning as experienced? Is the latter a perceptible reality, or a logician's fiction? Is every work reducible to a state of consciousness?

First we must distinguish the man and the craftsman. The artist's conception of his art, and the scholar's of his science, do not necessarily correspond to the meaning inherent in the art or the science. The physicist's interpretation of his theory is often borrowed from

[17] Autonomous when it tries to construct an intelligible system or to explain an intellectual development, inseparable when it interprets a relation verified by causality.

philosophical memories or from popular doctrines. A novelist, who thinks he is a realist, may be a poet. All these propositions are as unanswerable as they are trite. But there is more to it than this. A poem no longer belongs to its author. The latter at most might explain, when lines are obscure, the symbolism he used. So, then, the experienced meaning is either the meaning inherent in the work, or it does not constitute the privileged object of historical understanding.

The historian imagines an inherent meaning which would express exactly the craftsman's intention. The *true Kant* is not the Kant who is true, but the one who lived. It is an illusion to think that the creator always knows what he is doing or always accomplishes what he intends. It is false to confuse the reality of the consciousness or the truth of the monument with the experienced meaning. Even if we admit the possibility of such a coincidence, what difference would it make, since the historian does not recognize it, and he arrives at this fictive or real truth not by way of passive fidelity, but by an active attempt to recreate? He himself determines *by theory* the nature of this truth.

If Weber's conception were put in vague terms, it would easily be made to sound probable. Of course history is concerned, not with abstract ideas, but with living men. The uncertainties show up as soon as the values of the terms are made specific. What is this life we try to re-experience? What is meant by experienced meaning when we speak of a poem or of a philosophy? Weber's mistake was to take the ideal goal of understanding as a given object and to approve as legitimate only one of the lines which historical research follows.

* * * *

If the notion of experienced meaning is abandoned, does it not seem that Simmel's objection appears to have increased in importance? There would, by definition, be a multiplicity of *objective meanings,* all interpretations not contradictory in themselves and with the texts would be *de jure* legitimate, so that reality would lose all fixity, as interpretation would lose its exact goal.

The argument seems to us doubly inexact. To begin with, the historian is not like the reader of a detective novel. He does not seek just any solution which he can by dint of cunning justify. The only interpretation he cares for is the one that is philosophically valid, historically probable, compatible with the psychology of the creator and the epoch and with the rules of rational reflection. Now, in this way, the claimed multiplicity of objective meanings is considerably reduced.

Again, the uncertainty also comes from the necessity of choosing a certain system of interpretation, that is, of determining a certain conception of philosophy. Will it be said that the interpreter must adopt the one shown in the doctrine he is studying? Let us admit that this may be so for understanding an isolated work. Immediately, Simmel's scepticism is discarded, but a new question arises: if we set aside the plurality of possible theories, if we situate ourselves inside a system, can the understanding of ideas as ideas be universally valid?

Actually, it is hard to put the question in isolation. A philosophical idea scarcely exists by itself. The diversity of meanings is primarily due to the diversity of the contexts into which it may fit. Shall we say that the Kantian theory of forms of sensibility represents, at the least, an autonomous part? But is it not necessary to compare the texts relative to time, which figure in the *aesthetics* with those of the *analytics*, of the *first metaphysical principles of the science of nature*, etc.? And, depending on the interpretation of the criticism itself, is not the emphasis either on the strictness of the *forms*, or, on the other hand, on the creative spontaneity of the mind? The nature of thought, especially philosophical thought, makes the detached idea incomprehensible, the fragmentary interpretation absurd.

So, then, it is in connection with totalities that our question is asked: can a doctrine be interpreted in a universally acceptable way? Two affirmative answers seem conceivable. The truth may be contemporary or it may be retrospective. Either the interpreter *coincides* with the author's thought, or else his system of reference is absolute.

Let us look only at the first possibility. Even Max Weber, in spite of the fiction of experienced meaning, stressed the rôle, inevitable and indispensable, of selection. Now does not selection make some deviation between the original and the reconstitution inevitable? Nothing prevents us, as good positivists, from reducing the part played by selection. We do not retain all of Kant's ideas, or at least we shall arrange them in such a way as to retain the order they originally had in Kant's own mind. But the doctrine is not totally one, it has no single centre; on the contrary (and this is more or less true for all great philosophers), the diverging tendencies are apparent (the critique of dogmatic metaphysics and the residua of it, a critique substituted for the ancient philosophy or a new metaphysics, etc.). Will it be said that the historian does not have to overcome contradictions: he exposes them just as he discovers them in the texts? Agreed, but he still must arrive at a *single* interpretation, or the diverse tendencies are, not reconciled, not juxtaposed, but organized. Now, this organization, *which is not inherent in the documents*, is the historian's own doing.

The interpretation of Kant is gradually changing in Germany because instead of asking how metaphysics may be transcended by criticism, the question is how to re-establish a metaphysics beyond the old condemned metaphysics. How can a supra-historical philosophy be attained, as long as man is the prisoner of the historical process? The best of these books invent no ideas at all foreign to Kant. They expose propositions neglected because they disagreed with the traditional conception. They expound solutions implicitly given for problems which Kant did not *consciously* face, but which he inevitably resolved because *they force themselves upon everyone*. Of course there is not much between the arbitrary interpretation and the philosophical restoration of the authentic interpretation. But the difficulty can not be avoided by invoking the obligation of equivalence. The interpreter never puts himself in the place of the author; he does not succeed in doing so, and at heart he does not wish to. History is not a duplication of what once was; it implies a creative restoration from which science itself cannot break away.

The modality of historical judgments depends on the relationships of the historian with the historical individual; between the accidental contact of two individuals, or of two epochs, and the integration of a proposition, either scientific or philosophical, into the system of total truth, there intervene all the forms of intellectual history. The truth about the past is accessible to us if, like Hegel, we rise to an absolute point of view. It escapes us by definition if we ourselves think we are historically determined and partial.

* * * *

Doubtless there will be the objection that we have taken too favourable an example: the most positivist of historians will admit the indecipherable ambiguity of Kant's work. The example was used only to illustrate the idea, or rather the two inseparable ideas: the past, in so far as it is intellectual, is by essence *incomplete*, and the *recapture* of the past implies a sort of revival.

The sense of these two propositions changes according to the context. A scientific truth, in its mathematical expression, is definitively fixed, at least within certain limits. A deductive theory, likewise, as long as its principles stand, knows no other history than that of a progress. Only in this case the system is incomplete and the revival of the past depends on the extension or deepening of already acquired knowledge.

However, the work of art is *ambiguous in itself*, since it exists only for minds and admits neither rational expression nor verification separable from living consciousnesses. The Parthenon, the gaiety of Rheims, do not signify for us what they meant for the Athenian or the medieval Christian; they do not arouse the same feelings, or represent the same values. The contemporary and the historian, even though they share in the same admirations, are never united. This explains why the history of art develops according to art's broken rhythm. Men's relations with the ancient creations, men's relations among themselves, govern both developments.

But it might be said that this spontaneous understanding only governs the selection (one is not studying cathedrals when one is considering them as *Gothic*), and that knowledge, as soon as it becomes scientific, frees itself from this dialectic of epochs and styles which recognize each other by confrontation. In fact this is not so at all. A civilization curious about the whole past, like ours, selects the monuments, at least those whose aesthetic worth it admits. In addition, the historian who goes beyond the establishing of facts and dates does not evade the uncertainty of meanings, because the latter constitute the very nature that one is striving to grasp. The representations of art exist for minds, and become different for different minds and environments. *The plurality of images does not conceal, it defines the essence of the work.*

The case of philosophy is by far the most complex, because it seems to be intermediary. The element is elusive, as in art, but a progressive system is conceived, as in science; a doctrine is addressed both to the living man and the scholar, and lends itself to aesthetic enjoyment as well as to an interpretation aimed at truth. No creation is more concerned with history, none claims a supra-historical value with more assurance. For some, Plato is a contemporary, for others he shines in the light of the primitive mentality. Nowhere does the multiplicity of portraits measure so accurately the value of the original.

Every intellectual activity fits into a tradition in and by which it is defined. There is no scholar or artist who does not start out with a momentum of acquired knowledge, nor is there transmission which does not correspond to a sort of re-creation. Even in the field of positive science, the review of what is known assumes, not submission, but power of mind capable of demonstrating and as it were inventing anew. When it is a question of works in which man engages without yielding to constant norms, the same freedom is manifest. Each age chooses its own past, drawing from the collective treasure; each new life transfigures the heritage it has received, giving it another future and imparting to it another meaning.

Thus are explained the posthumous fates of monuments, the inevitable alternation of oblivion and renascence, the enrichment of masterpieces by the admiration of the centuries. This explains why no fact, provided it be not purely material, is definitively excluded from the present actuality. Only those beings no longer having anything in common with the living can be entirely dead. The limits of virtual presentness coincide with the limits of human unity.

III. THE UNDERSTANDING OF MEN

HISTORICAL narrations link events, but the facts themselves are intelligible only by means of men's *motifs*—at least the immediate motifs. Troop movements, if the military organization, the goals and instruments of the war were unknown, would constitute only a chaos of absurd perceptions. The understanding of actions, although decisive for the historian, assumes the understanding of men's consciousness.

We shall first describe the essential types of this understanding. Then we shall put the logical questions.

* * * *

When a man in a blue uniform holds out his hand to me at the entrance to a railway station platform, I know immediately the *motif* of his action. However, the *ego* to which I respond is, so to speak, completely disindividualized; any other person, in his place, would have acted in exactly the same way. The consciousness which I understand is impersonal as is the gesture I perceived. This example offers the maximum of simplicity. In fact, end and means are immediately clear to me; I do not need to look for either the ultimate goals or for the personal *mobiles*; I am in the presence of an official, not of a personality. The various types of understanding are easily classified starting with this elementary example.

The understanding of an act consists, as we have seen, in grasping the goal sought (we shall speak, in this case, of rational interpretation or interpretation of *motifs*). This goal may escape me: why did Hindenburg turn over the government to Hitler? Why did Mussolini decide to conquer Ethiopia? Most historical problems, often declared insoluble, belong in this category.

The inquiry in such cases moves along two lines. Either we seek, in Italy in 1935 or in Germany in 1933, the facts which make Mussolini's or Hindenburg's decision reasonable. We assume in the case of the Italian dictator the wish to keep himself in power or to assure national greatness. If the economic or financial crisis endangered Fascism, if the conquest in Africa were the only means of increasing the power and glory of the country, the move becomes intelligible. The same applies to the choice of Hitler as Chancellor if no other government remained possible. Let us say then in a general way that the inquiry into *motifs* ordinarily consists, not so much in analysing possible objectives, as in discovering in the world of the individual data such that the decision will appear to correspond to them (means adapted to the assumed goals of the actor).

However, instead of exploring the environment in order to account for the means, one can also search the consciousness in order to get at the plan or plans conceived. Was Mussolini dreaming of a great native army, an instrument of the future Italian empire of Africa? Was he merely trying to distract the country from want and poverty? Is it the typical dictator's reaction to domestic crisis? Did Hindenburg look upon Hitler as the saviour of Germany? The only man capable of restoring it and avoiding civil war? For each example, the questions could easily be multiplied.

The historian, though, is not satisfied with these somewhat impersonal goals. The administrator, it matters little whether minister or dictator, merges with his function only so long as the goals of his conduct are of the supra-individual order. There is no doubt that to understand Richelieu's diplomacy it is necessary to know his conception of French policy, that is the goals he assigned to it: once the doctrine is posited, the individual disappears, and there remains only the minister. On the other hand, if it is thought that Mussolini was seeking only his own glorification, the intoxication of power and risk, the decision ceases to be impersonal. It may still be rational if it was the best way of reaching the goal (even if the latter was selfish), but its reasonableness must be measured by the preferences and knowledge of the actor. We shall speak of *partial rational interpretation* in cases where the analysis of the personality is avoided, and of *total rational interpretation* when the attempt is to include the whole personality.

Rational interpretation, even when total, is not in itself sufficient. In order to account for the final intentions[18] which cause men to act, recourse must be had to another explanation. It might be suggested that everyone receives his set of values from his milieu. No doubt, but the question arises anew for the values of the group. In the last analysis, we either limit ourselves to observation and understanding based on these data, or else we show another rationality, one which links the classification of ends with the personal or collective impulses.

Psychology does not answer only these questions. At times it is indispensable in the simplest cases. Certain acts manifestly do not

[18] I use the word *intention* here as equivalent of *motif.*

result from deliberation: this treasurer gave the order to buy under a delusion, a certain leader was no longer master of himself. Moreover, the interpretation by *mobiles* fills in the gaps of rational interpretation (either partial or total). It accounts for irrational goals (Napoleon's megalomania) or for irrational means (ones not adapted to the goal).

Theoretically, rational and psychological interpretations are complementary and not mutually exclusive (except in cases where the *ego* remains impersonal because the actor disappears wholly behind the public official). As soon as we have to do with an individual we can question ourselves about the *mobiles* of his decision, even if it is reasonable. In practice history goes beyond the rational interpretation especially in these three cases: either the *motifs* are uncertain (what did he intend?), or else they seem not very reasonable (he should not have acted thus), or the historical character himself is interesting (the great man).

For simplicity and brevity we have logically divided the various forms of understanding, which are in fact more or less confused. It is easy to show that we are not concerned here with an arbitrary construction. Besides, it is enough to ask: how does one account to oneself for the conduct of others except by first assuming intentions and then linking those intentions with impulses. These abstract distinctions merely set in order the spontaneous processes of those who understand human actions, that is, each one of us as well as the historian.

* * * *

Let us consider first the fragmentary interpretation, either psychological or rational. According to the discussions above, we should always be confronted with a plurality of *motifs* and an uncertainty concerning the *mobiles.* This plurality cannot be overcome, since reconstruction after the event cannot get at the one intention, even supposing that the actor conceived only one plan; and this uncertainty is linked with the ambiguity of *mobiles* and with the possibility of an indefinite tracing of the regression.

We have just pointed out that historical decisions show the same characteristics. There is no need to repeat the discussion, but merely to show a few distinctive features.

The interpretation of *mobiles,* in general history, usually resorts to popular psychology. Sometimes it merely expresses observed facts in psychological language. The intrigues of a certain parliamentarian are explained by ambition, Mirabeau's treason by the need of money. Even when it analyses the character more thoroughly, the interpretation more often than not sticks closer to lived experience than to scientific fact. If we look through a recent work such as Mathiez' *La Révolution Française,* we find nowhere any terms taken from an admittedly scientific psychology. Elementary feelings—fear, ambition, debauch, combined with rational *motifs* and rash impulses, suffice to account for lines of conduct in that epoch, despite their diversity and individuality.

It does not follow that a private decision, for example Robespierre's decision to impeach Danton, is explained without ambiguity. If we go beyond the rational interpretation, if we do not admit that the decision expresses only the wish to defend the Revolution by eliminating traitors and rogues, we immediately imagine a *mobile*: rivalry between revolutionary leaders. In most cases, similarly a likely *mobile* is not hard to find. How can this probability be changed into truth? By showing that it is in agreement with the documents? Doubtless, but the documents give us not *one mobile*, but several. Also, whether the account is by the interested party or by the observer, the testimony must always be critically examined. Of course, the known relation between jealousy and desire to injure is an example of a typical sequence. It would in a way play the rôle of the law guaranteeing the necessity of the singular succession. In this sense the explanation by *mobiles,* partial but based on documents and guaranteed by a rule (more or less vague), would pass as objective.

Unfortunately this objectivity—already pointed out in connection with knowledge of self—remains quite theoretical for it does away with neither the plurality of *mobiles* conceivable and compatible with the sources, nor with the arbitrary nature of the choice.[19] Even more than *motifs, mobiles* are always multiple, imperceptible even to the actor. Under cover of this uncertainty, the preferences of historians show up plainly; the history that used to be taught was full of characters worthy of popular novels, heroes and traitors; good and wicked people move across the stage, some burdened with crimes, others with virtues. The recent, so-called scientific, historiography of the French Revolution, is shot through with such conflicts, the most famous of which opposes the 'Dantonites' and the 'Robespierrites'. The favourite acts in the interest of the revolutionary idea (a type of rational interpretation tending towards the impersonal), or glorifies the individual, represented as the servant of a cause. The wicked one always obeys his passions; even when his conduct was opportune and effective, personal *mobiles* are blamed.

One of the most striking arguments of those who criticize the science of history is based on this impossibility of knowing the inmost

[19] Especially choice of the system.

thoughts of the actors, that is, of explaining the acts which merge with the events.

In reality this lack of knowledge is far from being as serious as is commonly imagined. To begin with, the historian does not so often meet with these decisions whose origins he vainly seeks. Most actions which come into the account pursue goals known to all. The intentions of the general, the soldier, the merchant, of those in public office who exercise a specialist activity, are immediately clear. Economic behaviour appears as the type of an intelligible behaviour based on a certain end. Rational interpretation develops without obstacle as long as the *other person* remains impersonal or rational.

Of course one may reasonably object that individuals do not always *adapt themselves* to the circumstances, that they do not passively submit to the pressures of others and of events. It is impossible to interpret the inconsistent behaviour of Louis XVI, between the meeting of the Etats Généraux and the 10th of August, without fathoming the mixture of cowardice and patience, of Machiavellianism and submission, which appears in his contradictory attitudes. And if we take one of his decisions (for example, to veto a decree of the Legislature), one would doubtless have to choose between the rational *interpretations* (even more so between the *mobiles*). Political history is forever running into such decisions, which express the individual rather than the milieu.

Of what importance are these uncertainties? Whether Louis XVI acted in good faith or hypocritically, the facts are there. He refused certain decrees, accepted others, he swore fidelity to the Constitution and tried to flee. Is it not proper to distinguish between the intentions inherent in the actions and the secret thoughts which preceded or accompanied them and which the historian can disregard? Gestures, even the simplest of them, are intelligible only by conscious minds (movements of the hand by the meanings of the written words), but only *motifs* expressed in action are important.

It might perhaps be dogmatic to say that the historian is uninterested in what has not become outwardly observable, especially since the borderline between realized intentions and vain ones is vague. States of mind are part of the object, and the narrative is often interrupted in order to apprehend and elucidate them. But these attempts are at least suggested by the subject matter: the succession of events is broken when it seems effectively cut by the intervention of a character; one is disturbed by the *motif* which is not consistent with the act; *mobiles* are called in to make up for the insufficiency of the rational interpretation. In all these cases the plurality and uncertainty are, so to speak, given in the documents, in life itself. To prove this intervention or this contradiction—that is the task which the historian must, and does indeed, accomplish, however doubtful the results at which he arrives may be.

It is generally imagined that the interested party could have told us the absolute truth. In fact, the actor reconstructs afterwards, like the historian, the period of his consciousness. He often knows better than the observer, especially the distant one, what he intended (the goals he conceived of before acting). But this superiority arises from the information at his disposal, not from a sort of infallibility or privilege of position. Hence it is apparent that in cases where evidence is not lacking the uncertainty does not mean a checkmate for science, but expresses a sort of ambiguity bound up with the essence of human consciousness and the gap which always separates knowledge and life.

Fragmentary interpretation, according to the preceding discussion, would be uncertain rather than relative (under cover of this uncertainty partiality takes the bit in its teeth). Is interpretation of the whole, whether psychological or rational, *essentially* relative to the interpreter?

To interpret a line of conduct, we put into logical form the deliberation which theoretically preceded it and which had perhaps remained unexpressed. We must put ourselves in the place of the *other person*, determine what he knew, conceive what he intended. If we associate an act with an individual, we are logically accountable for the reconstruction of a whole body of knowledge and a whole hierarchy of values. Is this an impossible task, beyond the bounds of science? By no means: in fact, as soon as we are concerned with men or with distant periods of time, we have no other recourse. Historical understanding broadens; it aims not so much at the understanding of individuals as at comprising a conception of the world.

One example will be enough to illustrate. Monsieur Lévy-Bruhl's works aim at the exact rediscovery of the original logic obeyed by the primitive mind. The effort of detachment is exerted as far as it is possible. Instead of interpreting the *other person's* reactions in the light of our technique or ethics, it would be forbidden to mix these two *mentalities*. By strictness in method, we should assume that they are mutually alien.

But is there a contradiction between the assumed otherness and the postulated fidelity? Can we think the primitive man's thoughts? Can we classify values as he did? Let us first take note of a sort of practical incapacity (due to the insufficiency of information or to a deficiency of our imagination). Abstraction from self and sympathy with others demand rare talents and perhaps are never entirely complete. But that is not the question. Since we are concerned not with sharing the feelings of another but with reconstructing the system of his intelligence and his morality, the possibility of understanding cannot in principle be denied (on condition that there is a minimum of community between the two worlds of thought). The danger is that relativity may re-enter from another side. Let us admit the ethnologist's competence. The fact still remains that the way of thinking, isolated by him, did not exist for primitive man as it does for the interpreter. Primitive man is the *other* for civilized man. This relation governs the choice of concepts used. M. Lévy-Bruhl uses the categories in their modern form: second cause (regular antecedent and not effective force), principle of identity, to define by contrast the forces set in motion and the participation conceived by primitive man. Because of this, we imagine another system of reference and a different selection—that is, a different interpretation (even supposing the interpretation to be strictly according to the documents).

This relativity seems to me fundamentally inevitable; it follows from the results obtained in the preceding chapters (*The Understanding of Ideas*). As we said, the interpreter commits himself to the interpretation which he proposes because ideas exist only by means of a mind, and because two minds never manage to coincide. The interpreter of states of consciousness does not take as object the idea in itself: he knows only ideas as lived, but he still proceeds by way of the rational interpretation, and that is always integral to the historian who, if only to oppose, always understands the *other's* world in and by means of his own. The image of the other, in science as in life, always reflects the communication between two persons.

But suppose we leave global vision to the arbitrary caprice of the biographer; does not scientific psychology (psychoanalysis, for example) make it possible to establish *objectively* the character and history of the individual?

Without going into a study which would lead us away from our subject, we shall first remark that a psychoanalytical interpretation is, by nature, partial; it neither eliminates nor lessens the value of other interpretations: the religious asceticism which the psychoanalyst attributes to sublimation is, as such, still offered to the psychologist or to the historian of religion. Besides, the psychoanalysis of an individual case always depends on the psychological theory of the historian: the interpretation, then, would be unambiguous only if a single theory were admitted and proved. Finally, it attains the status of truth only if it has available enough documents. Now, documents are, by definition, lacking in so far as historic individuals are concerned, since only *analysis* (medically speaking) could supply them. Notwithstanding these exceptions, assuming the occurence of all these conditions, assuming that the observer reduces his *personal equation*, psychological understanding does attain objectivity, even though, like all scientific knowledge, it is incomplete, because the original experiences are never known and because the exploration of the unconscious is indefinite. The relations between excitations and reactions, between feelings and *drives*[20] and conscious thoughts, are nonetheless true, as judgment on facts and sequences conforming to laws is true and may be confirmed by evidence.

A fortiori, under given circumstances, the interpreter, more perspicacious than the actor, is able to apprehend the true desire in spite of the justification. The ambiguities of self-knowledge denote first of all for the psychologist an intricacy of documents, not an insurmountable uncertainty. On condition that we observe the person, his behaviour and affections, we succeed in determining both his actions and intentions, his clear wishes and the inclinations sometimes unrealized by himself. But the psychologist does not proclaim the conscious to be fictive or illusory and the unconscious to be real: the justification is quite as real as the desire. Moreover, if *drive* and justification move in the same direction, it is impossible to estimate the part each plays in the determination. If they contradict each other, no decision could be predicted in advance, nor could a retrospective conclusion be drawn from the act to the corresponding *drive*. The reasons which individuals attribute to themselves are not without significance.

Finally, these interpretations are valid in so far as they are established by psychological *analyses*. Without *analyses*, the search for *mobiles*, at least in history, must, to be objective, proceed by way of rational interpretation (above all when it is a question of social groups whose impulses are imagined rather than observed).

We thus come to the last problem, the most interesting, that of the relations between the two systems of interpretation.

Let us first recall an observation already made. The preferences of the historian dictate the choice of the system. Explanation *from above* and explanation *from below* are always successful. We remember the expression: 'no man is a hero to his valet', to which might be opposed that 'everybody is a hero to someone'. Lucidity and naïveté, the desire to belittle or to enhance combine to multiply and oppose the different interpretations of a single line of conduct.

On the other hand the interpretation of the *mobiles* can, in the

[20] (*pulsions*)—we use the technical term adopted by French psychologists.

extreme, arise spontaneously from the observation of the act: we look for the *mobiles* rather than the *motifs* of the man who angrily lashes out with his fists. Logically, the psychology still comes after the rational understanding, but the latter is in this case limited to the realized intentions which are given in the perception. The priority of the rational interpretation is, then, valid in a general way.

Moreover, in history, the rational interpretation is, if one may say so, *privileged,* because the intervention of *mobiles* tends to dissolve the singularity of the historical phenomenon. All revolutions are easily explained by resentment, since they all offer, at the outset, the class situation which justifies the hypothesis, but for this same reason the most interesting thing is lost sight of, namely, for example, the features which make the modern labour movement incomparable with Spartacus and the slaves. Moreover, the historian's liberty knows no limits. Some will attribute to a base *mobile* all historical movements they wish to depreciate, and, inversely, to a noble one those to be exalted. On this point we may instance Scheler's essay on resentment, according to which the eighteenth century Revolutionists obeyed their need to topple superior values because of envy, and the Christians responded to a heroism which transcends these, by humility. This is an entirely arbitrary decision, for neither one of the two doctrines, as such, implies resentment, and the men in both cases doubtless felt it, as do all men, in uncertain proportions.

Pareto's treatise offers an even more striking example of the sophisms licensed by hesitation between the two systems. The *logic* of behaviours should be measured by the knowledge and values of the actor. Now, Pareto goes back from the rational interpretation to the *residues,* but without trying to understand the significance men themselves attributed to their acts. As a result he is forever mixing a critique of political ideologies—a critique implicit in his own theory —and a psychology of society, a psychology foreign to history, which retains only universal characteristics and justifies hopeless conservatism. Let us say that, in order to draw a conclusion from *motifs* to *mobiles*, it is important to grasp the *motifs* in the universe of the *other*: it suffices to attribute one's own preferences or knowledge to others to make them hypocritical or absurd.

But, it will be said, is it not possible to evolve one or more historical psychologies and, as a result, remain a psychologist without misunderstanding history? On this vast problem, let us limit ourselves to a few observations. In fact, the psychology called historical depends usually on a rational interpretation. One succeeds in sympathizing with a way of feeling or reacting; beyond a conception of the world, one understands the life which went on in that world. Does the historian then show the psychic structure of the type of men? Let us admit that usually *mobiles* serve to explain behaviours sufficiently stripped of their particularity to fall immediately under general rules of concepts.

There are studies of social or historical psychology, if by that we understand a description of characteristics peculiar to a group or an epoch. In the same way, psychoanalysts question the permanence of neuroses: according to education, the early situations in which the child develops and the collective tabus, different complexes result, or at least the basic urges assume differing appearances. Nevertheless it cannot be denied that the psychological explanation tends to generalize facts and men, that is, in the last resort, to make of them illustrations or examples of truths. In any case, assuming success—which is by no means excluded—in particularizing resentments or revolts, the fact would still remain that any psychology rises by definition to the level of supra-historical relations or ideas: the real question is to know at what level of formalism it reaches them. (Is the Oedipus complex a datum superior to historical change; is it not necessary, more formally still, to speak of complexes which create the relations, variable with social groups, between the child and the people around him?)

Whether it is a question of *motifs* or of *mobiles* it is the historian's duty to detach himself and to think like others, even were it to bring to light later unconscious impulses. Alone in their totality, the systems of experienced facts and values and *analysis* of the individual would be of a nature to overcome the uncertainty inherent in partial interpretations, but global interpretations, by the selection and reconstruction which they imply, remain stamped with an inevitable relativity.

* * * *

So far we have assumed that the interpreter wishes to put himself in the place of his model. For the biographer, this is not the case, for he simultaneously uses all the systems of interpretations. As a result the ambiguity is due essentially to the place given to each of them, and thus the idea of truth disappears.

The biographer does not naïvely accept the conception which the interested party had of himself. Auguste Comte, for example, gradually discovered and built up a past in which people and events were arranged according to the rôle and significance which the religion of humanity reserved for them. Such a biography is a document for the biographer. But a biography, in its turn becomes a document for the future biographer. The most complete interpretation, one which would unite all systems and show their connections, would not be definitive, because the value given to each, never inherent in the object, would still depend on a decision. As was said above, there is for man no truth of existence. Each interpreter composes a picture; God alone would grasp the unity of an ultimate will.

IV. THE UNDERSTANDING OF FACTS

THE SERIES of judgments which make up the account have to do first of all with events. Now, events are by nature neither the result of an individual decision, nor the manifestation of ideas. Does conceptual reconstruction bring to light intelligible relationships which are inherent in reality in the cases where it does not trace back from acts to actors?

We shall first discuss, using examples, the understanding of facts. Then we shall specify the requirements of objectivity.

* * * *

Let us take two traditional examples: 'John Lackland went that way' (it has often been said that this is all that interests the historian), and the battle of Marathon (or Waterloo), the favourite example of Simmel and of all the literary critics of history. Can we in this case speak of objective understanding?

If the historian limited himself to fixing the visible event (John Lackland went that way), the latter would indeed be free of the uncertainty bound up with knowledge of the psychic, but by the same token it would be stripped of all intrinsic intelligibility; material data would be observed, the unity of which would be arbitrarily constructed by the judgment of the historian. Such is not the case: the fact is not merely the physical arrival of John Lackland at a certain place; it is also his intention in going there, or more exactly, it is the act of going from one place to another. Taken in its perceptible reality, the fact would be assimilable to the fall of a stone; historically, it is at once both perceptible and intelligible, for in the formula which expresses it only the *realized motif* is retained, and so ambiguity is avoided without giving up understanding. In this sense the observation, the announcement, of a historical fact—at least one of this category—attains integral objectivity.

But, it may be asked, would the other example give the same result? Quite the reverse; the variation between the event and the narration appears here with such obviousness that scepticism in its various forms, from Stendhal and Tolstoy to Cru and Valéry, has always cited military history as its proof.

We shall set aside the problems suggested by Tolstoy: the part played by those in authority matters little; it is for the historian to estimate it anew in each instance. (We shall explain only the historian's tendency to overestimate it.) Nor shall we raise the question of faithfulness of description, either literary or historical. In the first place, that is a question of documents (and of their criticism) which we have excluded from our study. Next, at least in so far as literature is concerned, there would be reason to distinguish *truth of detail* from *veracity of the whole.* With an accumulation of facts substantially exact, one does not necessarily *communicate* an authentic impression, one does not always *convey* the human truth of war. Now, we have excluded the problems raised by historical *expression.* Of literary criticism we retain only the opposition between the reality, formless, chaotic, accidental, and the order of the narration. This reflection of the novelist (the battle of Moscow in *War and Peace* or the battle of Waterloo in the *Chartreuse de Parme*) falls in with the logician's analyses. Simmel insists, indeed, on the impossibility of isolating the *atom*, an impossibility from which he concludes the inexistence of laws of history (for true laws are valid for constituent elements), and then the existence of a limit to division, for in order to restore the continuity of the experienced development, the isolated fragments must retain sufficient duration and singularity.

That the historian never succeeds in detaching a *historical atom*, since the act of the least important soldier would refer us to the man's past and to the circumstances of the event, we readily agree. That, on the other hand, the historian *reconstructs* and does not *reproduce* the fact, could not be more obvious. But after all, that is not the essential distinction between the collective fact (such as a combat) and an individual fact; in both cases what is substantially given offers the same multiplicity; the unity, whether it be the effect of perception or of memory, comes from the mind; it results from a sort of *conceptual translation.* The difference is related to the degree of complexity. The plurality of actors entails the plurality of experiences undergone: each one has observed or endured the event in his own way. Does the historian's account adopt one of the spontaneous versions or does it rise above the relativity of viewpoints and individual impulses? Is it an individual perspective or an objective reconstitution?

The battle as experienced by the general has nothing in common with the one endured by the private. Surely the battle related by the historian is closer to the former than to the latter, because, in order to grasp the intelligibility of the whole, he must, of course, have recourse to the battle plans and orders from the top, since troop movements, at least at the beginning, show the succession of these understandable *motifs*. Then the shock of battle is observed and the results noted: the left advanced, the centre was pierced. The account then aims neither at the experience of those in command nor at that of the men; it retains something of both, lumping together the plans and orders of the former and the action of the latter. Above all it avoids the relativity of the individual's consciousness and point of view by sticking to visible, indisputable facts.

The *conceptual translation* of these facts (understanding of the *motifs* realized in behaviours) brings us back to the preceding example. The intentions of the commanders and the acts of the soldiers are to a large extent real and objectively understandable (uncertainty reappears if the commander's conscience is probed, either to explain a certain inopportune decision or to show the final intention of which the realized intention was only the first term).

No doubt this battle seen by the historian is *ideal*, in the sense that it has reality only in the mind: is it also *idealized*? That is a question less of a characteristic of the science than of an inclination of the scholar. As the narrator, because of an unconscious nationalism, places himself on one side of a battlefield (whereas he should, like an aerial observer, be above the adversaries), as victory appears in the carrying-out of a strategy or a tactic, as the fight, in its actuality, tends to disappear, as dead, wounded, participants and sometimes even technical means are overlooked, there is an unconscious slipping into legend. Logically, the narration, which in its intelligible texture is the work of the historian, is, nevertheless, valid for all.

Two reservations only must be made. We have called the first operation by which a fact is constructed (advance of the left wing) a *conceptual translation*, not a selection. In effect, no event is eliminated even though none is described. The conceptual expression *represents* a multiplicity of data, grasped as a whole, in their entirety or in their result. But to the extent that, below the level of the constructed fact, the historian notes one or another episode, he chooses freely. This elementary selection is often insisted upon as though it were of a nature to compromise the objectivity. Actually, these notations are intended to suggest an atmosphere or to evoke a situation. The arbitrary character of the choice is of small importance. On the other hand, the concepts by means of which we retrospectively organize the battle run the risk of bearing the mark of present-day military knowledge, just as our understanding of modern warfare may be falsified by memory and tradition. Techniques, strategies, tactics, have changed: the historian perhaps projects his own categories into the past. This anachronism is partly legitimate, if the act had come before it was consciously realized, if the present theory throws light on a line of conduct which itself was unaware of it.

A final objection: is the battle in its totality still intelligible, or must victory or defeat merely be observed, like fair or foul weather? A battle has the same structure as history in its totality. Made up at once of reasonable intentions, unpredictable encounters, and material forces, it appears by turns intelligible like human behaviour or work, and absurd or at least determined like the stone's falling or the struggle between animals. It is understandable or not depending on the level from which it is viewed. The incoherence of individual motions is followed—thanks to the discipline of the troops or the perspective of the observer—by the ordered vision of the commander or of the historian. But these events, already organized, do not steadily unfold according to a plan; accidents still occur, and in the final analysis men meet in combat, and courage, material means, or Fortune decide the outcome. Of course there is still a logic at this level. But at times order dissolves into chaos, panic seizes the crowd. And one wonders whether the microscopic facts and accidents, overlooked in favour of the overall pattern, do not constitute the true and effective reality. Everywhere one sees desires or reasonable reactions, and the outcome, of a sort not desired by anyone, is surprising. The mystery is both at the root and at the top. The constituent part and the totality remain elusive, but between these two extremes objective knowledge is constructed.

* * * *

Let us now examine two quite different examples of *institutional events* (that is, occurences within institutions). A bank president decides to raise the discount rate; a judge announces a verdict. To understand these actions, the psychology of these individuals matters little; knowledge of the banking system or of the law suffices. It is a special case in which the rational interpretation evolves within a social logic.

The fragmentary understanding of the economic event is free from the ambiguity of the individual's consciousness. The technique of the behaviour, fixed in writing, is offered for objective observation. The information needed by the interpreter is not related to special psychological data. In the example we have chosen, everyone knows immediately the objective at which such a measure is generally directed. The inquiry would bear upon the exact goal to which it corresponds in a given situation (to curb speculation, to stop credit inflation and price rises, to protect the currency, etc.). Again, circumstances nearly always point out the goal which the historian discovers by study of the setting of the event. The rational interpretation of an economic event, then, attains a universal validity, as does the conceptual expression of the fact, with the difference that the economist constructs less than the historian because he finds in reality itself the intelligible relations which he contents himself with reproducing.

Can such an interpretation be indefinitely expanded? The banker, in his thinking, foresees and calculates the reactions of *others* to his decision. So in principle the same interpretation would remain possible as long as the conduct of the individuals obeys the same logic observed here, a logic of interest, of maximum profit: the system would lend itself to a total reconstitution to the extent to which the exclusive influence of desire and economic rationality would assure its independence.

Such hypotheses, as we know, never entirely correspond to reality. There is often some measure of irrationality even in the procedure relative to the banking discount, either at its inception or in its outcome (arguments outside the realm of economic rationality). The movements of floating capital today obey not so much the variations in the rate of interest as they do the anticipation of profit or loss contingent on parity of the medium of exchange. Let us say that generally speaking, economic behaviour does not entirely conform with the schema (all the more so since the State's interventions imply the consideration of alien and often ill-specified goals).

If we left out of account the difference between concrete man and *homo oeconomicus*, between the actual economy, always more or less influenced by outside phenomena, and pure economics, could there be developed a *total rational interpretation*, universally valid? To answer the question it would be necessary to outline a critique of economic theories. Let us merely take note of the data on which the answer would be based. Is economic rationality, either for one society or for society as a whole, unequivocally defined? Does the complexity of situations and impulses allow the prediction in advance of a decision, once a certain definition is admitted? In other words, are the goal and the means sufficiently determined, even abstractly, to authorize the reconstruction of an ideal functioning?

Whichever it is, there would still be a variance between this reconstruction and the actual course of events. The historian would make use of the theory, but only as a means to get at the concrete result.

The judicial action is more complex. If we consider a contract between two individuals, we have to distinguish the contract as made in its legal meaning, as an ideal jurist would interpret it, and the, perhaps divergent, intentions of the two contracting parties, the goal each of them hoped to attain, their estimate of the value of their agreement (a value perhaps not coinciding with the judicially admissible validity). In other words, a legal action between private persons involves two understandings, which are always mutually indispensable: one because of the *motifs* of the contracting parties, the other in the judicial system. Let us call the first the historian's understanding, the second the jurist's, because the latter considers the meaning as experienced, while the former, inversely, meaning as experienced via judicial meaning.

The action of the judge is more complex: the result is often objectively perceptible (so many years in prison, or such and such a fine), but these perceptible facts express the decision which is itself defined by an interpretation of a special case according to existing rules, presupposing an interpretation of the law and of the actions involved (and sometimes of the individual consciousness of others).

Piecemeal understanding, whether of a contracting party or of a judge, brings us back to cases already studied. It is without the ambiguity of individual consciousness when it sticks to the meanings of the texts (of the contract or of the laws), without going into the *motifs* of interested parties or legislators. Always, whether it comes from the historian or the jurist, it appears as a reconstruction of either a judicial whole or of judicially experienced events. If it sticks to the perceptible facts, it is objective *de facto* and *de jure*; but if personal intentions must be considered, it is uncertain; objective *de jure*, but not necessarily *de facto* if the judicial meaning (of a text, of a private act, or of a law) is to be unambiguous.

It is not important, for our purpose, to pursue or to study this analysis more thoroughly, since it is infinitely complicated in its details, given the multiple forms of judicial understanding. We only felt it important to put the same question in connection with law as for economics, that is, the possibility of a total universally valid interpretation. Not that it involves the same answer, but, on the contrary, because it leads to entirely different observations. The economic system would be both rational and real. The judicial system reconstructed by the historian would be ideal, or at least ideational.

The notion of *judicial reality* is ambiguous. Either, in fact, men's behaviour is considered as real, in which case, real economic law at a given time is law as it was effectively applied. The existence of a rule is defined from without by the probability of sanctions in case of violation. Such a reality would be multiple, incoherent, composed of both observable acts and psychological states. Piecemeal judicial understanding would be a special instance of historical understanding as a whole, either of consciousnesses or of exteriorized facts (with the single complication that the rational interpretation would operate by way of at least partially rationalized systems). Or, on the contrary, judicial reality would be that of the legal imperatives. Legal science, a reconstruction as rational and coherent as possible of the system of a certain body of laws, would be like the ideal expression of the interpretation to which the jurist proceeds. In this case the ideology would be defined with reference to *pure law*, to the intellectual nature of the law, and not with reference to life.[21] The distinctions between public and private law, between law and the State, would be ideologies (although conceived by many people and hence effective), because they would have no place in the intelligible edifice of the law as the scientist would reconstitute it.

Is it possible for the understanding, taken in itself, either of historical reality or of the pure reality of law, to attain universal validity? It is indeed difficult to separate the plurality of systems from the plurality within a system. Supposing that there is such a thing as an original and naïve judicial experience, the historian, in order to understand it, reconstructs it, and science attributes a strict unity to multiple and often contradictory data. In determining an object as well as in organizing it, the historian at least commits himself by the concepts he uses. Whether the varieties are subordinate to a universal idea of law, or whether they are opposed in their distinctiveness, the substitution of a retrospective order for the chaos of actions and psychological states inevitably links history with theory.

These examples seem to lead to two conclusions: first, the possibility by means of the objectivity of judicial technique and texts, of noting and objectively understanding actions without connecting them with individual consciousnesses. Second, at one moment or another the inevitable return to psychology because a social system, always closed in upon itself, collides with external forces, and especially because reality itself appears at one time at the level of the intelligible, and at another at the level of behaviour and lived experience.

* * * *

It might fairly be objected against our analysis of impersonal understanding that, being totally objectified, an event is no longer historical because in its historical essence it is never confused with its material

[21] We refer to Kelsen's doctrine.

vestiges. It prolongs itself because of its mental reverberations. The political and social results of the king's flight, are an integral part of the fact, so that it is difficult to discern the limits of the fact.

So considered, Simiand's work is especially interesting. By using statistics, he succeeded in establishing the circumstances under which labourers and entrepreneurs consent to increase the intensity of their work. In this way he outlined a classification of tendencies corresponding to a socially defined way of life. Objectification in this case is total, and yet the fact, accessible to all, is still historical: the action is not distinguished from its visible results.

Neither institutions nor *mores* come into this category. On the contrary, they both share in the uncertainty of consciousnesses and ideas. Collective customs, also, offer special difficulties because they often seem gratuitous. They express feeling rather than utility. Perhaps once rational within a system of beliefs, they have been maintained by the force of tradition. Understanding in this case consists not so much in ascertaining the knowledge or values which made them intelligible as in realizing the certainties, interpreting the symbols, sympathizing with the human attitudes.

Consequently, all the fragmentary interpretations we have recognized would become insufficient. They are useful, but only up to a point. It is life as a whole we are trying to grasp, a totality which is gradually constructed by bringing together these partial comprehensions. But by the same token, the advantages of objectification disappear. In spite of the massing of evidence, total understanding, unless it is intuitive, emphasizes the rôle played by decision. For the unity towards which we strive, the unity of an epoch or of a culture, is nothing but the fictive source of works and actions which are all that is directly accessible.

CONCLUSION

The Dissolution of the Object

ONE fundamental idea emerges, it seems, from the preceding discussions: *the dissolution of the object.* No such thing as a *historical reality* exists ready made, so that science merely has to reproduce it faithfully. The historical reality, because it is human, is *ambiguous* and *inexhaustible.* The plurality of spiritual worlds in which human life unfolds, and the diversity of contexts in which ideas and elementary facts take place are both equivocal. The meanings of man for man, of the masterpiece for its interpreters, and of the past for succeeding generations are inexhaustible.

The three steps which we have distinguished, the *recapitulation* of the idea, the *construction* of the fact based on the experience of those who lived it, the *organization* of the various states of consciousness, offer differences. The *constructed fact,* limited to its objectively recognizable characteristics, is free from uncertainty, but this objectivity is conceptual rather than given. Moreover, even if we set aside the enrichment of the fact by its results (similar to the enrichment of the idea by its corollaries), history, so conceived, is never objective, because by detaching itself from man, it loses its essential character.

The recapitulation of ideas (in the broad meaning of the word) immediately involves the historicity of historical knowledge. The pure idea calls for a system, the idea still active in life for a new understanding. The one is revivified by the unlimited progress of knowledge, the other by the unforeseeable changes in living. Hence the impossibility of distinguishing knowledge of the past and development of the mind.

As for the organization of consciousnesses, it ends inevitably with the observation of a relationship. The individual whom we conceptually re-create is, as far as we are concerned, the *other* or the *same*; we separate him from or bring him nearer to ourselves; he is the model or the enemy. Even if he were indifferent, he would still be so to us.

In each case we have also observed the necessary attempt at detachment, towards objectivity. That knowledge which would choose a system in accordance with subjective preferences (the rational interpretation in order to aggrandize, the explanation by *mobiles* to depreciate) would be partial, would fail to reconstruct the system of values or learning which makes it possible to sympathize with the actor. In the same way, the understanding of ideas would become arbitrary if it were entirely freed from the psychology of the author and went so far as to confuse epochs and universes, under the pretext of making the past alive or of demonstrating the eternal truths of the works.

This dialectic of detachment and appropriation tends to justify much less the uncertainty of the interpretation than the freedom of the mind (in which the historian has a share as well as the creator); it reveals the true goal of the science of history. This science, like all reflection, is, so to speak, as practical as it is theoretical. The ideas sought are ones we wish to integrate into the contemporary system; the monuments handed down are called upon to enrich our culture; the lives reconstructed must serve as examples or as references, since man recognizes himself and determines himself only by comparison.

Objectivity is perhaps beyond this relativity. Just as the unity of the account would rise above but not fail to recognize the plurality of intellectual worlds, so also understanding, without neglecting the revival of the works, would rise to an ever wider validity, subordinate to that of the present and of the theory. Truth contemporarily possessed would make possible the understanding of previously acquired truths.

Third Part

EVOLUTION AND THE PLURALITY OF PERSPECTIVES

INTRODUCTION

The Concept of Evolution

WHETHER fragmentary or global, the understanding studied in the preceding part was always static. Inevitably our analysis remained abstract and, so to speak, artificial. We were contrasting, according to the standard schema, subject and object in order to measure the difference intervening between the experience as lived and the construction, between the model and the portrait. The time has come to re-establish the continuity; historian and historical individual differ, but they belong to the same whole. Thus we bring in again the essential dimension of historical reality, *evolution.*

Strictly speaking, the word evolution applies to ontogenesis, to the development of potentialities contained within the germ plasm. Unity inheres in both the identity of the being which changes, in the solidarity of the succeeding phases, and finally in the irreversible orientation of the progression towards an end implied by the initial state, if not included in it. In the first place, one might well ask to what extent historical movements merit the term 'evolution'. Three criteria would be decisive: do the changes take place in a single, enduring and identical entity? Is the origin of these changes within the entity? What are the relations between various moments, and in particular between the initial and the final state?

This problem, which we may call the *nature of historical evolution*, certainly arises. But we shall not approach it directly by relating the various forms of development with the typical characteristics of evolution. As a matter of fact the stress is not always on the development of interrelated forms; the fecundity of time is emphasized. The newness of the forms, not their former presence in the embryo, seems essential. In the paradoxical alliance of the words *creative evolution*, the idea of creation is stronger than that of evolution, as is epigenesis than preformation. It might also be said that philogenesis, rather than ontogenesis, was taken as a model. Historical movements, then, should be judged by two divergent criteria: that of unity and continuity on the one hand, and that of the depth of the changes on the other.

However, the simultaneous use of these two criteria would not suffice. The decisive question would still be the alternative of objective and subjective. Here, as everywhere else, science, inseparable from reality, involves two contradictory interpretations. Either we insist on the activity of the historian: is it not enough to show connections between certain economic changes to create the fiction of an economic evolution? The conceptual expression suffices to give a certain unity to events. The perspective of the retrospective spectator, who sees the past tending towards the present, lends a direction to the development. Or, on the other hand, we may consider the movement itself, of Germany towards an authoritarian government, of capitalism towards a planned economy. Is not the account limited to reproducing the whole as existent within the object? As it is in the animal kingdom, evolution would in human affairs be the primary datum.

We should like to avoid a metaphysical fiat as well as a purely logical compromise (such as that of styling historical evolution as *wertbezogen*, referring to values). So, we shall resort once again to description. It allows us immediately to set aside schematic solutions. For example, in the guise of nominalism, some people adopt the subjective thesis. Now of course when confronted with ontogenesis, historical evolution is always to some extent metaphorical; it does not offer in evidence the support of a biological nature, but it would not do to conclude arbitrarily that the unity of the development is entirely fictional (even if the latter resolves in the end into a multiplicity of individual facts). In other words, we admit to begin with the objectivity of evolutions as we do of wholes, but also their plurality and ambiguity. The historian does not artificially make up totalities of dispersed and incoherent elements; he recomposes totalities inherent in the world of history.

In reality this decision is not the proper object of our study. We are trying to point out the limits of objective knowledge. The consideration of evolution raises two questions: how is the past related to the present? Is this relationship to the future a source of relativity and of uncertainty, or does it, on the contrary, make it possible for us to show, after the event, the truth in history?

We shall again consider the distinctions made in the preceding *Part*, and then go on from the understanding of ideas to the history of ideas

(Chapter I), from impersonal understanding to the narration and the history of facts (Chapter II). In Chapter III we shall contrast the two possible interpretations of retrospective rationality; finally, in the last chapter, we shall examine the problem in its most complex form, that of historical evolution.

I. THE HISTORY OF IDEAS

WE SHALL again consider the problems of the *history of ideas*, beginning where we left them in Chapter II of *Part* II. We showed that the historian considers ideas in themselves as well as states of consciousness as shown by ideas, that he must himself determine his object by choosing a *theory*. We finally pointed out the variation between the experienced meaning and the retrospective meaning, a variation which is the essential element of the posthumous reconsideration of intellectual productions.

First, we shall try to specify the nature and content of these theories, presuppositions of the investigation. We shall ask whether history-reality of science or of philosophy does not of itself impose a certain *theory*. We shall show what *perspective* within a certain theory means; finally we shall note the involvement of historical knowledge with history itself, an involvement which confirms a certain objectivity without eliminating the plurality of perspectives.

* * * *

Let us take science as an example; as a matter of fact we observe various ways of retracing its development. The positivist Western science would for Spengler be attributable to a peculiarity of modern man; the Faustian desire for power has forged an instrument, just as Greece built up a static and harmonious representation of mathematics and of the Universe. Other sociologists, without opposing absolutely incompatible conceptions of the world, linked mechanistic physics with a philosophy itself expressing a vital attitude or social relations: the substitution of causal relations for essences and qualities implies the arbitrary division of nature, shown on one plane, and subjected without defence to the technique. Finally Marxism, far from seeing in the development of science the progressive revelation of Reason, would bring it into association with capitalism. The natural sciences, a historical phenomenon like all human creations, would be inseparable from a system of economy.

This example offers a special simplicity (and that is why we confine ourselves to this rough outline of the various methods). Indeed, everyone will recognize the rights of the inner interpretation as well as of the sociological one. It is quite proper to refuse to admit that they may be contradictory or incompatible. One can understand Kepler's laws in the author's psychology, and on the other hand see the meaning they have in present day physics. In the same way, more generally, we trace the formation of the modern *theory* of science starting with the natural philosophies while discovering the propositions set up during that time, which are still valid. The historian goes back to states of mind and social conditions without leaving out of consideration the value of the works, that is, their truth.

This combination of different interpretations is not peculiar to the case of positivist science. However, the *theory* of science enjoys, with reference to the *theory* of philosophy, two privileges. No one debates the existence of a science as science; moreover, in our civilization we recognize as such science of the Western type (at least in the case of mathematics and physics). In addition science of its own accord discriminates between true and false, so that agreement is established on the present day content of mathematical or physical truth. Thus, both the plurality and, within the intellectual universe, the ambiguity, stand eliminated. (There would be reason to modify these statements a little: the certainty is valid only for raw results and for the equations which express them; the imaginative representations and the general interpretations evolve as philosophy, not as science.)

The question of the rhythm of the evolution then has a different meaning, depending on whether we think of the evolution of ideas in themselves or of the evolution of scientific ideas integrated to the different epochs. To the extent that the past of the sciences is referred to the present, scientific development inevitably takes on the appearance of a progress. *The theory of a universe is by the same token the theory of the evolution of that universe.* Since science in its present state is either more nearly approached or more complete than previous science, progress is inevitably the law of history, on condition that the word progress is taken in its broad sense: we used to imagine, too simply, progress as an accumulation, whereas physics develops by renovation, by review of apparently indubitable principles.

On the other hand, if we examine the rhythm according to which science has *in fact* developed, we observe regressions, discontinuities. One period was fertile, another sterile. Some things learned were forgotten, the very idea of science and method has varied. Does this mean that the rhythm of real history depends on observation alone? Undoubtedly so if this history depends on a juxtaposition of data; it is for empiricism to establish the date at which a certain conception was first stated. But history is also, and above all, the organization of systems, and depending on whether we link the science with cultures or with economic systems, the pace of the movement is liable to change. Can different versions be simultaneously valid? Of course one may be rendered more likely than the others, at least empirically; it would be shown, for example, that determining conditions are social or economic rather than cultural. But logically the diversity of conditions is conceivable, and for that very reason so is the plurality of the interpretations that a philosophy of science or of general history would make it possible to classify, if not to reduce to unity.

Let us now consider the history of science (as such): does it entirely escape relativity? There is still, it seems, a factor of renewal: the present state, which governs the concrete organization of the past, often confers upon ancient results both another place in the edifice of knowledge, and a new value. The Newtonian conception of the emission of light, for a long time condemned by experiment, has taken on a meaning refused it until just recently. Instead of retracing a rivalry decided in favour of one adversary, we now see, at the end of the process a sort of reconciliation which does away with the conflict itself. Of course it may be said that the example bears upon a theory and not a law. But history uses concepts more or less involved with those theories which are an integral part of acquired positive knowledge, and the result is that it partakes of their vicissitudes. As long as science is incomplete, and that doubtless means as long as mankind continues to live, a body of knowledge is renewed either by the consequences drawn from it or by the context into which it is inserted. If by *perspective* we mean the view of the past ordered by reference to the present, then the history of science (as science) admits many and changing perspectives. History—as the reconstitution of earlier science—is involved with history as the development of science. The awareness of its past by a discipline is merely a form of its own self-awareness.

In the last analysis, then, the real question would bear on the *historicity* of science (not on the history of science). Of course it has developed in time, it has been subjected to external accidents, it has often wandered, it has stopped, or even gone backwards. But are mathematics and physics now what they necessarily had to be, or on the contrary, what a contingent history has made of them? The contingency we have in mind is no longer the one arising from their dependence on human or social psychology; we are thinking here of an essential contingency such as that of invention as contrasted with discovery. Could we have made progress, following Michelson's experiment, except by means of Einstein's theory? It goes without saying that we do not claim to offer a solution: we lack the competence, and it is for specialists to answer. It was important only to carry the discussion this far: if the system of science is or becomes progressively necessary, history is definitely eliminated, since the present state could have been encompassed at one stroke by a more powerful mind. The perspective would disappear (or it would itself obey a sort of progress) and the science of the past would be useless at that moment when history would come to an end by being dissolved in suprahistorical truth. Once again history-science shares in the fate of actual history.

* * * *

In the case of philosophy the fundamental difficulty is to find a definition which approximately limits the domain properly belonging to it. In addition, the historian determines his object by choosing a certain theory of philosophy (which is also a theory of its history), but this last affirmation will doubtless meet objections; a sort of scepticism or nihilism will be seen in it: if philosophy does not reveal its nature through its history, how will the historian avoid arbitrary decisions?

Refutation will be tried from two different points of view: if history is considered as the laboratory of philosophy it will be claimed that history itself will make the decision, and the historian with positivist tendencies will hesitate to recognize this part played by an inevitably philosophical decision, and will strive to discover in the facts the law of the development.

The first problem may be stated as follows: 'What is the nature of this history? Does it necessarily remain like the history of religions, a source of private opinions linked with the greatness or decadence of a certain social group? Or has one the right to say that it corresponds, like the history of the sciences, to a progressive discernment of the true and the false?'[22] Without doubt *history* must be understood in the objective sense. But if the *discernment* is not apparent for all (and the very fact of the question proves that it is not), it is for history (in the subjective sense: knowledge of the philosophical past) to effect it. Hence the remark: 'such a question is not one that it is possible to decide *a priori* by the dialectic of words. . . .'

The *dialectic of words* could not, it is true, decide any question *a priori*, but such an expression too easily hides the true difficulty. The *science of the past* is asked to remove the doubt affecting the essence of the movement of philosophy. The historian will be called upon to

[22] L. Brunschwieg. 'De la vraie et de la fausse conversion.' *Revue de Metaphysique et de Morale*, 1931, p. 29.

prove that history (reality) is a progressive discernment of the true and the false. But this is not one of those questions empirical method decides *a posteriori* by the accumulation of facts. And to the extent it does decide, is it not because it is already oriented by the answer it is to make?

Science realizes this discernment because it has available a criterion, experimental verification. What is the criterion of *philosophical verification*? According to the very letter of the doctrine to which we allude, it is the history of the sciences. So we immediately see why the *dialectic of words* was rejected. The choice of this criterion is anterior to the investigation and could not be justified by it; the choice represents a part of the decision by means of which each historian determines his object by adopting a certain *theory* of the spiritual universe. It is clear that the history of the sciences allows discernment of philosophical truth only on condition that the very *theory* in question be admitted: namely, that philosophy completes its mission with the awareness of scientific progress.

But, it will be said, of what use is such a decision? Scientific history is neither *narration*, nor *progress*; the former is before understanding, the latter beyond positivist method. Philosophy we do not have to define, but to gather together the multiple and changing definitions of it which situate it between art, religion, and science. Besides, the term philosophy is still abstract and suggests a false problem: what the historian recognizes are men who philosophize.

No doubt these remarks suggest *one* of the conceivable methods. When it is a question of an author, one devotes oneself to the *experienced meaning*, when concern is with the system, one retraces the succession of doctrines and the revolutions in thought on the level of collective existences. One reduces the number of *postulates* to the extent that one succeeds in coinciding with mental states. Our opinion is unchanged concerning the criticism outlined in the preceding *Part*: experienced meaning is a fiction. In spite of everything it indicates a direction of the effort of interpretation: the historian aims at the meaning given to the work by its creator. Could he not in the same way follow the development without adding to or subtracting from the complexity, the multiplicity, of the reality?

The question remains whether, under these conditions, there still exists a *history of philosophy*, that is, whether the observed diversity offers the minimum of unity or continuity which establishes it as *history*. The conceptions, the objects, the methods of philosophy have varied. At one time it applies itself to the totality of things knowable, at another it is reduced to reflection on science. Sometimes it is almost merged with religion, and sometimes it opposes religion and demands autonomy. Of course if one showed by comparison a certain number of features characterizing all doctrines commonly called philosophy, one would arrive at a vague definition such as: meditation by man on his fate, his place in the universe and the final problems of knowledge and existence. But in this case one can specify in advance the rhythm of the movement: such a philosophy passes through unpredictable alternatives, changes meaning and function with the times, is tied to the alternatives of enthusiasm and wisdom, of romanticism and rationalism. And there is nothing beyond these vicissitudes except man himself, ever questioning and always ignorant.

This refusal to decide is then the equivalent of a decision. We showed, in the case of science, that one observes the development *de facto* but that one theoretically determines the development *de jure* (or, if you wish, one observes the development of ideas in actual life, determines the development of ideas as ideas). The distinction also applies here. One observes the succession of schools of thought, but the intrinsic rhythm—the progress, orderless succession, dialectic, exploration, the eternal antinomies—is given immediately by the concept of philosophy. For example, philosophy conceived as awareness of science is certainly legitimately a progress (progress towards the discovery of its vocation, progress towards a more exact and more lucid consciousness).

As for positivist history, it hesitates between the traditions from which it is derived and which it tries to transcend. Between the history of sects and the theory of evolution it seeks a middle way. The first leads to sectarianism or to scepticism, the second justifies the necessity of time and traces in the past the gradual attainment of reason. The history of mankind rises to the level of a history of philosophy to the extent that it retains either the alternative of the first method, or the inherent rationality implied by the second. In the last analysis, the history of philosophy expresses either an ever renewed interrogation, or the development of knowledge and wisdom (and still there would be here only a history of man philosophizing: unity would come, not from the philosophies, but from psychological types or situations).

All these analyses lead back to the formula: 'there is no philosophy in the past except for the one who philosophizes'. Or again 'every philosopher possesses the past of his philosophy'. These expressions seem commonplace and obvious to such an extent that we should scarcely have called attention to them if, most of the time, an attempt were not made to evade them by appealing to science itself (in this case historical science) to decide. As a matter of fact, the fear is that the philosopher, if he must at the same time discover his own truth and its history, may be subject to the whims of his personal aesthetics.

There is, at the source of this fear, a misunderstanding. The priority of theory over history is *de jure*. In fact, the theory is elaborated as the philosopher explores the past. The priority implies simply that the facts impose no doctrine and that a philosophical proposition, even one which formulates a definition of philosophy, can admit no other proof than a philosophical one; or again that philosophy be defined by a basic interrogative, by bringing everything back into question.

* * * *

We could take other examples. In the case of art we should observe the plurality of *theories* and *perspectives* arising from conceptual expression (history of styles), from showing the relation with the present in a history of the mind or in the development of a style (the point of arrival governs the whole movement). In the same way history-science would partake of the rhythm of actual history; the dialectic of styles is reproduced in a dialectic (partly independent) of the theories of styles; the succession of works in a series, equally unpredictable, of their interpretations; actual history and history-science possessing a certain autonomy, but in fact subordinate to the destiny of souls (in Dilthey's sense).

There would be no interest in resuming those analyses which, schematic as the foregoing ones, would offer nothing new. Besides, in this general work, we necessarily limit ourselves to first principles. It is important only to go back to the proposition with which *Part II* ended, that is, that history-reality and science—does not exist in itself, but by and for a historian. Libraries contain manuscripts of texts considered philosophical, documents reveal sequences or systems of ideas, we discover elementary histories in facts; but we never succeed in composing in this way a history of philosophy unless, by the decision we make about philosophy we give it unity and evolution.

Let us apply this conclusion to religion and we shall immediately grasp the most difficult problem. It seems that there is no history of religion, either for the unbeliever or for the believer; for the latter because religion has no history, for the former because there is no such thing as a religious order of thought transcendent to psychic or social phenomena. Psychology of religious experience, ecclesiastical sociology, the diffusion and struggle of revelation in the world, can be seen of course. For a history to be properly religious, churches would have to be changing in their essential meaning, or man's aspiration towards faith would have to be the essence of religion. But churches preserve and transmit an immutable revelation. The communings of lonely individuals with their God, scattered through the ages, do not form a whole. And faith is not religious if it does not come from God. In this sense, the dimension of history is fundamentally opposed to a philosophy of transcendence.

II. THE HISTORY OF FACTS AND OF INSTITUTIONS

IN THE last chapter of the preceding *Part* we discussed the understanding of events, objectified either within social systems or by conceptual expressions and for the historian. We now resume the analysis where we left off: how are these elements organized to recompose the development?

Traditional logic uses the notion of *selection.* The historian would choose from the strictly established facts, and this choice would correspond to subjective preferences. Criticism of the mere concept of fact is usually overlooked, as though the elaboration began only with the assembling of the data. On the contrary, if our study up to this point is valid, it would be important to distinguish, first, *conceptual expression* and *elementary selection*, and then *historical selection.*

We shall explain the traditional theory of selection and try to show how, on the basis of impersonal understanding, a historical perspective is set up.

* * * *

Logicians and men of letters both recognize the need for a choice. The latter, hostile to history, see in choice the condemnation of this pseudo-positivist tradition. What is this so-called science, which instead of explaining keeps on narrating as it pleases, since it retains or disregards at will the information amassed by erudition? As for the logicians, they have argued two questions. They have asked what was the norm by which the discrimination was effected: *value* or *efficacy*? Moreover, they have tried to show the effects of selection on the validity of the account: is it a source of universality (the same facts according to one system of values would be universally historical) or of relativity (the historian freely goes into questions which he asks of the past and which express his curiosity and position)? In short, is it objective in the same sense that the historical process would be sure to be, as memory which spontaneously simplifies, recapitulates, and transfigures? We have elsewhere discussed these conceptions at some length; we shall merely recall as briefly as possible the results here needed.

Rickert's theory (selection by values as principles of universality) is limited to putting into logical form the commonplace idea that everyone picks from among events those which for one reason or another *interest* him. Now this way of expressing it, to be philosophically productive, ought to strip interest in history of its subjective character. This was certainly Rickert's intention; he thought he saw, at least within a given collectivity, actual agreement about values, an agreement that would guarantee the objectivity of the choice. We have shown that in reality this solution is still illusory. For the same facts to appear effectively in different accounts, *all* the values of the period under study would have to be known. Moreover, this logical objectivity, limited to one period, also assumes total detachment on the part of the historian with regard to his own society, faithfulness without reserve to the extraneous object; a detachment and a faithfulness which seemed to us logically and in fact unattainable. Finally, the idea of selection contemplated by Rickert is the popular idea; if it is a question of grouping or of organization his theory is of no use just when it becomes indispensable. With the same data, the most contradictory general views are composed.

The so-called conception of the *effective* seems no more satisfactory. The only historical facts would be those which have had an effect on subsequent development. But how is this influence to be estimated? At what moment in time does one place oneself? What term of reference will one use? Is it the effect on the present which matters? No historian, in this case, applies the rule. How many events preserved in collective memory exert, apparently at least, no influence on the present? Abstractly, the inadequacy of this criterion is easily shown: effectiveness is measured by reference to something, at a certain date. Thus we are driven back to another choice on which the original distinction will depend.

It is not that these two theories do not correspond at least partly to the selection actually practised by historians. On the contrary, any number of examples may be cited to justify both of them. Ravaillac's or Charlotte Corday's dagger thrusts are historical, not the deed of an apache in a dark street. The same natural phenomenon may or may not come into an account, depending on its human consequences: the storm which destroyed the Armada, the Lisbon earthquake, are historical. And yet, statues by Phidias are, for us, immediately historical. The two formulae correspond to the traditional ideas: historical meaning and intrinsic meaning.

In so far as the logical alternative (is selection objective or subjective?) is concerned, we have adopted the second hypothesis. A subjectivity which, in the profound thinking of Weber, is less arbitrary than historical, is inherent in the scientific task. Selection consists not so much in discarding certain data as in *establishing the object, analysing the values, defining the ideal types*; in a word, in organizing the world of history in accordance with certain concretely defined questions. Weber's error was having admitted a radical and over-simplified distinction between two procedures, selection and causality, thus maintaining the fiction of an entire objectivity. In reality it is most important to specify the various aspects of selection and to describe the elaboration of the wholes.

If one confines oneself to abstract formulae, the indifference of historians to literary criticism and logical proofs is explained. After all, they care little if Frederick II's greatcoat disappears from the chronicles; no one will forget the plan of the battle. Consequently the choice with which they are reproached, even if they admit its existence, is still part of their work, marginal to their preoccupations. In order to prove that the determination of what is essential and the orientation of the account are subjective, one cannot be content with such primitive examples. What is at stake is the nature of historical experience.

* * * *

The objectivity of understanding, in the example of the battle, was of a special order. It was constructed and not passive; the historian does not reproduce what took place, he neither relives nor brings back to life any of the experiences undergone; he tells the story of an ideal battle which an aerial observer might perhaps have understood, who was careful only to note visible actions and results. For the individual stationed at the level of the constituent elements these conceptual expressions become possible only after the event. The impression and contemporary view are fragmentary and nearly always biased; impartiality requires distance, but does distance also make it possible to overcome particularity? Or, on the contrary, are conceptualization and retrospection factors of relativity?

The historian tends to recognize only that part of the past which has prepared the future, which has been in the meantime realized. But he can resist the temptation and discover events with no consequence, decisions which history has proved mistaken. The vain resistance to the movement has its place in knowledge. But if we abandon the ordinary idea of selection, the question occurs in another form; all the data are retained, but are they not *represented* differently, depending on the future which they have effectively had?

Even in the example of the battle the account is oriented towards the outcome. Of course the facts are given as they occurred: so much ground gained or lost, such and such losses; all these material details are forever fixed. But each one is fitted into a system, the conduct of the soldier into that of his company, the attack by the left wing into the general tactics; and in the same way, the early advantages, on the day of Waterloo, fit into a whole which is completed and defined by the defeat. The emphasis in the narrative, the setting of episodes, are governed by an interpretation which is never wholly contemporary.

So far we have paid no attention to the retrospective character of understanding because in the example chosen the definitely achieved goal (since it is in the past), does not compromise the validity of the interpretation. But at all levels the same operation is performed. The historian connects the facts with each other, builds spatial and temporal systems which by definition look to the future. A prophet after the event, *he puts history into perspective*, and his perspective is tied in with the present, a true present or a present fictionally carried back into the past, in any event posterior to the development being traced.

However, the idea is simple and ordinary. If we had not tried to define it sharply, examples or formulae would have sufficed us. The rise of Boulanger is not like Hitler's because the latter attained power. The attempt of 1923 was transfigured by the Third Reich. The Weimar Republic has become a different thing because of the Nazi dictatorship which has given it provisionally the significance of an intermediate phase between two empires. The experiment of the *Front Populaire* will gradually reveal its importance to historians yet to come: depending on whether it leads to a new socialist government or to reaction, it will appear and will be truly different, and that is why there is no history of the present. Contemporary people are partisan and blind, as participants or victims. The impartiality expected by science demands not so much the quieting of passions or the collecting of documents, as it does the observation of results.

* * * *

We have given in a general way the idea of perspective. It is now important to make it specific and to examine it more thoroughly. Perspective assumes different appearances depending on whether one looks at a partial fact, basing observation on its presently known consummation, or at a still incomplete evolution. In addition, it is necessary to distinguish the *static revival* of a period expressed in a language suggested by a new situation, and the *historical revival,* the tribute to a master by his disciples, to one regime by the one succeeding it. In short, it is advisable to reintroduce all the complexity of the object. Every material fact is by definition achieved, unchangeable. But the historical event always has interest for conscious minds, and is connected, directly or indirectly, with the present. The plurality of interpretations comes together with the plurality of perspectives. And the real problem becomes the difference between the act and the mind of the actor, between the development and the ideas men have of it.

The opposition between finished and incompleted evolution is absolute, if two fragmentary evolutions are compared, the Boulanger plot and Hitlerism, for example. But it suffices to consider larger systems and to integrate them in the final whole, human history, to make up a continuous series.

The French Revolution has, in the ordinary sense of the word, been over for a long time. If we treat it as absolutely past, it appears, in its objective features, forever crystallized. But as soon as we try to grasp it in its very life we inevitable project upon it the shadow of our present struggles. It matters little that most revolutionaries did not consciously realize the class opposition between proletariat and bourgeoisie. It is enough that these distinctions make it possible to interpret a certain number of events in order that the *socialist history of the Revolution* may be legitimate, even if it tends to understand men differently from the way they understood themselves. All periods are susceptible to this revival through newness of interest of the present in the past. But most of the time this revival derives from the perspective setting. If there is a socialist history of the Revolution, it is that the victory of the third of the States General brought into question the destiny of the fourth. The bourgeois revolution is claimed by the socialists because for them it leads to the social revolution. In this sense, the great Revolution, theoretically complete on the 9th Thermidor or the 18th Brumaire, has not yet come to its true end. We feel contemporary with it, so that we transfigure it by our conceptual system (on which selection and organization depend), by the perspective setting, and finally by political passions (which inspire value judgments and give character to the account). In this case, historical impartiality has not yet triumphed over the point of view of the partisan.

In the same way one could show the triple actuality of the struggles which tore the republics of Athens or Rome. Historians still take sides for or against the democracy, for or against Caesar; they still explain the social or economic problems of antiquity in the light of our problems; finally, they still orient partial developments towards their goals, such as the period or culture as a whole towards its terminus, or towards the succeeding stages of human historical change.

These are abstract distinctions, no doubt, since political interest will often inspire other choices, and since in its turn it derives from the present which finally suggests the orientation of the whole. These distinctions were, nevertheless, necessary. Each of these realities answers a specific intention. The partisan is a contemporary at heart; he becomes judge, apologist, or critic. Static revival assumes the past to be *other*, but *other for* the present. Perspective overcomes the opposition of present to past, includes the two terms in the unity of a movement. In short, the relativity of perspectives connected with the development is immaterial to the antithesis of subjectivism and objectivism. It is the evolution itself which makes the past *other*, by giving it another future.

* * * *

History is a body of knowledge which is expressed in words, and results in sentences. The decisive problem is, then, the problem of concepts. We spoke above of static revival through the historian's language. Is it not necessary to apply the remark to a more general conception?

We could not develop here such a conception, which is an essential part of a methodology of the social sciences. It is important only to justify the diversity of historical concepts, without admitting either Weber's rather naïve nominalism, or Rickert's theory of givenness without form. The immanence of wholes, the thesis of Dilthey's objectivism, in no way does away with the plurality and relativity of *ideal types*.

Let us admit that the historian's concepts are borrowed from the mental states of the actors: the ambiguity does not disappear on that account. We have observed it, at the elementary level, in the examples of judicial phenomena and of a battle. The historian who does not admit any partiality must place himself above the differences between judge and litigant, between soldier and general; but at the upper level he finds new uncertainties. A historical idea, as efficient as was for a long time that of the Roman Empire, varies with men in each period as it does with the periods. The reality of the Roman Empire for the historian does not and must not coincide with any lived experience, as if the definition of ideas were retrospective and the historical development transcendent to mankind.

Will it be objected that no one will look for valid concepts in the minds of anonymous and powerless individuals? Is not capitalist rule offered quite obviously to external observation? The ideas individuals form of capitalism are of little importance, it is enough to describe the facts. But there again we encounter, even if we disregard ideology, a multiplicity of definitions implied by the nature of the real and by the situation of the historian.

Capitalism constitutes a whole, the different elements distinguished, the complex character of trade in time and space, the supremacy of the profit motive (substituted for the desire to provide for needs), the application of science to techniques, the rationalization of production, the separation of factory and home—all these features combine in a peculiar unity. For this reason a definition, unless it is reduced to an enumeration, demands a choice which, once again, does not consist of forgetting and retaining, but of fitting into place. The diversity of possible choices, then, is due to the human quality in the historical world, to the existence of totalities and to the uncertainty of the organizing principles, to the multiplicity of points of view assumed first by the man who lives and the one who rethinks life. We refer the reader to *Wirtschaft und Gesellschaft*: he will get an estimate of the number of questions that can be asked of a political regime.

Finally, the originality of a regime is determined only in and by history. If capitalism disappears without the disappearance of the complexity of trade, we shall still have as a character of the period private ownership of the means of production or opposition of bourgeoisie and proletariat. Depending on whether the future system will be one of planned national economies without the elimination of the present classes, or on the contrary, will be of the soviet type, the meaning of capitalism in the evolution will vary. The definition of a period depends on the one that follows it.

* * * *

Three arguments demonstrate the relativity of notions without bringing in nominalistic logic or specifically *critical* ('criticiste') method: the ambiguity of mental states and diversity of appearance depending on level of observation, the reality of wholes and the plurality of points of view, the change of perspective. If, then, it is asked why a fragment of history is not defined and, as it were, perfect in itself, we shall not again say as in the preceding *Part*, that the mind is inexhaustible and that the atom cannot be grasped, but that historical reality lies essentially beyond individual destiny.

We saw an example of this transcendence in the case of the battle. The combatants together produced the event desired by none, experienced by none, as it exists for the historian. The multiplicity of behaviours ends with a global result which, as a collective product, does not express and perhaps does not satisfy any one participant. A movement such as National-Socialism is historically defined not so much by the enthusiasm of the masses as by the institutional and human changes it finally brought on. A totality like the Roman Empire is both an idea and a power immediately visible and effective. To take different examples: in one place the difference between the individual and the whole appears, or again, between a revolution and its results (that is, between human desire and its effect on society, an event and its results); finally, there is the difference between State and individuals, a myth and human lives. We could, using other examples, ring the changes on the idea, which we shall sum up by quoting the old saying: men make their history, but they do not know the history they are making.

III. EXPLANATION OF ORIGIN AND RETROSPECTIVE RATIONALISM

THE PRESENT derives from the past, and the historian tries by studying the latter to understand the former. But, in *Part II*, we have just seen that the perspective of what no longer is comes from what followed it. We thus come to a sort of antinomy, since retrospection inevitably retraces the order in time and since true knowledge should follow that order.

We shall first study the relationship to the present of *explanations of origin*, and then *retrospective rationalization*, that is, the interpretation by consequences. We shall ask, in short, whether it is possible to avoid this dialectic by always remaining contemporary with the development. But our study will be directed by two fundamental questions: is a historical succession intelligible in itself? Is the true nature of an activity or of man himself revealed at the beginning or at the end?

* * *

Let us consider, to begin with, the history of ideas; we have two cases to be noted. Either the succession is that of two ideas taken in their intrinsic meaning, or understanding is external. Let us look first at the first hypothesis. The transition from the Cartesian plurality of substances to Spinozistic unity, from the new technique of vaulting to the Gothic style, from Michelson's experiment to Einstein's relativity—all stand as immediately intelligible. It is enough to establish the situation to account for the answer; to set up the antecedents to understand the consequences. The intrinsic rationality which links one term to another is here communicated to the historical series. Understanding, directly unique, remains dependent on a *theory*, since this reasoning is defined only within an intellectual universe.

It is clear that such understanding goes back to the origins *exclusively*. It follows the development, without explaining the beginning; it assumes both the intellectual universe and the specific will which manifests itself in that universe. History, and especially sociology specializing in genealogical inquiry, always start with a philosophy, a science, an art, or an embryonic reason. One sees in an activity, tending towards a different goal, an intention destined to acquire complete autonomy. Technique, or magic, appear as the origins of positivist science if either of them allows as a component the observation of natural regularities. The taking on of form is reduced to a dissociation; the illusory impression is given of a transition from one species to another.

These explanations are, quite obviously, relative to the present from which the start is made. The opposition between the continuity suggested by Durkheim and the discreetness insisted upon by M. Lévy-Bruhl, between primitive thought and rational thought, is caused by the differing definitions of rational thinking. For primitive thought, the general and imperative character of the concepts is typical of reason; for rational thought, it is logical identity and positivist causality. In the same way the opposition between the various interpretations of science (technique or magic) expresses an uncertainty less empirical than philosophical. (Similar remarks would apply to the relations between religion and philosophy.) According to Scheler, problems of origin are always metaphysical. Let us say that in any event history alone never suffices to solve them.

The relativity of explanations of origin represents one of the forms of relativity peculiar to all accounts oriented towards the present. One constructs the evolution of philosophy which ends with phenomenology as well as the one leading to critical idealism. Everyone retains, from among past authors, those who lead to his own thought; within systems, what is saved and what is denied. As a final judgment this cannot be condemned, however provisional it may be, but it is important to exhibit its assumptions. Merits and sins are weighed in the scales of a truth which belongs to the judge. National-Socialism finds for itself a line of descent in German thought; Communism would succeed in doing the same.

If, instead of seeking ancestors within a universe, the germ of the universe itself is looked for, the selection is similar, but in this case it is involved with a determination of essence. Everything depends, as we have just seen, on what is regarded as typical in a certain activity, and a definition, then, is either absolutely valid or legitimately arbitrary. Historical perspectives are multiple unless they are appended to a philosophical truth.

There will perhaps be the objection that we should have held the other hypothesis and put explanations of origin in the class of interpretations from the outside. Science is born of admiration or of need, religion of natural fears or of the sacred feeling awakened in the individual by the collective being, philosophy of primitive representations, mythological or theological, of which it is a later form.

In this case, indeed, the foregoing remarks would cease to be valid. On the other hand, these ventures at once fall before the objections pointed out in *Part II* above. One does not, by establishing the determining conditions, fix the specific meaning of an idea or of an experience (a religious one, for example). These interpretations, then, are either equivalent to phenomenologies (pure description of life), and in that case they are in contrast to other phenomenologies, or else they claim to be causal, in which case they are relative to a previous grasp of the phenomena. And this brings us back to the first hypothesis. Explanations of origin, then, always imply theories, in the sense in which we understood the word. They are dependent on a philosophical justification, not on an amassing of facts or on a historical account.

We find a similar illusion in the history of institutions. Certain sociologists have sought the simple societies from which all the others would come. Durkheim thought that the early forms of the ban on incest help us to understand the family organization or the sexual morals of today. The study of aptitude would suggest principles valid for our own existence.

There are several problems here. If, as Durkheim said also, the causes of an institution are found within the society to which it belongs, the reconstitution of the successive phases through which it has passed has nothing to do with the truly scientific explanation. If it is a question of the economic regime, it is the laws by which it functions today, not on account of how it came about, that is primarily of interest (Simiand insisted on this). The opposition here is not absolute though, for both beyond and within these laws, history still has its function.

Furthermore, for Durkheim the horde was the primitive and homogeneous segment from which the gradual make-up of complex societies was traced, the clan, the whole group from which there emerged by dissociation, family, religious, political groups, etc. From the totemic clan to the modern family, he sketched out a continuous movement, the matriarchy, the undivided agnatic family, the patriarchal family representing intermediate forms. He was inclined to confuse logical results with actual successions and to assume a history which would be that of humanity. The idea of *cradles of civilization* would be properly cited against evolutionism. But, without resorting to provisional scientific results, the fragility of these hypotheses can be shown. Neither the diversity of institutions nor of societies is subordinate to a few principles of classification. Social species and, *a fortiori*, the periods of human development, vary with the concepts used. And it is not certain that a historical totality is reducible to a collection of fragments.

We shall not insist, either, on the limits of the comparative method and of sociological generalization. The essential idea which inspires this research and which we wish to bring out, appears as well in the study of incest as in the *elementary forms of religious life*; the essence of a social reality would be revealed at the start, a rule to which we shall not oppose the contrary one: stick first to the case in which the fact is presented with maximum clearness. Both start from a hypothesis which is at least questionable, that is, the assimilation of history to a development from the simple to the complex. The capitalist economy is of course more complex; it is, especially, different from elementary barter. For social regimes, it is much more a question of fixing the limits of the wholes than of constructing a human evolution.

In the case of intellectual works, the prejudice in favour of the primitive unites with the attempt at simplification. One hopes that by grasping the meaning of the true or sacred in the embryonic stage, they can be brought closer to practical or profane activities. This is a double illusion: a work is defined by its end more than by its causes; man, if not created in the image of God, gradually attains humanity. Furthermore, the vendor in the market performs, perhaps, the act constituting mathematics; the actual want of discernment does not eliminate the specificity of the act (of the intelligence of the relations, in this example).

It is true that theories of knowledge often appear as explanations of origin which, consequently, would not be reconcilable with any philosophy. It is not that the causes in this case suffice to define the essence, but all doctrines interpret the nature of the categories at the same time that they do their formations.

* * * *

Retrospective rationalization in knowledge of self consists of substituting for the development of consciousness a series of *motifs*. In history it consists above all of grouping events so that the whole will appear as intelligible as the decision of the leader, as necessary as natural determinism. Now, assuming that each individual line of conduct is reasonable, is the global result still so?

The question is not of the sort which can be decided by a yes or a no. It is easy to cite the uncertainties of contemporaries, their contradictory anticipations; but it can quite properly be said that the historian sometimes knows the truth of a period better than those who participated in it. The rhythm of the economic phases is perceptible only afterwards, and yet it is objective. Why should not the same be true for the irreversible evolution of capitalism towards another regime?

In the first analysis, we shall confine ourselves to the two following observations. The reasonable explanation of a victory is always to be found, *post eventum*, either in the military organization, or in the valour of the leader, or in the plan of the battle, or in the technical means. In the same way, for a revolution, in the states of mind, social conflicts, etc. But this probability, always reached at a certain level, proves first of all the resourcefulness of the mind. In each case, the whole must be examined, and it is rarely fictive, rarely also inherent as such in the reality. But—and this is our second observation—retrospection is infallible, because it accounts for a past future. To reduce to unity the multiplicity of possible interpretations we should have to show a determination: with a certain factor given, the result could not have been otherwise. Only the study of the antecedents can prove the future necessity. But by the same token one forsakes understanding and appeals to the method of verification by cause.

Retrospective rationalization thus comes into the history of ideas. Distance makes it easier to distinguish schools, periods, styles. From a closer view, one sees only individuals; from afar, broad outlines appear.

Let us set aside this organization of the wholes which would call forth the two observations just made. Does not the history of ideas as such always lean towards anachronism, since it assumes a *single* will in its essence, of which the whole evolution would be the manifestation and the present system the achievement? As far as Husserl could see, phenomenology achieves the intention of Cartesian idealism, that is, to grasp in transcendental consciousness the principle of all certainty.

We do not have to inquire empirically whether this evolution was necessary or not. Necessity, which is in question, depends only on reflection; it is entirely ideal, since it links the various moments in science or philosophy. Historical truth, in this case, would merge with a systematic truth gradually elaborated.

However, retrospection runs another risk: the sameness of intention does not do away with conflicts between periods; consideration must be teleological to show the true end of the activity; but in order to be historically true, it must be free of contemporary bias. Hence, we have a reciprocal movement from past to present, so that we may compare them, and, by means of this comparison, realize at once *our* certainties and those of others. The reciprocity is all the more necessary because the present comes from the past, is often its logical result: there is always the temptation to attribute to teachers the knowledge which their disciples have, to ancestors the responsibility for their descendants. In the realm of ideas, *retrospective rationalization* implies and demands a justification of the development through the validity of the result, but it must be combined with the explanation of origin, which completes it and rectifies it. Thus, we come upon the primary idea of evolution: the initial state and the final state, inseparable, refer each to the other.

* * * *

But could not this dual transcendence be avoided, and could not one be always contemporary with the event? Of course, the simple narration which tells of the movement of things and beings tends towards this ideal, and possesses special value. It notes coincidences, antecedences, results. No sociology, or philosophy of history will replace this authentically naïve presentation of men in action. The well-known book by M. Mantoux furnishes an example, for one sector of society which apparently lends itself least to the application of this method, that is, economics. It has the merit of showing personalities as well as wholes, decisive dates as well as global movements. It proceeds from numberless and anonymous lives to the peculiarly historical development without sacrificing anything.

Such an account is quite different from popular narratives, bound up with each moment, looking neither forward nor back. History is truly the art of hiding the to-and-fro of retrospection to origins, thanks to a work of elaboration applied to all aspects of the world. Success demonstrates how anachronism, as well as unintelligible juxtaposition, is avoided.

In the history of ideas, the balance is harder to maintain. Cartesianism is of course the result of medieval philosophy as well as the origin of modern philosophy. All interpretations set it between past and future, and, too, they all lean towards one or the other. If some sort of truth were established in and by the author's psychology, it would not be final; one would have the right to put the Cartesian idea above the system—the critical idea above Kant's system.

And yet, this practical impossibility is not the main point. The historian is not trying to relive each historical moment, because he is trying to tie together the two ends of the chain. The sociologist and the philosopher, one seeking the simple society, the other its final expression, obey equally profound tendencies, because historical evolution, like biological evolution (either individual or of the species) would imply knowledge of the embryo and the adult, of origins and of end. It may be that the sociologist's ambition is as illusory as the philosopher's: we do not attain the final state, but neither do we reach the initial one. We are a part of the evolution, we find ourselves both by means of the goal we have set, and by the history we attribute to ourselves. By this dual reference to past and future we organize the movements which, incomplete in both directions, permit only relative and provisional understandings.

The doctrine of evolution in biology comes both from documents showing various fauna and flora at different times in the earth's past, from positivist philosophy seeking a mechanistic interpretation of apparent finalities, and from a naïve confidence in the value of imagined causes. Once the Lamarckian or Darwinian factors, which answered all questions because they gave a sort of verbal expression to the unknown forces which one would have liked to know, were discarded, history remained only a word, a question asked, or an indication of mystery.

In the same way, in the human order real development is not immediately intelligible: social changes, successions of empires, the rise of peoples, all these changes are not clear in themselves (at most we understand that they are changes, but it is necessary to give reasons for what we observe), they demand an explanation, as does the diversity of living forms. To show the particularity of each period or existence is merely to note the basic fact.

It is different in the case of the intellectual movement, where the beginning is given at the same time as the specific intention which defines a determined universe. It is immediately understood that no state of knowledge is definitive because science implies the effort of ever greater approach to truth. It remains to establish the influences favourable or unfavourable to this evolution. But when all is said and done, the progress of truth is not explained, any more than is a fragmentary truth, by anything other than itself.

In contrast to phylogenesis, history is not arrested. We do not see humanity in its adult state. Thus, each of us imagines it as he wishes it to be or foresees it, an imagining forever uncertain if it claims to be an anticipation of reality, one perhaps inevitable and legitimate if human nature is not to be accepted, but created.

IV. HUMAN EVOLUTION

IN THE preceding chapters, we studied problems presented by special histories. We noted the two contrary and complementary moves, towards origin in order to situate the present, towards the things of today in order to understand the past as realized by its future. In this chapter, we consider general history, that is, the history of man. Three orders of questions come up as a result of this broadening of the object. First, how unify the various sectors of the reality, how bring together the systems of interpretation? In addition, we shall look for the means of organizing, within one and the same evolution, different totalities. Finally, in connection with global development, there is the same uncertainty discussed in the preceding chapters: what is the rhythm of history, the nature of theory, the connection between different phases, the validity of the perspective?

* * * *

The *dissolution of the object*, of which we spoke in *Part II*, makes possible a true continuity between the present study and the preceding one. There are not, in the proper sense, any elements or atoms. Historical facts are already reconstructions, and even when individual, they are historical to the extent to which they are connected with collective things. At all levels, we are faced with systems inscribed in reality (systems of common representations or of modes of acting which tend to be reproduced). We have, through the intermediary of spontaneous retrospection, pointed out the transition from the narrative to the evolution. Does the same method make it possible to include the whole?

Total history would be a *history of men*, in the plurality of their activity and their universes, from their ways of feeding themselves and their barter to their style of worship. But would not such a history be partial, since it subordinates all systems of interpretation to one which it considers conclusive (as we pointed out above in connection with Dilthey's *history of souls*)? The expression *history of men* suggests at most a programme; in place of the Dilthey plan, nearer thought than action, the man who would be substituted for the soul would be a producer rather than a believer, a worker before being a dreamer.

Furthermore, *systems of ideas*, as well as *social systems*, exist, but only the historian gives them form. Whether it is a question of a period, of a generation, of a school, or of a nation, it would be as absurd to deny the things held in common as it would be to slight the task of interpretation. The individuals of one generation, marked by the situation in which they arrive at consciousness, often have a certain identity of aspirations or of reactions, but it is the historian who picks out common intentions and particular traits, who separates data which, in a certain perspective, seem to be characteristic of a time. The selection which we predicate is based neither on incoherence (Weber), nor on the infinity of the real (Rickert), but on the most incontestable fact: the interval which separates the historian from his object, the realization of consciousness from consciousness itself, and the observer from the party concerned.

It might be opportune, in connection with each of the concepts mentioned, to pursue the dual analysis of the objective system and of retrospective understanding. We shall not attempt this; it would take too long, and it is not indispensable. In effect, no matter how diverse historical unities may be, whether they spring from milieux or from will, from technique or from religion, they are partial, they connect individuals with multiple groups, they divide society into fragments. The totality which we are looking for, then, would have to overcome, even more than the particularity of the system of interpretation, the plurality of personal or collective activities. The real problem is that of the order to be established between the disparate elements of all life and culture.

One could, at first glance, consider a sociological order. In the same way that we analyse a method of production, exchange, and distribution (a multiple analysis, since it must take into account technical, legal, social relations, ownership of tools, of sharing of taxes, wealth, etc.), a political system (number and designations of governments, degree and basis of their authority, relation of governed with rulers, their reciprocal attitudes) why should our analysis not extend to the totality?

Nothing, indeed, forbids it. But understanding, whether static or dynamic, must choose between an increasing number of concepts and perspectives as it becomes wider—unless the whole is more determined than are the elements. But in any case this determination is not contemporary. Considered objectively, a society decomposes into institutions which doubtless combine, but do not contain an imperative or exclusive principle of unity. Politics and economy are always closely interrelated within a collectivity. It may be more convenient to begin with one or the other according to circumstances; one may show how the hierarchy of authority is adapted to returns from wealth, but sociologically there is not any one way of considering the organizations, or even less one single way to subordinate some to others or to follow their transformations, whether interdependent or autonomous.

We shall raise the question in the next *Part* of the help given by the inquiry into cause. For the present, we should like to show the plurality of understandings and point out the origin of historical totalities in a certain conception of man. Once again, we in no way deny the objectivity of systems, at whatever level they appear. All cultures are perhaps individuals condemned, one after the other, to a lonely death. But a reconstruction, unless it is agreed that it is only one among others, ought to be subject to a *true* plan, not merely a possible plan, but the only valid one. This plan is inscribed neither in minds, which are not unified, nor in behaviours, which are, for each and for all, multiple and sometimes incoherent. A static sociology, a cross-sectional snapshot, shows the schema of operation. As for a *statics* such as the *Système de politique positive*, it is no longer the summary of a provisional state of things, but the end of history; it is, in a particular form, a *theory of man*, since it fixes the value to be given to the various activities and relationships which are to bring people together. In other words, it determines the life to be imposed on mankind: the unity of one period is fundamentally that of a given sort. It matters little whether we speak of values or culture; the opposition between reality and ideas disappears; it is a question of man himself, of his goals in life, of the imperatives he obeys, of the works to which he dedicates himself—in a word, of the meaning he gives to life. Thus there is revealed the kinship between history and philosophy, since this totality is the one considered by every philosophy. General history should be a history of philosophies as lived.

* * * *

History—even natural history—demands, as we have seen, a dual unity: the unity of a whole in which the disparate changes take place, and the unity of an evolution giving direction to the movement. The unity of spiritual histories exists through the decision of the historian who thinks in terms of a certain order of values or truths and seeks their origins. Factual history begins with immediately given wholes and gradually rises to the level of institutional realities more and more vast and lasting; thus a certain orientation becomes apparent: the account given of an empire or city state, Rome or Athens, finds within the framework of the object a beginning and an end, distinct periods, from founding to decadence. Would that history which rose above nations and particular cultures be stripped of this dual unity?

It would be hard to indicate the point where the break would come. The history of Europe is as real as that of nations (national histories, in any case, do not go back as far as the former). And we follow a continuous line, to Rome and Greece, and consequently to the peoples who influenced the culture of classical antiquity. But, if we adopted this method, if we limited ourselves to a search for our ancestors, we should sacrifice a large part of our past. To understand the history of man, we must start not with ourselves and our times but with the multiplicity of empires, civilizations, and epochs.

As long as one is thinking of a totality, whether of a time, a state or a system of evolution, the historian can set out to identify himself with individual or collective life. We have demonstrated the impossibility of this ideal, and that a posthumous revival is inevitable. But, when one is thinking of several unities, the historian no longer claims fidelity; transfiguration becomes voluntary and calls for other procedures. The distinction between what is important and what is negligible no longer obeys criteria inherent in the object, but it obeys present values, or the demands of comparison and of retrospection.

Historical comparison, by definition, consists of noting similarities and differences. Institutions (political systems, for example) are looked at from a certain point of view (number of governments); the different kinds (oligarchy, democracy, etc.) are noted. The more the points of view are combined, the more modes are distinguished in each of them, and the more richness and fecundity is gained by the method. Note Weber's political sociology, where, starting with three concepts (the charismatic, the traditional, the bureaucratic) there is worked out a study which makes possible the application to one society of several qualifying factors, each of which isolates and characterizes a certain aspect of collective existence.

The transition from comparison to evolution makes other demands. If it is a question of a partial evolution (for example, political), it would be advisable to grasp the continuation and line of changes; both sociology and the philosophy of history create spontaneously, by their interpretations, that indispensable unity which goes from military to industrial societies, from mechanical to organic solidarity, or from the past in its entirety to the advent of liberty, the end of civilization. This movement need not be explicitly regarded as a progress (although in fact it nearly always is); it is necessary, and sufficient, that the various succeeding forms of government have enough in common to belong to one development. If the question is one of global evolution, the historian must first constitute the totalities, in order then to link them together. As contrasted with the comparative analysis used by Weber, the historian would in this case choose a rule or a few rare rules of organization to which he would subordinate all others; for example, he would consider methods of production and exchange or mental structures; human periods would merge either with the different types of economy, or with the various stages of the development of the mind.

Doubtless it would be possible to avoid the schematism of the law of the three states, or of liberty for one, for several, or for all, to recognize the diversity of historical forms, to trace the multiple lines and detours of the evolution. In any case, unity comes from the identity of a problem (intellectual, or social) set for all mankind, from the continuity of solutions men have found throughout the centuries, and, eventually, from the orientation towards a universally valid solution.

To what extent is it possible to organize such a history, one in its immensity? We shall meet the question again further on. We only wished to trace to its end the labour of reconstruction, the beginning of which we have seen in partial and impersonal understanding.

* * * *

In Western thought, the meaning in history derives from Christianity, which makes of each existence a solitary adventure in which the salvation of the soul is at stake, and gives to mankind as a whole, by means of its mission, one single destiny, between the fall and the redemption. Secularized in the idea of progress, this philosophy nonetheless maintained the double unity on which the existence of history depends, the unity of men and of their development. Certainly, the biological idea of evolution replaces the mystical concept of the reversibility of sins and deserts. But it is not certain that the historian of today still recognizes an evolution; is humanity like the individual who progresses from puerility to wisdom? As for the history of the species, it is even more mysterious than that of societies.

If it is a question of science or of technique, it is easy to show progress, on condition that the accumulation of knowledge, the increase of power, be considered as preferable to ignorance and weakness. In the same way, and more generally, as a function of a value—liberty, i.e. the guarantees of the individual against the police or administration—it can be argued that such and such a change in law or government is for the best. Once the goal is set, judgment goes back to an appreciation of the means. But a philosophy of progress is incommensurable with these objective appreciations (based on a certain hypothesis), for it consists of admitting that the totality of societies and of human life tends to grow better, sometimes even that this improvement, regular and continuous, is to go on indefinitely. Essentially intellectualist, it proceeds from science to man and to social organization and is optimistic, since morality, logically and in fact, would go hand in hand with intelligence.

The reaction against this doctrine has today taken the most varied forms. People question the reality, or at any rate the regularity, of progress. Too many events have revealed the precarious position of what is called civilization; what were apparently the surest gains have been sacrificed to collective mythologies; politics, unmasked, has revealed its essence to the most naïve. Thus logical and factual criticism has been levelled at the reasoning which drew conclusion from science to man and society. A departmental activity, positivist science develops according to a special rhythm without either the spirit, or even less the conduct of man, following its accelerated movement. Reason is no longer either the supreme good or the conclusive force.

Besides, what does this so-called progress signify? Between a collectivist society offering itself as an absolute value, and a liberal society aiming at broadening the scope of individual independence, there is no common ground. The succession from one to the other could be judged only with reference to a norm which should be above historical variations. But such a norm is always the theoretical projection of what a particular collectivity is or would like to be. Now, the world of today knows too well the diversity which is obvious within itself to succumb to the artlessness of closed groups, or to have the presumption of those who measure themselves by the past and by others with the confidence of their own superiority.

It is not certain that the concept of evolution can resist this dissolution of values, this disappearance of the goal of history. Its function was to explain and justify diversity. Instead of the antithesis of true and false, of good and evil, it showed the necessity of progress, the historical truth of errors or, more generally, of preceding phases. If we abandon the comparison of the ages of life and periods in the past, if the final state, having sunk to the level of the others, no longer gives the movement any direction, do we not come back, for our philosophy, to the history of sects, for sociology, to simple succession? Finally, let us note the results of sociological study, the increasing importance of the idea of *cradles of civilization* (as opposed to the evolutionary doctrine), the recognized singularity of cultures. *History-evolution*, today, is degenerating into *history as development*. Always creative spiritually and socially, history is without a goal, has no set terminus; each epoch exists for itself, alone and inexplicable, since each time chooses a different end, and since there is no real common bond between these scattered elements of humanity.

* * * *

In appearance *history as development* represents a sort of liberation. Instead of applying a rigid plan, the historian happily sets out to discover all the singularities; he strives to recognize and understand them in themselves. Whereas the believer in progress subordinates and sacrifices, as it were, the past to the future, the philosopher of development is one with life, and respects it, since each of its moments bears within itself its own *raison d'être*.

But this liberation ends in a sort of anarchy. Of course the objection will be that the procession of historical totalities, even without orientation, makes up a history. It is still to be determined whether totalities do not owe their existence to the residues of evolutionist and intellectualist philosophy. It is conceivable that global unities are empirically discovered (for example, Spengler's cultures, or Toynbee's *intelligible fields of investigation*). Let us set aside the arbitrary uncertainty of these delimitations; let us confine ourselves to one observation: this would lead to a plurality of independent histories, the supra-individual law of which would be fundamentally irrational, like the laws of matter and of life. These histories would have nothing human left; they would be fatalistic; their mystery would make the science of the prophet-sociologist almost incomprehensible.

The unity of man's development, unintelligible if it is real, ineffective and transcendental if ideational, must be both concrete and spiritual, like that of an individual or of a collectivity. It must rise above the duality of nature and mind, of man and his environment, for man is seeking, within and by means of his history, a mission which will reconcile him with himself.

CONCLUSION

Development and Evolution

IN THE preceding *Part* we looked in vain for a truth which would fit the reality. Did we, by reintroducing the fact of evolution, bring to light a new factor of subjectivity, or did we attain truth at a higher level? The two theories are at first glance equally tenable. The *Social Contract*, or National Socialism, though ambiguous in themselves, could be determined in and by means of a biography of Rousseau, or German history.

We found to begin with, for general history as well as for special histories, the plurality of systems of interpretation. The history of philosophy has a different rhythm depending on whether it is characterized by the search for truth, the effort of aesthetic construction, or the *résumé* of the eternal discussions about inexplicable antinomies, depending on whether it expresses an immutable man or changing human natures, whether it anticipates a positivist knowledge or answers to a specific and fixed intention. Between these hypotheses, neither the learned restoration of texts nor of systems will make it possible to choose. Also and even more clearly, man, the centre of history, is productive, sometimes of gods, and sometimes of techniques, perhaps of both at once, but the interpretation of a universe or of a culture depends on a theory not derived from empirical facts.

Moreover, in all forms of history we have shown the relativity to the present of the historical view, the static and historical revival in the interpretation of facts and of institutions, the relativity of explanations of origin, the tendency towards retrospective rationalization suggestive of the necessity of development—but the future becomes proportionately more distant. In the case of general history, the orientation of the *perspective* tends to merge with the *theory*, as judgments of fact become indistinguishable from appreciative judgments. *Theory* establishes the importance of the various activities, at times even a material criterion of value for a given activity: the historian's decision about himself more and more governs the whole view of history.

Does this mean that the consideration of evolution implies a relativistic conclusion? Actually, we do not yet have the right so to conclude. Let us admit the mutual involvement of retrospection and the present: the validity of the former depends on the nature of the latter; history as reality could be a revelation of truth of such a sort that history as science would gradually participate in this progressive truth.

Historical understanding sets out in two divergent and even opposite directions. It aims either to interpret a period in itself, or else to put it in its place in a larger totality, to subordinate it to a movement which transcends it. These two tendencies correspond to two aspects of reality which no one saw better than did Dilthey. On the one hand a man, a society, have their centre, their meaning in themselves. They make up a whole in which each element is related to all others and is explained by them. But on the other hand, an adventure, even if it were personal, takes on its exact meaning only retrospectively because the outcome is always capable of changing what went before it. In one case truth, contemporary with life, is shut inside the limits of closed unities; in the other truth, as historical, appears gradually in memory or to the distant observer. Dilthey never clearly pointed out the opposition; he never succeeded in reconciling his taste for biography and his desire for a universal history.

These two tendencies in research correspond, of course, to two views of history, two philosophical intentions. Some see the past, their own and that of collectivities, dispersed in fragments; others see it unified by the evolution which leads up to the present. Some discern first of all the singularities, others the identity of man and the continuity of traditions. Some discover in each moment and in each existence its own justification, others believe in progress and think that the future constitutes the goal and *raison d'être* of anterior stages. This conflict is not merely theoretical; it is tied up with differing sets of values, with the antithesis of life and thought, of beauty and truth.

Is it irreducible? Of course one could state exactly the claims of each interpretation according to different aspects of reality, and according to different works. But even when all had been said and done there would still be a fundamental antinomy. A philosophy of evolution implies the essential and final unity of history. A philosophy of development gives consent to the anarchical juxtaposition of diversities. Man, the prisoner of an epoch, integrated in a society, defines himself by placing himself and freeing himself from the tyranny of the past by choosing his future. But, is this decision, which is necessary for those who live as it is for those reflecting on the history of philosophy or the philosophy of history, is it, like personal preferences, an arbitrary thing, or can it claim the universality of truth? On this question depends the modality of the knowledge which the individual gains of the collective destiny, that is, of himself.

GENERAL CONCLUSION OF SECTION II

The Limits of Understanding

THE EXPRESSION *limits of understanding* is ordinarily taken in the psychological sense. Jaspers and Max Weber speculated about the extent of comprehensible phenomena. The question was particularly difficult for Jaspers, who was studying pathological facts. When one understands the content of a delirium one does not necessarily understand the relation between the original trauma and the mental disturbance. And one almost never understands why and how certain neuroses bring on physiological symptoms.

We set aside this aspect of the problem; it has no significance for history. Weber, it is true, had raised an analogous question, perhaps even merely transposed Jaspers' question. What are the frontiers of the field which is created by the sociology of understanding? The answer he indicated was not unequivocal, for he did not clearly distinguish non-conscious and non-comprehensible (in theory, not in practice) and he tended to confuse rational and comprehensible. Failing to discern clearly the understanding of *mobiles*, to analyse affective understanding (which he only mentioned), he traced out the decrease of intelligibility from *final rationality* to tradition.

On the other hand, he recognized the mechanical, instinctive, reaction, or the reaction of a madman as a typically incomprehensible fact. This observation is doubtless valid, but the sociologist will insist on another question, for him conclusive. It is a matter first of all of situating reasonable behaviours, of outlining the limits within which historical events or social institutions present themselves for understanding as personal actions, and beyond which limits the facts no longer seem to correspond to a thought and obey a blind determinism.

We have already, in the preceding section, examined the diffusion, so to speak, of elementary intelligibility; we have noted the surprising character of certain totalities. We shall resume this study in the next two sections.

We shall dwell still more on the other two contrary and complementary meanings of the same expression. Understanding implies an objectification of the psychological facts; what sacrifices does this objectification involve? But, on the other hand, we have also seen that understanding always commits the interpreter. He is never like a physicist—he remains a man as well as a student. And he refuses to become pure scholar because understanding, beyond knowledge, aims at the *appropriation* of the past. The above question will, then, be inverted, and will be one concerning the consequences following an imperfect objectification, and the conditions presupposed in communication between minds.

If one were to divide the life of the soul into superimposed layers, from the psycho-physiological state up to the act of mind, one could locate the matter of understanding, the psychological given, a sort of extension of an act within a consciousness attached to a body. We shall not discuss Scheler's metaphysical constructs; we shall merely point out—a proposition implied in our previous analyses—that it is illegitimate to give an ontological reality to conceptual distinctions. Without failing to recognize the diversity of its aspects, we have considered psychological life in its concrete totality, as it is offered for immediate observation or for reflection. Consequently we have never observed any fusion or assimilation of the *egos*, though we have never questioned either the common possession of basic beliefs or the priority of common ideas and emotions, or the grasp by different minds of intentionalities to a large extent identical, the equivalent of the sharing towards which, according to Scheler, historical understanding tended.

In the same way, we have recognized from the outset a sort of perception of others. But this perception does not cause us to share an alien life, it presents it to us objectified. The fidelity of the historian has nothing in common with the immediate impression of the witness, although both demand the capacity to step outside of oneself and to imagine another existence. We reconstitute a system of preferences or of behaviour without, most of the time, succeeding in feeling the soul whose intellectual structure we have, as it were, laid bare.

On the other hand, lacking any intuition of the intentionalities or others in visible expressions and symbols, we do not consider accessible what Scheler called *Gesinnung*, the *moral intentions* of a being. As spectators we have global images of others; one appears as noble, another ordinary. But the *Gesinnung*, assuming that it merges with the moral quality (which is far from being necessarily the case, since, because it is constitutive of each individual, it eludes conscious choice and has nothing to do with merit) never appears as total and unambiguous. It defines itself as an impulse, love or desire, inclined towards a certain set of values. Now, one never arrives at a final impulse and the analysis of goals is essentially indefinite. The *moral intention* which can be conceived and which is distinguished from both *motifs* and *mobiles*, since it implies an appreciation, does not entail any perfect understanding.

To no greater degree is the subject in its totality or in its free decision given to the spontaneous intuition of the spectator or to the patient reconstruction of the historian. Whether liberty is conceived as the ethical exertion or as the source of all life, it disappears in the case of the other person just as it does for oneself as soon as it is crystallized in the past. A whole destiny is perhaps the effect of a single choice, the choice of intelligible character, of a world of values, or of a lot in life. Confused with its results, liberty would no longer be distinguished from a fatality: whether the choice could or could not have been other than it was, once made it is and it remains, and one observes it, determined like any reality. Only a feeling which would reproach us for our choice would make us conscious of our alienated power. Others, then, are indistinguishable from their conduct and from their psychological states. If they change we shall complicate accordingly the idea we have of them, but they will not stop being what they are. They become separate from their fate only for those who treat them as persons, and who, without penetrating the mystery, admit the power of creation.

A double limit to understanding is thus set by the fact that the latter assumes an object; moral quality is beyond the *motifs* and *mobiles*, liberty and totality are within the dispersion. Living contact gives us at times the sensation of the quality, long familiarity and the intelligence of certain acts make it possible to come close to the essence of the individual. But in the last analysis the gap between possession through knowing and communication through being remains. To eliminate the restrictions of objectification, knowledge should yield place to participation. But one only is oneself—one thinks or imagines others.

Of course this knowledge, in the end, transcends itself. Just as one *is* one's own past, so one incorporates the wealth passed on by others. But at this moment science disappears. The past still appears in so far as it is an integral part of our mind or life. To explore it we detach it from us and project it outside. If, after recognizing it we assimilate it again, we are for that reason no longer historians—we then again become historical beings.

This communication between persons seems to contradict the attempt at objectivity which we have analysed in all forms of understanding. In reality, the interpreter's commitment is, in every way, indispensable, since human facts, ambiguous and inexhaustible, lend themselves to multiple understandings.

Men live the judicial or moral experience, the historian determines it by reconstructing it. The spiritual elements insert themselves into different totalities, the historian puts the wholes in order and marks out the essential. All the moments of a life or of a universe come together in a development, the historian composes the series and, depending on his perspective and values, fixes the relationships between the phases, and the meaning of the movement.

The historian struggles at times to reduce as much as possible this connection between science and the present. Either he reduces retrospective organization to a sort of juxtaposition or conceptual expression, or else he takes limited fragments separately, without integrating them to an evolution. But, in the first case, science would tend to disappear in proportion as the rôle of the decisions diminish and as one came theoretically closer to a total objectivity. In the second case, one would succeed in avoiding the relativity of perspectives, but only to fall back into the plurality of images.

What matters more to us than the search for empirical exactness, the importance of which is methodological, is the intense effort to attain universality beyond particularity. Does the individual succeed in encompassing the history of which he is a fleeting atom? As a scholar, does he succeed in retracing the development of his science? As a man, does he manage to think in terms of the various human groups and to follow their succession? Logically, the sameness of mental reasoning or of human nature, however formal the community so created, authorizes an integral understanding. But we must still rise above the limitations of the individual mind and of each moment of history. Universality of knowledge would demand of the historian and of history a disindividualization, the presence of truth—an acquisition in common—in the consciousness of the historian, the interpreter of all men.

SECTION III

HISTORICAL DETERMINISM AND CAUSAL THOUGHT

INTRODUCTION

Directions of Causal Inquiry

CAUSE is originally conceived as the agent or the efficient force which produces the effect. If the meaning still given to the word today were analysed psychologically, there would usually be found a residue of this anthropomorphism or mysticism. Cause would be like a human power or, at least, a creative dynamism.

But this metaphysic does not stand up to the requirements of logic. In order for a causal relation to be demonstrated positively, it is not important that the link of cause and effect be intrinsic or essential, but it is necessary that it be perceptible and verifiable, that is, conformable with a rule of succession. The cause becomes the constant antecedent, the regularity the sign of necessity.

The development of the notion of cause does not stop there. The constant and necessary antecedent occurs only at an elementary level of scientific organization. The examples J. S. Mill cites to justify his definition are almost outside science. Practically, we say that the condensation of water vapour is caused by the difference in temperature between the side of a glass and the surrounding air. Scientifically, one would have to calculate the conditions of temperature and pressure under which condensation is produced, without choosing, except for pragmatic reasons, a cause among the conditions. In physical science they rarely speak any more of *the cause*, or even of *the causes*: they try to discover, by combining functional relations, the concrete data.

Of course, in the sense in which Auguste Comte put the search for causes in opposition to the discovery of laws, modern science aims at causes. No regularity established by observation alone satisfies our curiosity. And more than ever the tendency is towards representative hypotheses, in order to elucidate the atomic structure of matter. But, whatever be the meaning the philosopher gives to the notion of causality, the cause of one law (for example, gravitation) could, in the end, be only another law from which the first would be deduced, or a representation of things at a lower level (a representation which itself is reduced to relationships). So that one never arrives at either a supreme principle or a final element.

Starting with these commonplace remarks, the problems of historical determinism are easily brought out. The sociologically inclined critic asserts the absolutely necessary transcendence of metaphysics by logic. Instead of the force or the *motif*, let us look for the constant antecedent, unconditional (the more general, the less conditioned). The observation of the concrete data does not give the true explanation: it demands comparison of multiple examples in order to distinguish the accidental from the necessary. History would give way to sociology (traditional discussions revolve about this problem).

But would it not be possible to carry over into the theory of history the transcendence of Mill's logic by means of contemporary epistemology? The true aim of science is to substitute for subjective appearances verified and objective relations which dissolve both the objects of immediate perception and the objects-as-causes of elementary science. The three stages of our study will be causality in a single sequence, regularities and laws, and the structure of historical determinism. They indeed correspond to the questions which authentically and spontaneously arise.

Causal thought in history begins with the child's or the judge's query: whose fault is it? It aims at establishing responsibilities, but it rises finally to metaphysics: who rules the world? Is it ideas or interests, individuals or crowds, men, fate or a God? Between the practical concern and the philosophical reflection there stretches out the field of scientific experience. The idea of cause seems indispensable for the bringing together the scattered phenomena by means of universally valid relationships. Without it, sequences would remain accidental and indistinguishable from chance encounters.

To put it another way, three different intentions direct the analysis of causes in history: the intention of the judge, that of the scientist (coordinate and opposed), and that of the philosopher, higher than the other two. The first sticks to the antecedents of an event, the second tries to set up links of co-existence and succession, and the third tries to bring together and compare the two inquiries, set in their place in the context of historical determinism.

Of course, the intransigent positivist will recognize as properly scientific only the scholar's intention. And he would justify by the traditional formulae such as 'there is no science but of the general', his scorn of the historian, preoccupied with unique circumstances which account for an event unlike any other. But a theory of this order, far from being really positive, would be arbitrary, for it would do violence to the spontaneous progress of knowledge. The judge's concern remains legitimate as long as fatalism or sociological determinism is not evidenced, and the philosopher's reflection as long as the results of science, far from satisfying our curiosity, seem to depend on the personal beliefs of scholars.

To start, we do not have to choose, but to recognize the problems. It is necessary only to specify a few simple distinctions which will guide our exposé. The problems of causality in history are, some of them formal, others material. What is the influence in history of masses and of great men, of ideas and of interests? Such questions are material. We regard as formal, questions relative to the logical conception of historical causality. Moreover, we must, again, separate formal and material. In the formal sense any causal inquiry concerning an event is historical. The expert is in the same position as the historian. But on the other hand the nature of the historical facts carries with it consequences for the scientific construction. The historian does not, like the expert, observe natural phenomena, but human agencies and their consequences. The procedures, the results, depend perhaps on this structure of the reality.

However, these beginning remarks suffice to distinguish understanding and causality. Understanding is concerned with the intrinsic intelligibility of *motifs*, *mobiles*, and ideas. The latter aims first of all at establishing necessary links by observing regularities. Constant succession is the schema of causality, to use Kant's expression. To the extent that the sociologist tries to discover causal relationships, he legitimately ignores, he must ignore, the probability of rational sequences; he treats historical phenomena as extraneous or, to use the classical expression, as things.

We shall study first historical causality, that is, the analysis of the causes of a single fact. Next, we shall ask whether and to what extent the world of man allows relations comparable to those of the physical sciences. In other words, the first *Part* will be devoted to historical causality, the second to sociological causality. In the third *Part* we shall bring together the results obtained, and shall try to answer the following questions: what is the nature of historical determinism? What are the limits of causal thought in history?

First Part

EVENTS AND HISTORICAL CAUSALITY

ANY historical investigation is, by definition, retrospective. Any causal exploration is, then, regressive: the historian starts with the effects and goes back to antecedents. But a fact always has a number of antecedents. How can we determine the true cause? Practically, it will be said, the choice is a function of curiosity or of self-interest. But is not such a choice arbitrary? Under what conditions does it assume scientific value?

On the other hand, if we consider an event in all its complexity, we could not isolate it from the moment when it occurred. It is unique and singular. How can one establish the causes of a phenomenon incomparable with any other and which is seen only once? The need to simplify the effect thus allies itself with the choice of the antecedents.

We shall first show according to which schema there is brought into an argument the potential generality, indispensable for distinguishing the causal relationship from the simple succession, without leaving out of account either the localization or the originality of the event. Then we shall try to specify the meaning and limits of this causality, by comparing the three concepts of chance, of responsibility, and of cause.

I. THE SCHEMA OF HISTORICAL CAUSALITY

THE APPARENT inconsistency in historical causality is due to the impossibility of distinguishing, except by repetition, a succession contingent upon a necessary relationship. Even if Napoleon is the cause of the defeat of Waterloo, I shall never be able to prove it, because this sequence, unique in time, peculiar in quality, could not recur. Hence the oscillation in the logical theory of history between scepticism and sociologism; the historian recites the story of events in their established order, but the *motifs* which he attributes to the actors offer only an illusory satisfaction to the mind. Of course the connection between one detail and another often seems to be probable, because it is familiar, because we have ourselves experienced the impulses moving historical characters, because we all fall back in practice on the explanation by *agents* or *forces*. Nevertheless, these accidental connections have no place in positive science. On the contrary, once the laws of the social order were known it would be easy to establish the causes of historical facts. Various logical schemata are available: either one divides the antecedent phenomenon A and the consequent phenomenon B into elements connected by laws, so that in conclusion A may be called the cause of B; or a phenomenon B (e.g. inflation of the assignat of the Revolutionary Government 1790 ff.) will be called the effect of various phenomena A, A^1, A^2 (over issuing, speculation, war, etc. . . .), each one being a cause or condition favouring B; or the particular series AB will be directly deduced from the general relationship (every dictatorship ends in foreign ventures, the Fascist dictatorship is the cause of the Ethiopian war).

Scepticism and sociologism seem to us equally inadequate. The connection between one detail and another is certainly met with in historical accounts, but when speaking of *motifs* or *agents* or *forces*, this type of interpretation is not exactly defined. We saw in the preceding Section that psychological accounts constitute only one type of intelligible relations. And, moreover, none of the logical schemata mentioned and which are usually offered in a more or less clear form by the logicians seem to us characteristic, or essential. *De jure* all three are possible and legitimate. *De facto* the most interesting schema is the one Weber pointed out. It alone will make it possible for us to explain the true nature of historical causality, to distinguish truly between historical and sociological causality, to connect judgments of causality, expressing a *retrospective probability*, both with the historian's curiosity and with the structure of the world of history.

* * * *

Let us first recall the logical schema. If I say that Bismarck's decision was the cause of war in 1866, that the victory at Marathon saved Greek culture, I mean that except for the Chancellor's decision, war would not have occurred (or at any rate not at that time), that the conquering Persians would have prevented the Greek 'miracle'. In both cases the effective cause is defined only by confrontation with the possibilities. *Every historian, to explain what did happen, asks himself what might have happened.* The theory merely puts into logical form the spontaneous practice of the *man in the street.*

If we are seeking the cause of a phenomenon we do not limit ourselves to adding up or bringing together the antecedents. We try our best to *weigh* the peculiar influence of each of them. In order to effect this discrimination we take one antecedent and think of it as having disappeared, or changed, and try to construct or imagine what would have happened under that hypothesis. If we must admit that the phenomenon under study would have been different in the absence of this antecedent (or in case it had been different), we shall conclude that it is *one* of the causes of a part of the phenomenon-effect, that is of the part we have had to assume as transformed. If the Greeks had fallen under Persian rule, subsequent Greek life would have been partly different from what it was. The victory at Marathon is one of the causes of the Greek culture.

Logically the investigation includes the following operations: 1. analysis of the phenomenon-effect; 2. discrimination of the antecedents and isolation of one antecedent, the efficiency of which it is desired to measure; 3. construction of unreal developments; 4. comparison of mental images and the actual events.

Let us assume provisionally, in order not to complicate the description of the logical schema, that our general knowledge, of a sociological order, permits unreal constructions. What will be their modality? Weber's answer is that it will be a question of *objective possibilities*, otherwise called sequences conforming to known generalities, but only *probable*. The theocratic government would not have been a necessary result, but an *objectively possible* result of a Persian victory. The circumstances making that regime (unrealized) *objectively possible*, would in any case have combined with other events which would have been favourable or unfavourabe to that evolution. The correct formula, then, will be one of probability: a Persian victory will be called an adequate cause of a theocracy; it would have produced it in a very large number of cases, or, more exactly, in a comparably larger number than the cases in which it would not have done so. An effect is called accidental with reference to a certain group of antecedents if the group leads to the effect only in a small number of cases (a number small in contrast with the number of those in which it would not lead to it).

These two conceptions of sufficiency and accident apply not only to unreal constructions. The causal explanation of an event, the measure of potencies is a matter of stating exactly these judgments of sufficiency and contingency. Let us look at the case of the Revolution of 1848: its *immediate cause*, as commonly expressed, was the shooting on the boulevards. No one questions this connection. But some reduce the importance of the final incidents by saying that if they had not occurred the Revolution would have occurred anyway. This assertion, strictly expressed, is equivalent to saying that if the shootings are thought of as not having occurred, the other antecedents, taken together, are sufficient cause for a revolution. On the contrary, if a historian thinks that the situation made a revolution possible but not probable, the sufficiency of the shooting will accordingly increase (to express it exactly, it would lead to the revolution in a moderate but not a great number of cases; in this sense one would still say that it more or less *favoured*, more or less increased the number of favourable chances). In short, revolution will be accidental with reference to the situation if in most cases it does not occur. Naturally these cases are fictitious and exist only in and by our thought. These judgments are on that account no less capable of validity, or at least of probability.

These reasonings of retrospective probability make it possible for us to give exact meaning to expressions met with in everyday life as well as to those of history. An immediate antecedent is only the *occasion* of an event when, as seen by the historian, the event under consideration must inevitably have occurred, given the historical situation. (Even here the occasion may be important if the moment exerted an influence on the subsequent history.) An event is always accidental in a relative sense with reference to a certain group of antecedents. But one may speak of an accidental determinant if the effect is accidental with reference to the totality of the antecedents with the exception of a few facts (for example, the shooting). An event may be considered a *turning point* in history if, accidental or not, with reference to the antecedents, it is the sufficient origin of a long or important evolution. One will speak of a *nexus of events* if, being the originally adequate beginning of an evolution, the event under consideration was an accidental effect with reference to one group of antecedents, but the sufficient effect with reference to another. Just as the statesman, in terms of the possibilities which he glimpses, draws the outlines of the world upon which he exerts his influence, so the historian, by a retrospective meditation of the probabilities, shows the articulation of the historical process.

* * * *

The conclusions drawn from causal analysis belong to two different types: either the battle of Marathon is *one* of the causes of the Greek culture, Protestantism *one* of the causes of capitalism; or the shooting is an accidental cause of the Revolution of 1848 because the political situation was the adequate cause. Is not the judgment of the second type of minor importance? Does not the claim to evaluate the degree of adequacy of a cause exceed our curiosity and resources?

If one refers to Weber's exposition one cannot strictly maintain the distinction (and that is why we have simultaneously shown the various aspects of the theory). The conclusion of the first type implies the notions of adequacy and accident. Indeed, to establish that an antecedent is a partial cause, we must construct the unreal development which would have been the adequate effect of the circumstances (once the antecedent has been eliminated or modified), find the consequences which were called for by the various antecedents considered separately or all at once. In all the cases, we express judgments of objective possibility which correspond to more or less sufficient relations between historical facts. Of course, when the inquiry ends with a judgment of the second type, the logic of the probable comes in more directly. In order to say that the Revolution of 1848 is the accidental effect of the shooting it is necessary to imagine a fortuitous structure, defined in its basic characteristics by the political situation in France at that time (just as the structure of the game of pool is defined by the form of the table, the holes, the ball, etc.), and to consider the shooting as an accidental circumstance (like the varying impetus of each shot), which no regularity connects with the outcome.

In fact, the real distinctions lie elsewhere. Weber explained both the theory of causal rules and the analysis of a single constellation. As soon as we try to establish rules, the idea of chance plays only a negative rôle. Just as a law in physics is valid only with the reservation 'other things being equal,' so the social and historical rule applies only under normal conditions. If the rule is said to be adequate (and not necessary) simply to reserve the possibility of external accidents, history's case is in no way different from that of the other sciences.

On the other hand, when the historian tries to explain an event, he uses generalities (it matters little whether they are specially established for the purpose or are otherwise known), which he collates with each other and with the conjuncture. As long as it is a question of showing the influence of one antecedent, this comparison will usually be enough. But to discern the efficacy of an unusual datum, one will usually have recourse, implicitly, to the construction of a *fortuitous structure*, and within this structure one will make a mental calculation of the adequacy or the contingency of the effect. Weber examines, then, at the same time, the probability essential for any causal relation, for any historical regularity, and for any analysis of a particular case. It is advisable that, without failing to recognize their likeness, these forms of probability be separated.

The distinction we have just made (does the historian want to establish rules, or analyse a particular example?) makes it possible to solve the problems raised by this interpretation of causality, considered as a retrospective calculation of probability.

* * * *

To what objections is this theory open? To begin with, it could be said that constructions of the possible are always fanciful and that consequently these reasonings have no scientific value. We shall come back to the question later. One might question the import of this schema which would be of use in exceptional cases. We shall come back to the extension of this singular causality. It remains for us to examine immediately a third category of difficulties, those pertaining to the schema itself. Is it legitimate to distinguish objective possibilities (legal cognitions) and the accidental facts, to divide conditions into constants and variables? Does not this schema, in addition, imply a circle in the investigation and a relativity in results?

Let us start by considering the first case, that of general rules. We have seen why Weber attributed to them a quality of sufficiency, not of necessity. The whole of reality is not thinkable. A necessary relation applies only to a closed system or an isolated series. Referred to the concrete, any law is probable; circumstances, alien to the system or overlooked by the science, are apt to interrupt or modify the foreseen evolution of the phenomena. Any application, any technique, demands a margin of safety (for example, it may be a question of the resistance of materials). In the same way, one does not determine retrospectively the one cause or law of the collapse of a wall or bridge, but the circumstances which would make the catastrophe more or less likely.

In addition, the historical reality and circumstances especially justify, as we shall see later, the rôle of probability. Let us suppose that the judgment of sufficient cause (development of Greeks under Persian rule) is based on analogies, that is, the Persian policy in other countries. The analogy between the case under consideration and the other examples is only partial. Moreover, the facts which are being compared are fragments of social totalities, separated perhaps arbitrarily, checked by decree at a certain date. Our judgments, then, when most favourably considered, are adequate and not necessary, since abstract relations are not the whole of the concrete singularity, because historical comparisons involve something of the arbitrary, and isolated systems are always subject to outside influences.[23]

This interpretation is adequate as long as it is a question of rules. Besides, Weber often refers to the opposition between *nomological* and *ontological*, between law and raw facts. But he also suggests another opposition, of adequate causes and accidental causes, one which implies as we have said, the fiction of a *fortuitous structure* defined by the constant causes creating, in favour of a certain event, a more or less strong probability. Of course, such a description of *fortuitous structure* is antropomorphous. In each drawing (of a number in a game, or of sex in the laws of heredity), all circumstances, both constant and variable, intervene in the same way. There is nothing to prevent, as long as we do not forget the human meaning of the formulae, our distinguishing the conditions (physical structure of the game, ripening of the gametes, condition of the organs) which throughout a large number of gambles stay the same, from those which vary each time (impetus of the ball, position of the spermatozoids, etc.). Now, the

[23] We shall make these observations more specific below when we study sociological causality.

historical reality lends itself at least partially to comparision. Accidents, like casting lots, have a certain independence; they are multiple and depend on multiple causes. Of course, there would be reservations, greater or smaller, depending on the case. Accidents are linked with situations differently from the way in which the varying causes in a game are linked with the constant causes. But the historical reality is discrete enough for the fiction to be legitimate.

Shall we say that the probability is subjective and expresses our ignorance, or that it is objective and corresponds to the nature of the real? The foregoing analyses justify neither alternative. For an infinite mind, the difference between what is *thought* and what is *perceived* would disappear. Humanly, it is inevitable. So, if probability is subjective, it is a question of a transcendental subjectivity, not a personal one. It arises fatally whenever a scientist tries to foresee and explain a singular fact. As for the probability born of the partial character of historical analyses and of causal relations, it exists in our minds, not in things. One can imagine an infinite mind grasping the whole determinism of the process. But such a utopia holds neither interest nor meaning for logic. For the infinite mind would understand the determinism of events at each moment, in its particularity. Now, we are asking whether general relations are probable as a result of our ignorance or in the world of history itself. There is no proof that certain partial sequences are sufficiently separated from the whole to take place automatically, given the first term of them. We ought not to cite the principle of determinism, for it links the total antecedent with the total result: the real at a time t is the cause of the real at a time t^2. It does not follow that relations obtained by dividing, simplifying, or organization of the data on a macroscopic level, are necessary.

There remains the other objection: the investigation would proceed in a circle. The objective possibility is determined by the elimination of the accidents, the accident is determined with reference to the objective possibility. This circle seems at once both incontestable and non vicious. For the two procedures, the establishment of generalities and the explanation of the event, are interlinked because they represent the successive stages of the scientific operation (in history as in the other sciences). Once an adequate connection is shown, it is used to fix the efficacy of the exceptional circumstances in some particular example. The superimposing of reasonings about probability is then inevitable and legitimate. There is an unending comparison of particular cases to bring out adequate rules, then a use of these objective possibilities in the historical analysis.

But, it may be said, the real circle is different: a result is commensurate with reference to a certain group of antecedents, contingent with reference to another group. An event is said to be accidental within a certain *fortuitous structure* which is determined by a chosen set of conditions.[24] We recognize some accidents with reference to certain antecedents, that is, with reference to a certain historical change, but not accidents in the absolute sense. But this relativism does not in any way seem inacceptable. It is not a question of writing a Uchronia (a history reshaped as it might have been), but of articulating the narrative of the development, of outlining the various evolutions, their intersections and relationships, of restoring to the past the characteristics of actually experienced political reality. Probable and relative judgments are adequate to this task.

II. CAUSALITY AND RESPONSIBILITY

THE LOGICAL schema of causality remains formal in every sense of the word. The expert studying the causes of a railway collision tries to specify the particular circumstances immediately preceding the accident (lack of prudence, bad visibility, etc.) and the relatively constant facts (condition of the track, signal system, etc.) more or less favourable to the catastrophe (which increased the number of variable causes of a nature to provoke it). Both expert and historian deal with the question of *responsibilities*. In the same way that we shall try to specify the positive meaning of chance by confronting current usage with strict definitions, so we are going to try to define the meaning of a *historical responsibility*.

* * * *

Moral responsibility, legal responsibility, historical responsibility all share a common rôle: the establishment of causes. The fundamental difference concerns the order of the causes: the moralist views the *intentions*, the historian the *acts*, the jurist *compares intentions and acts* and measures them with *judicial concepts*. *Historically* responsible is the man who by his acts sets in motion the event, the origins of which are sought. Such a judgment should have no moral implication; as seen by the historian as such, war and revolution are in no degree crimes, but facts, among others, of a frequence varying according to the centuries,

[24] Hence a certain ambiguity of language, even in Weber's. Generally when we say that such and such a fact is the accidental cause of a certain event, we mean that the event is accidental with reference to a set of antecedents making up the constant causes of the fortuitous structure. The accidental cause is the variable cause which leads to an exceptional draw. But one can also, at times, give an opposite meaning to the same expression, and define the accidental cause as the *opportunity* by which an effect implied by the situation is realized.

observed in all cultures and all periods. Let us suppose that the historian is studying the responsibilities for *one* war. Can he succeed? Is the question scientific?

First of all, the historian must keep the fact in its singularity, in the exact moment when it occurred. Will it be called an ill-put question, which only the sociologist could answer by establishing the causes of wars? Not at all; under the most favourable hypothesis, he will point out the antecedents *most often* or *always* met with before a war. Assuming that one of these antecedents appears in the case under consideration, still all would not have been explained. There would still be the question *by whose action* and *why* war broke out *at that moment.* Will it again be said that the situation in Europe had for several years made war inevitable? Perhaps, but that is a problem of historical causality: by analysing the singular constellation we estimate the probability of conflict created by the diplomatic, the economic, the social system, etc. However great be the evaluation of this probability[25] (and doubtless it appears rather great to the historian of today, as it did so appear to the contemporaries), the question of the immediate causes retains its importance. Put back into its historical perspective, the occasion (and for the same reason the efficacy of the occasion) will lose its importance in proportion as the distant or underlying causes (the situation) approach necessity. It would still be important, at the least, to fix the responsibility of the *moment.*

The problem is sharply defined: it is no longer a question of anything but the immediate causes. The standard difficulties then come up: how choose between the antecedents? at what moment start the inquiry? Taking 1914 as an example, the origin of the crisis is apparent in the facts themselves, with one reservation; some historians begin with the Austrian ultimatum, others with the Serbian plot against the archduke. However, there is agreement on one point: the primary antecedent which made war likely was not the assassination of the archduke, but the Austrian ultimatum. Beginning with this initial fact, the investigation becomes complicated by reason of the multiplicity of actions and their interconnections. In connection with which decision will the question be asked: 'what would have happened if . . . ?' For example, *if* the Russian mobilization order had not been signed so soon? *If* the statesmen of the Entente had known of the change of opinion at Berlin on the 29th and 30th of July? Or, *if* they had been willing to take advantage of it?

[25] Moreover, the evaluation depends first of all on the hypothesis made concerning the *evolution* of this system: would political and economic tension in Europe have continued to grow if war had not come in 1914?

The responsibility for actions is measured *either by the results they brought on*, or *by the consequences which another decision might have had*, or, finally, *by the initiative shown in them.* The refusal to consider the Serbian answer hastened the declaration of war on Serbia and, resultantly, greatly increased the chances of war. The partial rejection by Serbia of the Austrian ultimatum may be blamed by reason of the consequences which unreserved acceptance would almost necessarily have had. But even the historical responsibility depends also on the order of succession: no one will offer the argument of French refusal of the German ultimatum, considering the extent to which that refusal seems the inevitable answer to demands in every way unacceptable. The risk increases that the historical judgment may be involved with legal and moral considerations. The *initiative*, at the beginning, can scarcely indeed be estimated by the most empirical historian without taking into account diplomatic and moral regulations. It will be asked whether the Austrian ultimatum was or was not justified, legitimately, politically, morally, etc. This question also permits a partially scientific answer. The customs of international law are known. However, the discovery of the part played by Serbian officials makes Austrian severity less scandalous today (without any change whatever, with reference to consequences, in responsibility).

But other difficulties arise. The historian does not take one by one all the antecedents, for he would never exhaust them. He puts together his account according to the logic of the intentions. Inevitably, he goes into a psychological inquiry (in the broad meaning of the word—*motifs* as well as *mobiles*). So a new risk arises: *the measurement of the responsibilities of individuals by their intentions.* Now here there is an error of principle: the historian analyses intentions in order to understand decisions, to discover their causes. But the *causal imputation remains essentially distinct from the psychological interpretation.* The official who neither foresaw nor desired the consequences of his acts is responsible if the historian thinks that these consequences were objectively predictable and probable. Of course it is important—for intentions are also historical facts—to remember that on both sides, and in proportions perhaps the same, there is seen the acceptance of or the desire for war. In any event, it remains absolutely necessary to separate the historical responsibility from the moral responsibility. The blame for the actions is neither eliminated nor made less by the inconsistency or the purity of the motives.

The problem of the origins of war, then, is subject to the objective solution only if various conditions are met, various exact statements given form. Remote, and immediate responsibilities are, *de jure* and *de facto*, independent. In one respect, complete innocence remains compatible with complete culpability in another: the man who did nothing to create the tension making war possible may have made the moves which made it fatal. Besides, the question of remote responsibilities may admit a number of answers depending on the moment at which the historian views matters. The opposition offered by France to German advances may have aggravated a situation made more dangerous later by Germany's attitude.

As far as immediate responsibilities are concerned the answer can claim to be neither simple nor unambiguous. The act or acts which caused a probability of war are established, but there is hesitation about the intentions of the actors (weakness, desire for war, a liking for and acceptance of the risk by the gambler), about the diplomatic, moral legitimacy of these actions, about the degree of initiative to which they bear witness (to what extent were they caused and determined by the antecedents?). In connection with all actions, the same distinctions would be prescribed, namely, *efficacy*, *intention*, moral or political *legality*, *initiative*. It is enough to read the books devoted to the origins of the war to trace out the interplay of these uncertainties. The legality of the Russian mobilization is questioned (did the declaration of war on Serbia, the technical difficulties of mobilization justify it?); one questions the rôle it played (its consequences), the intention it makes manifest (prudence or desire for war), the initiative it expresses (the actions of the Central Powers made it inevitable, or probable, or admissible, etc.).

If all historians consented to these analyses, could they come to agreement *de jure* or *de facto*? Logically, there would still be two sources of uncertainty: on the one hand, the unreal constructs necessary in estimating cause (with reference to antecedents as well as for results), on the level at which the historian places himself, never carry conviction: on the other hand, it is almost impossible to separate the estimate of initiative (theoretically of the order of cause) from moral or political legality of action (without reckoning that the supposed intention is again brought in).

Finally, to form a synthetic judgment, one has the choice of various methods: either to consider the attitudes of the *dramatis personae* at the successive moments of the crisis (example: the Austrian statesmen wanted a diplomatic success at any price; the Germans gave them *carte blanche*, then took fright); or, one may keep strictly to the decisive actions, those characterizing the beginning or turning points of the crisis (the Central Powers committed the acts which made war possible, the Allies, later, those which made it certain). We also remember the expressions answering another question (intentions): all the parties concerned wanted, hoped for, or at least accepted, the war.

* * * *

Is such an analysis of causes assimilable to an investigation of responsibilities? We purposely omit the judge's effort of reconstruction of the facts, comparable to the first stage of historical study (criticism of texts and establishment of *what happened*). Apparently the judge or moralist starts with an *offence*, indicated by moral or judicial rules, then he goes back to the guilty party (the one committing the offence) and finally estimates the degree of that party's responsibility. In the case of the historian we see a comparable procedure, one proceding from fact to the agent (or agents), but we perceive neither offence at the beginning nor any estimation of responsibility independent of the degree of causality. Let us look more closely at similarities and differences.

War, we were saying, as seen by the historian, is not a crime. The historical investigation, then, would start with an arbitrarily chosen fact; of small importance are the humanitarian or patriotic feelings inspiring this choice. Next, responsibility would be established empirically, but this responsibility would have to do only with the *acts*. On the basis of action, efficiency is the true criterion. The excuse of the leader who 'had not intended that' is rightfully challenged. Causality becomes indistinguishable from culpability, since the latter lies uniquely in the *to-act-or-not-to-act*, in the direct or indirect results of the decisions.

Consequently one can ask whether the primary fact, far from being arbitrarily chosen, is not defined in the same way as is the responsibility. So much zeal was not expended in studying the origins of wars as long as they were considered the normal way of settling national rivalries. This investigation, even today, is thought to be vain and superficial by philosophers who see in war the supreme test of collectivities. If no one claims the initiative, or dares recognize the lawfulness of it, it is perhaps because war now appears as a historical *fault* (in the double sense of the word).[26] The fault, even in this case, would be less designated by a revolt of conscience, transcendent to the order of events, than by history itself; defeat, the fall of empires, such are the supreme crimes, beyond ill or good will. If these remarks are admitted, the absence of a fault (at the beginning) like indifference with regard to intentions, would express, not the opposition between historical

[26] It goes without saying that the moral condemnation borne by the pacifists is always confused with this intuition of anachronism.

causality and legal (or moral) responsibility, but the specific quality of an *ethic of history*, immanent in the behaviour and destiny of men.

But, it will be said, there still remains a difference. Historically, it is rare, perhaps impossible, to establish an entire responsibility; neither an individual nor an act is the sole cause of a historical event. The fault is always relative since it is defined by the fact that it increased the chances for the catastrophe, or decreased the chances of avoiding it. In the same way the opportunities missed, or grasped, are defined. Of course the jurist who indicts the criminal, the one who started the fire, or who killed, has the impression that he gets at the unique and authentic cause, but it would be dangerous to conclude from this that he makes use of another concept of cause and holds to the dynamic idea of the creative agent. In reality, in such a case, deed and doer are one, they are not opposed like effect and cause. On the other hand, the moment intermediary agents step in between the behaviour of the guilty and the illegal deed, the moment the blows are but one of the causes of death or excess speed but one of the elements of the situation in which the accident occurred, we again find a causal analysis similar to the historian's: one weighs the responsibility of the guilty party by determining whether the circumstances in which the criminal deed produced the condemned effect were normal.

Of course, criminal responsibility, if not civil responsibility, implies, in addition, a certain moral responsibility, or, more precisely, a guilty state of mind.[27] The latter is, so to speak, a part of the definition of misdemeanor or of crime.[28] So it is normal that the degree of responsibility be estimated by the state of mind of the guilty one, either at the moment of the act, or permanently. It can even be said that essentially one seems to determine the state of mind of which the conduct is the sign and expression. Now, it is striking that, as soon as attention is directed to the degree of responsibility, the causal analysis is reintroduced with its division into elements. Negligence passes as guilt to the extent that it seems efficacious (except for it, the individual would not have committed the offence) and not inevitable (a different line of conduct is normally conceivable). Drunkenness lessens responsibility because, retrospectively, it seems to diminish the chances of a different decision (it makes it less possible, the misdemeanour more deterministic). Moreover, lucidity is an aggravating condition since we believe it increases the chances of abstention, in so far as the past

[27] Cf., for these problems, Kaufman (Felix). *Die philosophischen Grundprobleme der Lehre von der Strafrechtsschuld*, Leipzig and Vienna, 1929.

[28] We saw in the preceding Section that an act is understandable by reference to a certain intention (sometimes impersonal).

is concerned, and for the future it increases the unfavourable ones (chances of another crime).

Actually, this attempt to fit exactly the punishment to the crime is not usually interpreted as empirically as we indicate here. An essential guilt, founded on free will, is usually assumed and the circumstances of the offence are taken as outward signs either of freedom, or absence of it. In fact, this liberty, accessible objectively, is based, like historical liberty, on an analysis of the antecedents: liberty appears greater in the proportion in which we recognize as smaller the sufficient number of antecedents to be changed so that the event would have been different (in addition, this change must not be excluded by any one antecedent, must even seem possible independently of any other variation). The historian analyses the situation, the psychologist the character and the situation. The total loss of consciousness or of lucidity[29] eliminates all possibility of variation (since a variation is always assumed to be the action of the individual). Bad upbringing or poverty weaken resistance to temptation. The greater the aggregate of antecedents leading to the crime, the more liberty, and responsibility, are reduced (with the added complication that, depending on whether the past and the character are considered, or the situation, opposite results are likely to be obtained).

May it be said that this relative liberty, which demands only a fragmentary determinism, is not enough to justify a morally authentic guilt? A full discussion would lead us away from our subject; let us limit ourselves to a few observations.

God alone would know the essential responsibility, since He alone would discern the final intention of the individual. Man, left to himself, must make the distinction between each man's guilt for himself, and guilt seen from without, for others. One may, through remorse, become conscious of an offence, and consequently, of a liberty having neither degree nor limits. But this liberty can not be grasped by the spectator. All jurisdiction, inevitably social in character, designates the content of guilty behaviours, if need be, the reprehensible state of mind (inferred from various signs); it knows nothing of liberty, and consequently of the will to evil.

These two forms of ignorance are, however, not comparable, but rather contradictory. Liberty would be excluded by a determinism previously created; the unknown future seems fixed before it exists if, for the human fabrication, there is substituted the illusion of a necessity contained in reality, or again, if our retrospective construction

[29] We could say that lucidity and consciousness are integral parts of the *state of mind,* objectively perceptible, which merits punishment. An offence implies a certain intention.

and the actual development are confused. We experience liberty as long as we remain contemporary with our act. Afterwards, we explain the decision by referring it to its antecedents as though it had been determined. At most we succeed in giving an idea of an intelligible liberty by restoring to the past its character as an anterior future, instead of viewing it in its retrospective fatality.

As for the moral judgment of others, it is positive as long as it keeps in view the outer reality of conduct or the nature of *motifs* or of *mobiles*; but these data, perceptible or psychological, are equally alien to the ethical order. Just as Kant was not assured of the morality of any act because a selfish twist is always liable to compromise pureness of heart, so we explain all acts contrary to the accepted rules without coming upon a will which freely chose evil for its own sake. The alien consciousness, the moment it is objectified so as to be understood, allows multiple and incomplete interpretations; it excludes an absolute judgment. Of course there are other ways of evaluating people—according to their human quality, the values they represent, the efficacy or the objective morality of their behaviour. We only wanted to show the impossibility, if a will is defined by *motifs* and *mobiles*, of conceiving it as either absolutely good or evil, for the twofold reason that it is *ambiguous* and *intrinsic*.

Once again, historical responsibility is in the image of true responsibility, at least that which it is given to men to know, a relative and fragmentary responsibility, involved with the retrospective probability through which historical determinism is constructed.

III. CAUSALITY AND CHANCE

According to the above analyses, judgments of historical causality would go back to retrospective calculations of probability, a probability bound up with the scholarly process and with the character of the events. And we found, in the logic of causality, the notion of chance which lies traditionally at the centre of the theory of history.

In this chapter we shall examine the problems presented by these two concepts: Must accidents be defined in a relative and formal fashion, as in the preceding paragraphs? Do accidents really exist, if we may so express it? Is it possible, once the meanings of the terms are clearly defined, to formulate strictly the classical questions?

* * * *

It is easy to analyse the different meanings of the word chance, based on the Aristotelian theory. According to Aristotle, the fact of fortune or chance is unrelated to any law, occurs neither always nor often; it is rare. The rarity, however, tends to become confused with contingency. Regularity proves the existence of a necessary connection, singularity its absence. These rare and contingent facts belong in different domains. Either it is an intelligent agent who, instead of attaining the desired goal, arrives at another, or it is a thing (or animal) which reaches an end which is not its authentic end. Fortune and chance, then, characterize the realities existing *in view of something.* All of Aristotle's examples, still classic because they so well illustrate the commonly held idea, lend themselves to the same interpretation by means of the *error of the nature of final causes.* The debtor happens to come to the market place, and meets his creditor. Someone digs in the ground to plant something, and finds treasure. A frightened horse runs away and the flight saves him; a stone falls and strikes a head. In all these cases the result is not the one the agent, or nature, intended. Thus, between a monstrosity and the encounter between the debtor and creditor, from Aristotle's point of view, there is no fundamental difference. His logical and metaphysical theory opposes, in a hierarchical world, the accident to the individual's realization of his goal (outward activity or form).

It is enough to analyse Aristotle's examples to remind us of the two ideas forming the basis of Bergson's and Cournot's theories. The three-legged stool which stands straight, the stone which strikes someone, are so many events suggesting an intention. The mechanism imitates the finality. The human character of the effect, by a false application of the principle of equality, tends to extend to the cause. The intelligence apparent in the events is found concentrated in the representation of the evil genius, which we call chance.

In addition, Cournot's theory consists of analysing not the connection of fact and the pursued and unattained goal, but the origins of accident. The meeting of creditor and debtor on the square, of the stone and the man's skull—all these examples can refer to Cournot's formula: the coincidence of two series or the coincidence of a system and a series. Each series obeys a strict determinism, but the encounter itself knows no law. The idea is clear and now standard, but series and systems are still to be defined. How does one manage the definition in history?

* * * *

Every event is derived from several series. Whether it is a question of the War of 1914 or the Hitlerian revolution, many causes would be easily discernable. The assassination of the Archduke is the end of one series (the activity of Serbian revolutionaries, Panslavism), the Austrian diplomacy in the Balkans is another series, as are the Russian and German diplomatic policies. But in addition, if the war were viewed in the light of the extension of European diplomacy, there might be seen the end of a system. Depending on the point of view, the same event appears fortuitous or otherwise.

Of course the formal analysis of the preceding chapter solves this apparent difficulty, giving strict form to the reasonings of historical aetiology, but at the same time it deprives the concepts of order and chance of any absolute value. It is the historian himself, who, in terms of the known regularities, the normal evolutions, organizes the texture of the development. An event may be said to be accidental with reference to one system of antecedents, adequate with reference to another. Chance, since many series have come together; rational, since at a higher level an ordered whole is found.

But does not chance denote a category of data materially defined? When, in history, one speaks of chance, one immediately thinks of a certain type of facts, as though the positive concept (Cournot's) were enriched by residua of the Aristotelian or the Bergsonian meaning, as though the systems and series were delineated in terms of human interests. Thus, chance is invoked whenever natural phenomena break into the course of history (earthquake, a statesman's illness, weather conditions determining the outcome of a war, a battle, etc.), every time disagreement between cause and effect (petty cause, great effects) becomes striking, or even each time a *great man* seems to exert an influence on the outcome.

These cases are easily classified under the formal definition. Natural phenomena immediately form a distinct series. Moreover, the historian collects into a whole social, economic, or institutional conditions, so that the decisions or initiatives of individuals assume the character of accidents, whereas, with reference to the individual they may well be adequate. One goes so far as to imagine that the overall realities are more determined than are partial facts, so as to conceive of an essential distinction between the former and the latter. And yet, overall realities are made up of individual behaviours, bound up together in the reality or by the historian, and chance is only relative.

There is of course nothing to prevent the support of a material meaning by which accidents would be the partial data (individual initiatives, chance meetings, etc.) which correspond to the variable causes of the *fortuitous constructs* assumed with a view to causal analysis. But again it is necessary to remember that material meaning and formal meaning are not the same. Formally, any phenomenon may be accidental. Formally, the sudden development of German industry between 1870 and 1874 is accidental with reference to the former condition of the economy, since it originated in the war indemnity, that is, a political fact outside the order of economic cycles. Shall we say that an accident defined with reference to all antecedents, to the whole situation, would be absolutely and not relatively fortuitous? But, to begin with, one could ask if there are events which nothing in the past prepares for and explains. Moreover, even in this case, the event would not be accidental in so far as it was isolated or individual, but because it would represent a break with previous development. We should still be left with the positive and formal meaning, for a chance (materially) is often necessity's executor.

As a matter of fact, if, like Cournot, the historian included the whole system of history, if he were bringing out the inner meaning of Providence, accidents, defined with reference to this system would become absolutely fortuitous, as it were. Because, with the multiplicity of systems, ambiguity would disappear: the two ideas would fuse, or at least the distinction between them would matter little. Let us assume, for example, that history leads necessarily to a united Europe. The historian, armed with this knowledge, would contemplate fearlessly the late conflicts in Europe as remnants of an epoch drawing to a close. Partial or otherwise, these chance events would fall into their places as such in the *true* perspective of the past.

In other words, the impossibility of confusing the two ideas is due first of all to the uncertainty which lies in the fixing of the limits of series and of systems, to the plurality of fortuitous constructs which the scholar is free to set up or to imagine.

* * * *

The preceding remarks could not fail to be disappointing. Indeed, one hopes that the philosopher will decide between historians and sociologists, theorists of chance and theorists of necessity. Of what use are these logical formulae which in the end express the spontaneous practice, unless they make it possible to solve or at least to state clearly the real problem?

First, our schema confirms what was pointed out in Section I, in connection with compensation for or elimination of accidents. For whilst this elimination by time seems in the long run to be likely within a system (defined by an adequate causality), the same is not true for accidents occurring at decisive moments or at points where systems intersect. The economist observes cyclical changes, discovers hundred-year and short-term movements, puts chance events in their places (war, politics), events exerting no influence on the evolution of the economy beyond a certain time or extent. But this whole evolution is perhaps ruled by a fragmentary factor extraeconomic in character. Moreover, the coincidence of a depression and a political crisis is apt to produce a revolution (example: Germany, 1933) the consequences of which seem incalculable and remain unpredictable. The Russian revolution, perhaps resulting from an accumulation of favourable chances the outcome of which at least depended on several fortuitous factors (leaders, results of battles, etc.) ushers in an economic system whose intelligible and necessary development emerges from this beginning.

Common sense suggests—and reflection confirms—that the margin of uncertainty is neither always fixed, nor always unlimited. Of course, in all periods certain eventualities are excluded; there is no retrogression from big industry to craftsmanship, and political power shows the force of certain features to which submission is inevitable. In this sense it can be said that there are limits within which Fortune rules, but those limits are vague and indeterminate. One could not say, from the outset, that chance events play no other rôle than to speed up or slow down an immutable fate spelled out in advance. In times of crisis it seems that possibilities multiply, each quite different from the others; when Greek liberty is at stake, the play of contingency appears immense.

No general proposition, then, could anticipate the results of a study which with each example must be renewed without prejudice. The theories on this subject give expression to philosophies basically alien to the uncertainties of history. The antithesis of global and partial determinism is confused with the antimony of liberty and necessity. An absurd confusion; moreover, metaphysical ideas in fact entail concrete statements. What is the use of preaching human liberty which, belonging to all, would belong to no one? Created by all men, history would be desired by none; blind result of numberless conflicts, it would be chaotic because of the very fact that it would obey contradictory wills. Either the individual is considered, in which case he is freed from slavery not by metaphysical formulae, but by showing him the conditions and the moments of his power; or else it is humanity that is considered, and then this idea must be defined: is it enough that the past does not carry the future in itself, or must the whole of history be governed by conscious reason?

The argument about great men leads to similar conclusions. The two lines of argument which clash monotonously seem to us as unanswerable as they are inadequate. Determinism rightly reminds us that certain elements cannot be changed at will (in order to prove the efficacy of chance). All facts are interconnected; the striking detail perhaps expresses a lasting general fact (the missed opportunity, the bad choice of leaders). In the same way, the great man expresses a group or a time. The work of a conqueror, such as Alexander for example, corresponded to a historical demand; sooner or later the unity of the ancient world would have come about and the two cultures, Greek and Asiatic, would have interpenetrated. But no less properly it could be said that history does not always find the man capable of accomplishing the tasks imposed. Moreover, if the conquests of Alexander and Genghis Khan had not been prepared by circumstances, if a technical superiority had not made them possible, it is obvious that genius would not have been enough. Nevertheless, this possibility might not have been exploited. It is the same for the founders of religions, Luther or Mahomet. And it will always be proper to ask what marks the individual has left; what traces are left among events by the fact that historical necessity was fulfilled at a certain time, in a given manner? What traces in the cultural creation? To what extent does Protestantism bear the stamp of Luther, or Islamism that of Mahomet? If the Prophet had been another man, would the two religions be different from what they are?

It would be easy to follow this traditional controversy. But the above questions show why it leads nowhere. As long as abstract formulae are insisted on, it is as possible to justify determinism as the cult of heroes. The individual and the situation must be analysed to specify what reality finally owes to each. Now, this analysis (like any causal inquiry) must be renewed in each case. The problem admits of no general solution; it is not even authentically philosophical because it depends on scientific research.

However obvious these remarks seem to us, we are certain of not winning conviction, so spontaneously do the undemonstrable assertions of determinism arise from the perspective of history. One recognizes, first, opportunities and decisive moments grasped or missed, but, always and everywhere, whether it is a question of a military victory or the crumbling of an empire, there are discovered underlying and *valid* reasons which retrospectively confer an apparent necessity upon the effective outcome. It is forgotten that the opposite outcome might perhaps have permitted an equally satisfactory explanation. In other words, retrospection creates an *illusion of fatality* which contradicts the contemporary *impression of contingency*. Neither one is *a priori* true or false; the future often rectifies the judgments of the participants. At least the contemporary impression implies no dogmatism, contrary to the retrospective illusion. Consequently, the burden of proof lies with dogmatism.

All vast reconstructions share with retrospective prophecies the privilege of infallibility. Now, as we are about to see in the next chapter, the investigation of cause by the historian is directed not so much at tracing the broad outlines of the relief of history as at preserving for or restoring to the past the uncertainty of a future. The historical narrative, like the language, recognizes multiple *actualities*; it is enough to go back to any moment (no matter how far back) to define with reference to this fictive present the three dimensions of time. The historian avails himself of this mental power, and thus succeeds in distinguishing the fatality of that which, having been, can no longer not have been, from the massive necessity that would crush the individual and would imply a predestined future.

IV. LIMITS AND MEANING OF HISTORICAL CAUSALITY

THE LIMITS of historical causality are of two orders. Some are due to the schema itself, others to the nature or lack of knowledge we have at our disposal for the construction of unreal changes. The meaning of historical causality, based on these analyses, will appear of itself: if we were never capable of answering our questions we should still be right in questioning for the purpose of restoring to the past future its future quality.

* * * *

We have already seen, in the preceding chapters, that the determinism of retrospective probability recognizes only relative concepts. Rules and events, the sufficient and the accidental, appear inseparable in the organized experience of the historian. Of course reality suggests this organization, but however well founded the scholar's decisions may be, they are rarely the only ones possible: the question might have been put at another time, for the evolution is continuous and one rarely gets back to the very beginning; no certain choice of antecedents nor any certain analysis of the effect is categorically prescribed.

This liberty of reconstruction shows up again in the choice of the *level.* One historian will place himself on the same plane as the participant, another will overlook the microscopic analysis and trace the overall changes leading to the event under consideration. The problem of the immediate origins of the war, for a Marxist, would have little importance and interest. The capitalist economy, twentieth century

European politics secreted so, to speak, a general conflict; the incidents of the last days matter little.

These remarks specify the character of the results; they do not compromise their validity. Another reservation, more serious, will question the correspondence between schema and reality. Is there in history the equivalent of constant causes? Even if the question is answered in the affirmative, it is no less apparent that this causality is, so to speak, *instantaneous.* One goes back in thought to a moment in the past, one *stops* the evolution, sets the course of the constant conditions which were nevertheless changing, in the direction of the event one is studying, or in the opposite direction. One has measured the effectiveness at the chosen moment; but what would be important to know in order to specify exactly the rôle of *underlying forces* and of the detailed events would be the development of the constellation. Now, in our unreal constructions we imagine the results of the situation, not its changes (in the preceding chapters, we did not make the distinction).

In this way, then, the essential differences between the ideal history and the procedures of the empirical sciences become apparent. The dreamer chooses and arbitrarily suppresses a fact (one perhaps inseparable from the whole), imagines what happened, tries to enter into the details of this fantasy. The scholar asks only whether by causing a fact to vary he gets, *at the moment at which he places himself*, another event. He is satisfied with showing that 'something would have been different'. Most of the time he would not, without great difficulty, say more. In any case (at least at a lower level) he is not able to follow the consequences of his hypothesis, to such an extent does the interplay of causal series in reality surpass the power of our intelligence. Suppose the French had lost the battle of the Marne? Suppose the order to retreat had not been issued to the German army? Suppose America had not intervened? Of course the possibility of different developments is glimpsed, and, in terms of those evolutions, probable and quite different from actual history, the importance of a given victory or of American intervention are estimated rather highly; without concealing our inability to reconcile science and ideal history, without denying that at a higher level one at times distinguishes the probability of the global development which accidents, seen from close up, render apparently contingent.

Thus we come back to the problem we have so far set aside: Do we have the means for the retrospective organization of determinism in accordance with probability? Of establishing that causality, relative and instantaneous?

* * * *

Before even studying historical generalities, we can show why and how the historian arrives, in practice, at hypotheses of causality which at least are likely. Let us suppose that he puts himself on a lower level, that he is considering individual actions, the exact decisions of a given moment. What would have happened if the Tsar had not signed the order for general mobilization? The historian has no rule applicable here; former actions are too particular to be subsumable under a law. But, thanks to this singularity, the historian can make guesses relying on other data (Austrian mobilization was decided on before Russian mobilization was known, etc.). It may be said that the case is exceptional; if Austrian mobilization had been the answer to Russian mobilization, one would have to attribute to the latter a share of cause of the other, which perhaps would have been decided upon anyway. We are not trying to cast doubt on this uncertainty, but only to point out the idea; the closer we approach the absolutely concrete, the less available knowledge we have, but the more the facts themselves stand in its stead. That there may have been, in the Austrian ultimatum, in the declaration of war on Serbia a very great deal of initiative and that this created a possibility of war, no one doubts. And, in the same way, no one doubts that the battle of the Marne, after the defeat at the frontiers and the retreat, was a sort of miracle, that, with reference to most of its antecedents, it was accidental. Would the war have ended if the battle had been lost and if Paris had fallen? No one can say so. But on the other hand, everyone will admit that the probability of French defeat would have been considerably increased, that it was by that hypothesis very great.

So then, at this elementary level, in what cases, at which moments, does one suspend the narrative in order to substitute for the judgment of reality a judgment of at least virtual necessity? Almost inevitably, whenever the account seems to be interrupted of itself, when an individual performs out of character, a political decision does not fit the circumstances, an evolution is determined, begun, or stopped by an accident. Whether one compares the act and the personality, the personal decision and the environment, a historical movement and an accident, reality has the structure implied by the causal analysis, and the causal analysis suffices, not to measure exactly, but to discern the efficacy of an antecedent or the contingency of a fragmentary fact. Now the historian usually claims no other results. No one will ever know what would have happened if the Archduke had not been assassinated in 1914.[30]

[30] Conjectures would have to be made as to the evolution of the political and economic system in Europe.

Let us suppose, on the contrary, that one puts oneself at a high level. What are the causes of capitalism (defined in a certain way)? Here the analysis of the antecedents will rely on analogies, on at least approximate rules. Some such conclusion will be arrived at as: Protestantism is one of the causes of capitalism[31] (of certain aspects of capitalism). But, between what one can say at least with likelihood, and what one would spontaneously like to know, there is still an immense gap; for is the causality of Protestantism to be considered great or small? Max Weber's formulae show a hesitation which reflects a lack of knowledge. How measure the degree of efficacy? At the time one thinks one is observing it, how take the various causes into consideration? How to know, with reference to the future (which future?) which is today the past? The final question which everyone asks would be put in terms of the common expression: 'Would it, in the long run, have come to the same thing?' Without Protestantism, would the capitalism we know today exist? Now this question definitely exceeds our knowledge, and may have no meaning; for we should have to specify *which* capitalism, *which aspects* of capitalism. By the way the question is put, one substitutes the global totality for the events being analysed, but, on analysis, would not the causal concept disappear? One can try to trace the consequences of the antecedent under examination; but, assuming no present datum is directly connected with Protestantism, it does not follow that the latter's influence is exhausted; for the interplay of causes makes it impossible to untangle the web of influences. What would have happened without this distant religious phenomenon no one knows or ever will know.

Between the microscopic and the macroscopic, between observation of facts and the comparison of generalities, we should find many intermediate cases where both methods would be useful simultaneously. It is at this middle level that the investigation of causes leads to the most precise and positive conclusions. If, for example, it is a question of an economic phenomenon such as the devaluation of a currency, it is possible to show, without question, that in a given case it brought certain results. This is a causal judgment whose modality is reality. The historian shows that in a given case (Belgium) devaluation brought about the return of capital funds, the lowering of the rate of interest,

[31] We are concerned here only with an example. We are not considering the truth or falsity (according to the documents) of this theory. For this thesis requires not only the analysis of other forms of capitalism and of various antecedents. It is necessary first to establish by observation the particular development of capitalism in areas where the Protestant spirit predominated, the priority of the one with respect to the other, and the impossibility of attributing to another antecedent the responsibility of the development.

the restoration of the margin of profit, etc. He proves that: 1. No other event explains these phenomena either within the framework of the national economy, or in world economy (they do not occur at the same time in other countries of the gold standard area, no other antecedent accounts for them); 2. These phenomena are linked with the cause by intelligible connections (the return of capital funds is explained by self-interest on the part of investors); 3. The causal relationship is deduced by empirical or scientific rules: in a given constellation, devaluation produces such and such results. Such is the form of causal judgment in history.

Immediately, we come back to the simple schema we discarded above: singular sequence goes directly back into the general relationship. But at the same time this schema appears as a particular instance of the complex schema. The first applies when conditions are normal (predictable within the law) or constant (only one antecedent varied), external circumstances are ignored, and causality, deduced from law, appears as assured in the case under study. But if other antecedents had varied at the same time as did the value of the currency (national unity instead of political conflict, a different policy with regard to credit, public works, etc.), we should have recourse to the complex schema: to estimate the influence of the various antecedents by analysing the degree to which each one was determinant. Or again, if the classical effects of devaluation did not occur in a certain country, we should try to see the exceptional circumstances which prevented or diverted the classical consequences of manipulation of currency. As it seems desirable, we go back from the complex to the simple schema, or vice versa. The essential thing is to recognize the significance of the schema in the reconstitution of the human past.

* * * *

One might, it seems, keep to the simple schema as the only positive and fruitful one. It avoids unreal constructions and is limited to the determining of factual responsibilities. But it is just this pseudo-positive interpretation which appears to us mistaken. Unreal constructions must still remain as an integral part of science, even if they do not go beyond an uncertain probability, for they offer the only means of escaping the *retrospective illusion of fatality*.

After the event, the origins of romanticism are easily discovered in pre-romanticism; one is consoled by the thought that the lost opportunity did not really exist, that the human decision would have come up against the tyranny of things. The idea of continuity, the idea of necessity, come spontaneously from the perspective of history, because we begin at the end, because we know what has been, but not what would have been; we work out the future, today, the past, of events and decisions, and we are prone to fail to recognize the contradictory complexity of the reality.

Moreover, we are always free to organize a global movement by bringing together incoherent facts, since, semi-godly creators of the historical development, we freely choose the level at which we place ourselves in order to eliminate accidents and bring order out of chaos. The microscopic examination, the evocation of possibles, refute this claim. These systems, scholarly achievements because they imply superimposed probabilities, could not themselves transcend the modality of the judgment of probability.

We have seen how the historian's interest guides the selection of antecedents (which the schema in no way determines). The moment of a decision or of a conjuncture is isolated in order to give the account the tone of contemporary experience. For men in action know the uncertainty of fate, the reaction of the individual to the world, of the will to character, at the decisive instant brought back to life by the historian whenever he confronts a future which has become real with the other eventualities at that time considered, but which today stand condemned. The word responsibility regains its meaning because, freed from a counterfeit enslavement, we no longer can fall back on an obliging necessity to excuse failure or cowardice.

The retrospective evaluation of probabilities regains the deliberate thought which would have been possible in the ideal case in which the actor would have had all the information accumulated by the historian. This identification in no way compromises the dignity of the scientific analysis. The positivist, in all innocence, believes that the future is unpredictable and the past fatal. But the historian's past has been the future of the characters in history. If the future bears the stamp of an essential unpredictability, the explanation must respect the nature of the event. The historian will no more be refused the right and duty of imagining what might have been, in order to understand what has been—even if his imaginings are still uncertain—than will the statesman be advised to act blindly according to his desires, under the pretext that all his calculations are liable to be mistaken. Anticipatory calculation is a condition of reasonable conduct, as retrospective probabilities are of the true account. If decisions and moments are neglected, one substitutes for the living world a natural world, or fatality. In this sense, historical science, the resurrection of diplomacy, becomes contemporary with its heroes.

The formula is valid on condition that it is remembered that, above partisan passion, it insists on being impartial and is acquainted with the future.

CONCLUSION

LET US try, in order to complete and clarify our results, to compare our interpretation with the theory Simiand gave in the *Revue de Synthèse Historique* and to the *Société Française de Philosophie*. The main arguments are familiar: each causal relationship must be deduced from laws; in order to choose the cause from among the antecedents, it is necessary to isolate the most general and least conditioned antecedent; and this isolation requires the establishment of regularities; hence the assembling of multiple cases and, in order to make comparison possible, the expression in conceptual terms of the phenomenon which results.

We have also recognized that every causality implies at least a virtual generality. Otherwise the sequence would remain unique, hence accidental, unless a mystic bond, intelligible or psychological, linked cause and effect (intention and act, will and conduct, force and fact), which would cause us to forsake the causal concept. But the conclusions drawn by Simiand go far beyond the premises. The cause of an explosion, says he, is the expanding force of the gases, because the law applies to every explosion, because the 'force of expansion' is the most general antecedent. Now, the example clearly shows that Simiand substitutes one problem for another: the cause of any war is not the cause of the war of 1914. The historian, in this case, is not comparable with the physicist, but with the expert. To have been ignorant of and denied the specific nature of the historical investigation—such, in our view, is Simiand's first error.

In addition, Simiand has likened historical generalization to scientific analysis. He recommended expressing the effect in general terms: the revolution of 1848 would be the overthrow of an unpopular government by a minority opposition. How did he fail to see that this conceptual expression differs in its nature from the isolation of the factors? In physics, for example, the law of gravitation, or Mariotte's law are general with reference to a particular falling body, to a certain variation of volume or pressure of a gas, but each of the functions makes it possible to grasp one concrete aspect of all the facts conforming to the law. On the other hand, Simiand's formula substitutes an idea for an event, it organizes into an ideal unity various and complex behaviours, it sums up, it simplifies, it neglects the date and certain characteristics of the effect. No matter how much one discovers and multiplies laws, one will never explain what one didn't know at the beginning; or at least it would be necessary to combine the singular data with the abstractions—in other words, to reconstitute the unique constellation by the method of the judge or the historian.

Doubtless Simiand would have cared little for this line of argument, for his theory, apparently logical, covers on the one hand a philosophy of history, on the other, a methodology. If events, dates, individuals, accidents, were inefficacious, Simiand's logic would borrow its truth from that *sociologistic* doctrine. He denied such a dogmatism, for it was especially important for him to lead the inquiry in a certain direction. Against the pure narration, the liking for the anecdote, he demanded the causal explanation, upheld the necessity of abstraction, of comparison, of generalization. Such a method gained additional value for him since he applied it to an order of phenomena in which it is incontestably prescribed.

It is the mixing of these three distinct arguments, logical, philosophical, and methodological, which keeps eternal controversies going. Methodology always reflects scientific practices which are legitimately different. Whether it is better to regrasp historical totalities in their singularities or to compare similar or analogous institutions which are present in different civilizations, the alternative seems to me bare of significance. The results aimed at are different, and the fruitfulness of the procedures is evaluated by trial. As for the philosophical question, it is vain, because it is just as impossible to affirm as it is to deny universally the efficacy of accidents or the similarity of facts distant in space and time.

Of course, Simiand's logical arguments remain partially valid. It is true that historical analysis is more exact as it makes use of a more fully elaborated sociology. But in the absence of such a sociology, history does not lose its way in simple juxtaposition. Between the arbitrary choice of a condition baptized 'cause' without justification, and the determination of the most general antecedent, which dissolves the singularity of the fact, of the moment, and of the contingency, there exists a selection which the historian's curiosity directs, but which is, nonetheless, given its assumptions, objective.

Second Part

REGULARITIES AND SOCIOLOGICAL CAUSALITY

'As a matter of fact, everything that concerns man is stricken with contingency.'

Vidal de la Blache.

SOCIOLOGY is defined either by opposition to the other social sciences or by opposition to history. In the first case, it appears as a specialized discipline whose object would be either the social order as such, or society as a whole. In the second case, sociology is characterized by the attempt to set up laws (at least regularities or generalities), whereas history is limited to narrating events in their peculiar sequence.

We shall keep to the second definition, without other discussion of the autonomy and organization of sociology. We call sociology the discipline which demonstrates general relationships between historical facts. The preceding *Part* leads up to the present study in two ways. As a matter of fact, the analysis of a unique constellation demands the use of rules, whether it is a matter of weighing the efficacy of a group of antecedents or of constructing an unreal evolution. Besides, the historical investigation of causes, though it may correspond to one aspect of human development, does not result primarily from an objectively given structure: it expresses one aspect of historical interest. *A priori*, a different interest remains just as legitimate, for example, one which would centre on the global determinism of situations or of masses, on the inevitable recurrence of typical sequences. Both complementary and divergent at the same time, sociological and historical causality complement each other.

Besides, this *Part* will, nevertheless, present a quite different character. In connection with historical causality, it was a question of showing the logical schema by which historians spontaneously and unconsciously proceed. Thus we could choose imaginary examples without going into the exact description of the scientific inquiries. On the other hand, the logical schema of sociological causality, universally admitted, raises no difficulty. It is sufficient to refer to J. S. Mill's logic and use the methods of presence, absence, and concomitant variation:[32]

[32] cf. Simiand's exposé in the first volume of *Salaire, l'évolution sociale et la monnaie*, Paris, 1932, and note the rules he indicates for counterproof (in order to be sure that the two terms do not depend on a third and are independent).

cause, as seen by sociologists, is the *constant antecedent.* It is then advisable now to go beyond the schema and analyse some concrete inquiries in order to show the philosophical problems. Moreover, the schema leaves unexplained the decisive procedures of the science.

According to contemporary epistemology, the physicists's task is not so much to apply Mill's methods (even in elementary science) as to divide up the data in such a way that the antecedents in several different cases may be compared. When the facts lend themselves to enumeration and comparison, the essential, we may say, is accomplished. The exact nature of the disciplines appears first of all in the organization of the experiment. So, the questions we shall meet will be, for example: within what limits does one try to establish regularities? Within a single society, or by comparison of analogous phenomena in distant cultures? In order to witness the recurrence of the same sequences, at what level does the sociologist place himself? What must be his method of simplification? How does he divide the facts or the wholes?

However, we shall not have to go into the technical details of these problems. In fact, for one thing, we shall consider only their philosophical or logical aspect: it is not too important whether researchers, depending on the nature of the reality, use the comparative or, on the contrary, the statistical, method. The diversity of procedures answers a normal need of science. Again, our limited goal is still, first of all, to set the limits of historical objectivity. Consequently, we shall try to specify the nature of causal relations, their modality, their relationship with reality, their full significance. Thus we shall arrive at a definition of some of the traits distinguishing sociological causality.

We shall look successively at natural causes, then social causes. Since both imply the comparison of the phenomena integrated to distinct totalities, we shall, in chapters III and IV, stay within a historical totality, the repetitions developing on an *identical basis*, and we shall study the causes established according to statistics (frequencies or concomitant variations), and, at last, the cause assimilated to the prime mover of a cyclical movement. Of course there are many other forms of sociological research. However, these chapters will let us recognize the most usual types, and providing we use the examples without being tied down to them, the conclusions should maintain a sufficient generality.

I. NATURAL CAUSES

As we said, sociological cause is always defined as the constant antecedent. Hence the return, in this chapter and the next, of the same questions: on what level, within what framework, are we to observe repetitions? How isolate the terms one wishes to bring into relationship? But in this chapter another question dominates our exposition. We are studying the *non-social, non-human* causes of social, human phenomena (we shall call them, in order to simplify, the *natural causes*). Now, the idea of connecting an antecedent and a consequence which are heterogeneous seems questionable: is not social determinism autonomous, sufficient unto itself? Would not the *geographical thesis* be absolutely false, even as a working hypothesis, and not merely extreme or doubtful? To use Durkheim's formula: is not the cause of a social fact always another social fact?

This is the last question we shall try to answer, without losing sight of our main problem: of what nature and modality are judgments of sociological causality, and, specifically, of judgments connecting a natural cause and a social effect?

* * * *

The term still most used today to express the action of the environment on man is *influence*. The mystic or magic overtones giving this word its particular resonance have often been pointed out. We need not concern ourselves here with these uncertainties. The term simply reminds us of the two aspects of the problem. On the one hand, we try to show sequences or regular coincidences between geographical data and human phenomena. But, on the other, we want to understand regularities. Causality would not be an end in itself; it calls for a psychological or rational interpretation: the influence of the environment resolves itself either into an effect of the climate on temperaments (and consequently on societies), or into the intelligent use of the land and its resources by man.

We shall not study the different modalities of this concrete expression. Our only interest is the procedures by which general propositions are made in accordance with formal rules. It is also useful to recall, in order to evaluate the results exactly—success and failure—of the causal inquiry, that when all is said and done it is man himself—and his behaviour—which is in question.

The *geographical thesis* (no longer met with in the writings of geographers) would consist in the assertion that geographical conditions *determine* the lives of collectivities. Expressed in terms of causality, it would be summed up in the following: 'The same social phenomena correspond to the same geographical conditions.' The difficulties are immediately apparent. How can the *same* geographical conditions, the *same* social phenomena, be determined? If one descends to the concrete individuality, one never finds two islands exactly alike, or two valleys, or two plateaus. Even less two tribes or two ways of life. Is this a facile and superficial objection? The rule of indiscernibles does not prohibit the intelligible organization of the facts. Of course, but it was useful to remember that the terms which were supposed to be united are *constructed* and not *given*. The decisive moment of the inquiry into causes, then, is the isolation of terms and the definition of concepts.

In what direction will the geographer turn if he aims at causal relations? Let us say to begin with, very brutally, that he sticks to mass data. Only aggregations interest the geographers, says M. Vallaux, for example,[33] since only mass facts, groupings, natural regions, or human orders, concern him. It is not apparent, moreover, that even at this level geographers have succeeded in showing necessary relationships. There is no correspondence between a way of life and a similar natural region, nor a single historical destiny and a similar geographical situation (expressed in terms of island or plateau). Let us speak neither of chance, nor of indeterminism. The question is methodological, not transcendental. When we wish to cast light on the peculiar efficacy of the environment, we either leave other factors out of account, or assume that they are constant. The principle of causality—a philosophical truth—does not imply that one order of causes, all by itself, determines a given effect, or that one cause may be entirely isolated. No *a priori* theory could foresee the texture of determinism.

However, the results of this macroscopic analysis are not without value, even though they do not reduce to necessary relationships. A *negative* conclusion often has a positive value, so to speak. That a complex civilization requires sufficiently favourable geographical circumstances in order to develop, that outside of certain latitudes human societies have never risen above a rudimentary stage of development—such propositions, partial and prudent, far removed from the dogmatism formerly dreamed of, have, nevertheless, a scientific character. For in spite of positivist illusions, it does not depend on the scholar alone to discover everywhere a strict determinism.

People are always debating as though, logically, we have no choice except between necessity and an absence of any connection. In reality we have available a third hypothesis, namely, as Weber said, a more or less close connection between sufficiency and accident. An environment may *favour* a way of life without imposing it (that is, produce it in the majority of cases—imaginary cases, of course). This hypothesis is all the more likely in the humane sciences because the causes are particularly entangled with each other. An isolated factor is not enough

[33] C. Vallaux, *La Science géographique*, Paris, 1925, pp. 80 ff.

to determine a global effect: neither the concomitant conditions of a relationship nor the two terms of the relationship are, from one appearance to the next, identical enough for necessity to become evident on a macroscopic level.

Of course, we have no more right to deny than to affirm *a priori* the existence of necessary connections. We are only trying to distinguish between the *postulate* of determinism and the hypothesis of necessary relations between abstract and general terms. And besides, we can suggest the greater or lesser probability of the affirmation or negation. (Negation is even more likely if history is taken into consideration.)

As a matter of fact, the geography of history is more descriptive than causal. One would like to set up, in the context of a political or economic development, a single terminus, the cause of which would be a geographic situation. For example: the insular character of England would be the cause of her maritime fortunes, her mineral wealth of the advantage she had acquired over her rivals in the nineteenth century. But it is easy to answer that England has not always been a great sea-power, that she learned much from foreign sailors, that she has not always been economically superior to her rivals. And many regions, notwithstanding their mineral resources, are economically backward. If we wish, in this case, to use causal language we can at most speak of sufficient cause and accident: the coal mines favoured nineteenth century economic expansion. Of course, one example proves nothing, and the justified objection would be made that this is, after all, an example of a false causal relationship. But a special case illustrates difficulties of general significance. How, as a matter of fact, could historical facts be theoretically and wholly explained by geographical data? The historical fact would have to have the same duration as the natural fact. Now, the most stable historical facts (economic, social, etc.) change rather rapidly without anyone noticing the previous or simultaneous changes of the geographical data (*a fortiori* for facts such as the foundation and growth of cities, etc.). Since all social phenomena are part of history, the natural environment would account for them at most only partly, since the so-called effects appear or disappear, whereas the causes stay constant.[34] (At least the social phenomena explicable by geography are considerably reduced if we demand that they be as invariable as geography.)

Of course, there is the possibility of abstracting social phenomena from the evolution: either the development of a culture considered as a

[34] The constancy is, of course, entirely relative. The natural environment changes throughout historic time too, slowly if it is a question of natural changes, sometimes very rapidly if it is a question of the transformations wrought by man himself.

whole is organized into a single term, or a certain characteristic presenting throughout the duration a relative stability is, in imagination, isolated. But at this level one runs into a new difficulty, for the historian no longer has enough examples available: where is a country to be found comparable in all ways with England, except for the geographical situation? Now such experiments would be necessary to measure the causal effect of that situation. Where can there be found an environment similar to that which the valley of the Nile and the regular rises of the river created for Egypt? To the same extent that the Egyptian bureaucracy seems to us manifestly related with water control and the demands of a rational technique, to the extent that it is a response to the challenge of circumstances, to that same extent it is impossible to say that it is an inevitable result of environment, and difficult to estimate exactly the causal responsibility of the environment in this social organization, and the originality of that organization.

So then, we must again abstract and generalize. Generalize the cause: instead of the Nile, one will think of a river (or delta) and will ask what are the characteristics of the cultures developed along rivers (Egypt, Babylon, etc.). Abstract the effect: one will isolate a certain feature, inseparable in reality from many others, but which is found to be similar or at least analogous in other cases. It is conceivable that necessary relations can then be set up (in a given region the agriculture always is of such and such a sort). But this necessity unfolds on the level of an intelligible experience, it is partial and, as it were, external to reality. Concretely, it signifies that man's initiative develops within certain limits. The social characteristics imposed by a certain environment indicate the minimum demands which any human creation must meet.

There remains one last recourse—microscopic analysis. Of course it will be said that, considered as historical facts, neither methods of agriculture nor the distribution of farms and villages nor mine workings nor even the locations of cities or the tracing of roads, depend exclusively on geography. All these have changed with time, and history alone tells us why a certain city enjoyed, at one period, a splendid prosperity, why it then declined. But does not the distribution of water supplies explain, in a given area, the distribution of dwellings; the contour of a region, the laying out of lines of communication and the positions of cities? Let us make a distinction here between the language of understanding and that of causality. Geography, which *describes*, shows how, in fact, men have profited by circumstances. And in this sense it makes the way of life and certain institutions understandable. But it does not prove that men have adopted the only conceivable solution of the problem which nature put to them. So, with the same distribution of water supply, it is not unaccountable to meet with another distribution of human groups. The presence of a city at a certain place is, it seems, easily explained by a certain geographic reason (confluence of rivers, river mouth, water supply, etc.). But certain situations, very favourable in this sense, have not been taken advantage of, and certain urban centres are geographically paradoxical: in one place artificial ports have been dug out while elsewhere natural ports have remained neglected.

Does this mean that human geography is never explanatory and can scarcely be called a science, in this sense? For our part, from a strictly logical point of view, we shall not so conclude. Either, in fact, the geographer will answer that he helps us to *understand* human behaviour as it uses nature to create societies—that he explains the reasonableness of it; or, beyond intelligible relations, he will hold to the causal language, but that language, recognizing sufficiency and accident (that which often or rarely produces effects), ignores necessity because in fact man is not subject to the constraint of environment. If the modality of the judgments is what is possible, it is because contingency characterizes all human decisions, even those expressed in institutions.[35]

* * * *

For our part, we should adopt both this theory of the causal relations (possibility and not necessity) and the material significance of this contingency. Man is neither the prisoner nor the slave of his natural environment; far from being passively subject to it, he contributes to its creation. But another interpretation could be, and has been, given of this weakness in geographical causality. Sociologists have seen in it their fundamental error of the geographical thesis (a thesis existing today only among those who fight it). Geographical data, they say, producing now one result, now another, are never explanatory. Is it conceivable that the same cause may, in different circumstances, have different effects?[36] This is as much as to say that it is not a cause. An inevitable checkmate, a sociologist of the Durkheim school will affirm; one social fact necessarily has another social fact as its cause.

We do not have to come to a decision in this ancient quarrel between sociologists and geographers. We are concerned only with the philosophical aspect; now, first, it has a methodological aspect: instead

[35] The contingency here referred to is not metaphysical. It is possible that the totality of the conditions necessarily determines the effect, but geographers and historians admit only *external* (natural or social) conditions. The contingency we speak of implies only that human will (perhaps itself determined) may be effective.

[36] Cf. Simiand, *Année sociologique*, vol. XI, p. 723 and Halbwachs, *Année sociologique* n.s., vol. I, p. 902.

of describing, somewhat at random, all the phenomena found in a certain area, would it not be better to isolate and compare? Isolate the style of houses or the structure of the villages, observe these phenomena under the most varying conditions, compare in order to bring out the true explanations, that is, the constant antecedents (the antecedents of a certain style of house, of a certain distribution of habitations). In other words, sociologists set comparative against monographic method, and causal relations, denoting constants, against the juxtaposition of heterogeneous geographic and social phenomena.

We have no authority to decide which method is the better. We can simply point out that the goals of the two methods are not the same, consequently, one does not exclude the other.

As for the argument that one social fact is always caused by another social fact, without discussing it fully, its justification is apparent. That between the environment and an institution some collective agencies always intervene, we should admit without objection. That is another aspect of the initiative which nature always allows man. There is the illusion that, by speaking of collective agencies the idea is made specific; race and temperament, from which different reactions might, it seems, result with respect to a single situation, are excluded. In fact, since men always live in groups, a certain state of social consciousness must come in between environment and behaviour, even if this state expresses a hereditary predisposition.

Must we go further and say that social facts only are causes? Shall we go so far as to deny the influence of the environment on the development of life in common, that of natural resources on density of population, of crops on economic prosperity? We should have to deny the obvious: even though not a necessary cause, even though operating through the instrumentality of a social fact, a natural phenomenon is, nonetheless, capable of efficacy (in the sense of historical causality: if we assume this phenomenon to have been changed, the social reality would be different). Shall we say that we have the right to take no further interest in these natural phenomena because some social facts would be capable of having the same influence?[37] This would be a singular argument: sociology studies what occurs; it matters little that the action of nature may be replaced by that of society; since it exists, it commands the scholar's attention.

We see no reason, then, to deny *a priori* the import of geographical interpretations. Society does not represent a closed empire; nature is one of the factors determining its existence.

* * * *

[37] Cf. Halbwachs, 5 *semaine de Synthèse, Science et Loi,* pp. 190–191.

It is no easier to show racial causality than environmental—the opposite is true. Of course, there is no talk of liberty with regard to race any more than with regard to environment. But the main difficulty, namely, that of isolating the effect of a cause, is in this case more acute.

Let us suppose that the historian wants to explain certain events (decline of Athens or of the Roman Empire) by means of racial phenomena. Will he, first, manage to establish the facts, that is, the simultaneous changes in size and make-up of the population? Once the facts were established, he would have to work according to the schema we discussed in *Part IV* above. But would he find other cases to compare? A historical event is always preceded by historical antecedents capable of accounting for it. In order to weigh the efficacy of one antecedent (especially a transverse antecedent subtending, so to speak, the social development), it would be necessary to compare enough other analogous cases to estimate what is properly attributable to the one antecedent.

So, this method is abandoned and the attempt is made to establish regularity of succession. One then considers not so much events as wholes (a superior culture, in its original features, would be ascribable to the influence of racial heredity). But at this level the same difficulty arises: two cultures always differ through several circumstances. By what right can all the responsibility be attributed to one among them? There remains, it is true, the positive demonstration: all the higher cultures, at least of a certain type, would be the achievement of one and the same race, a demonstration which would at least create a rather strong probability.

But here another difficulty arises. How recognize races, and especially their psychological dispositions? Usually, various methods are combined: direct observation of individuals—which would show at least the frequency of certain talents within certain populations—comparison of races and classes so as to show the diversity of the hereditary data according to social groups, which are themselves the reflection of racial groups, and finally the comparison of cultures, historical works being regarded as the expression and proof of innate qualities. Let us add that racial theorists usually recognize two propositions which are at least debatable:[38] the hereditary transmission of psychological tendencies as well as of physical and physiological traits, the possibility of isolating, at least in thought, pure races (even though all races are, in fact, mixed).

[38] The race theorists usually add some scientifically undemonstrable propositions, such as the absolute superiority of a certain race, the harmfulness of miscegenation. Others bring races and social classes into relationship, and hold that the heredity of certain classes is of inferior value.

We need not go into the discussions, currently impassioned, of the fixing of racial limits, the choice of distinctive characteristics, the possibility or not of distinguishing races and evaluating their cultural capacities. It was merely important for us to point out the difficulties involved in the search for biological causes in history. The difficulties are of two kinds: if an aggregation or a historical event is considered, it is difficult to discern the proper efficacy of one cause, especially a natural cause outside the order of the social phenomena (not to mention the quasi-impossibility of establishing exactly the antecedents of that order). Again, in order to construct the end cause, that is to say, a certain heredity, it would be necessary to circumscribe either a physiological group pure as to origin, or a historical group. In fact, there is hesitation between the former and the latter, and, far from a direct constitution of racial cause, there is already recourse to the historical (still to be explained) in order to define the end cause.

The conclusion we should like to draw from these rapid remarks is, however, not the one usually proposed by French writers. They conclude, indeed, the falsity of the affirmations by the impossibility of proving them, or at least they do not clearly distinguish between certain theories which are less accurate than famous or political, and the general idea of an influence of racial peculiarities on the course of history. Now, to the same extent that it seems to me difficult to prove, just that far it seems reasonable to admit, that the different racial groups had different heredities at the beginning, heredities which have showed up throughout history, and that their action has perhaps been considerable, even though we are today incapable of discerning and demonstrating it. The conditions of the causal investigation explain why in all strictness racial causality has up to now rarely, if ever, been verified.

* * * *

It seems, at first glance, that race and environment constitute the two terms of an alternative. Does not the study of the complex of individual and environment make it possible to explain animal conduct? For man, a third term must be added: the inner environment, so to speak, that is, society. Furthermore, it would be vain to compare these three terms and to claim to estimate the efficacy proper to each one. For they are not comparable to three forces of which the resultant would be social phenomena. In collective life, heredity expresses itself, and perhaps nature enters in. These three factors, the results of a pragmatic distinction with a view to a positive inquiry, represent neither three divisions of the reality, nor three autonomous potentialities. Thus, at least for race and environment, the relations shown do not go beyond probability, an expression of an objective possibility. Men make use of certain of their talents according to the various conditions in which they have to live. Societies exploit certain available resources according to their preferences and their history. Social life itself chooses from among the given facts, material and human.

The modality of causal relations shows not so much the failure of the analysis as it reflects the structure of reality.

II. SOCIAL CAUSES

TO HAVE an idea of the diversity of causal inquiries undertaken by sociologists, it is enough to examine Sorokin's book on sociological theories. Sorokin interprets, in fact, almost all the theories in terms of causality, and he passes in review the schools—geographic, ethnic, anthropologic, racial, bio-social, economic, etc.[39]

Let us consider, for example, the demographic facts. We shall ask about the effect of birth-rates on death and marriage rates, the effect of density of population on welfare, political organization, social ideals (equality, etc.). Let us take the economy: we shall consider the relationship between one type of economy and the political state, economic crises and wars, crime, etc. One could in the same way bring into relationship religion and the other sectors of social life (economics, politics, family life, etc.). We could multiply the examples indefinitely.

What are the most striking features of the results obtained? To begin with, what is the modality of the causal relations? Of course, these questions are expressed very vaguely and it would be well to particularize them. One may ask: what is the effect of economic crisis on the rate of crime? Or again, what effect does increase in population exert on migration? Or, what influence does capitalism have on family organization, unemployment on suicide? Now, certain of the answers establish co-variations. Economic depression and unemployment cause the crime and suicide rates to rise. These co-variations are based on statistical studies; we shall examine them in the next chapter. The other answers belong in the category of influences, favourable or otherwise. Density of population itself, whatever it may be, neither creates nor destroys the well being of the people or the democratic regime, but a certain density *favours* prosperity or egalitarian ideals. In the same way, depressions favour revolutions, as does unemployment a low birth-rate, as protestant ethics does capitalism. In other

[39] We used the translation into German. Sorokin (Pitirim), *Soziologische Theorien im 19 und 20 Jahrhundert,* Munich, 1931.

words, we should again find here possibility (a more or less sufficient relation), but not necessity.

Besides, none of these causes would be absolutely a cause, since it could enter as an effect into another relationship. Neither density of population nor depression represents a primary fact. Must one accept this universal interaction, or does sociological determinism demand a supplementary postulate?

We shall try to analyse sociological determinism, first by discussing Durkheim's theory as it appears in the *Règles de la Méthode*, then by describing Weber's application.

* * * *

Durkheim declares, in the *Règles de la Méthode sociologique*, that sociology must, like natural sciences, explain, that is, elucidate by causes. It is easy to perceive the methods he condemns, namely the psychological, teleological, or the ideological and historical methods. On the other hand, it is harder to distinguish the characteristics and procedures of truly sociological causality. Let us start with the criticisms in order to try to understand the assertions.

Psychological explanation is excluded because the social phenomenon is *sui generis*. Association, life in common, give rise to original data. In addition, Durkheim seems to identify psychology with a psychology of the individual as a type (normal, civilized). How can one account for a social fact, for that reason historical, by means of characteristics common to all men? Also, to cite the goal or function of an institution is to admit that it was created consciously, voluntarily. Now this artificiality, incompatible with the regularity we see in social facts, does not correspond to the reality: the whole is primary; it is the whole that moulds the consciousness of individuals, and produces the collective organizations, the theoretical justification and the origin of which are confused by the individual. Let us accept these two arguments, which are foreign to the causal problem we want to examine here.

The critique of historical method is not so clear. Durkheim explicitly attacks the metaphysicians of history. He takes, as an example, Comte's law of the Three States, and reproaches him for implying the unity of human development, of breaking up the social species, of assuming a mysterious tendency in evolution; finally, of seeking in the past the cause of the present and the basis of prophecy. 'If the main causes of social events were in the past . . . the different societies would lose their individualities.'[40] Explanation would become impossible.

[40] Durkheim, *les Règles de la Méthode sociologique,* Paris, 1901, 2nd ed., p. 147.

There lies the origin of the fundamental conflict which Durkheim's theory sets up between sociology and history. Now, the alternative *present* or *past*, or *history* or *society*, seems to us vague and, it must be said, not very intelligible. There are conceivable two types of relationships: one type shows the association, regularly observed, of two or more social phenomena; the others show the constant succession of two facts. But there is no difference of nature between these two types of relations, between the static correlation and the dynamic law. Present conditions could not be understood without referring to the group's past, without analysing the interdependence, a constant datum, of various institutions.

Why does Durkheim insist, against probability and traditional application of theory, that only concomitant causes are true causes? He seems to think of each society as an independent whole sufficient unto itself. In addition, he substitutes for society, as we see it in its concrete complexity, the *social species* and its *constitutive characteristics*, which would be the sole object of the scientific study. He imagines that in this way he gets rid of all the accidents that are evident in history. The real nature of collective life is caused by the *inner environment* and, in the last analysis, by density of population (material and dynamic) which is consecrated as the primary fact.

But how can such a declaration be justified? How define the idea of *primary fact*, of *determining factor of the collective evolution*?[41] Of course, Durkheim states these things in positive terms: a fact is primary when it is general enough to explain many others. But according to this, the economic system, or the technical, is also a primary fact. No one questions the possibility of establishing any number of relationships in which density of population would be the cause: such a density regularly entails one or another political, economic, or moral phenomenon; but it, in its turn, demands an explanation. Hence, why would it be primary? Why the only determining factor?

Now this postulate, which is in no way indispensable to the causal inquiry, has as its real function to hide the prime necessity of selection,[42] and the fragmentary character of sociological determinism. By speaking of *constitutive characteristics* of the social species, by disdainfully eliminating superficial, historical, data, there is suggested an absolute opposition between these two orders of facts, and there is bestowed upon a perhaps legitimate choice a scientific blessing. And in addition, under the pretext that the inner environment determines multiple

[41] Durkheim, *les Règles de la Méthode sociologique*, p. 143.

[42] It has, in Durkheim's theory, other functions which we cannot examine here. Above all, combined with the concept of social species, it forms the basis of an anti-historical sociological realism.

consequences, the easy shift is made from the idea of general efficacy to that of an absolute primacy. Or again, we go from morphological observation to causal interpretation in order to give exclusive value to a convenient method of procedure, to an arbitrary order of succession. There is reluctance to see that, at least at first glance, sociological relations are, in so far as they are causal, scattered, because they are not organized, like physical laws, into a deductive system. Lacking the perception of this major difference, there is the struggle to introduce surreptitiously a system either by consecrating a certain factor, or by confusing description and explanation.

Will it be said that Durkheim's theory is based on the results obtained in the *Division du Travail*? In reality and on the contrary, the causality demonstrated in this book is made false by the same errors we pointed out in the *Règles*. In the first place, the demonstration relies on one of those striking alternatives which Durkheim loved and used with extreme dialectical cleverness. What are the causes of the division of labour, he asks? Individual or social? Tedium, the desire of accrued wealth—the hypothesis is insufficient. Only social causes are left, and more particularly one cause internal to the structure of collective living, namely volume and density of population. In reality, the very terms in which Durkheim states the problem seem inexact. In fact, the division of labour, generally understood, does not represent a determinable and isolatable fact. It may be vain to look for the causes of a global phenomenon affecting contemporary societies as a whole. In any event, it would behove us to analyse the different aspects of the phenomenon in order to discover its antecedent or antecedents. Now, Durkheim does not engage in this systematic review (one can conceive of other theories than the desire for happiness, tedium or social bulk), and he asks another question, peculiarly historical, namely: how was the transition from primitive groups to the division of labour made? It is as if he were sure in advance that all societies had gone through the same stages, obeyed the same laws and as though it were possible scientifically to show *the one* cause of the historical process *as a whole*. Obviously, Durkheim is a captive of the old philosophies of history which he claims to be replacing with science, but the premises of which, alien to scientific practice, he retains. The alternative of *individual or society* is just as arbitrary as the alternative of *history or society*.

So, in theory as in application, Durkheim is bound by a sort of realism which is almost metaphysical. The social totality must have all its causes in itself. The evolution of history, as a whole, must be explained by one prime factor. Whereas, in fact science, which is above all causal, begins with analysis, that is, the decomposition of wholes into elements, whose connection one tries to establish.

* * * *

No one has affirmed with as much energy as has Max Weber this necessity of selection which we have just recognized. (We mean by selection, here, the organization, the construction, of terms united by causal relations.) Therefore, it is suitable, in order to see the possible varieties of this selection which precedes or accompanies the causal investigation, to go back to *Wirtschaft und Gesellschaft*, a work on sociology which is both static and dynamic, systematic and historical.

The questions directing Weber's study are very general: what influence does economy have on law? religion on economics? political constitutions on economics? But, definitely—and here is the essential thing—it is not under this general form that they are answered. It would be impossible to say *absolutely* what the influence of the political system on the economy is, but one can ask what action a charismatic power exerts on the scientific management (rationalization) of the economy. The terms of cause and effect are each one elaborated by the mind, exactly defined, and the characteristics which are retained for the definition originate in a conceptual abstraction which separates the elements *without always taking into consideration the real inseparability of the institutions*. A bureaucratic or charismatic power is linked, in each case, with a whole social organization. Moreover, charismatic powers are found in the most diverse civilizations, from the prophets of Israel or Islam down to the contemporary demagogues. The different examples, brought together under the concept of charism, possess in common, then, only a certain number of traits; nay more, their resemblance exists only for the observer who, situated at a certain point in history, rethinks the past with the assistance of such notions, as are suggested by the contemporary situation. (The same remarks would hold for the rationalization of an economy.)

The relations connecting these abstract and general terms are then unreal in one sense, like the terms themselves, and they never lead to necessity. Protestantism *favours*, it *does not determine*, economic behaviour of a capitalist sort. Capitalist economy *favours* rationality of law, but there are many forms of reasonableness, some of which have remained alien to the British system of law. Even the predictability of the law, needed by capitalism, is not *necessarily* produced by the latter.

If the conceptual structure limits the exactness of the results, it yet broadens the field open to the comparative method. For it is the historian, by the concepts he uses, who designates the points where differences and likenesses show up. Egyptian and modern bureaucracy are of the same genus. Using the three ideal types, *bureaucracy*, *traditionalism*, *charisma*, sociology succeeds in grasping all the varieties of political administrations. On the other hand, this extension of the comparative method seems to compromise the exactness of the results.

The objections raised by Weber's method are apparent in the above remarks. Does not the lack of necessity in the established rules result from the procedure? If one shut oneself up within one society instead of comparing societies in other respects very different, if one demanded examples identically *based*, would not the causal relations reach greater precision? Again, instead of a retrospective division, taking no account of actual interlockings, would it not be proper to have regard for real unities? Neither all the comparisons nor all the selections would have equal value and fruitfulness: instead of subjecting them, as does Weber, to the sociologists' varying interest, could they not be referred to the structure of the social whole?

Beyond all question, there can be seen two tendencies in the sociological reconstruction: either the sociologist rethinks the past in terms of concepts expressing the questions and problems of the present, or else he does his utmost to stay contemporary with each society. In addition, the sociologist's ambition is often to discern, by the comparative method, real unities or typical changes. We shall study the reality of statistical patterns in the next chapter. Further on we shall again come to the ideas of structure of the social whole and of laws of civilizations. For the time being, we content ourselves with pointing out the two tendencies, and with holding that at the point of departure, no system of concepts could claim precedence. As long as any one system has not been justified by a philosophy of history, *a priori* or *a posteriori*, all of them are legitimate, since they all express certain questions asked by living men, and, by the same token, bring to light certain aspects of the social order.

Besides, from a practical viewpoint, the systems claiming to reproduce reality derive from interests which evolve with history. The classifications of the statistician making a study of suicide also express extra-scientific intentions. If Durkheim was the first to grasp the influence of civil standing on the frequency of suicide, it was because he was concerned with presenting the argument of the breaking up of the social ties. The quality of the results is not compromised for this reason. One can merely say that in the first analysis, if the sociologist engages in a statistical investigation, the same thing holds *a fortiori* for a theory in which the totality of social phenomena should find room.

* * * *

Does the modality of causal judgments depend on the answer to the above problem (objective or subjective selection, retrospective division or contemporary analysis)? Are causal relations susceptible to the status of necessity? Let us specify first the reasons why the rules found in *Wirtschaft und Gesellschaft* are at most sufficient. To begin with, they isolate the relationship of two terms which in fact are never separate, and consequently outside influences could not be ignored, even in the statement of the relationship. In addition, the action of one term on the other is not in itself compelling if it is a question of a general term; the different examples are liable to show so much diversity that the consequences may not remain constant. Finally, since these relations correspond to social sequences, to series of human decisions, a sort of essential contingency must be considered, one which is due to our ignorance of individuals or the liberty of persons.

Let us look at an example in which the causal relations are especially clear: the exact effect of currency devaluation. Inevitably we shall speak of sufficient rather than necessary effects. In fact, depending on the circumstances, devaluation has different consequences. In one instance it is intended to maintain the domestic purchasing power of the money, and does not produce a price rise (England); in another, the goal is to give relief to debtors and cause a rise in prices (the United States). Let us re-express the example: the more general the causal term, the more diversity offered by the presentations, the further, from necessity, the connection between cause and effect becomes. Besides, it could be said that devaluation stimulates the return of capital invested abroad. But here again it is a question of a tendency: depending on the financial policy of the government, the confidence of capitalists, the safety of foreign investments, the inflow operates or not, at a more or less rapid rate. Let us put it still another way: concomitant conditions make the result doubtful, they create a possibility of deviation or inhibition. Finally, the most general effect of devaluation is the unequal increase of different prices, the lack of balance between wholesale and retail prices. But here again there persists (without recalling the other two arguments) an uncertain factor, internal to the relationship itself, for the adjustment of prices is accomplished by human behaviours. Now, psychological reactions to devaluation vary according to memories of inflation, confidence, and national pride: panic may sweep away all prices in a sudden tide, scientific predictions may be belied by human folly.

This example suggests the various means of doing away with the uncertainty which substitutes sufficiency for necessity. First, an effort will be made to state exactly the terms of the relationship, so that all special cases correspond to the concept. But as we come closer to the concrete, we eliminate the general. When all is said and done, the uncertainty has disappeared, but, also for that reason, necessity, for we are confronted with a historical causal relationship, not a sociological one. And we come back to the example discussed before. The effects of the Belgian devaluation can, indeed, be shown. Under the given circumstances (relatively stable at that moment), devaluation restored a margin of profit, brought on a wholesale price increase of 25%, of retail prices of 10%, etc. The modality of these judgments is one of reality rather than necessity, or at least the necessity is linked with such concretely defined relations that they occurred only once. However, it is still a question of cause, for on the one hand the review of the antecedents does not turn up any other phenomenon, the variation or sudden appearance of which explains the observed facts; again, the generally sufficient relations give to the actual series the logical characteristic of a causality.

Consequently, foregoing the attempt to find relationships both necessary and real, ideal necessities will be sought, fictional ones, as it were. Some abstract statements of economic theory are often consecrated as laws. Thünen's, or Gresham's, laws are admittedly unreal; their necessity is valid under normal conditions, 'other things being equal'. As for the uncertainty of human impulses, it is reduced to the minimum whenever the sociologist considers typical behaviours concerned only with universal tendencies (such as the desire for the greatest prosperity possible).

In other words, sufficiency tends either towards the necessity for unreal and fictional relations, or towards the reality of historical sequence. The three types of propositions are, in any case, only separated by differences of degree.

* * * *

Weber said that all causal relationships should have a dual sufficiency: causal and significant. Understanding makes it possible to grasp the *motif* or *mobile* of a statistical co-variation, or of the influence of a given political administration on a given economic order. If we admit that the investigation of cause is guided by selection, understanding, under the guise of conceptual perception, would come before causal relations, just as it would follow them in interpreting regular series. Now this is obvious: only the expressions are peculiar to Weber—the ideas voice the practice of all sociologists. With the causes of suicide established statistically, questions are asked about the *mobiles* making suicide more frequent in a given situation or in a given group. And to analyse the causes, the facts must still have been isolated and defined.

This dual intervention of understanding in causal inquiry is the result of two characteristics which until now have seemed to distinguish historical determinism. Causal relations are dispersed, they do not fall into a pattern, so that they do not explain each other as do the classified laws of a theory in physics. Understanding makes up for this dual deficiency; it makes the regularities intelligible, it brings them together conceptually.

III. SOCIAL CAUSES AND INDIVIDUAL CONDITIONS

Limits of Statistical Causality

SUICIDE is one of the favourite subjects of the French school of sociology: extra-scientific reasons explain this extreme interest. In the superlatively anti-social act of the person in despair, Durkheim saw the influence of collective reality, as though the individual was still a member of the group at the very moment when he decides to escape from it. At the same time, the increase in the rate of suicide illustrated the crisis in our civilization.

We choose this example of statistical causality for quite different reasons: the conditions favouring experiment and the many problems posed by interpretation of the raw results. Indeed, nowhere is the opposition so evident between social causes and individual conditions or circumstances, between statistical patterns and real life. So, our analyses, based on this one case, would bring to light certain limits of statistical causality.

* * * *

Statistics make it possible to trace the variations of the suicide rate from year to year, even from month to month. Moreover, by comparing frequency according to classes, regions, civil standing, etc., we get the equivalent of an experiment. We review the influence of the various factors isolated, for the most part, thanks to the stability of other factors (if regional rates are considered, the influence of age, civil or professional standing, etc., is eliminated). The main difficulty comes from the insufficient separation of the various causes: to estimate the exact part played by religion, we should have to compare the rates for two groups otherwise exactly alike. As a matter of fact, social groups having different religions always show other dissimilarities.

This statistical experimenting succeeds in setting up propositions of the following type: celibacy or widowhood increases the frequency of suicide; marriage, children, make it less. Each society shows a relatively stable rate, or at least a rate whose regular change seems to obey laws. Wars, revolutions, seem to bring the rate down. Or again, regions predominantly agricultural have lower rates than industrial areas, etc. Such are the bare figures which must be universally accepted (once the accuracy of the statistics is admitted). Interpretations begin with the translation of the figures into ideas.

Durkheim thought it was legitimate to analyse, on the basis of the statistical data, the mechanical aspect of suicide, to describe the psychological types involved. The higher frequency among celibates would show one of the causes of voluntary death: egoism. In the same way he distinguished two other categories: the altruists, and the abnormal.

Now this method seems overbold. Durkheim finds that the state of celibacy, widowhood, divorce, etc., favours suicide. From this he draws the conclusion that celibates kill themselves because they are self-centred. Let us admit for the moment the truth of the deduction. This sociologist still forgets another fact: there are fewer suicides among heads of families, but they do occur. Shall we label them egoists? To what psychological type will he assign them? Durkheim reasons as though the higher frequency in one group were the equivalent of its occurrence in contrast to its absence. Thus he forgets that certain cases fit into no category.

Broadly speaking, the error would be a double one. To proceed from the raw result: a given status makes a given fact more frequent, to the determination of types. It would have to be admitted that 1. some co-variations entail one, and only one, psychological interpretation; 2. statistical patterns are real. Now the psychological interpretation is always possible, often probable, also often uncertain: could it not be said, for example, that celibates have less resistance to despair, or that they are exposed to more temptations, or that most of them are neurotic, etc.? As for the reality of statistical patterns, it cannot be supported in this case. Not only is suicide the act of an isolated person; not only would the union of desperate individuals be at most that of a common anarchy or egoism. All the social causes of suicide merely cause variation of the evidence; they imply, then, other factors, either individual or psychological.

Durkheim refused to accept the most advisable explanation, the one which immediately agrees with the figures and according to which the allegedly social causes would simply be *favouring circumstances*. As he saw it, the stability of the rates would show the existence of great collective forces, as real as cosmic forces, which alone would have the efficacy necessary to drive individuals to the point of committing this unnatural deed. The motives given by people to justify their decisions as well as the psychological antecedents would be, at most, conditions; they explain that the collective force is incarnate in one individual rather than in another, that one chooses the rope, another the water. Heredity or insanity create a favourable situation, but none of these factors are ever the cause, for they never determine the act itself. Only social forces, which each year demand and get their tribute of victims, are truly causes.[43]

This time we are fully involved in mythology: metaphysically, a difference is conceivable between condition and cause, between what leads up to and what achieves, between what makes possible and what makes necessary. But logically, scientifically, how is such a distinction to be applied? Either we shall consider a particular suicide and call attention to the many antecedents, among which certainly social data appear which are outside the individual or inherent in his personality. The choice of a cause among these conditions is arbitrary. At most it reaches the relative objectivity specified in *Part I* above: in terms of a certain interest, one discerns either the decisive impulse or the exceptional event which inspired the act. How can it be said that such an investigation will always arrive at the social antecedent?

Or, we consider a great number of suicides within a group set aside by the sociologist or given in reality (celibates on the one hand, a region or small community on the other). In this case we can say that the structure of the group is expressed by a certain frequency, but as soon as we try to specify the causes, factors representing merely favourable or unfavourable conditions are defined, and are never sufficient to justify the phenomenon: neither all neurotics nor all abnormal people kill themselves.

Positively, the necessary task would be not so much to set up types[44] or to find an allegedly authentic cause, as to select and evaluate the influence of various causes. This is on condition, of course, that the idea of *collective forces*, which alone would justify a language foreign to logic and science, is given up.

In any case, Halbwachs abandons it completely. The *egoistic current* would again become, for him, the fact that egocentricity is, in a specific group, further developed in intensity and frequency. The constancy of the indications is due, not to the permanence of *collective forces*, but to

[43] Cf. Durkheim, *le Suicide*, Paris, 1897. 'For every people there is a collective force of determined strength, which compels men to kill themselves,' p. 336. Cf. also pp. 365–366, p. 53.

[44] It is, of course, not impossible to constitute types of suicides: the psychologist certainly does so, perhaps the sociologist, but with more difficulty as long as he refuses to study individual cases as well as statistical rates. The variations are in fact so small that they scarcely authorize the inference from the general to the particular, from social situation to psychological attitude.

the impossibility of distinguishing social factors and individual circumstances. After all, it is the global condition of a society which accounts for statistical relations (each of them isolating the action of one social cause, of one aspect of the collectivity). We would fully accept this description, to such an extent does it seem to us to correspond to the raw results and to close observation. Situations which increase suicide rates seem to the desperate person to be reasons for forsaking life. Bankruptcy, chargeable to economic crises, is, at the same time, both an individual motive and a social cause. And yet Halbwachs would not accept this interpretation, since he insists on proclaiming the *essentially social* nature of suicide. The difference of opinion appears in the controversy with the psychologists.

* * * *

The quarrel of the sociologists and the psychologists is known (and we assume it as known);[45] we confine ourselves to the logical connection of the two contradictory lines of reasoning. We shall set aside questions of fact or technique, such as the accuracy of the statistics, the importance of abortive attempts, etc. The psychologists' arguments are of two types: either they show that the factors allegedly social correspond at the same time to psychological factors (celibates, Protestants, Jews include a majority of neurotics); or else they rely on observance of individual cases to claim that only individuals who are constitutionally neuropathic (ones constitutionally low-spirited, cyclothymics, hyperemotive people, etc.) are capable of killing themselves.

The first objection, in effect, brings back into question certain interpretations of the statistical co-variations. It calls for other statistics (about mental illnesses), which are, of course, hard to supply. As it stands, it makes some of the commonly accepted sociological explanations doubtful. As for the second argument, it presents, logically, a dual deficiency: first, the observation of singular cases authorizes judgment that many suicides are neuropathic, not that all suicides are neuropathic. Second, even admitting the last statement, the observation of the particular would still leave a gap. Only a macroscopic statistics could reveal to us certain social influences. All neurotics do not commit suicide. To prove the efficacy of civic or social situations, we should have to have statistics, difficult to establish, which would give us the frequency of suicides among neuropathics in terms of those situations. Statistics prove the influence of the collective factors: a brute fact involving two interpretations which are perhaps simul-

[45] Cf. the book by A. Delmas, *Psychologie pathologique du Suicide,* Paris, 1932, and M. Halbwachs', *Les Causes du Suicide,* Paris, 1930.

taneously valid: either there are two classes of suicides (psychological and social), or, among the neurotic cases, social causes would control the selection.

To what extent do the figures furnish the means to go beyond this carefulness and this partial confession of ignorance? If, in other societies, there is observed the presence of neuropathics with no suicides, the legitimate conclusion will be that a certain collective representation is an indispensable condition. Again, if one could examine at first hand a sufficiently great number of cases, one would discover the proportion, if not the part played, by the psychopathic antecedents. Lacking statistics, lacking these comparisons of societies and this analysis of individuals, one must be content with the undeniable co-variations and acknowledge the plurality of the interpretations, perhaps unequally probable, but which also surpass the provable results.

Psychologists and sociologists are so captive to their preferences as specialists that they alike refuse to separate strictly the established fact (statistical co-variations or microscopic examination) and hypothetical interpretations. The psychologist sytematically denies the macroscopic data, which cannot be distinguished at the level on which he places himself.[46] The sociologist concludes that because it is impossible to discern, there is no real distinction. Halbwachs refuses to admit that there are two types of suicides. He uses the curious argument that if there were, they would not be indicated by the same concept, as though the characteristics common to all voluntary deaths were not enough to justify the term.[47] He correctly observes that mental health depends, at least partly, on social life (which multiplies mental maladies, elects the individuals of a certain temperament, etc.). But by what right does he proceed from the interconnection to the confusion of the causes? Halbwachs then cites the identity of the mental conditions of all who renounce life; the suicide is isolated, he is outside the community, it matters little whether this solitude comes from the illness or from the situation, from the anguish of mind or from bankruptcy. But the sameness of the mental condition, assuming that the sociologist describes exactly what takes place in minds, neither does away with nor solves the question, for the same condition (or, more precisely an analogous condition) may come from different causes. Now the question is to find out whether this solitude comes from inner causes or from external accidents. And on this point we have not made progress

[46] In addition, Delmas asserts that an *inherited* predisposition of a pathological order is an *indispensable* condition. The most striking weakness of his thesis is, of course, this assertion, which is fragile both psychologically and sociologically.

[47] Cf. Halbwachs, *Les Causes du Suicide.* Paris, Alcan, 1930, p. 407, and Durkheim, *Les Règles de la Méthode Sociologique.*

unless we again assert that the same condition results inevitably from a single cause. This is an especially contestable assertion, for, at first glance, it is apparent that the individual excluded from a group by social decree is not to be confused with an uneasy person who, lost in his distress, forgets the group which is prepared to welcome him.

Now let us note again that the figures agree just as well with the thesis of the two classes of suicides as with the opposite thesis. It is enough that half the suicides result from social causes for the observed co-variations to be intelligible (for that matter, the constancy of pathological suicides from year to year is at least likely). But if we admit that all suicides imply both psychological predispositions and social circumstances, the co-variations explain themselves again (as if one admitted suicides of the pure type and of mixed type). It does not follow that the alternative is devoid of significance: we are justified in asking whether only those whose inherited temperament condemns them to despair give up living, or, more generally, we question the influence of both of these factors. Of course, we have no thought of proposing a solution. It merely seemed important to show that there is no contradiction between microscopic and macroscopic examination, between psychological and sociological data, but only between two theoretical systems which refuse to recognize themselves as such.

* * * *

The example just analysed seems to remind us of the traditional problem of the relationships between the individual and society. We are still under obligation to specify in what sense this problem depends on the philosophical analysis, how it affects present questions of sociological causality.

We often wonder whether a phenomenon, suicide, marriage, death, language, reason, is social or not. A peculiar question, fundamentally badly stated. All human phenomena are in one way or another social, since they occur within collectivities which could not fail to influence them. For the philosophical discussion to enter in, we must add the word *essentially*. We will ask whether reason is an essentially social thing (such a question, though, does not involve a causal answer). Or again, the question will be the priority of the whole or of the element, the autonomy and originality of the whole, the value of both of them. It may be that these old arguments are fostered mostly on ambiguities, but at first glance they still have meaning.

On the other hand, as applied to the interpretation of statistics, the *social-individual* distinction (social causes and individual conditions) has been revealed as illusory. Whether it is a question of suicides or automobile accidents, how are motives (personal) and circumstances (collective) to be distinguished? Speeding and lack of skill favour accidents. But this would not prevent determining statistically social causes, such as the number of cars, days of the week, etc. It would not occur to one to hypostasize a dangerous curve into a force transcendent to the individual which would take its toll of victims every year. It is important then, not to assert that a fact is social—an assertion as indisputable as it is vague—but to specify in which sense it is social, or again, to analyse the nature of the patterns disclosed by statistics (the alternative of real and imaginary patterns is still too simple and abstract).

We can put into a first category the phenomena which are both vital and social. The average height in a collectivity, the frequency of a certain disease, depend on biological character as well as on the way of life. Of course, we properly recognize phenomena of *total sociology*: a common life is expressed in figures just as is the heredity of a population. But these general statements partly mask our ignorance: to evaluate the influence of a given factor we should have to resort to statistical experiment or even to descend to a lower level (average heights or average incidence of diseases yield only global results). Such patterns are not so much fictional as they are heterogeneous, and the same is true for all those that bring together such various data, which deal with animal life and society.

By contrast one will speak of homogeneous patterns (or of a known homogeneity) when one succeeds in isolating a cause. For the biologist, the pattern made up of a pure lineage would be ideally homogeneous. In that case, all differences (in height, for example) are attributable to environment, which in its turn is reducible to a plurality of partial causes (hence the distribution of heights along the line of the bell-shaped curve). The sociologist never knows such perfectly homogeneous patterns, but all the statistical experiments, such as in the case of suicide, have, as their goal or result, the successive study of the various factors. Differences in age or civil status disappear (compensate for each other) when frequency by regions is studied. In the same way, the wage-level in the area of Paris may be taken as a whole without considering qualifications, age, etc. But these two examples, however much alike they may seem, allow two different interpretations. For we go from the notion of *homogeneity* to that of *reality*. The homogeneity of a pattern, which is always relative, assumes merely that the other causes are active somehow or other. On the contrary the Parisian wage-level or changes in wages from one year to the next have reality as patterns. Neither this level nor this change represents merely a sum or an average. It would be the salary of each worker, rather, which would be determined by the totality. In economic life this power of the wholes is met with at all levels. The broadest unity rules the narrowest, world prices govern, the solidarity of the citizens of the realm and of local markets determines the efficacy of the anonymous forces which, although they derive from personal decisions, end by imposing their law.

But that is only one type of the real pattern. Birth or marriage statistics apparently allow another interpretation. However personal the decisions may be which commit a person to matrimony, the annual occurrence of it nevertheless exhibits great stability. But in that case, it is not a question of the independent or effective totalities, not even of a collective feeling taking possession of everyone. The readiness to marry, living conditions, remain about the same from one year to the next in any one group; the variations in the statistics show either a changing psychology or a different make-up of the population, or, finally, changed social relations. The pattern still is real in the sense that it reflects globally the structure of a collectivity.

Between economic patterns and those of social statistics (marriage, birth) there come in psychologically real patterns (changes in opinion, waves of optimism, social classes, behaviours peculiar to an economic group). For example, there is the attempt to divide income rates into naturally separate classes: instead of arbitrary fiscal classes, true scales are sought, the upper and lower figures limiting a type of income corresponding to a way of life. But on the other hand, a class is real not so much because of a level or way of living as because of its self-awareness. Beyond the figures, the sociologist is interested in the class feeling revealed by no statistics. The common mentality of a group, then, is defined in two ways: either the individuals have the same reactions or they have the feeling and desire of their solidarity. (These are the two extremes between which most examples occur.)

The list does not claim completeness. Bio-social patterns, patterns made homogeneous by isolating one factor, independent and effective totalities, rates of social statistics, psychological unities—all these categories interconnected by series of transitions—would call for detailed study. The outline of a theory of sociological patterns should merely make it possible for us to generalize the conclusions suggested by the example of suicide.

There is much insistence today on the macroscopic view. The sociologist discerns in indices or frequencies, social realities existing only in and for the whole. But they forget to insist on the diversity of these patterns and on the obligation always to complete statistical evidence by qualitative analysis. Simple description, then, forces solution of absolute antitheses, either philosophical or methodological. An atomic view and a holistic vision equally falsify the given. Microscopic and macroscopic examination, mutually indispensable, complement and rectify each other. There is no such thing as a single interpretation of fortuitous structure and of statistical groups, because there are diverse types of social phenomena. It would be wrong to say either that all causes are active in each case, or that constant causes are always opposed to varying causes. No one of these representations gives us in advance a knowledge of the reality.

* * * *

Are co-variations, like the sufficient relations of general sociology, scattered? As first understood we should have to say they are: the sociologist interprets psychologically a given relation, set up according to the figures. The explanation does not consist in deducing the relationship from a more general one, but in imagining a psychological drive (*mobile*).

And yet, according to some writers, the sociologist combines partial relationships in order to grasp the global collectivity. Hence causal inquiry would tend toward synthesis, and not, as we have so far indicated, toward separation of the factors. Of course, the sociologist, once he has discovered multiple and fragmentary causes, uses all the results simultaneously, so as to picture to himself either the final cause or the totality of causes. But in proportion as he gets nearer the whole, he abandons the language and the method of causality. To consecrate a way of life as cause is to sum up in one word the conclusions of the investigation, both in their complexity and their contradictions. Transcending lacunary determinism, the sociologist describes and comprehends social life in its entirety.

IV. CAUSE AND PRIME MOVER

From Causality to Theory

SIMIAND'S doctrine and practice are centred in a doctrine of causality. In view of the sensation created by Simiand's work, we could not fail to compare our ideas with the essential texts, the early articles and the introduction to the *Salaire*. However, we shall not stray from our path. Simiand's economic researches will furnish us with an example of causal analysis within a certain society, on one and the same basis with the multiple appearances resulting from the cyclic character of the phenomena—a case we have not yet considered. In addition, we shall, for the first time, observe organized relations, nearly a system, but we shall see at the same time how the advance is no longer from fact to necessity, but from reality to theory, that is, to rational fiction.

In other words, this study will seek the following goal: to justify our interpretation of causality by showing that neither Simiand's explanations nor his concrete investigations contradict it; to elucidate Simiand's conceptions by comparing what he accomplished with what he tried to do, by distinguishing the modalities of the various propositions expressing verified connections.

* * * *

Simiand never distinguishes between the nature of the results he claims to get and the methods he considers indispensable to give the results scientific dignity; or rather, he makes no distinction between means and ends, between methodology and epistemology. Hence, he does not specify the limits within which his edicts are valid, he assigns equal value to rules of very general import which are an integral part of any causal logic, and to special rules which reflect the peculiar structure of the economic reality. Let us look at Simiand's rules in order to show the significance of each of them.[48]

Selective review is a necessity in any causal investigation: in order to find the cause among the conditions, to isolate the constant antecedent, it is imperative to enumerate all the data present before each occurrence of the fact which is to be explained. Implicitly or explicitly, in one form or another, all scholars recognize this imperative, to which Simiand gave ideal expression, and in so far as possible they all do their best to obey it.[49] But in certain cases the review will be likely to be indefinite. And, before any enumeration it is important to construct the antecedents in such a way as to substitute for the innumerable facts a limited series of factors.

Identity of basis makes this selective review easier, and the causal analysis stricter. The more alike the antecedents from one occurrence to the next, the more value in the comparison and certainty in the proof. But in so far as this rule is opposed to the ordinary use of the comparative method, it is not absolutely valid. As a matter of fact, for it to be applied, there must be multiple occurrences which are substantially the same (with identical bases); this is certainly true of economic phenomena with alternating phases. But this particular structure is not found in all sectors of the social whole. More, the comparison of some-

[48] In what follows we assume that Simiand's rules are known, and refer once and for all to volume I of the *Salaire, l'évolution sociale et la monnaie.*

[49] Simiand's criticisms of samplings, of overuse of examples, are noneheless pertinent. He has also specified the necessary counterproofs to J. S. Mill's method.

times widely separated civilizations complicates the situation because the institution occurs in each one in an original constellation. But as we have already seen, sufficient relations are still demonstrated, the interdependence of historical phenomena is established, whether they are concrete facts or abstract characteristics. The two types of research, identically based, and by comparison of societies, are equally legitimate, depending on the inclination of curiosity and the nature of the object.

The rule of *complete, effective* and *continuous phenomenoscopy*, claiming to transpose the methods of the natural sciences, also gives particular expression to the necessity experienced by the economist who feels that he is in contact with reality. Since the fundamental characteristic of economic life is cyclical change, since progress is made by a series of crises, the sociologist applies himself to tracing one by one the interconnected fluctuations. Otherwise, skipping from one period of stability to another, he would neglect the very principle of the evolution; namely the creative instability. The rule may still have some meaning outside the field of economics. In any case, it is well to grasp the continuity of the development. But how is it possible so to stick to history, when it is a question of qualitative phenomena, not understandable through indices or coefficients, when it is a question of events suddenly occurring rather than evolving in some regularly alternating rhythm?

This same structure of the economic reality explains all the other precepts: that of *independent wholeness*, which concerns the delimitation of the object, *homogeneous segregation*, valuable for research; the *superiority of successive relations*, the necessity of *arrangement in series of dependent connections*, of *preferring the closest relation*, all of which affect the nature of the results being considered. The first two are obviously linked. They require that the patterns isolated by the scholar be real, whether it is a question of the global whole which will constitute the field of inquiry or of partial patterns defined by some coefficient or other. We pointed out above the different meanings of the expression, *real pattern*; we distinguished between homogeneity and reality of the patterns, also between the various shades of reality. Now of course it is the scholar's function, when such patterns exist, to discover them. The precautions advised by Simiand to verify the homogeneity of segregation are of great value. But it is not the scholar who is responsible for the existence or non-existence of the pattern. If these rules reflect an application to a particular subject matter, they are nonetheless valid, but their general extension is again open to challenge.

The same is true for the last three rules as a group. Of course, it is possible to maintain in a general way the superiority of the causal relation over the functional one, of the cause which is closely related to the effect over the more distant cause. But after all, these propositions obviously predict the conclusions which Simiand will reach. The preference for serial dependent connections anticipates his definition of the economy: a succession of instabilities. If dependent connections must be arranged in series it is because *there is a constant order in reality itself*, according to which the variations of the different factors are interrelated, starting with a *primum movens*. And, in order to overlook no one of the intermediate agents, to estimate the extent of the interdependence, it will be necessary to set up at the beginning the closest relationship, and to retrace one's way, step by step, to the initial cause.

So, Simiand's theory, as we see it, must be viewed on the basis of his application of it, and not inversely. All the rules give expression to the experience of an economist (excepting the one concerning selective review, which states strictly the obligation of any causal analysis as formulated by Mill). These remarks are not intended at all to disparage the doctrine, but merely to make it intelligible and to limit its application. Now, what especially concerns us is the nature of the results, of the causal relations. Our observations, just above, have suggested that we must, to understand them, study, not Simiand's theory, but his work itself.

As a matter of fact, in his early articles,[50] the theory is still independent of the specialized disciplines. And, did not Simiand remain consistent to the end? Must we not judge our ideas by the conception of causality developed at the *Société de Philosophie*? It is true that Simiand always advocated the schema as stated at that time, but in fact, it does not exactly correspond to his practice. We have already shown that the historical investigation, though Simiand did not explicitly admit it, influenced his thinking. We shall now proceed to show that the determination of cause as the *most general, the least conditioned antecedent*, is only a logician's fiction, which tallies with no scholarly procedure.

* * * *

If we follow his logical argument, Simiand's intention would be to distinguish the cause among the conditions by applying this formula: *the antecedent linked to the effect by the most general relation is the cause.* We have already discarded this theory, at least as a theory of historical causality. The historian does not look for a cause comparable with the expansion force of gases, which would explain any explosion. He thinks

[50] *Revue de Synthèse*, 1903. Communication to the *Société Francaise de Philosophie*, 1907.

rather of the smoker's match or the watchman's carelessness. But would this theory be valid sociologically? Would not the *true* cause be the least conditioned antecedent?

In order to answer the question, let us simply ask: how is the cause of the increased rate of gold reserves determined at the beginning of ten year fluctuations? The elimination of the other factors is effected by four successive operations: the cause must be present at the beginning of each phase, it must explain the whole change, it must show the same alternations of growth and decrease as the global change, and, finally, it must be the primary term of the dependent relations within each cycle. Let us review these conditions one at a time.

The scholar who pursues an inquiry on this basis looks upon each cycle as one occurrence of the phenomenon. The cause, then, must be general, that is, it must have been found in each cycle. This generality, or more exactly, this constancy, is the sure sign of causality, since it expresses the regularity of the series.

But, to find the one antecedent which will be consecrated as *cause*, other operations are imperative. Not the elimination of the less general antecedents, but the constitution of a macroscopic fact of such dimensions that the minor data and accidents may be eliminated. What Simiand is looking for is the cause, or causes, of the global variation in wages or, more exactly, the broad outlines of its growth interrupted by phases of decrease or stability. Now, neither strikes nor political events could be the cause of this general movement, since the increase begins before and continues after the periods during which strikes are frequent, and because strikes show no overall variation comparable to that in wages. Of course, it can be said that the global movement is general whereas the facts are limited. But this opposition has nothing to do with the opposition between logical generality and particularity, and it would be better to oppose the global, the bulk, the total, with the particular, the accidental, the component. (The increase in wages in any one year, or in ten years, is a historical event just as unique as the increase for any one worker, but it is a total event in comparison with the fractional events of which it constitutes the sum.[51])

Moreover, since the gross fact (the one to be explained) offers alternatives, a supplementary elimination is immediately available: the constant data, assuming that they are a permanent condition, are not the cause of the cycles. Scientific and technical progress, the psychological trends in social groups, figure among these permanent conditions. Technical progress is indispensable to the B phases so that

[51] Even though this sum may, perhaps, have an independent reality, in so far as world prices govern all other prices and ,as a result, all economic phenomena.

employers may pay wages which are no more than nominally less, thanks to increased production and higher individual productivity. Again, the resistance to nominal pay reductions is an indispensable condition of the change because this *creative inertia* compels employers to apply principles of scientific management to their business.

Subsequent to these three types of choice, are there still left several antecedents from which the most general would be chosen? Not at all. There are still several factors whose order of dependence is analysed. The *value* of production, which runs approximately parallel with wages, is broken up into two elements: quantity and price. Going beyond prices, and leaving aside once again volume of production, we arrive at the volume of currency in circulation, and finally, beyond that, at the rate of increase of the metal reserves.

What is the logic of this causal countermarch? As a matter of fact, it follows two rules: to grasp the simple factors, and, *once the interaction of the two movements is demonstrated*, to draw the usual conclusion from priority to causality. It is the currency in circulation, and, primarily, the gold reserve, which sets off the series of actions and reactions, all of whose phases are indispensable but whose dependence is more or less remote with reference to the *primum movens*.

Setting aside the generality which consists of the regular appearance before each event, the successive eliminations have nothing to do with the greater or lesser generality of the antecedent. The increase of circulating currency is neither more nor less general than the rise in prices—it is only anterior or posterior. As for the *expression of the effect in general terms*, we may, of course, find its precept in the formation of the global wage movement. In that case, the priority of the sociological investigation would be the same as the sociologist's duty always to place himself at a certain level. Now that obligation is easily explained when the global change has autonomy and homogeneity (as in economics). It still remains to be seen when the historian, in his study of the object, turns up an analogous structure.

On the other hand, the principle of division into series of the dependent relations plays an important rôle. It is this principle which explains the internal order of cyclical determinism, and which demands regression towards the primary term. Since this connected series of factors is inherent in the reality, certain statements of the problem of cause have preference. It has been asked[52] why Simiand twice discarded volume of production. Could we not look for the cause of the face value of wages in phase B (a livelihood equalling an increase in

[52] Cf. Landry, 'Réflexions sur les théories du chômage et du salaire.' *Revue d'Economie politique*, Nov.–Dec. 1935 and March–April, 1936.

wages), and, in that case, would we not necessarily arrive, via volume of production, at mechanization and technique? Simiand, I believe, would not have questioned the possibility of establishing, by abstraction and isolation, such a relation, but he would have held that certain relations have preference because they express the dynamics which are inherent in the social economy, whereas the others do not spring from the inner dynamism of the movement and the mechanism of the sequences (technical progress is explained by lower prices). This is all the more true since, for Simiand, this mechanism, as we see, was not merely *real*, but also *necessary*.

Simiand's causal study then, in its application, has nothing, or almost nothing, to do with his own theoretical formulae, and with J. S. Mill's logic (with the exception, let us repeat, of the principle of regular occurrence). The elimination of accidents by organization of the macrocosmic fact, the elimination of the stable data, by use of the choice of alternation as well as of the primary fact, the regression to the prime mover, all these procedures are foreign to the usual logic of induction, and to a large extent alien to the methods of the natural sciences. For no one has shown to the extent that Simiand has done—and contrary to his own explicit intention—the specific quality of science and of economic reality. The demonstration is all the more convincing in that it is involuntary. For where would there be found, in physical theory, the equivalent of this division into series of dependent relations? The representative theories which Simiand cites to support preference of causal relationship over functional interdependence have almost no resemblance to the connected series of factors which Simiand continually decomposes and recomposes. If a comparison were looked for, we should have to imagine a machine (an internal combustion motor) or, failing that, an organism so as to find this complex interdependence of a determinist system, arranged on the basis of an initial cause automatically reproduced by the final term of the series. Positive physics is as far removed from Simiand's economy as it is from traditional theory. Besides, as we are going to try to demonstrate, Simiand was revolutionary in the method he prescribed rather than by the knowledge he sought.

* * * *

The apparently paradoxical nature of primary cause, as demonstrated by Simiand, has often been noted. This fanatic of sociology sees, when all is said and done, at the origin of the whole economic process, a phenomenon as contingent as the rate of increase of gold reserves, that is, the discovery of new veins or the exhaustion of old gold mines. Now

Simiand, always in the name of a natural science, in any case more fictional than authentic, was, in his own words, looking for a rational explanation.

The reasonableness of an explanation seems, as he sees it, to come from two characteristics; generality, and necessity. The general quality of the causal connection discovered in a single experiment seems to him at least probable: the same alternation of phases, obeying the same mechanism, would be apparent in other, independent, wholes. Let us accept this proposition, all the more probable since the prime cause of the phenomenon is outside the French economy and is a part of the economy of the world market. Besides, from any view point, the causal relation of M–A would be *universal*; the subject would in one case be singular (the historical individual), in the other, general (several, or even all, of the economies of complex exchange).

In still another sense the relation is general. As a matter of fact, the alternation of phases of expansion and contraction of currency offers at least a certain regularity: it will probably be repeated in the future.[53] Besides, even if the *precipitating fact* (the discovery of new gold fields) did not occur, non-metallic currency could make up for the shortage so that *alternating inflation and stability* would, whatever the circumstances, still be the rule.

But there is still more. Neither this general nature of the subject nor this approximative and probable regularity sufficed for Simiand. If need be, science would be content with a necessity dependent in some way on a contingent fact, but reason permits raising the following hypothesis: the development of the economy, or rather its progress (that is, a bigger slice of the cake for everyone) could not have been realized any other way. And, in a page deserving of fame,[54] worshipping what he had burned, Simiand offers sacrifice to conceptual method and tries to prove that except for the variation of the different prices which itself is conditioned by the expansion of circulating currency, economic progress is inconceivable. In an economy of direct barter, the increase in volume of production would not interest the producer, since, with prices dropping in proportion to the increase, he would get, for his increased production, the same value in other merchandise.[55]

The judgment of this demonstration matters little. Two facts seem indisputable: the demonstration could not be attributed to oversight

[53] There is, to a certain extent, a self-regulation, since lower prices make gold mining more profitable.

[54] *Le Salaire*, II, 516–517, and *Les Fluctuations economiques à longue période et la crise mondiale*, Paris, 1932, pp. 53–54.

[55] Simiand also above all shows that the desire to protect the profit made in period A is the indispensable incitement to economic progress in phase B.

or to a fancy; Simiand insisted on it to the extent that he himself said that he had been convinced by his own conclusions only after he had confirmed them logically (he reproached one of his critics for having neglected to do this). Again, this demonstration follows from the conceptual method which he had so bitterly attacked. Now, this necessity —*things could not have been otherwise*—does not seem to me comparable with the modality of physical judgments which simply establish causal relations valid for closed systems or for conditions abstracted from the real. The scholar says: given a certain antecedent, a certain consequence necessarily results. Strictly, he formulates the laws according to which, *in fact,* natural phenomena follow each other; he expresses in equations the structure of the universe as he finds it. He does not demonstrate that it could not have been other than it is. The necessity that Simiand envisages is of a different nature. It is founded, like the necessity of all economic theories, on the psychology or the logic of human behaviours: without price changes, producers would get no profit by increasing production; without price drops they would not have the courage to carry out technical progress. To the extent that men cannot be other than they are, economic necessity is categorical and not hypothetical, since it expresses both the recurrence of the same situations and the permanence of human tendencies. Simiand imagined he was reducing the science of economics to the sacrosanct pattern of mathematical physics; he discovered, by another route, an economic *theory.*

We do not mean, by these remarks, either to belittle the greatness of the work or to underestimate its originality. For this theory, consistent with tradition, was due to be established by other methods. Instead of being anterior to the empirism, the fruit of a simplification and a schematization, it comes after the experience from which it is directly derived. Thus, it integrates a richer reality, one closer to history. It abandons the fiction of the *homo oeconomicus* of the classicists or even of the Austrian marginal school; the mechanism of the economy operates through the agency of actual men. Social groups are moved by impulses, the scale of which seems constant and which, in spite of their intrinsic irrationality, finally produce a result fortunate for all. The reason inherent in the economic system is collective and not individual. Simiand recalls it to mind: intelligence lies with the world and his wife. But his *collective reason* is above all similar to the *ruse of reason.* As in the philosophical consideration of history, so here, individual passions appear *in fact* at the service of ends of which they are ignorant.

Nevertheless, the return from experience to theory is not accomplished without difficulties and ambiguities. As a matter of fact, one of two things is sure: either the necessity is bound up with the real causal relation, or it is valid only for an ideal schema. Let us examine these two hypotheses.

Can we say, following Simiand himself, that the movement of the economy could not have been other than it was? Certainly not. It was not necessary that the mines in California be discovered exactly in a given year. We understand here by contingency both the possibility of conceiving the other event and the impossibility of deducing the event from the totality of the previous situation.[56] It is an accident then, which contradicts the necessity of a rational truth and that of a sufficient relation. Now it is not enough to say that the increase of non-metallic currency *could have* produced the same result. In order to make the real evolution necessary, one would have to prove—and no one, I believe, has tried it—that this increase would have occurred at the time when the mines were discovered and that it would have determined the same expansion, first monetary, second economic. Lacking this, the difference between what would have been and what was, brings back, with the efficacy of a coincidence at the beginning of a global change, contingency into history, even into the history of the economy.

Will it be said that this necessity is obviously applicable only to the broad outlines of the development? All right, let us accept that interpretation, which agrees with the alternative we just stated. The alternation of the phases is necessary because both phases are indispensable to the progress of the economy, because one tends to create the conditions making the other one possible or inevitable. But Simiand was conscious that this necessity was not inscribed in the facts, and that is why he had recourse to conceptual reasoning. Indeed, it would have been possible legitimately to ask whether the same progress might not have been made at less cost, whether it would not have been possible (or if it would not be in the future) to avoid the cycles which represent so much individual suffering and poverty. Why should not the increase in productivity make possible a continuous growth in the volume of production and, hence, of real wages?

Simiand had a right to limit himself to a retrospective observation of fact: as a matter of fact, this cyclical movement has occurred regularly and has brought on certain effects. But he must have had the impression of a partial failure; perhaps, he unknowingly clung to the traditional theory as his model—the theory more or less confused with

[56] There is neither a *categorical necessity* (psychological or logical), nor *hypothetical necessity*.

positivist science. In addition this necessity alone justifies fully a privileged position of the problem of cause. Without it, the relation of technical development to real wages would become just as valid as that of currency in circulation to nominal wages.[57] Finally, the scholar needs this necessity—that *it could not be otherwise*—when he deduces scientifically an imperative of action. For he must give an answer to men who want progress without being willing to pay the price for it: you cannot have the one without the other.[58]

Let us add, finally, that this necessity is derived both from observed human psychology and from economic experience. The hierarchy of trends suggests it, as does the regular return of the inciting cause. It is enough, then, to take individual reactions in a capitalist regime as eternal to rise from fact to theory, and to declare the observed mechanism necessary.

However plausible and attractive this confusion may be, it is dangerous. It is important to separate clearly three types of results. *Historically*, the abundance of gold following the discovery of the mines in America or Africa was the cause of a rise in prices and of an economic expansion (a new factor within a given constellation). *Sociologically*, the rate of increase of gold reserves, following the pattern of the examples of the nineteenth century, would govern the alternating phases of economic cycles and would be their *primum movens*. *Theoretically*, if the psychology of the economic individual does not change, if the successive situations which determine conduct cannot be brought about otherwise, the economic factor is necessary in the sense that the same results would not be attained by any other means.

So then, assuming even that the integral truth of Simiand's conclusions be admitted, *the necessity is not real*, and *the reality is not necessary*. The necessity applies to a schematic reconstruction and not to the economic movement as it in fact occurred.[59] And again, it would

[57] Cf. Landry, loc. cit. For the past, this relation is still nonetheless subordinate to the mechanism of the cycles.

[58] It would be easy to show why Simiand had little chance of being heeded. But that would be to depart from our subject. In reality, the science as he conceives it does not satisfy all the conditions of a body of knowledge practically useful. (*a*) it is retrospective and does not allow any attempt at innovation; (*b*) it is based only on recurrence and recognizes less what particularizes each new crisis; (*c*) it is situated at a level that does not correspond to the interests of the practical man. Then, like any theory which takes note of the ruse of reason, it has Machiavellian implications. Men must continue to be ignorant of the mechanism which their passions, blindly, set in motion.

[59] There still persist many obscure points, because the schema is barely indicated. Is the alternation of long term phases necessary? Does it represent the normal functioning of this schematic economy? Or, on the contrary, are short cycles necessary, long phases being (theoretically, or even sociologically) accidental?

be desirable to specify the importance of this abstract necessity. Would a socialist economy, totally planned, experience the fatality of the cycles? Is not this fatality bound up with a system of free prices, perhaps with an international economy in which world prices represent for all national economies the controlling factor, or, as someone has said, the modern form of fate?

Economics is a privileged field for causal analysis. Historical relationships are numerous and precise, sociological relations are both close to reality and to necessity (sufficiency approaches necessity). Finally, historical and sociological causality are supported by a theoretical necessity which Simiand tried to read, somehow, into the facts, but which in the long run he, like all economists, had to demonstrate by making use of a conceptual method.

* * * *

If we had to describe Simiand's philosophy and method in one word, we should speak of *realism.* All the procedures of science must follow closely the structure of the object. Shall we call it sociological realism? Doubtless, but also scientific realism, for it seems never even to occur to Simiand that the scholar may be free to construct his concepts as he sees fit, according to the drift of his curiosity, so obvious is it to him that the scientist is bound by the material which he is elaborating, and to such an extent does the system seem inherent in the mechanism of economics. One question, and a decisive one, then, still remains. In what instances does causality thus lead to theory; in what instance does there exist a *system* of causal relations? In short, do history and society, *as a whole*, offer a structure such as we find in economics?

CONCLUSION

LET US quickly sum up the results arrived at in the foregoing chapters, and draw from the description the sequels with respect to the limits and objectivity of sociological causality.

One might say, generally, that all causal relations in sociology are partial and probable, but that these qualities assume, depending on the cases, different values. Natural causes never imply necessary effects because nature never imposes upon human societies any sort of exactly defined institution. Social causes are more or less adequate, and not necessary, because rarely does an effect depend upon a single cause. In any event, the partial determinism develops regularly only in a single constellation which is never exactly reproduced.

Thanks to statistics it is true that causal relations, assuming conditions are normal, become both certain and necessary (or very nearly necessary). Celibacy increases the number of suicides, political crises decrease it. But these causal formulae show an inner probability because of the fact that they are global and macroscopic. With reference to the individual, they express an increased chance of a certain event.

To be sure, these macroscopic determinisms are not inevitably unreal. On the contrary, economic systems, such as world prices for example, although they are created by an infinite number of individual decisions, do constitute a compelling force for some other system or line of conduct. And at times, it is on a higher level that the regularities and serial connections of causality appear, as if the determinism of history were operating over the heads of persons, beyond the individual consciousness. In such a case, causal relationships, otherwise incoherent, seem to be organized into a system, and the effective series approach a necessity (theoretical, and no longer sociological).

With the modality and the essential types of causal relations thus specified, we can put the other question, no longer that of the limits of sociological causality, but the question of the objectivity of that causality. To what extent are these relations dependent upon the historian?

Abstractly, the answer is easy: selection, preceding experimentation (comparison of examples, constitution of antecedents, etc.) is subjective; verification, once the selection is admitted, compels recognition by all who want the truth. These results are still provisional, since it still remains for us to study causal systematization and the antinomy of objectivism and subjectivism. But the features just pointed out already suggest the point at which the difference between natural and social cause would be noted: physical laws know no intrinsic uncertainty comparable to that created by the variety of human reactions. The positive sciences seek the origin of mass relationships even in the elements, whereas the regularities in the social order appear only in aggregates. The extent of sociological relations, then, is limited, because they are interconnected by terms which are constructed rather than analysed, and involved in historical totalities rather than isolable. So it is immediately apparent why the definition of the science by causality presents a problematical and paradoxical character: in certain social disciplines, description or understanding is more important than the alleged necessities; in all of them, conceptual construction precedes or accompanies the investigation of cause; in no case, finally, is the latter sufficient in itself, whether it calls for a rational theory or demands a systematization.

Third Part

HISTORICAL DETERMINISM

IN THE Introduction to this Section, we pointed out the three intentions of the judge, the scientist, and the philosopher, which direct the causal investigation towards three goals: the responsible cause of a single fact, the necessary relations between isolated elements, and the characteristic nature of historical determinism. We must tackle the last problem, apparently the most extensive. In fact, the preceding analyses already contain, virtually at least, the solution. Besides, the philosopher aims only at the synthesis of the partial results.

We shall first have to compare historical and sociological causality (Chapter I), in order to reconcile historians and sociologists, in order to put necessity and chance in their places within the object. Again, causal relations, both historical and sociological, have so far appeared, except in the case of economics, scattered and incoherent. The main question then is whether to *transcend* these partial relations or to *systematize* them: we shall examine the attempts to transcend and to systematize in Chapters II and III. Is it possible to set up social and historical laws, to list the various orders of causes, to fix in a general way the hierarchy, the subordination of these various factors? All that will remain will be, in Chapter IV, to study historical determinism from a double—objective and subjective—point of view, as a structure of reality and as an elaboration of the scientist, in order to specify, in the Conclusion, the limits of historical causality—limits which themselves extend in two directions: what is the extent of causality in the world of history? What is the validity of the determinism, that is, how far is retrospective construction dependent on the present and on history?

I. HISTORICAL CAUSALITY AND SOCIOLOGICAL CAUSALITY

THE DISTINCTION governing the preceding exposé is principally formal: historical research sticks to the antecedents of a singular fact, sociological research to the causes of a fact which may be repeated. The divergence of interest was enough to account for the different bearings of the two disciplines. In fact, the schema simplifies the original data and, in the very course of the exposition, substantial oppositions—social-individual, social-historical, partial-global—came along to complicate the primary opposition of singular-general.

We should like, in this chapter, to bring together the results of the two preceding *Parts*, from the double point of view, formal and material, to compare the two types of causality so as to show that they both retain their legitimacy; and that, far from contradicting each other, they imply each other. Thus, we shall be able, for the last time, to hark back to the *sociologistic* prejudice in favour of social and general cause, and to show the place which belongs, in science as well as in action, to historical investigation.

* * * *

The logical opposition of singular versus general occurs at all levels. The historical particular, whatever its extent may be, lends itself to a historical analysis: it is enough that the historian should show its originality. Max Weber studied the causes of *Western* capitalism and cast light on the characteristics making it incomparable with the other forms of capitalism (observed in antiquity or other civilizations). More generally, Simiand's study leaves room either for an analysis of the data at a lower level, or for an inquiry into the exact features of each cycle, or, finally, for an attempt to show the irreversible development of the system throughout the alternating rhythm (not to mention the origin of accidents at the beginning of cycles). In these three senses, economic sociology calls for a historical study.

Neither the sciences nor the problems are inscribed in the reality itself. Hence the impossibility of defining cause as the antecedent linked with the effect by the general relation, a fictitious rule which Simiand never followed. For, as we have seen, either one sticks to the fact in its historicity, and then one does not get to the most general antecedent, or else one begins by generalizing the fact, by placing oneself at the macroscopic level, and then there will be no need to discard the particular antecedents—they will already have been eliminated in the construction of the terms.

Moreover, as we noted, abstract relations never exhaust the unique constellation. We can now account for that inevitable margin (which does not, as Simiand thought, require the metaphysical idea of individuality, nor of personal will, mysterious and free). In one sense this margin exists in all the sciences; its existence is recognized by the requirement of a coefficient of safety in order to proceed from theory to application. But in history, it has a special meaning because, as we have seen, history's generalities are partial, imprecise, and scattered. To state the cause of revolutions in general, we had to ignore the individuals who started a given rebellion at a given moment. The sociologist who would be satisfied with general causes, then, would slip from logic to metaphysics; he would assume, as admitted, the doctrine denying the efficacy of individuals and of coincidences. (We may add that, if this doctrine were true, the historian would not perform a vain task by listing the chance occurrences which have carried out the designs of fate.)

Finally, laws are not always the most instructive results. The history of the French Revolution is at least as interesting as the rather paltry generalities which characterize the conclusions of a comparative study of revolutions. Greek art is certainly more stirring than the laws of the development of the arts.

But there is still the sociologist's objection: interesting or not, are not the generalities the essential condition of any causal inquiry? Does the historical investigation not necessarily come *after* rules and comparisons? Is it not the margin between combined generalities and the global situation that limits the efficacy of accidents and the proper object of the historian? To answer, it is important to connect the formal oppositions with the material, to keep in mind the various types of abstract propositions.

Do not the historian and the sociologist study different facts, or at least the same facts from different points of view? For Durkheim there was no question but that the sociologist ignores the *superficial* accidents of the development and concentrates his attention on the *constitutive features* of the social species. And in Simiand's examples, the elimination of individual data is indicated as a methodological rule. On the other hand, the historian of politics is keenly interested in the adventures of Mirabeau, Robespierre or Danton, and they have no place in the sociologists' construction.

There is no doubt that one may easily proceed from the formal to a material opposition, that historical curiosity may turn into a curiosity about accidents, or that the demand for laws may lead to an exploration of the sectors of reality where regularities are to be found. It is important only to forestall two errors. First, material and formal opposition are not identical (we have just seen that the historian places himself at all levels and considers all the orders of facts). Second, the distinction between the social and the historical (or the individual), often suggested by the real, never corresponds to an essential difference: it is always relative and partly subjective.

The constitution of a society belongs to history. It changes as time goes on, sometimes suddenly as the result of accidents. For, even though the latter do depend on the constitution of the society, they nevertheless react upon it. The separation is conceptual and of mental origin (which does not mean that the density of population may not be largely independent of historical events, nor that each society may not be characterized by a density which often remains constant throughout the most changing political eventualities).

Nor should one confuse the opposition of social versus individual and that of necessity and contingency. Of course, facts considered as peculiarly social, economic systems, systems of ownership, organization of agriculture, etc., show a more coherent evolution, less subject to personal initiative, more intelligible in their broad outlines. But one must keep to the logical and relative meaning of the terms adequate and accidental, necessary and contingent. In all historical spheres, in all circumstances, formal relations will be noted. Moreover, the necessary is never real; it is usually macroscopic, results from a conceptual organization of the elementary facts. Even though this global necessity may give expression to a necessity actually imposed on the individuals, it should not be confused with a fatality transcendent to events and people.

The extent to which the collaboration of the sociologist and the historian is possible, is apparent, and to what extent the historian can make use of the sociologist's results. If they both study the same fact with logically different intentions, they will rely on each other. If, on the contrary, they study different facts or place themselves on different levels, they are apt to ignore each other.

We do not imagine a historian studying post-war Germany, who would not make use of the general relations concerning the phenomena of transfer of property, rates of interest, the reconstitution of capital, etc. In the same way, a problem such as the origins of capitalism calls for the use of historical generalities, at least of analogies and comparisons. On the other hand, what good would the sociology of war (causes of war in general) be to the historian analysing the breaking out of the World War, or the sociology of revolution to the historian of the Revolution of 1848? The whole of the historian's work develops, in such a case, along the line of facts which the sociologist, immediately and *en bloc*, ignored or expressed conceptually. The details of official decisions, the diplomacy of the week before the European conflagration, all that belongs with the accidents which the sociologist deliberately, and often disdainfully, ignores.

We can now answer the question of the priority of one type of causality over the other. In one sense the priority of sociological causality is obvious: in order to prove the necessity of a determined consecution, there must be available a rule, if not a law. But this priority calls for certain reservations. In the first place, if the establishment of a rule requires a simplification, a macroscopic grouping making it no longer possible to get back to the event, the historical investigation does not follow the sociological research because it is wholly independent of it. Second, when it is dependent, it is still often first because the situation must be analysed in order to bring out those elements which may be generalized.

Is it even necessary to reintroduce a scale of values between the two forms of causality? Assuming an analogous modality in the two types of judgment, are not their strictness, their subjective probability, different? To be sure, social regularities are often better established than are historical sequences. But it is important to compare historical and sociological relations belonging to the same order of facts. It would be too easy to compare with the rules of economics the unpredictable successions of political events. Political regularities are neither more precise nor better elaborated than single sequences. On the other hand, the historical sequences of economic phenomena are as well, sometimes better, elucidated than the generalities. The effects of a given devaluation of currency appear to us more clearly than the effects of devaluation in general.

Will it be objected that the difference of value is due to the difference in levels, and that, as Auguste Comte said, in history, one would see the whole better than the detail? The saying is true, doubtless, if we compare our knowledge of the individual act and our knowledge of a limited whole (for example, the whole of February 6, 1934 on the one hand, and the first shots fired on that day, on the other). Even so, this impression must be mistrusted, for men have made, without knowing it, a history they did not intend. By the conceptual expression of the events, in broad outlines, there is danger of resorting to a subjective and arbitrary version of them. Perhaps the moderate interpretation[60] is no more definitive than the partisan interpretations (Fascist plot or revolt of the French conscience). Does this mean that this example justifies the general conclusion that the whole is better known than the detail, but the interpretation of the whole is more exposed to the danger of being subjective? Many reservations would have to be made. We know more about a certain textile industry in Flanders in the Middle Ages, which documents make it possible to reconstitute in detail, than the proportions of various enterprises at that time, the volume of international trade, etc. Shall we say that the limited whole (a certain battle, a certain industry) is better known than the more extensive whole (the economic situation)? Here again it would be important to distinguish between different cases. Certain political

[60] Cf. *La Journée des Dupes*, November 11, 1630, when Richelieu's enemies were discomfited by the failure of a plot against him.

changes are clear to us in gross, but not in detail (National-Socialism). In other cases we do not know whether the global change (the check of Protestantism in France) has a total unity or whether it resolves into a series of accidents. The more independent reality the totality has, the more valid is the global knowledge, even if there are elements of which we are ignorant. On the other hand, the more the totality is confined to a historian's view, the more ignorance our alleged knowledge hides. The main point then, once again, would be the reality or unreality of the totalities.

* * * *

The comparison of the two sides, considered formally, confirms the legitimacy of the two types of causal inquiry. Does the comparison lead to new results in the material order? Do not the regularities eliminate chance, or, at least permit a return to the ideas already suggested concerning the elimination of accidents and the rôle played by coincidences in the process?

Nothing of the kind: the determinism established by the sociologist does not prove the truth of *sociologism.* The regularities do not imply either the disappearance of, or compensation for, series whose origin is contingent.

Without going back to all the arguments given above, let us look at the partial causal relations we have observed. Whether conceptual expression isolates concrete phenomena, or constructs abstract terms, in all cases these rules do not abolish accidents either without or within the partial determinism. At the starting point of regularities we sometimes find accidents (discoveries of gold mines) the consequences of which are indefinitely prolonged. Does not the particular sharpness of a certain depression (a sharpness attributable to certain non-economic details) provoke effects (revolution) with unpredictable results? Finally, macroscopic necessity always runs the risk of representing a cerebral view. It does not imply that particular facts may not have been effective at a lower level. The causes of the world-wide coalition against Germany are seen in the political situation, and so there is no difficulty in reconstructing an evolution which, from the rapid rise of the Empire to the anxiety of its rivals, leads to the adventure and defeat. But if the outcome had been different, would not causes just as profound have been discovered? (In the same way that it is easy to imagine *profound causes* that German historians would have found for the defeat of republican France.) Now, perhaps the outcome depended on the Battle of the Marne, which was in its turn subject to a multiplicity of individual initiatives. Let us put the remark in general terms: the macroscopic determinism established by rational elimination of the effect of accidents or by showing the effect of such and such a macroscopic datum possesses at most, objectively and subjectively, a probable value, for it is itself the result of the accumulation of partial data which could have been different. It disregards rather than compensates for the chance elements.

In truth, two hypotheses would limit the extent of these remarks. If the global change, such as that of the economy, were real in so far as it was global, the events, on a lower level, would seem incapable of stopping it or turning it aside. In another connection, if a determinism takes in the whole of society, one would conceive the disappearance of accidents which would record the conjuncture of partial determinisms.

To go further, then, it would be necessary—and we thus come back to the questions asked at the end of the preceding *Part*—either to transcend in extent the fragmentary regularities, or to attribute to macroscopic relations a sort of objectivity. We shall try, in the following chapters, to answer these questions.

* * * *

Is it illegitimate to stop with this conciliation? To maintain simultaneously history and sociology, chance and regularities? We do not think so. Quite to the contrary, the interpretation of the different causalities proceeding from specific intentions makes it possible for us to reduce the apparent paradox, to dispose of the pseudo-problem.

The historical investigation, as we have seen, responded to a reaction against the retrospective illusion of fatality; hence the effort to resurrect, or more exactly the effort to put oneself back at the moment of the action in order to become the actor's contemporary. Now the search for responsibilities, the denial of the determinism which puts the event back among the normal succession of events in a historical totality, in a word, the attempt to imagine that things could have been otherwise, almost inevitably leads either to discrete data (as opposed to a constellation), or to singular data (as opposed to common characteristics). The sociological inquiry, by its nature, tends in the opposite direction.

Let us suppose that the sociologist is analysing the causes of suicide. Because of the very fact that he considers it a social phenomenon, he withdraws it, as it were, from the control of personal free will, tears it away from the history and temperament of the individual; he takes suicides as a whole, their frequency, and analyses the circumstances according to which the coefficient varies. By definition he ignores the accidents, either outward or internal, which may have determined a given suicide; he stresses only the regularities because he is looking for these only. Of course he might still seek without finding; if the social antecedents were neither favourable nor unfavourable, the sociologist would be likely not to get from the figures the regular co-variations at which he aims. But at least the *nature of the answer is implied by the question.*

In the same way, the moment the sociologist states the problem in general terms (what are the causes determining wars?), he assumes that they are *determined*; he forgets, or does not wish to remember, that the time and the singularities of each war are the result of individual initiatives or of conjunctures, that is, of facts apparently foreign to any rule. *In order to construct the determinism, the sociologist by professional obligation assumes its existence.*

Now, let us recall again that determinism is not merely the application to history of the general principle of causality, but a certain philosophy of history. It matters little that in each case the total antecedent necessarily leads to the total consequence. The determinism assumed by the sociologist unfolds at a certain level, it involves the efficacy, predominant, if not exclusive, of certain factors. In other words, the sociologist spontaneously concerns himself (sometimes uniquely) with situations, masses, macroscopic regularities. He calls upon an allegedly universally scientific postulate to justify his specialist point of view.

Certainly the traditional historian's philosophy, which puts the accent on the fragmentary facts, chance, individual actions, is equally suspect. And we do not think of preferring one to the other, since we say that there is no choice, generally, between two special perspectives, between two aspects of history. The philosopher does not have to arbitrate the pseudo-philosophical arguments of the scientists. Reflection reveals the origin of the quarrels and their vanity.

The man of action uses sociology and history simultaneously, since he thinks out his decision in a situation both unique and global, and in terms of elements susceptible to recurrence, hence capable of being isolated. The elementary rules make predictable the consequences of the event which the personal decision is going to introduce into the web of determinism, but the singularity of the situation leaves room for initiative and innovation at the same time as making the partial regularities specific. The practical man demands both these regularities and these chances. Without the latter, he would be reduced to the rôle of the agent of fate. Lacking the former he would be free but blind and consequently powerless. If the macroscopic determinism were at once both total and real, the individual person would have no other recourse than to carry out a transcendent decree (since it would be situated at an inaccessible level); or else he tries to find in the reality, beyond the *means* and the *possibilities*, the supreme goal which he *must* pursue. In that case the partial determinism, shot through with accidents, is not enough, it would be necessary to read the law of evolution which willy-nilly would drag men onwards to a known and pre-determined future.

II. LAWS OF HISTORY AND SOCIETY

ORIGINALLY, the idea of law has nothing in common with that of cause. The idea of cause applies to the force, the creative power producing the effect, the idea of law to the regularities the origin of which is sought in the commands of a superior power. The mystical residue revealed by analysis would be then quite different. Of course one could perceive the idea of a rule imposed from above, or that of a rationality which would preside at the necessary recurrences of the same sequences. In particular, the laws of history, and above all, economic laws, retain something of these extra-scientific characteristics.

In positive science, cause and law seem inseparable; since cause is defined as the constant antecedent, any causal relation implies a law, at least if Auguste Comte's idea is held: Law is a constant relation of coexistence or of succession. Indeed, how are the two concepts to be distinguished? It is advisable to list a number of distinctions.

In the first place, cause is inferior to law. One will speak of the causes, not the laws, of suicide, because the established relations are (a) macroscopic, (b) historical and singular (most intimately connected with a historical context in such a way that any generalization seems doubtful). In the same way, the effects, not the laws, of currency devaluation are pointed out, to such an extent do the effects, variable with conditions, seem resistant to abstract expression. In this sense the law would denote a first transcending of causality both in the direction of the general and the microscopic (besides, the closer one gets to the elements, the greater the chance the relationships have of recurrence and of thus acquiring an extended field of application).

But in another sense it is, on the contrary, the cause which represents a transcendence of law. The cause of gravitation, so long sought, was supposed to reveal the working of distant attraction. We see two types of explanation of a causal relation: either the law, with greater validity, from which the first primary explanation would be deduced, or else the representative hypothesis, the minute data which would allow reconstruction of the mass facts (for example, the atomic theory in connection with the theory of gases). These two hypotheses are perhaps equivalent if, little by little, all their supports are resolved into relations so that the data, on the lower level, lead back in their turn to equations. (Of course we set aside the philosophical interpretations of the principle of legality and causality.)

To what extent has this effort towards the explanation of laws an equivalent in history or sociology? If, as we have seen so far, sociological relations are incoherent, we should be confronted with a fundamental difference, since it would be impossible to discover the explanation of one law in a higher law. On the other hand, the regularities allow of a psychological explanation; the search for the *motif* and *mobile* would be the equivalent of the causal explanation in the natural sciences. It might even be said that, in one case as in the other, the effort is directed towards the same goal, namely reality. Conscious individualities represent the element, the human life underlying the observed regularities the final support. Without entirely denying the analogy the differences predominate a good deal. The effort towards reality ends in fact with diametrically opposite results. In one case the search is continued indefinitely through connections which become more and more exact, and in the other it quickly settles on some psychological or rational accounts which, in spite of their uncertainty, bring the inquiry to a close.

Or one could, with Simiand, consider that causality has as its characteristic to point out the meaning of the connection established between two factors. Instead of functional interdependence (quantity of currency and price), one notes here the order of succession. We have seen, in connection with Simiand's theory, the importance of this observation (arrangement of dependencies in series, determination of the prime mover). We do not think that the comparison with the representative theories (the mechanistic tradition versus the tradition of energism) is justified, but however it is expressed, the idea plays a decisive rôle. Instead of getting lost in a multiplicity of functional relations which seem to leave a free choice of the goal upon which the voluntary action bears, one would succeed in specifying the primary factors governing any economic change.

We need not return to this point, already examined above. We have summarized the well-known distinctions in order to offer a final definition, the only one we shall go on with. In fact, we are interested here only in the laws of society and history which take note of an extension of causal thought. Now, in the case of social laws, we find two forms of this extension: certain economic laws would organize into one system, others would apply to all societies, and would show the necessary characteristics of human groups in all times and everywhere (the law of the élite, the law of the distribution of wealth). Again, historical laws are distinguished from the sociological relations studied by the fact that they are *essentially* historical. They are valid for irreversible changes: linguistic laws stating the regular change from one form to another or laws of politics stating the typical succession of forms of government or of constitutions. Finally the question will be to know within what limits such historical laws exist. Will there be found laws for the total development, or only for isolated sectors of historical reality? We shall study these three points: (a) social laws, (b) partial historical laws, (c) problems of the laws of history as a whole.

* * * *

We shall not study theoretical thought. That would be the subject of another book. We shall limit ourselves to a few remarks to show that, whatever the logic of theoretical thought, our conclusions would not be compromised. The extent to which the idea of economic laws is ambiguous, to which it still holds irrational left-overs, is common knowledge: the idea of *commandment* breaks to the surface of these so-called establishments of fact; the economic order seems to be clothed in special dignity, as though it corresponded to a providential harmony. That is why no one has ever asked the question which, for theory, would be the same as the one we ask of history: is there, *even logically* (*de jure*), one and only one economic theory? Is the question paradoxical? Not at all, for every theory involves a simplification of reality, a rational structure based on more or less fictive hypotheses. *A priori*, nothing bars a choice by economists from among several primary hypotheses. Shall we say that only one of them corresponds to the reality? Yes, of course, if the theory, as in Simiand's conception, is inherent in the reality so that the mind has only to decipher it. But we have seen that experimentation does not suffice to prove the theory, and that conceptual reasoning intervenes to confer a rational necessity upon the relationships brought out by experience. Hence doubt returns: is it not possible to conceive of other forward moving economic organizations? Are economic cycles, with their cortège of ruins, indeed a law of nature, or, even more, an imperative of collective reason?

However, it may be that with this *logical plurality* we are confronted with *factual plurality*. Hence the contradiction between the concrete explanations. Indeed, one of the methods of causal analysis most used by economists is equivalent to a comparison of the schema with the real. For example, theoretically, unemployment should disappear if wages were in approximate balance with marginal productivity. Since unemployment, instead of doing this, tends to become permanent, the fact is that one of the theoretical conditions is not met with: the rise of wages above marginal productivity becomes the cause of a phenomenon which contradicts the predicted order. It is immediately apparent that such an interpretation does not necessarily concur either with the investigation patterned after Simiand's method applied to determining the antecedents and their dependences, or, *a fortiori*, the determination of causes based on another schema (the Marxist schema, for example). In this sense, practically, just as there are different explanations of the same fact, so the scientists multiply contradictory precepts (save money, don't save money). Final judgment would require knowledge perhaps within reach but for the present not possessed.

We can, though, without compromising our own inquiry leave in doubt the nature of economic theory. The case of economics is in any case unique. There are other systems (for example, systems of jurisprudence), but they are ideational, not material, even though their intelligibility reflects a creation by history itself (and not by the historian). Moreover, the theories are valid for a certain economic structure, historically special. Aside, perhaps, from certain very general propositions which would be acceptable for an *eternal economics*, the propositions of the *classical economists* fit the case of capitalism and are applicable only to it; economic cycles presumably would not occur in a wholly planned economy. The theories (except the Marxian) merely show the working of the system, the mechanism by which it is reproduced. The knowledge of history, with its difficulties, again becomes indispensable in order to observe and describe the irreversible evolution of the system itself. Finally, every theory is partial and abstract; none fully explores either economic life, which is always shot through with political or psychological influences, or, *a fortiori*, the totality of a social system such as capitalism. Theoretical systematization, then, would at most provide historical thought with one element which would reveal its insufficiency and unreality by confronting it with the concrete.

* * * *

As an example of a static law, valid for every society, we shall take Pareto's formula of the distribution of income; always and everywhere there would be a pyramid of riches, with many poor at the wide base, a few wealthy ones at the narrow summit.

Let us admit to begin with that this law has been verified for all known civilizations. It does not follow that it will still be true for future regimes; at least that prediction involves some risk. As a matter of fact, the comparison of societies with a view to establishing the sharing of wealth has the inevitable result of eliminating, if it exists, the irreversible evolution, and of ignoring the possibility of an innovation. After all, the most convinced socialists do not hide the fact that the economic equality (more or less complete) which they hope for has never yet been realized. That perhaps it may be rather unreasonable or imprudent to hope for it is granted. But their hope does not become absurd on that account, any more than does the likelihood of unlimited extension into the future of the law based on experience.

Let us also admit that this law may be confirmed at least to a certain extent in future society. Let us assume that it will be possible at most to reduce the distance from the base to the top of the pyramid (that is, lessen the gap between highest and lowest incomes), to increase the number of high or middle incomes. The significance of the law would depend on the importance attached to these changes with reference to the constant data. Is it important first of all to do away with extremely high incomes, or to bring those of the majority of the population up to a middle level? It is a question here of extra-scientific choices, and these control not the truth or falsity of the law, but the interest shown in it. Assuming that it does not prohibit the desired change, the margin of initiative it leaves is more important than the limits it may impose on action.

Generally speaking there are two remarks which must be made about laws of this sort. Firstly, they never prescribe any positive and imperative maxim. Indeed, they apply to the whole of a society, but they isolate one of its characteristics and are in that sense partial (the word should not be taken here in the spatial sense). Instead of considering distribution of wealth one can fix one's attention on the reasons why certain people should have wealth, on the occupations which confer privilege and power, on the human relations between economic classes, etc. So much for the various views the sociologist may assume for his analysis, the practical man in order to transform the social reality. Secondly, social laws of this type do not indicate a transcendance of sociological causality. In spite of their wider application—since they would be verified for all societies—in spite of their meaning for a global whole, they do not rise above the limits of the fragmentary determinism which the sociologist and the politician elaborate to explain the course of action without enslaving it, so that they can deal with reality without giving up independence of judgment.

* * * *

The existence of laws of history is the subject of endless controversy because the meaning of the term is ambiguous. If it is understood as any regular sequence of two terms, such repetitions are to be found in human history. The real problems, as we have found, have to do with the method of setting up relationships, the construction of the terms, the level on which regularities develop, etc. But usually the term, 'law of history' evokes a more precise idea of historicity. Now the more *historicity* is required, the more *legitimacy* tends to vanish. For, in the last analysis, the unique and irreversible process by definition allows no laws, since it does not repeat itself, unless, by a return to the beginnings, one imagines the orders of a superior power whose rules are obeyed by a universal movement. We are going to follow the progress, the beginning and end of which we have just noted.

It would be vain to distinguish historical from social laws among the examples of empirical rules which we have taken from Max Weber's work. In a given society, the relations connect coexistent terms as well as the antecedent of a modification. The action of the economy on the law tends to develop a certain type of legislation, to point that legislation in a given direction. Let us take a more specific example. The return in everyday life of charismatic power (dealing out jobs among those loyal to the leader, the cooling down of fervour, etc.) is characteristic of a typical change, which is at the same time irreversible in each occurrence, and legal, since the great number of examples bears witness to a sort of necessity.

It is easy to find partial historical laws. We may cite the example of linguistic laws. Sounds, meanings, as they go from one language into another, regularly undergo such and such a variation. This is a particularly favourable case, the change is irreversible and yet verifiable by experience, since numerous examples are known and since the motives, either psychological or physiological, account for the historical orientation.

As one rises to a higher level, the difficulties increase because the number of presentations diminishes, and the cause of the evolution becomes obscure. Let us look at another classic example, the succession of forms of government, a law of history going back to the Greek philosophers. First, it will be necessary to distinguish exactly democracy, aristocracy, tyranny, etc., so that the comparison of the historical cases may be exact. Next, to get enough presentations, either there must be a cycle, or the change must have been observed in several societies. The Greeks based their conclusions on this double verification. Today, we should not observe only favourable cases. Certain democracies endure without degeneration. Moreover, these typical changes are macroscopic, isolated, simplified; they substitute for each concretely historical series a schematic image, they isolate one political aspect of collective life, they bring together into a unity of concepts a multiplicity of events and actions. Their development is dependent on outside conditions. Their vagueness is great, since the rhythm of the process is indeterminate. Their recurrence is doubtful as long as the causes of this macroscopic regularity are unproved.

The long list of social cycles believed to have been noted will be found in Sorokin. Institutions, ideas, population, distribution of national income, the prosperity and poverty of nations—all these phenomena would be subject to the swings of the pendulum. According to Pareto, the élite reappear, and generally, an élite relying on force, courage, violence, is followed by a bourgeois, plutocratic élite, depending on ruse, intrigue and ideology. In the same way, in the matter of increase in population, there would be times of growth followed by decrease or at least of more moderate increase.

A priori we can neither assert nor deny that such cycles exist. Why should they show up only in economics? Let us note, merely, that the more interesting the cycles, the less demonstrable, and the vaguer the expression of them. That institutions, ideas, dogmas, come into existence, grow, and die out, is confirmed by experience. But no law seems to govern the speed of these changes, and this limits the value and usefulness of such generalities. In addition, the indefinite recurrence of the cycle has never been shown; over limited periods of time it is believed that they have been observed, but not throughout history as a whole.

Now, cycles and laws of history would show a transcendence of fragmentary determinism only if they fulfil one of two conditions: that they are applicable to a temporally entire history (so that the regularity over the whole time does away with accidents at least within the time studied); or that they are applicable to a historical totality (so that disturbing influences disappear and the macroscopic law may be imposed without resistance). Both conditions may be satisfied independently. To establish real and unending periodicity it would do to stick to the concrete, rather than to set up schemata. To show the laws of total evolutions, it would be necessary, on the other hand, to work out a systematic method of comparison. We shall briefly look at these two problems. Let us note first the results of the preceding analysis: partial historical laws are only one form of the fragmentary determinism studied in *Part III*, above. Neither the methods of verification nor the quality of the results are different. Whether the presentations be provided by a cyclical return or by a comparison of unconnected societies or periods is of small logical importance.

* * * *

Is it possible positively to lay bare the secret of the rhythm of history as a whole? This is the approximate statement of the final question suggested by the spatial or temporal extension of historical laws. We must set completely aside value judgments which are implied by the hypothesis of progress or decadence. For certain characteristics which can be objectively observed (increase of population, distribution of income, wealth of nations), science itself, not philosophy, would discern the pace of the historical movement.

In fact, the temporal extension is obviously unsuccessful. Neither for economics, population, even less for politics, can one perceive an eternal cycle which would transcend the breaks in historical continuity. Logically, on the other hand, one could conceive such an extension within historical totalities: one sector of the social reality might obey a law of alternation of phases from beginning to the end (at least of the totality).

Let us then consider first the spatial extension. Are there laws of cultural evolution, laws valid for the evolution of each culture, verified by the comparative observation of all cultures? Such a question obviously cannot be answered *a priori*. No one can foresee and fix in advance the outer limits of a macroscopic determinism. In practice, no law of this sort, accepted by all historians or by the majority of them, is known. In logic, is the idea of such laws absurd or contradictory?

What are the procedures, theoretically necessary, to establish them positively? To begin with, the sociologist demarcates the parts whose transformations he compares. As long as it is a question of partial laws, this demarcation, a special form of selection, is logically absurd; fruitfulness proves validity. In this instance, since we are looking for total and real evolutions, the unities of the science should reproduce the unities inscribed in history. To put it another way: it is the comparison that would gradually suggest the unities which are being looked for. Division and comparison, in fact, become interdependent. Practically, this division varies with the historian's interest: Lamprecht studied national unities, Spengler, cultural unities; Toynbee also sees cultural unities, but his *intelligible fields of study* are not the same as Spengler's.

This multiplicity of individuals makes it possible, next, to combine the singularity of each history with the element of repetition, without which law disappears entirely. According to the historians the similarities between cultures and the originality of each of them vary.

Then too, this synthesis of individuality and regular evolution necessarily leads to a biological metaphysics. The typical phases in Lamprecht, as in Spengler, correspond to the different periods of the biological process. Besides, the two attempts are quite different, for Lamprecht defines each historical period by a *dominant psychology*, extended from individual to collective psychology; and, in fact, the various terms (symbolism, conventionalism, individualism, subjectivism) serve above all as synthetic principles to organize material already known. On the other hand, this psychology suggests an explanation of the mechanism of the evolution, namely the laws of disintegration and reintegration. Spengler, on the contrary, manipulates, with a mixture of fancy and intuitive penetration, the discriminatory comparison, which brings out at the same time the parallelism of the phases and the originality of each total history. Is there any need to point out the arbitrary element introduced into these synchronistic structures?

Need we go further? Is there a contradiction between morphology and legality (in the sense given to the word by scientific knowledge)? The gap between macroscopic laws and elementary regularities seems immense. Moreover, repetitions here are inevitably fewer in number. Finally, the same terms are neither isolated nor constructed; analogies are claimed for histories which are incomparable. In order to transform the schemata of growth into laws, analogy and identity must still be assimilated; the succession of analogous phases would be confused with the return of the same phenomena.

However, the appropriate logical notion matters little. The point is to show the essential uncertainty and the intrinsic improbability of such panoramic views. The hypothesis is acceptable and even probable, that certain partial regularities (either of certain sectors, or of certain characteristics) can be shown by comparing cultural unities. But in order to arrive at inflexible laws of universal history, each individuality must be given an autonomy and an absolute singularity. Now the continuity of intellectual development (a continuity at least relative) is enough to make such a proposition at least paradoxical (which is not to deny the autonomy of each culture, nor the involvement of the mathematical truths discovered by the Greeks and integrated into the edifice of present day science, with the philosophy of the Greeks, and their attitude to life). The isolation of cultures again gives place to intercourse, trade, and borrowings. Later cultures do not begin at the same point as do early cultures. And, in the positive order, the reasons for the alleged fatality to which they would be subject are no longer apparent.

Against the dual Western tradition of the unity of human history and a millenary evolution towards a goal more or less fixed in advance, Spengler opposed the two conflicting dogmas: inevitable cycles within solitary cultures. But these dogmas, in any case, could have no basis of causal propositions. Indeed, in proportion as one rises to a higher macroscopic level, one organizes and selects, with increasing absolutism. Legal relations, positively interpreted, would at most denote partial developments, typical ones, made more or less probable by approximate comparisons. To sanctify them as destiny the sociologist substitutes metaphysical decrees for likely arguments. Unbounded individualities would blindly obey transcendent laws which, by some miracle, an individual brain was able to make out.

* * * *

The peculiarity of the law of history with reference to causal relations would, then, come back to an attempt to get to the macroscopic and the total, or to the claim to grasp the law of an irreversible process. It may be this last claim which plays the decisive part, for in the laws of evolution theological memories are mixed with positive ideas. Certainly the latter may be looked upon as the purified residue of providential mysticism. It is nonetheless necessary to stress the common ground which exists between them, the identical hypotheses justifying the bringing together of encyclopaedic sociologies and traditional philosophies of history.

Which are the questions of theological origin which science might return to and keep, because they do not logically transcend scientific knowledge? It seems, first, that the *trends of the evolution* may be the transposition of these laws immanent to the process which were imagined in and beyond the phenomena. Indeed, every person tries to locate himself in history, to mark the point at which the evolution of the system, economic or political, has arrived—a system with which he feels himself, willingly or not, involved.

Thus, today, one would note the most characteristic changes in capitalism since the beginning of the century, one would organize these various changes into a series; it would be enough to protract this singular series in thought to show the tendencies of the evolution. Logically, the latter would rely on a single presentation; they would be simply the extension into the future, in terms of probabilities, of a recognized past. The probability can be confirmed by analysis of the present, by bringing to light underlying reasons, in the structure of the economy itself, which account for the observed and foreseen changes.

Depending on the social sphere, these propositions range through all shades of meaning, from vague likelihood to a probability akin to certainty. Three factors determine this value. First, the analysis of the present which is the basis of the forecast is more or less akin to the theory of necessity, the ideal style of which would be the Marxist schema (decadence inevitably results from internal conflicts, the direction of the development is as fatal as is the present-day process according to which capitalism recurs). Second, the extent and exactness of the data interpreted. Finally, the degree of isolation of the sector whose changes are foretold. In the case of the economy the autonomy is extensive enough to verify rather generally the descriptive forecasts, barring accidental upsets (we are thinking here of prognostications such as the decline of liberalism and free enterprise, increasing intervention by the State, etc., not of previews of prices and price cycles based on regularities). On the other hand, the moment the field of application is extended, and as soon, consequently, as judgments rely on a largely arbitrary selection, the probability of the statements rapidly grows less. Each individual constructs for himself his own trends of the development. Each cites such and such an assembly of facts, and again the question arises: does universal history follow certain *tendencies* which the individual can get at from the facts?

Akin to these trends in the evolution are the *laws of tendencies* which point the direction in which a certain partial history is directed. In this way sociologists express one or another religious law; for example, the law of incarnation or spiritualization: the gods would be more and more personal, religions more and more ethical. But these so-called laws, if derived from mere observation, involve all the dangers of any sort of extrapolation based on fragmentary data. During a certain length of time one observes a movement in a certain direction; there is nothing to prevent reactions or deviations. Moreover, these laws take on a truly scientific nature if they are confirmed or explained by elementary truths, either psychological or logical. People have believed for so long in the forward movement of history that they have seen in reason the natural maturity of the human mind, and in past superstitions the equivalent of childish dreams. Lacking psychology or logic, one is reduced to pure empiricism; and so one historian will announce a law of alternation, and another a law of degradation. Perhaps we shall succeed in verifying these partial laws, but we should like to isolate the law of one partial evolution throughout the whole duration of a total evolution. Now, the science seems unable to satisfy the philosopher's ambitions.

We still find the same uncertainty as to the rhythm of one whole history or of history as a whole. We saw in Section II that the historian, by the values he chooses, by the positions he assumes, is able to determine it. On the other hand, it seems that objective science, at least the science of cause, cannot answer these questions—logically questions of fact—because it does not know that such laws exist. The ignorance is natural enough, for in order to see an irreversible or cyclical rhythm in the process, a determined direction, or even a definite lack of direction, one would need to find a simplicity, a regularity, and a continuity which accidents and the complexity of social events make impossible. The historian, forced to choose, runs the risk of substituting his own preferences for the experience, or at least of subjecting experience to his choice, unless he sees in the nature of man and mind an inevitable predetermination. Lacking that, causal thought ends only with more or less risky generalizations, with laws more or less partially constructed and statements of probability set up as fatalities by faith and feeling.

III. CAUSAL SYNTHESIS

SO FAR, we have not found the principles of systematization we were looking for. Neither the combination of historical and sociological causalities, nor social or historical laws answer the requirements of a synthesis because they do not overcome the dispersion and fragmentation of determinism. Social laws, from a certain point of view, cover a broader field, extend over a longer stretch of time, group facts at a higher level. With extension of them their uncertainty grows, but they remain partial and incoherent.

Now, all history solves, in one sense, the problem of systematization. A limited investigation begins at a certain point, goes to a certain point, the choice of starting and stopping places being external to causal thought. *A fortiori*, in a continuous account, the necessary connections demand organization.

We shall study three questions: does there exist, can we discover, a *primacy* of any one cause? Can *all* the causes be enumerated? Can constant relations be shown between typical causes? These three questions naturally remain subordinate to the fundamental query of this chapter: does causal thought of itself supply the principles of a systematization?

* * * *

Statements such as '*ideas make the world go round*', or '*the profits of production constitute the determining factor in the evolution of history*' are as banal as they are debated. But the claim to make such statements has rarely been submitted to criticism. Is it philosophical to ask whether it is ideas or interests which rule the world? Is it more philosophical to wonder whether the forces of production are or are not the *primary* or *exclusive* or *predominant* factor in history? We shall take this last thesis as an example, but we shall criticize it in a general way (the criticism would apply to any other theory of a primary factor).

Let us set aside the uncertainties relative to the constitution of terms: must we start with the forces or with the profits of production? Do the latter include judicial rules and certain political forms or only technique and economic organization? If the *primary factor* is enlarged without limit, will there not be the temptation to discover, within this term, the true first cause? Everyone is free to define as he wishes the profits of production,[61] and, whatever the definition may be, the latter could not constitute an exclusive cause.

Indeed, how can the proposition, that the profits of production *determine* society as a whole, be proved? There might be a static demonstration by means of sociological generalities; a certain condition of the term 'profit of production' would lead regularly to a certain condition of the term 'political regime', 'ideology', etc. Now, such a demonstration fails; equally developed capitalist regimes are combined with the most varying political constitutions, and the constitutions sometimes change in a country without these changes coinciding with or following economic transformations. Political change, for example, has a certain autonomy, although it does largely depend on the economic evolution. A historical demonstration would be conceived as follows: starting with any given event, causal regress would come to an economic cause and it would be the *true* or *last* cause in the series. That regress, starting with any event whatever, may go back to an economic phenomenon will be readily granted. It is only a matter of going back far enough; in addition, the various causes are too involved for one not to come quickly upon an economic antecedent. But the problem is to know why and how such an antecedent can be said to be the *veritable* or *ultimate* cause. We have analysed the workings of the historical investigation; it is inconceivable that anyone can say, in advance and generally, which antecedent is the determining cause. By what right do we stop in the regression? Beyond the economic antecedent other, non-economic, antecedents would show up. How can we give a meaning to the expression '*in the last analysis*'? How prove that it is always the situation which is the *authentic cause* of an

[61] Naturally, the sociologist is legitimately interested in the exact definition of concepts such as economy, technique, profits of production. But these definitions do not make possible a solution of the problem of cause.

event, and that this situation itself is the effect of the method of production?

First one would imagine a sort of metaphysical distinction between the essence and the appearance of the historical reality, the economy constituting the essence and the other data the appearance. But no one has ever given a strict meaning to this opposition, although, like all who want to grasp the broad lines of history without consenting to selection, certain Marxists often tend to disqualify the facts for which economics does not account by calling them secondary or superficial. Statically, economics would be the understructure; dynamically, in the last analysis, economics would determine the future order.

We can accept the static formula, but on condition that it is admitted that it is no longer causal. Indeed, to make of it a sociological truth, it would be necessary to construct the terms cause and effect (to a certain economic condition, a certain political condition) and we should come back to the impossible proof. But it is legitimate to *describe* a society starting with the profits of production, even though this validity must be based on arguments outside causality, and the fruitfulness of the method will vary, perhaps, with different societies.

In the dynamic sense the formula calls for the ability, starting with given profits of production, to foresee the future system; in the last analysis, collective ownership of the means of production will take the place of individual possession. What can one make of this forecast? If the economy obeyed a purely autonomous law, forecast and explanation would be equally possible. But the dialectic which goes from one historical totality to another in the past results not from an independent economic evolution but from the interaction of the elements (for example science quite obviously influences technique). In the same way, looking to the future, the evolution of the economy could not be compared to a peculiar movement which prolongs itself, unaffected by outside influences, but with the overall path of a complex development. By the same token, the accuracy of the forecast grows less. Let us suppose that capitalism, entangled in its conflicts, becomes incapable of progress, that men's reaction to the catastrophe is not fixed in advance, and the proletarianized lower bourgeoisie is capable of preferring some other regime than communism. As a consequence, the forecast would apply only to certain characteristics of the system (bureaucracy, concentration of industry, statism, etc.), but not to the totality or the detail of the future society, and *contradictory desires certainly affect the margin of indetermination more than they do the inevitable* elements, about which the doctrines are in agreement. Let us add, finally, that this possibility of a partial (probable) forecast is not characteristic only of the economy. Certain features of all future politics can be deduced from contemporary policies. The relative autonomy of each movement accounts for these fragmentary anticipations, as well as for the failure of the attempts to deduce from one factor all the others.

But it will be said that this strict unilinear causality does not answer the dialectical thought which would ignore a cause not at the same time being an effect. The main point would be the reciprocal action of the different historical forces, the economy representing the predominant one. We willingly accept this notion of *reciprocal action*, which is neither exactly Marxist nor specifically dialectical (reciprocal action becomes dialectical when it is inherent in a series, when the antithesis, by reaction on the thesis, the working by reaction on the creator, determines the access to a higher term which reconciles the first two[62]). *Coexistence is defined by mutual influence*. If two systems are under consideration, political on the one hand, and economic on the other, it will certainly be necessary to recognize the exchange of influences. But as soon as we come down to the detail, reciprocal action becomes the statement of a problem: in what way, at what moment, was the influence exerted? We do not claim that we always arrive at a one-directional relation; the formula of interaction expresses the limits of what we know and of our analysis just as much as the structure of the world of history. Perhaps the controlling term would be found at a higher or lower level.

As for the predominant rôle which is attributed to the economic factor in this universal interdependence, its meaning and importance are not clear. Of the exclusive or conclusive effectiveness of the economic factor we might conceive a philosophical proof, or at least one preceding the empirical investigation. But if all historical realities are efficacious, how can it be declared in advance for all societies, that a certain cause is predominant? Such a proposition limits itself to unlimited generalization of fragmentary results. Of course many Marxists, imbued with the scientific fanaticism of the last century, would rejoice that their philosophy should be a science, as their science would be a philosophy. But if materialism is reduced to the simple thesis of the peculiarly great rôle of the economic factor it will gradually become less important and gain probability in proportion as it loses in interest. For who casts doubt on the considerable influence of the economy in the process of history?

In order to assure that the doctrine does not degenerate into a vague

[62] Or, again, when the terms *deny each other, contradict each other,* instead of merely acting upon each other.

generalization of the causal influence peculiar to the economy, an attempt will be made to give a strict meaning to the idea of *predominance*. But this attempt is doomed to fail like the effort to justify exclusive efficacy. With reference to which term is this predominance to be estimated? Will one talk of a predominance which would be present in all societies, would appear in all historical phenomena? Such a conception, assuming that it was not self-contradictory, would call for unlimited demonstration extending over universal history. At present, it exceeds our knowledge, for many ideological, religious or political phenomena appear not to have the economic factor as their predominant cause. (What economic cause can explain the transition from polytheism to monotheism? the evolution of modern physics? the Crusades or the Wars of Religion?) In short, we come back to the same argument: the efficacy of the various antecedents is weighed in each situation. How can the result, unique and constant, of these special judgments be formulated in advance?

The propositions of popular Marxism just discussed (and, as far as we are concerned, any type of Marxism claiming to be a science and not a philosophy is a vulgar Marxism, because it is unconscious of its own nature), are the results of 'a double error': indiscriminate generalization of judgments valid for our time, and disregard of the philosophical significance of allegedly scientific formulae. Marx studied the society of his time and thought he saw that the structure of that society was mainly dependent on the economic regime. This proposition was no doubt correct, but it could not apply just as it was to all of the past. Also, this analysis of the present was combined with the philosophical idea that man was defined above all by his labour, and the history of man by the creation of the means of production, and even of the social milieu itself.[63] Hence the possibility of analysing the various civilizations in the light of the conditions determined by technique and the economic factor. The simultaneous disregard of the historical and philosophical origin of the theory has given rise to all the varying shades of popular materialism, all the wordy polemics over the first term, the exclusiveness or the predominance of the economic factor. This is a useless controversy, for systematization based on this factor does not and cannot come from causal thought (and our refutation would apply in the same terms to any other factor). As a matter of fact, the Marxist synthesis has been anthropological, not causal; its centre is a certain idea of man, and not the efficacy of a certain cause. We have

[63] He notes the relative autonomy of the economy and the fact that the individual's place in the routine of production governs his place in society. *Civil status* no longer exists—only *classes.*

not then, in the preceding pages, refuted Marxism, for the sufficient reason that we have not examined the essential ideas of Marxist philosophy, namely, the dialectics of history (the constitution of totalities based on profits of production, the intelligibility of the connections between one totality and another, a dialectic—negation and negation of the negation—of the historical process).

* * * *

The enumerations of historical causes or factors are countless. We have no intention of passing them all in review; only the principle of the classifications interests us; from logic to metaphysics, by way of history and sociology, all disciplines are concerned with these ventures.

To begin with, we shall distinguish the *horizontal* classifications—historical or, as it were, institutional, and the *transversal* classifications which are supposed to reproduce an objective hierarchy of essences. In between are the theoretical, psychological, or anthropological classifications, based on the tendencies of human nature. These distinctions do not exclude combinations. A classification like Scheler's tries to form a synthesis.

Logico-metaphysical classifications, like Meinecke's or Berr's, *biological, psychological, intellectual cause,* or *contingency, necessity* and *logic*, seem to us of little use. In practice, the historian never knows what, in the event, as it appears to him in its complexity, belongs to each category.[64]

Metaphysical classifications (Auguste Comte's or N. Hartmann's) would be exposed, if accepted as historical classifications, to the same objection. Of course the fundamental proposition that 'the inferior conditions the superior which remains autonomous' has perhaps a philosophical meaning. From it one would deduce relations of life to consciousness, of consciousness to intellect. But here again, it is difficult to proceed from this conceptual metaphysics to the reality of history. In addition, these statements, in so far as they are valid, lend themselves to direct proof (for example, the irreducibility of ideas as ideas), and this last method has the advantage of not leaving out of account the specific quality of the various totalities of history, of not transposing into causal terms the distinction between intellectual universes and the multiplicity of human activities.

A horizontal classification would of course avoid these criticisms. The institutions (churches, families, corporations, states, etc.) which

[64] On the whole, it is obvious that institutions evidence more necessity, and events more contingency; but what is the significance of such commonplaces?

the historian in most instances encounters, can be listed, but the division varies with societies and periods, and the scientists' curiosity. The result is at most a *memorandum* of causes, the function of which would be to remind the observer of the various phenomena to be noted. Such a classification would in no sense be systematization, since it leaves unknown the causal connections.

Only mixed classifications, which would show both the historical forces transversal to the development and the institutions which would be its expression or, as it were, its incarnation, would answer all the requirements. Such is the case in Scheler's theory. It is based on a distinction between material and ideal factors. The content, the *so-sein* of ideas, is always independent of the social reality, the intellectual act from the biological or historical individuality. The subject matter selects, among the ideas, only those which are realized in a certain period (it seems that Scheler is thinking both of the cultural realization of ideas and of the history of pure ideas). The influence of the élite would constitute the positive creative factor. Sublimely free, the mind is always without influence in the world. The real factors, in each time, determine present and future, and set the margin of uncertainty. Ideas have merely the power to stop momentarily, to slow up, or at most to guide, an evolution which goes on without them and, if they rebel, in spite of them. Scheler points to three real factors: sex (family), desire for power (politics), and desire for sustenance or wealth (economics). This theory of history is the transposition of an anthropological philosophy; we find the same freedom and the same helplessness of the intellect in personal and collective destiny. Institutions are tied in with instincts by way of the final goals to which they respond. Only the part played by the élite gives the structure of history its own character. And yet the transformation of the élite and of societies is explained by the psychological change of the governing groups (merchants succeed warriors). In the same way, the greater or lesser intellectual freedom with reference to the social body, the greater or lesser influence of mind, expresses a maturity in mankind which is reflected in the collective destiny. The successive predominance of the real factors, the law of the order of ideal factors (connections at various epochs between race, politics, and economy, between religion, philosophy, and science), is both anthropological and historical, transcendent to the development and verified by it.

We shall not discuss in detail these vast generalities, which are suggestive and dubious. We shall merely suggest our critical principles opposing such conceptions.

The transition from tendencies to institutions raises two objections.

Scheler admits that the whole man is engaged in every partial activity. If it were not for hunger and thirst there would be no economy, but if it were not for science, the modern economy would be inconceivable. In the same way, family life assumes both the sexual instinct and the understanding of legal standards. But how can we account for historically variable institutions by means of these supposedly constant impulses? The theoretical classification does not quite correspond to the historical classification. Ideas and feelings, needs and knowledge are always mixed and merged. Human nature, explained by an attempt at abstraction, appears only as a set of concretely irreducible attitudes.

Let us grant that the final goal, real here, ideal there, creates an opposition between the two categories of factors. The only consequence would be the autonomy of ideas (religion, science, philosophy) as ideas. Since ideas become forces by becoming integrated with passions, we again find a plurality of factors. And again the question will arise: how can one determine, *a priori*, the relation between factors the embodiment of which varies throughout the centuries in terms of a supra-historical anthropology? Moreover, the impulses, set aside by the philosopher, are expressed inseparably in all institutions; relations between factors must be directly observed and proved. Once again we are reduced to a psychology or a metaphysics camouflaged as a theory of history.

Let us admit that these propositions, as Scheler at times suggests, are the most general laws of sociology. How are we to conceive the primacy of one factor?

We have already granted the impossibility of getting at a primary and exclusive cause for the whole of the past. If one confines oneself to a certain culture, can one succeed in determining the governing element? It goes without saying that we are looking for a causal interpretation—not a psychological one—of this preponderance; there can be no doubt that human types vary according to the times. Scheler offers two formulae: he speaks of an *independent variable*, and of the factor fixing the *margin of uncertainty*.

The idea of an *independent variable* seems untenable. It would mean, as a matter of fact, the absolute autonomy of a partial evolution. Now, even during the period of capitalism the economic process is not isolated or independent. Politics, if it is the effect of an economic situation, reacts upon cause. Totalitarian regimes have given ample demonstration that the power of a State does not stop at the frontiers of trade.

Let us take the second formula, *margin of uncertainty*. It seems more acceptable because it is static and, in addition, it may be justified by incontestable arguments. In a capitalist system, certain characteristics of the social relations or of individual life are inevitable (class conflict, the influence of money, etc.), as though in fact the economy were outlining the limits within which the variations attributable to the other factors operate. In this sense, the formula still has an importance. It remains to be seen whether in each period one and only one factor is in this position, and whether it imposes a set of limits upon the other phenomena.

Let us consider any society. By the nature of the economy we can conclude the absence of certain institutions, if not the presence of exactly defined institutions, a consequence of the interdependence uniting the various parts of a totality. But, starting with a political, legal, or religious phenomenon, one would end with analogous propositions. A certain political system is not compatible with just any sort of economic system, nor a given judicial system with just any system of production and exchange. At the most, in each period the choice of a term is, if not obligatory, at least particularly convenient and motivated. But whatever the starting point, the conclusions are negative rather than positive; a given economic system excludes a given political regime (for example, a planned economy excludes formal democracy) or else the conclusions are stated in terms of trends: a given economy favours a certain type of government. In proportion as one reaches out for more distant phenomena, the tendencies become more vague. The margin of variations, defying clear definition, is no more than a metaphorical expression of social unity and of the breaking up of collective existence.

That these formulae are beyond our knowledge is best proved by the opposition between the ambition of retrospective explanations and the inadequacy of forecasts. Partial forecasts, projections toward the future of fragmentary causal systems established by experience, normally succeed. But the forecast relative to the future system (economic or social) is in the image of our global interpretation of the present. It fixes, in terms of such and such a relatively constant fact, certain characteristics of the other institutions (either necessary or excluded). With these absolute propositions the memory of historical syntheses is merged; as they appear in the past, societies appear to the observer as massive unities, expressions of an agency or a will which, after the event, acquires a sort of omnipotence. But, actually, man never lets himself be confined by any single intention; he shows his unpredictable freedom in the plurality of the worlds into which he projects his dreams, his hopes, or the multiple appearances of his real life. The unity of historical totalities, inevitably built up by the historian, is not the result of a juxtaposition or a composition of the elements, following a classification based on causes; it is immanent in the community, suggested by ethical truth or by the mission of man-mind.

* * * *

There is no prime mover of the historical process: Such, in brief, would be the conclusion of our study—a conclusion we could have drawn directly from the principle of any causal investigation, for *there is a contradiction between the affirmation, either a priori or a posteriori, of a causal primacy, and the systematic hypothesis of determinism, namely, analysis and comparison.*

We thus reserve the rights of other methods. The transition from one totality to another may be conceived as necessary, no longer in terms of observed regularities, but with reference to the internal necessity of the intelligible relationships. Perhaps the dialectic reconciles the antitheses which, to our understanding, become crystallized in insoluble contradictions. It is still necessary to maintain the distinctions, to keep from mixing up psychology, history and anthropology, from imposing on causal thought tasks which exceed its resources, and perhaps the resources of the human mind.

IV. HISTORICAL DETERMINISM

THE NEGATIVE results of the two preceding chapters bring us back to where we started. Scattered regularities combine among themselves and with single results, to sketch out the lines of the historical process and to outline the limits and anticipate the effects of action.

It remains for us to characterize the determinism of history, to show the material results implied in our logical analysis. Is cause compatible with the structure of the world of history? Can it be organized into an autonomous experience—into a total and intelligible unity?

* * * *

Current discussions relative to the use of the idea of cause in history usually revolve around the first of the questions just stated. Instead of defining cause as the constant antecedent, the determinism is conceived in the light of physical determinism in its strictest form. Thus the problem is created: are there laws of history? Does history obey laws? The problem is obscure, more metaphysical than logical; one tries to distinguish concretely different causalities (psychological, biological, even sociological), or else one opposes *historical contingency* with *natural necessity*, and strives to find an intermediary between them.

Of course, the antecedents which are viewed as causes are not the same in the different sciences, and in this sense historical determinism is psychological (*mobiles*, *motifs*, ideas are causes here). The mechanism of societies appears to differ from that of the physical phenomena as the latter, in its turn, differs from the life process. The comparison of these various determinisms is not without interest, but either essences are considered—and we shall leave aside transcendental considerations—or else the organized experiments are compared. It is not the idea of cause that changes, but the construction of the concepts, the organization of the connections. It was, then, *after*, not *before*, the logical analysis that the comparison of the structures should have been made. The latter are discovered as much by scientific observation as by phenomenological description.

Let us first examine the arguments of those who would rule cause out of the world of history. They may be reduced to two propositions: it is said either that the successions of historical fact exclude connections of cause to effect, or else that one cannot succeed in determining, given the nature of events, any isolable regularities.

We shall immediately throw out the first argument. Between cause and effect there is not only a constant bond; from the motive to the act, from the principle to the consequences, the mind discovers an intrinsic intelligibility (and it is possible that this intelligibility is found at all levels). But this intelligibility is not incompatible with necessity, which is not always of the mechanistic or physical type; the consequence, in history, does not correspond to the antecedent as does the motion of the ball to the blow it has received, or the expanding of a body to surrounding heat. Regular consecutiveness is the indispensable and sufficient condition. Of course there is no causal relation between the terms of an equation: $2 + 2$ is not the cause of 4. When the historian is dealing with ideas as such, and when he ends up with rational systems, cause disappears. But it would be enough to reduce these systems to psychic data in order to substitute, for the valid connections, habits of thought, which are historically peculiar and under the jurisdiction of determinism.

More serious are the other arguments, which invoke the contingent, individual, free, nature of events and, as a result, the impossibility of stating laws comparable to those governing nature. But this conflict is part and parcel of an already outmoded epistemology. Science no longer recognizes those absolute rules which, like the decree of a Creator, would force themselves on the world. As a matter of fact, either one is satisfied with approximate macroscopic relations constructed by the mind, or else one imagines the microscopic structure of matter; and then, far from arriving at the real atom, the scientist moves from one connection to another, and the final uncertainty is created by the intervention of the observer. In either case, one ends with comparison; it will be easier to accept the fact that all historical relations are elaborated with the assistance of a conceptual form of expression. In both cases, the final fragment and the whole elude objective knowledge, as though the intellect were forever banned from attaining an object fully satisfying it.

We have no intention, however, of denying the differences. The three terms 'contingent', 'individual', 'free', designate, metaphysically, metaphorically as it were, three characteristics of human development. Historical determinism, a retrospective organization of the facts based on the events, is alien to the alternative of necessity—contingency.[65] The historian would encounter this antithesis, understood in its strict sense, only if he rose above reality, above his situation as a scientist imprisoned in his own time, and as a man condemned to remain within the totality. On the contrary, if contingency and necessity, like accident and regularity, are opposed, it remains true that in the formal as well as in the practical sense, accident plays a special part in history.

In the same way, the metaphysics of the individual has nothing to do with the logical problem of historical causality. If absolute unity is attributed to the person (either individual or collective), actions or periods cannot be reduced to laws; each moment will express in its own way this unique unity. If, again, we set aside this metaphysics, all we have to do is observe and describe: men, in fact, are relatively closed wholes. Each has his own way of reacting, and if we get down to the level of the individual decision, it is often explained by the originality of the character rather than by general rules or by the circumstances. Practically speaking, the historian, except for the biographer, fits the act into the milieu. Supposing that the latter does not account for the act, the historian introduces as accident the part played by personality. He cares little for the metaphysics of the individuality; he analyses behaviours, their sources and results, and fixes the limits of sufficient and accidental relations.

If it is a question of a more extensive individuality represented by a nation or culture, he takes into account, even in the organization of cause, the *total* nature of the parts. Regularities established in and for a given society cannot be generalized as such. Abstractly, three consequences follow: the field of validity of the relations is usually nar-

[65] We have used the word 'necessity', in the rest of the book, in the current sense of causal determinism, except in the chapter devoted to Simiand, where we considered a categorical necessity, one at least partially rational.

rower; the normal conditions under which that validity is confirmed are more exact and complex; and finally, the causal connections (and especially the theoretical relations) sometimes come together into a system reflecting a historical construct.

In the same way we discard the doubts relative to freedom. Assuming that free will is admitted in its most traditional form, it would not affect the inquiry. As Max Weber pointed out, the typical act of free will is the reasonable one. Now, it is this act which is most understandable from the point of view of *motifs* and *mobiles*, the one most likely to recur in so far as the situation to which it corresponds may be repeated. Metaphysical freedom, then, compromises neither forecast nor explanation—rather the contrary.

It is natural that one who believes in freedom will tend to give less importance to deterministic interpretations. He will question their validity since, as he sees it, things might have been otherwise. But usually, without being fully conscious of it, the philosopher is thinking of a historical liberty having nothing to do with apparent metaphysical puzzles, that is, the efficacy of chance encounters, or the power of men (and especially of individual wills). The necessity he denies, which is entirely immanent, is one of institutions or of collective impulses. That there may be between metaphysical and historical necessity (or contingency) a sort of affinity we admit, but that is all. Physiological and psychological determinism would not keep certain individuals or humanity as a whole from rising up, perhaps victoriously, against blind forces or the tyranny of things.

* * * *

The real questions are *beyond* logic. They involve the autonomy and unity of determinism in history; and so far we have shown only its fragmentary and incomplete nature.

When the historian goes back from a fact which is to be explained to the antecedents, he spontaneously pays attention only to the variable data; he is almost never concerned with the relatively constant data (physical environment, race) which assuredly do not account for a given particular event, but which perhaps determine the general character of a history or at least one of its features. The sociological method must be used to show these influences, but at a level so macroscopic that verification is difficult, if not impossible. Professionally, the historian and the sociologist are interested in phenomena essentially historical and sociological. The historian tends to ignore causes which are transversal to the development (natural causes, race, and often population, except when there is a sudden variation in its density); the sociologist hesitates between denial and dogmatism, which usually express prejudice or ignorance, for the impossibility of separating the action from certain causes is not proof that the action is of little or no efficacy.

One of the uncertainties characteristic of the whole of historical determinism shows up here. How is this determinism itself to be explained? Does diversity of races produce variety of cultures? Generally speaking, it is environment that moulds mankind; or is it human heredity, as expressed in social environments—which themselves then seem to mould individuals? In short, is it the peculiar nature of social phenomena which gives an understanding of history? Between our questions and the answers which science can, in all strictness, furnish (comparisons which permit the opposition of man and environment or social conditions and race), there is a gap which metaphysics strives to fill.

The break is of course inevitable, but perhaps not so serious as one might be led to believe, for *the causes to be analysed merge with the terms which can be influenced.* Now these terms are first of all the social and historical facts which, in so far as politics is concerned, constitute both means and ends.

Science stops at the point where the philosopher assumes the rôle of the politician, where contemplation gives way to practice. The man of action functions on the level of the determinism in which he plays a part. The philosopher would like to understand it from a higher viewpoint. The practical man tries to weigh the possibilities created by or the influences acting on the relatively constant causes (or the transversal ones). The philosopher aims higher; he would like to weigh the efficacy of causes whose effects, always confused, are not easily or clearly discerned; he would like to embrace the whole, both social and historical, of a culture or an evolution.

* * * *

It is vain to ask whether history has an end, since Providence is no longer believed in. But it does not follow that the Hegelian Idea, a substitute for divine power, is condemned simultaneously with theological teleology. For Reason, whose Ruse is exposed by the philosopher, is perhaps merged with the rationality inherent in the chaos of history.

Everyone will agree that individuals obey their passions, that they get results they did not foresee or hope for, that men make their history unconsciously. The Ruse of Reason seems at first sight to express an aspect apparent to any observer of the actual process: the dissociation between the goals which the actors have in view and the results of their actions. This is the aspect which historical determinism, almost always macroscopic, grasps and organizes.

And so the problem of cause comes back, paradoxically, to one of finality. Historical events, transcendent over individuals, have been willed by no one. The two questions which occur are those suggested by the Ruse of Reason: are there *one* or *two* Ruses, a determinism of the whole or a number of partial determinisms? Is the Ruse even relatively intelligible, that is, could the result have been the goal of an intelligent will?

Causal research moves spontaneously in the direction of situations in which the personality disappears. Institutions and customs, historical movements (Christianity, National-Socialism), collective evolutions—in all these examples, private feelings are subordinate to communal passions, and individual conduct is subject to the goal assigned to all. So it is easy to describe those ruses by which men are sacrificed to ends which transcend them. But do these ends in their turn compose into an even virtual unity? Can they be compared with historical missions, which are reasonable as well as necessary? If mankind no longer recognizes either master or guardian, history has no unknown and fated end. But does man succeed in assigning himself a goal? Or can he at least, after the event, see the logic of what has taken place, without falling into the platitudinous and cowardly attitude of those who worship the outcome?

The peculiar thing about historical determinism is that it replaces the immediate understanding of the partial fact with another intelligibility, more doubtful, but at the same time superior to individuals and inherent in their association with each other, foreign to the individual consciousness and perhaps part and parcel of the human spirit. Determinism is inherent in reality and a construct of science, partial, and yet without limits set in advance.

The historian meets the final questions, products of theology but inevitable, viewing man in isolation. Science ends with philosophy, or rather, the two merge. The most absolute scientist spontaneously proceeds to organize fragmentary regularities, without which history would tend to dissolve into an incoherent plurality and lose the intelligible unity which defines it.

CONCLUSION

Causality and Probability

In the epistemology of the natural sciences, the two ideas of determinism and of probability are constantly compared. But it is important to distinguish the different values of this comparison.

1. The logic of induction is easily expressed in terms of probability. If both truth and reality are left out of account, only statements more or less probable remain. If, on the contrary, the probability is estimated by retaining (a) the idea of a correspondence between thought and object, (b) the idea of a truth which is more or less approached, then the probability will denote the divergence between the present and the final result, in which verification would attain certainty and approximation absolute exactness. Even in this *subjective probability*, the concocted schema steps in. Probability increases with the number and diversity of experiments, because the coincidences, which at the beginning would be apparent confirmations, would represent accidents more and more rare (the equivalent of an unusual series in a game of roulette).

2. The probability in errors of measurement is subjective; here the constructed schema intervenes directly. It is admitted that multiple causes determine small errors, some in one direction, some in the other; it is thus that the variation of readings from a certain ideal of precision is explained (e.g. the variations of height in a line of pure ancestry).

3. On the contrary, Mendelian probability is *objective*, in the sense that it assumes that reality has a fortuitous structure, which is the exact reflection of the artificial schema. As a matter of fact, the procedure is from observed results to assumed schema. There must be an argument along the lines of probability (subjective) to conclude the mechanism of the transmission of the sexes by their distribution (consequently the excessive variation between results and theoretical calculation demands a cause, that is, the discovery of some factor favouring a certain combination).

Mendelian logic is in practice complicated by the fact that a series of hypotheses (lethal factors, genetic changes, etc.) which are needed to account for results not in agreement with the forecasts, are added to the simple concocted schema. The further addition of reasonings of probability, from first results to the schema, then from the schema accepted to aberrant causes, then from those causes to new singularities (all these interpretations being in some way the reflection of numerical data) sometimes gives rise to doubts. One wonders how Mendelianism could be denied since it is becoming more complicated as new data are discovered. But this addition, it seems to us, expresses in a special way the essential unity of idea and fact in the experimental sciences. (Let us add that cytologic examination often confirms hypotheses drawn from statistics.)

4. Finally, probability—and this is the most common occurrence of the idea today—again comes into physics under a double aspect. The fortuitous microscopic structure (atoms, the law of large numbers) serves to account for observed macroscopic laws. Moreover, the impossibility of determining either the position or energy of the electron is expressed in terms of probability; on the elementary level, a necessity ordinarily put in terms of the change in the object inevitably caused by the intervention of the subject.

We easily find the equivalent of the systematic use, in the social sciences, of probabilities. The elimination of accidents in order to demonstrate totalities involves reasonings like those of the theory of errors. There is no reason why, within an area, the other factors of variation should not balance each other (in the case, for example, of suicide).

Besides, a certain number of sociological problems are like those met with in biology, such as that of finding the structure of the real, based on numerical results. In both cases, the main difficulty is the same: the interpretation of the statistics, the understanding of the phenomena beyond the figures. The comparison might even be carried further. The opposition between Galton's conclusions and those of the geneticists, the attempt to discern the influence of environment (a fortuitous structure, the plurality of independent causes, isolated by resorting to pure descent) and that of genes (a fortuitous structure of Mendelian type) both recall the difficulties met with by sociologists in expressing conceptually the observed co-variations and assigning responsibility to the various influences.

Of course the nature of the classification is still different in the two cases. The sociologist is no more able than the biologist to discover a collective reality (even one of hereditary make-up) based on individual cases. But the methodological necessity combines, in the case of the sociologist, with the specific nature of the facts, from which there results the special significance of statistics in the social sciences, a significance which is also variable with periods and collectivities; a very great significance in our mass societies (in the dual sense that the societies are very numerous and that individuals are in many respects uniform), a significance of minimum importance in societies where the personality, concrete and incomparable, plays its part.

We have thus progressed from the third to the fourth chapter, since the sociologist, like the biologist or physicist, analyses the changing relations between the micro- and macro-scopic. The microscopic here is on the level of the observer who constructs the macroscopic, or is subject to its power. For that matter, the comparison between atomic and economic theory is trite and for the most part inexact. Not only do personalities not collide with each other like atoms in a gas chamber; not only are they thrown off balance and bound together by collective passions, but also, even *de jure*, even in the ideal simplification, the structure of the reality is different. Broad economic trends are diffused throughout relatively homogeneous multiple systems; prices act as conductors because profit depends on price, and industry on profit, but in this mechanism, human tendencies play an indispensable rôle.

The equivalent of inductive probability is still to be found. We seem to glimpse two sorts—the inference from retrospective determinism and the induction from generalities. But in this instance, the analogy masks a real opposition. Probability depends not so much on extrapolation, which is essentially uncertain, of a verified relation, as on a sort of intrinsic complexity of reality. The event, which comes before the constructed fact, entails an uncertainty which the historian acknowledges in going back to the moment of the decision. This sort of probability also stems from the antinomy between partial and global. To show retrospectively the special quality of the event, the influence of the individual or the moment must be stressed by opposing it to the partial necessities. From another viewpoint, the unreality of necessary relations brings us back to the antithesis of the part and the whole, for if causal connection coincides with the series as observed only by losing entirely its general nature, it is because the constellations showing regularity are unique and because each of them is a part of a historical totality both unique and relatively one. So, probability would, in this case, be the result of the conflict between the *necessity of classification* and the *impossibility of isolation*.

The escape from this antinomy is either by relaxing the connection until probability is reached (the cause favours the effect or makes it more or less probable), or by rising, in the organization of the terms, to a macroscopic level, so that the concrete particularities are eliminated to begin with and the totalities become comparable because they are defined only by general features. Consequently, the two oppositions of the general and the singular, of the personal and the collective are again dependent on both historical curiosity and reality, oppositions which are *de jure* and *de facto* distinct, but the interdependence of which is not cancelled by the distinction. The antithesis of partial and global, that is of the individual versus history, is again encountered. So, it is not by chance that the last *Part* of this Section has ended with the concept of the *Ruse of Reason*. In the same way that the study of understanding ended with the question as to the ability of a consciousness to grasp the whole intellectual world, so the study of cause ends with the acknowledgement that probability applies to all causal formulae, because the individual tries to understand a macroscopic determinism. The same difference in size (reversed) which separates the physicist from the electron cuts the historian off from his object. In proportion as he rises to a higher level, he has more difficulty in apprehending the reality. Moreover, perhaps the failure expresses the illusory nature of the attempt. For the partial movements finally to be composed into one single movement, would it not be necessary for some integral vision or some providential will to lend reality to what, for man in isolation, is only the projection of a dream? The whole would become actual in an infinite mind.

GENERAL CONCLUSION OF SECTION III

The Limits of Causal Objectivity and of Historical Causality

In conclusion, we have only to compare our results with the guiding principles stated in the Introduction. To characterize the two inquiries—the singular and the general—we spoke of the intention of the judge and of the scientist. These two provisory definitions emerge from our discussion confirmed and rectified. Confirmed, because the judge, by postulate, tries to attribute the fact to an actor. So, instead of considering the global situation, he dissociates the antecedents; instead of acknowledging necessity, he limits himself to the moment and keeps only to the culprit, that is, he is concerned only with one isolatable datum without which the fact would not have occurred (as it did occur). But this intention is not only the judge's—it is also the historian's, who refuses to disregard unique circumstances; and it is the attitude of the practical man, who as a matter of principle sets the power of the forward looking and willing individual against the anonymous power of things. Depending on circumstances and on selection, it will be the judge, the historian, or the man of action, who will be considered. The investigation by the judge, having to do with the origins of the war; the historian's, which will inquire into the causes of occidental capitalism; the question asked by the man of action, both the one and the other, and also the one concerned with the rôle of leaders, of accidents and coincidences.

In the same way, the analysis of natural and social causes, the setting up of statistics and their interpretation—all this labour is quite natural to the scientist, who is concerned with regularities and likenesses. But how would the practical man anticipate the results of his decisions if partial relations did not determine the effects (at least the probable ones) of a generalizable fact? How would the judge arrive at his verdict unless he imagined, in terms of verified rules, what would have happened if the accused had acted differently? How would the historian show the influence of a group or of an original element if he were unable to estimate the particular efficacy of the other antecedents? The scientist's intention is, then, not unlike that of the historian and the practical man. But we have characterized it as truly scientific, because the politician, when all is said and done, tries to make his choice in a unique situation; the historian uses generalities, but he aims at the event, the development, or the incomparable totality. Only the scientist, strictly speaking, could be satisfied with regularities, even doubtful, scattered ones; he would resign himself to tracing the limits of knowledge to the point where the validity of laws vanishes.

But in reality, if the man of action is content with these two sorts of results, combined, but not united, the historian and the scientist always work out a subjective and decisive direction of the line of research towards a materialistic philosophy of history. This confusion is easily solved by reflection, but the confusion, as long as it has not been understood why a uniquely causal science is impossible, is a natural outflow of the dialectic of thought. In order to organize events and regularities in terms of each other and in a global order, and lacking any objective systematization, any science of history becomes philosophical; and that is why the philosopher's intention does not coincide with the two analytical inquiries, but transcends and seeks to reconcile them.

Thus are the limits of causal thought and its objectivity specified. We have shown exactly what *free* methods will lead to the setting up of cause in history or sociology in obedience only to logical and probable laws. At the same time we have shown the extreme extension of retrospective and fragmentary determinism. But, the *limits of causality account for the limits of objectivity.* Since no science of cause would be able to grasp the whole or be applied to a general development, the *organization of experience*, anterior to verification of constants, *conceptual structure*, inseparable from macroscopic study, and *synthesis of incoherent results* (inevitable in any continuous account, in any theory of society), must necessarily depend on other norms, must obey other principles. Historical determinism is hypothetically objective because it includes only part of the reality and could not, even by endless investigation, arrive at the total object.

SECTION IV

HISTORY AND TRUTH

INTRODUCTION

THE ANTITHESIS of the two terms *history* and *truth* is the only theme of this final Section.

We go back first to our basic question: to what extent can we reach an objective understanding of the past? But new questions inevitably come up. We have shown that, for partial histories, the real development governs the development of the retrospection: in that case it is the former that we must determine by means of a theory of the intellectual universe. If we limit ourselves, as we shall do, to general history, we must still specify the nature of the presuppositions and the rhythm according to which they change. Now, the theory of history is one with a theory of man, that is, a philosophy. History and philosophy are doubly inseparable: on the one hand, the evolution of historical interpretations would be subject to the philosophical interpretation; on the other, social changes would determine conceptions of the world, changes which are both causes and in part object of those conceptions.

In our first *Part* we shall assemble the results of our foregoing studies in order to set the limits of historical objectivity. In *Part II* we shall explain and discuss the doctrine of relativism, with a special attempt to specify for philosophies of history the meanings and limits of relativity. In the last *Part*, we shall consider the meaning of the essential fact that man has a history, with a view to showing the anthropological conclusions to which our study leads, and the questions with which it ends.[66]

First Part

THE LIMITS OF THE SCIENCE OF THE PAST

WE PROPOSE, in this *Part*, to answer the question we have asked as to the objectivity of historical knowledge. Since the results we shall show are, as it were, either dispersed or implicit in the preceding pages, our real task is to sum up and co-ordinate our preceding studies.

The last two Sections are quite independent of each other. We have

[66] This whole Section is only an outline. It points out the problems and suggests some solutions. To go deeper into the problems and to demonstrate the solutions we should have to exceed the limit we have set, and relate these thoughts to their beginning (the historical situation), and carry them to their conclusion (a philosophical concept of being).

often noted the necessary collaboration between the two methods, but, logically, the choice between them was still valid: either history links events and ideas according to the logic intrinsic in reality, or, it elaborates causal relations along the line of the regularity of sequences, without taking into account the intelligibility of man's desires. We now abandon this analysis. We shall try to interpret as a whole the construction and account of history.

Our first object, then, will be to compare understanding and cause. How are intelligible relations and partial determinism organized? Only then shall we be able to set the limits of historical objectivity, in the same way that we have, above, indicated those of understanding and of causality.

The outline of this *Part* is thus traced. Formal comparison, then material comparison of the two methods, will be our concern in the first two chapters: in the last two we shall try to show the limits of objectivity and the mutual involvement of science and philosophy.

I. UNDERSTANDING AND CAUSALITY

THE CONSIDERATION of Sections II and III together brings up many problems. The *problem of fact*: how do understanding and cause complement and combine with each other? The *logical problem*: does an intelligible relation require causal justification to take on scientific dignity? The *philosophical problem*: the historian or sociologist trying to establish causal connections deals with historical facts as though they were unintelligible. If that is the case, is it not for causality to step in, when understanding's resources are at an end, when the course of human development seems to resemble a physical determinism or a biological evolution? In other words, what is the place in the structure of the world of history, of rationality and necessity?

In this chapter we consider only the first two questions. We shall try to show the independence and inter-relationship of the two views, both in theory and in practice.

* * * *

We shall take as our starting point the idea, often expressed by Max Weber, of the indispensable union of cause and understanding. This statement seems to conflict with the thesis we have proposed by developing the study of understanding without appeal to other procedures. If every relationship must be, at one and the same time, both *sinnadäquat* and *kausaladäquat*, conformable to a logic (either psychological or intellectual) and to an observed regularity, no proposition would be scientifically acceptable, because of the mere fact that it would be intelligible.

Following Weber's examples, causal verification would perform three different functions. It should make specific the transition from type to special case, from rational to real, and from the plurality of likely interpretations to the true interpretation. Let us recall the examples already given: resentment leads to depreciation of higher values, an ethic similar to Christianity *may*, then, be explained by the wretchedness of the weak or the enslaved. But, to conclude the actual historical events by the psychological connection would call for a proof beyond the method of the order of historical intelligibility. Besides, a behaviour such as that of the 'economic man' who gets rid of bad money and keeps good money, is in itself reasonable; the theory fully satisfies the scientist, but it must be in agreement with actual human behaviour. More generally, all statistical co-variations call for understanding, and all forms of understanding for statistical confirmation. Finally, the interpretations given by the observer of other people's acts is not free of a sort of essential ambiguity. In a certain situation, no two people act the same, nor does the same person at two moments in his life; many impulses are always in conflict in everyone's heart. Apparently Weber conceived the necessity, in order to overcome this uncertainty, of a proof which would ignore verisimilitude, would observe the facts, and calculate the probabilities.

As always, Weber's examples illustrate real difficulties. But logically, the difficulties are incomparable with each other, and a basic distinction is not made.

It is true that the historian often hesitates between several interpretations which seem equally plausible. That is a special characteristic of the human disciplines, a characteristic involving important consequences in so far as method is concerned (in particular, the multiplicity of economic theories calls for a decision). But the verification authorizing choice is not always the same as a causal analysis.

It is either a matter of explaining a singular series of events, and in such a case the historian tries to show that his interpretation agrees with the documents. The truth of the proposition depends on the conformity of the account with the events. Or, it is a question of a general relation, and then cause comes in, but only in order to confirm the regularity (statistics suffice for co-variations within a given society, methodical comparisons are prescribed for sequences, either frequent or necessary, of wider generality). In other words, correspondence with the facts is still indispensable for any scientific judgment, since it constitutes the principle and guarantee of truth. The causal method is indispensable when the sociologist attempts to set up rules or laws.

Let us go back to the first example, the transition from the psychological type to the historical instance. Is it correct to say that the historian follows this deductive path? In practice he reconstructs what took place, tries to penetrate the consciousness of the actors, and arrives at the type in proportion as the interpretation, which is taken from the documents, becomes simpler and shows the most frequent or the most characteristic motives. As a result, the interpretation, progressively elaborated, has no need of posterior verification; it immediately possesses the validity it is capable of acquiring, even though it never loses the ambiguity which is bound up with the understanding of human life.

At times, the historian seeks a truth of a different nature: he tries to show that the effective *mobile* was indeed the one he has indicated (in the case of an individual behaviour); in that case he will proceed according to the schema of historical causality, and will weigh the importance of the various antecedents, etc. Or again, having turned sociologist, he will try to establish a general proposition: for example, the lower classes have a special affinity for a certain sort of metaphysics, the oppressed cling through resentment to democratic doctrines. Verification of constancy of succession or of the solidarity of the two terms will develop throughout a series of comparisons.

Weber, then, must have committed a double error. He must have failed clearly to distinguish intelligible propositions, the nature and end of which is the putting into words of what has been, and judgments of causality implying an at least virtual generality. In addition, he reversed the order of scientific procedures: the historian does not go from the type to the particular; he draws from the facts (or the documents) the type corresponding to the individual or collective conduct and which, considered as an intelligible interpretation, requires no other proof.

These distinctions, however abstract, have a real import. Let us consider, for example, Weber's own work on the Protestant spirit and capitalism. The discussions stirred up by this famous theory often lack clarity because the three phases of the work are not distinguished. First, Weber reconstructs, intelligibly, the capitalist and the Protestant mentalities. The ideal type he uses accentuates the original characteristics of *Western* capitalism in contrast with the other forms of capitalism, i.e. a free choice of a concept, a substitute for a concept of essence, which represents one historical individual and states in clear terms *one* of the problems of cause suggested by the complex totality. In the same way, starting with certain theological beliefs, Weber makes one way of living and thinking understandable. These two interpretations are valid as they stand, even leaving determinism entirely out of account. They are true to the extent that they conform to the facts; it is essential that the inferences were actually drawn from theology to life by the Protestants, and that the main characteristics of capitalism, as isolated by Weber, permit the reconstruction of capitalism as a whole, as it now is.

Moreover, Weber tries to establish two causal propositions: religious convictions determined Protestant behaviour, and the latter (consequently, indirectly, the convictions) exercised an influence on the formation of capitalism. To prove the first, he proceeds by reasoning and comparison: when situations were not yet capitalistic, individuals were already so. Protestant groups held only their ethics in common, and that alone accounts for the way they acted together. Besides, he tried to show by studying other civilizations, that capitalism required, in order to develop, certain intellectual conditions. The strongest criticisms bear on these two proofs—the interpretation of the Protestant spirit and of the capitalist mind (from their relationship) stand in any case. Even if the capitalistic behaviour of Protestants is explained by other causes, an at least possible influence of morals and religion will be admitted. Finally, supposing the last statement as denied, it is still true that certain Protestants have thought of their lives or justified them in these terms: now, is not the historian's supreme goal to understand the world in which men of the past lived?

Weber would doubtless have acknowledged these distinctions, but would have added that understanding or conceptual expression prepares for true science, which is always and only causal. The first step seemed to him tainted with a subjectivity inevitable and legitimate, but, as he saw it, that subjectivity was excluded by positivist knowledge. Now this solution seems to us both imaginary and inaccurate. In the above example, causality follows understanding, understanding puts the subjective questions, causality furnishes the objective answers. But understanding, if it sometimes serves to introduce the search for determinism, is nonetheless independent when it is limited to reconstructing the events or narrating the sequence of facts. Since it is singular, it in no way borrows its validity from the verification of cause. So then, either it is of itself objective, or else it depends entirely on this decision which Weber strove to reject at the start. Even more, it would infect causality with its subjectivity, rather than acquire from it a total objectivity. As a matter of fact, the relations established depend on the ideas used, on the divisions effected, which, conforming to certain regularities, do not eliminate the possibilty of other relations and other interpretations. Weber's logical solution, then, is valid only in cases where analysis of cause is exterior to conceptual expression; it is not valid either for independent understanding, or for the synthesis of understanding and cause. We have shown the autonomy; it now remains to describe the synthesis.

* * * *

We need not enumerate all the forms of explanation in history, which is not exhausted by the antithesis of understanding versus cause; the antithesis indicates, rather, the two possible modalities of any explanation. We shall merely describe, in a chiefly theoretical manner, the way the two procedures work together in history and in the social sciences.

In the first volume of his *Histoire de la Révolution Française*, Mathiez uses the word 'cause' just once, in connection with the *Assignats*. The depreciation of the bonds, even though set off by measures taken voluntarily (over-circulation), even though related to a change of opinion (loss of confidence) proceeds from a complex mechanism governed by nameless forces sprung from social reactions and relations which were both foreseeable and unintentional. This is a confirmation of the interpretation we have given of determinism and which stands as valid for specifically historical cause, either singular or elementary.

When an act is surprising because it seems ill adapted to the circumstances or because it is an innovation with respect to the past (environmental or individual), the historian tends to go back to the moment of the decision so as to repeat, with the actor himself, the leap from possible to real. Even in that case, as a contemporary and confidant of his heroes, he already shows the gradual transcendence of the development over individuals: destiny, for long uncertain, open to a different future, seems fixed when one starts from a certain date.

In the social sciences, the two procedures do not complement each other; they continually collaborate, according to the pattern indicated by Weber. But here again, the order in which they come is conclusive. As long as the effort is to verify rational constructions, there is no break with the evidences of daily living. The variation between the ideal type and the concrete is noted, without any choice of schema, since it is assumed in advance that reality will not exactly conform to either. On the contrary, the scientist who examines the data without prejudice, manages to establish relations he could not have anticipated, though he may be able, later, to explain them psychologically. He has the means to effect a discrimination between the theoretical hypotheses, even if he does need to show by reasoning the logic of the determinism which he has abstracted from the facts. To take only already analysed examples, let us cite the case of suicide among soldiers, a phenomenon as easily understandable as it is hard to predict, and Simiand's application, going from statistical experience to conceptual elaboration.

In an introduction to the social sciences, this last function of cause should be made of first importance. In history it is less apparent, because partial determinisms intrude into the whole movement and remain subordinate to understanding. In addition, the historian, because he tries to stay close to life, generally makes little use of sociological abstractions. He sticks to tracing events, sympathizing with conscious minds, and, by selection and organization of the data, to making existences and careers intelligible. When the action disappears along with its possibilities, when macroscopic regularities are neglected, merely for the sake of individuals, analysis of causes no longer has a reason for existence. Things happened thus, men were such and such; the mind finds satisfaction in contemplation or participation, as indifferent to uncertainty about what will be, as it is to the fatality of what has been. One then conceives a history entirely of understanding, but it becomes more difficult to conceive a uniquely causal social science. Once the co-variations have been shown, it still remains to interpret them, and the most positivist sociologist, the one most faithful to Durkheim's rules will never fail. In Simiand's work the final unity of the two methods appears with particular clearness. Causality based on statistical experimentation, and objective psychology taken from behaviours, combine so closely that human tendencies and gold reserves appear, in turn, as authentic causes. In reality, they are both determinants; modern economics shows this original structure. Men are subject to the law of things, since the amount of money, by means of prices (and especially world prices), governs the rhythm of activity, but it is men, who by their reactions to situations, create the history which they neither understand nor accept.

* * * *

This last example shows us the conclusion to which the formal comparison leads, and the question to which it leads. It is often said that the historian, unlike other scientists, considers a special type of causes, *motifs* or *mobiles*. These statements seem to us inaccurate, for the historian, when he tries to establish causes, reviews the antecedents, things, and institutions as well as the intentions of the leaders, and the mass sentiments. But it is true that he is always preoccupied with understanding the psychological mechanism by which the action of causes has been exerted. If this curiosity were non-existent, if the living ceased to be interested in the dead, history would be like the story of stars or animals. Starting with traces of consequences, we should try to infer the fleeting reality of a species which had disappeared.

Besides, in the example of economics, we include both men and environment. The *structure* of a totality authorizes a complete understanding. Now, is not the historian's ambition to grasp the structure of the whole of history? The question we have stated several times again comes up. Does the combination in reality of necessary relations and understandable conducts, and the collaboration of understanding and causality, make it possible to transcend the plurality of retrospective rationalizations and fragmentary determinisms?

II. THE STRUCTURE OF THE WORLD OF HISTORY

Plurality and Totality

WE SAW, in Section II, that after the event, witnesses, actors, and historians, work out different interpretations of the same events. In order to avoid multiple accounts, one tries to establish necessary connections. But partial necessity, in its turn, leaves us confronted with differing retrospections. Now, constantly we have reserved the hypothesis that global determinism would not be a construct of the scientist, but the law of history. In that case would not our conclusion again be challenged?

We shall try to show that no method, either synthetic or dialectic, resolves plurality into unity. In the facts as well as in the reality made up of facts and ideas, the historian finds a multiplicity, a reflection of the complexity of both human nature and the world of history.

* * * *

We have already used the term *structure* in connection with economic life. Apart from the distorted simplifications suggested by comparison with the atomic structure of gases, we have noted a certain number of characteristic features. In the first place, individuals are found in situations which recur regularly, a regularity due to two circumstances: the series of actions and reactions which brings back the initial conditions; second (and as important as this self-regulation) the effect of totalities, that is, the subordination of limited markets to wider markets and the predominant influence of certain prices and certain (monetary) factors. In the second place, human impulses are reduced, if not to the unity of one exclusive tendency, at least to a small number of tendencies in hierarchical arrangement and objectively observable (to the extent that the psychology of various social groups intervenes, it lessens or eliminates the regularity of the cycles, and increases the singularity of each of them). Is it conceivable that the whole of society offers such a structure? Doubtless it is not impossible to describe a society statically in a similar way but, either the description will apply to the ideally capitalist society, or it is the equivalent of a cross section. It shows how a certain society tends to maintain itself and to be reproduced. Just as the place in the process of production mostly determines social standing and class distinction in the capitalist regime, so are ways of life and thinking, or political constitutions tied in with the organization of the economy. But as soon as the living standard is considered, allowance must be made for preferences or value judgments, which are not reducible to a material determinism, *a fortiori* if the gradual change in social relations is considered.

Now—and here is the main point—neither a whole society nor one development could comprise a structure comparable to that of the economy. One does not find the equivalent of controlling prices; the groupings are *sums* or *quantitative amounts*; there is no regularity which brings back the same situations, nor any simplification of human tendencies. Political reactions vary with traditions or with the disposition of peoples. In their decisions, the masses and the individuals commit themselves, and the choice of one faction or the other, however primitive the *mobile* may seem, creates a margin of indeterminism. Consequently, history as a whole knows neither cycles nor secular change. Or, at least, they do not follow the economic pattern; they do not stop in advance, the consequences of accidents. The structure of the world of history is deterministic. Historical forces, like causes, cannot be reduced to the unity of an institution or the primacy of a *mobile*.

Do we thus adopt the subjective thesis in opposition to objectivism? The latter implies that the environment determines the man or that man's reaction be univocal and foreseeable. These conditions are given in certain sectors of society, but not in life as a whole (not in individual any more than in collective life). Neither the reality of partial systems nor the objectivity of fragmentary determinisms excludes the incoherence of partial facts and the uncertainty of the whole.

We arrive at similar results if we go back to the other problem of structure, the one concerning the connection between ideas and the real. We have analysed to begin with the plurality of the systems of interpretation, which led us to two philosophical conclusions (we set aside the methodological results). Intellectual values are, *as such*, transcendent over their origins and over all reality. The mind is a creative power, not a mere reflection of the world, or the expression of irrational forces. But, we had purposely set aside the possibilities of causal explanation. As a matter of fact, none of the foregoing remarks make it possible to specify in advance the limit of influence of a period or a society on a work. Objectified, taken as a series of psychological states, the work may be related to external causes, without possibility of affirming the existence of an unexplained residue. But this determination, *integral on a certain level*, does not compromise intrinsic meanings, because it ignores them.

In consequence, we should abandon Scheler's two formulae, the independence of the *So-Sein* as well as the powerlessness of ideas, metaphysical expressions of a *given* both more complex and simpler. There are no pure actions, really separable from experienced time duration, but to the extent to which *intentions* obey the laws of a specific logic, they are *de jure*, autonomous (and their contents are equally so for one who regrasps them). The plurality of created worlds, the duality of the psychological and the intellectual do not contradict the indefinite extension of historical inquiry, even though it were causal.

In the same way, the idea by itself is impotent—a statement which does not represent a proposition of fact, but a simple identity. A truth unadhered to is vain; when it has become a conviction, either individual or collective, it is, like any human reality, a historical force. It is useless, impossible, to estimate its efficacy in advance. Not only because such a question admits no general solution, but also it is badly stated, and dissociates inseparable terms.

There is no self-interest that does not disguise itself as an idea or justify itself, no passion which does not claim a goal either ideal or historically necessary. If rules are formulated it will inevitably be found that, by and large, feelings rather than reason, the environment rather than men's desires, control the historical process. But such generalities are as unanswerable as they are useless. To evaluate correctly the influence of ideas it would be necessary to take a special case and measure the difference between what a historical change accomplished and how it would have turned out if animated by another ideology. Or again, it would be necessary to isolate the consequences of a pure idea or reasoning (for example, to what extent have theories of welfare, independently of circumstances and psychological tendencies, dictated a certain conduct?). In a word, we should again find problems of historical cause which allow only particular and probable solutions.

Once again we end with plurality—plurality of intellectual worlds, of ideal as well as of real forces. A dialectic plurality, if you wish; between conditions and human desires, between the reality and the idea, there is established by mutual action a sort of relationship comparable not to a brute determinism or a sterile reproduction, but to the creative reaction of a conscious being.

* * * *

This structure may be qualified as *dialectic* in still another sense: dispersion does not exclude unity, nor does discontinuity exclude totalities (ambiguous ones).

The fragmentation of determinism is explained formally by the contradiction between the system and the analysis (which is essential in any causal thinking), materially by the impossibility of stopping the results of an accident or of composing historical movements. But on the other hand, any society shows at least unity of interactions between groups and institutions; order and authority which are indispensable for any collective life, and the orderly change which carries a nation or civilization along. The reality, then, is always total since at each moment and all through the duration it reveals a singular organization, lends itself to global understandings and yet eludes a single synthesis.

In the order of ideas we observe a similar opposition between the unity of man and the autonomy of intellectual universes. A concrete *theory* of a special history would show the extent to which man entirely commits himself in a partial activity. Is it true that in science everything takes place as though (as Dilthey put it) the body of knowledge had been separated from the living context, as though the subject were merged with the transcendental self? Outside influences favour or inhibit progress, they direct curiosity, perhaps they suggest certain concepts, certain representations taken from collective living; they do not change the results themselves. On the contrary, the content of a work of art is without doubt inseparable from the technical means, from the organization of society, from the intention of the man and the artisan; it is essentially historical not because it emerged in time but because it expresses historical beings and is addressed to them.

The dialectic of plurality and totality is, finally, found if we consider, for an individual or a society, the whole context of the works or of the life. The personal style of an individual all through his life, or the peculiar character of peoples, which is capable of lasting but not being revived, the single *motif* of each era which Dilthey tried to get at through the most varied activities and creations—all these unities have in common their reality, which is both incontestable and indeterminate. They are fragmentary for those living at the time, and if the historian can complete them he must still justify his retrospective transfiguration.

It is conceived that, depending on ages and social structures, plurality and totality may be differently composed. A society entirely rationalized according to Cournot's concept, or voluntarily planned along Marxist lines, would solve or at least minimize the incoherence of the historical process. A totalitarian society in which art, science, and religion would be genuinely integrated into the national-socialist conception of the world or adapted to the system of dialectic materialism, would extend and confirm the coherence of cultures. In neither case would the nature of the final unity be changed, since it would always be merged with the experience as lived and thought—that is, the systematic arrangement of all activities from labour to religion.

* * * *

This opposition of plurality and complex unities is as conclusive as that of chance and regularities, of development and evolution: all three together show the structure of human history. The third corresponds to the double effort at truth and the understanding of single human groupings; the one taken from Cournot's doctrine, and met with again in our study of chance and causality, expresses two of the fundamental characteristics of the reality in which the practical man acts. As for the one just explained, it specifies the conditions for political decision. No doctrine, indeed, is more dangerously utopian than one bringing together reasonable elements. One assumes the right freely to imagine an ideal society made up of fragments borrowed from the most varied regimes; one refuses to see that each social order has its greatness and its drawbacks, and that willingly or not one chooses the whole. As a corollary, the totalitarian thinking which would claim to make a whole society dependent on a single principle would fall into a fanaticism still more to be feared.

This opposition is no less important for the historian, not only because he tries to analyse the original organizations of the various civilizations, but because the concrete wholes denote the limits of legitimate and fertile abstractions and generalizations. To the extent that the capitalistic system is incomparable with any other economic system, the understanding of the system has more importance than the formal propositions claiming unlimited temporal or spatial application to it. In an operation of applied methodology, we ought to extend this study further. In this case, in conclusion, we shall merely make a philosophical observation. Our description ends, in a certain sense, with a material theory. The complexity of the world of history corresponds to a pluralist anthropology. Every totality is the imperfect work (retrospectively perfect) of a part of humanity; the complete unity would be the same as a goal placed at infinity. That goal would be the totality which the philosopher would embrace if man had exhausted his history, had stopped creating and put an end to his self-creation.

III. THE LIMITS OF HISTORICAL OBJECTIVITY

THE IDEA of *limits of objectivity* may be understood in three different ways. Either scientific propositions, beyond a certain extension, are no longer universally acceptable; or they are hypothetically objective, subject to a certain arbitrary selection verified by experiment; or, finally, all history is both objective and subjective according to the laws of logic and probability, but prejudiced in favour of an individual or a period which for that very reason could not demand universal agreement. In other words, where does science stop? At what point does it break away from decisions alien to positivist knowledge? How are presuppositions and empirical research combined?

It seems that in our survey we have here and there suggested one or another of these conclusions. Which one, in the last analysis, is true? Can they all be at the same time partially true?

* * * *

As a point of departure let us take again a human action and the two experiences, reciprocal and incomplete, of actor and spectator. Primitive accounts, of course, are those of witnesses or the parties concerned. Caesar was the first historian of the Gallic Wars, and the memoirs of contemporaries have the supreme privilege of presenting men and things just as they were observed and appreciated. These testimonies, though more living, are also more biased, in general, than those of the chroniclers or historians. They tend either towards intimate history, or towards special pleading or legend. The general telling the story of his campaigns may affect a sort of modesty about himself; the apologetic intention, however discreet it may be, even if all material facts are correct, nevertheless compromises the faithfulness of the interpretation. As for the intimate friends of the great man, they have the merit of bringing us closer to the historical personage, crystallized in his rôle, and the disadvantage of showing above all the backstage scenery. The great man was an individual just like others for most of his life. Each of his decisions was made in special circumstances and it is easy to see the influence of personal *motifs*. It is easy to make the transition from psychological lucidity to the liking for anecdote; one's ingenuity is taxed to discard myths, to reconstruct situations in all their prosiness.

This may be a legitimate reaction as long as it does not go too far and claim a sort of monopoly of truth. History's dimensions surpass plots, intrigues, scandalous or glittering chronicle. Royal historiographers are no more historians than are personal servants or courtiers. All of them furnish material and preserve the irreplaceable flavour of life.

The historian avoids these contrary biases because he subordinates the individual to his function and living experience to facts. He constructs the facts by first noting the results or global changes unknown by those living at the time. The *motifs* of the actors are generally inscribed in the completed actions, so that conceptual expression is free from the relativity of impressions (even though, on certain points, it is open to discussion and though the account by the conquered usually contradicts the conqueror's). Ambiguous if it gives the facts in a succession perhaps not the only one possible, the account approaches full objectivity in proportion as it tends to record only perceptible phenomena.

Whether it takes in a battle or a wider development (the French Revolution), understanding has the same characteristics, between mere juxtaposition of facts and their organization. Gradually the uncertainty becomes greater because the organization becomes more conclusive. For one interpretation to exclude absolutely all others, it should show necessity or rationality. Now, it can do no more than show probable successions. For though they do not prevent the building up of the world of history, the grouping of elements, the definition of facts, which become less and less reducible to pure substantiality, and the ambiguity of mental states and of contexts, all leave room for multiple and changing views.

So it is that the attempt is made to preserve in another way the prestige of impersonal understanding. Why not assemble the facts, established by the rules of criticism, using connections which are themselves objective, namely causal relations? There remains the question of the moment at which the problem of responsibilities will be faced, and the manner in which the division between antecedents and effects will be made. Nevertheless, historians and sociologists, unconscious of this difficulty, or at least indifferent to it, imagine that they have broken with the arbitrary procedure of narrators and psychologists. By abstraction and comparison, the sociologist tries to fix for a determined society, or for any society, regular sequences from natural to social fact, between social facts, between conditions and frequency and finally between two phenomena whose variations are quantitatively measurable. These relations, if we admit their verification by the rules of logic or probability, are valid for all who want truth, or else, practically speaking, for all who want *this* truth—that is, all who interpret the facts the same way and ask the same questions. A reservation which, purely theoretical for the scientist who is analysing the figures on suicide or birth, becomes conclusive for the historian who gets down to individual facts, or for the philosopher who is trying to take in the whole character of the development.

Determinism is always fragmentary; *instantaneous* if it is a matter of explaining one event, *partial* for explaining regularities. As for the laws to which some philosophers aspire, they lack probability to the extent that they are supported by ever rarer examples and more unlikely analogies; they isolate certain of these boundless evolutionary processes without certainty of encompassing either the decisive forces or the essential realities. There is no such thing as a systematization of cause, any more than there is a *primum movens* of history as a whole.

The three meanings we applied to the limits of objectivity, then, are applicable in turn. The logical relations, hypothetically objective because they depend on conclusive selection, become more and more arbitrary as they take in wider movements. But the global vision into which determinism fits is marked by a special intention which governs the choice of facts, the nature of concepts and the organization of relationships. This intention, as it widens the object, tends towards a final term which is the historian's concern. This is, when all is said and done, the present, which, being incomplete, is determined with reference to the future, imagined and unknown by the men who are destined to create it.

If we now consider, not the real atom, but the intellectual atom, we observe under another form the necessity of *appropriation*. An intellectual element is never contained within itself, never fixed; it needs an act of re-creation to bring it back to life—that is, to be again thought and felt by a mind. The interpreter commits himself—and his commitment, depending on the worlds involved, assumes a different value.

In a science characterized by an increasing approximation or, by accumulated knowledge, the historian needs only to reconstitute the approach of present conditions to trace an advancement. On the other hand, in the realm of philosophy, commitment implies a personal decision because there is no agreement about the nature of the universe. In these two cases, the historian, like the creator, must become a scientist or philosopher, but scientific theory is commonly recognized, as is the independence of truth; the theory of philosophy and of art is as variable as the present with which the past is related.

In no case is the psychology of production the same as the understanding of the monument. But the distinction in one case is due to the isolation of thought within the psychic context, in the other to the creative power of the individual as a whole. The goal of knowledge is determined, like the laws to which it is subject. In *gratuitous* works, there is complete liberty. So, the ambiguity applies to the definition of the intrinsic interpretation itself. This interpretation hesitates between the understanding as experienced, which again feels the beauty, the artistic understanding which tries to analyse the impression on the spectator or the structure of the object, the eternal or particular conditions of aesthetic values, and historical understanding which considers the human or spiritual attitude of which the works are the expression or transfiguration. All these forms of understanding are renewed with history; the first one because it is like the communication of two persons, always relative to each of them, the last two because, either isolated or brought together in a history of style, they partake at the same time of human contact, of conceptual expression, and of an unfinished development.

The history of philosophy is uncertain like the essence of philosophy, intermediary between discovery and creation, or both at once. It proceeds from man, an imperfect reality which it expresses or knows. The intrinsic interpretation, then, would apply to a historical meaning, a meaning either of origins or of object. Any political or moral doctrine may be reduced to the intention of an individual or of a group; inner understanding would show the truth (the present or desired state) of the individual or group. It is by the setting in a whole development, by the deepening of the historical meaning, that the transition is made from simplification to intellection. Or again, a true philosophy, that of the State for example, would contrast with an ideology by the fact that it would define a concept applicable to all special forms. Truth would merge with totality.

We made the distinction above between two forms of renewal of understanding: the *static renewal* which is due to the historian's otherness, and *historical renewal* linked to the perspective. The first condemns the effort to be contemporary to failure, the second dooms to relativity the attempt at global understanding. One gives expression to the infinite wealth of human types, the other to the imperfection of a world of which each fragment would be defined only in and by a whole universe. But, more profoundly, the final principle of the renewal lies beyond this opposition, in the freedom of the man who both creates and re-creates. The atom, like the whole, is inexhaustible in so far as it is a property of the mind.

Actual history and ideal history are, taken separately, not enough. They both refer to human history, the first because spiritual worlds come from man and in the final analysis are explained only by him, the second because events are interesting only in so far as they affect life. This total history demands, as does intellectual history, decisions which, as in actual history, control the conceptual organization and the direction of the development.

In the knowledge of others, uncertainty is due to the possible conflict between actions and consciousness of them, the personality or the behaviour and the individual's idea about it. In knowing a historical character, the difficulty is the same at first. But others are added, which come from the plurality of worlds at each moment, from the ambiguous relations between various human groups. Statically, where is the principle of unity of a totality to be grasped? In a perspective, how are common traits and original characteristics discerned? How are the singularities in a development including diverse periods and cultures to be brought together?

Apparently these three decisions are independent of each other, and the last one implies the other two, since it organizes the images of different times and the social comparisons within one evolution; but it is in reality primary in so far as it expresses man's own decision about himself by measuring himself against the whole of the past. Basically, it constitutes history (in the philosophical sense); history exists, as a matter of fact, as soon as there appears, with the permanence of a problem, the unity of a development directed towards an end. For a partial history it is necessary and sufficient for one activity to be common to all the collectivities; for a universal history, since community of interest could not extend to all activities, it would do for one of them to be accepted as characteristic of mankind's mission as a whole.

* * * *

These conclusions might be summed up as follows:

History may be treated as an objective reality, in which case knowledge is doomed to an indefinite progress towards an inaccessible end. Since the scholar tries to grasp the whole of each moment, the whole of the historical process, he resorts to a comprehensive understanding, but the latter steers clear of neither the particularity characterizing all ways of looking at things, nor the relativism accompanying the incompleteness of the movement when related to an ever new future.

Second, history can merge with the development of intellectual worlds. In this case the science of history originates and ends with the appropriation by the living mind of ancient works. It is a means by which the individual may situate himself and what he accomplishes in the whole evolution in which he collaborates. The review of the intellectual past is one aspect of each individual's awareness of his historical destiny.

Finally, history is like a human life, and knowledge, like knowledge of self and of others, is directed by a decision with a view to the future and understands others only with reference to the subject. This dual dialectic is indefinitely pursued, as the historian discovers himself by discovering what the world is and what he wants.

These distinctions are valid if it is added that history always partakes of mind and of life, and that it is always objectified by and for the historian.

IV. SCIENCE AND PHILOSOPHY OF HISTORY

THE PHILOSOPHY of history is, in France, a literary genre so discredited that no one dares confess interest in it. It is contrasted with science as fancy is with exactness, intuition with knowledge. The uncertainty of documentation, the vastness of vision, the claim to submit the complexity of reality to a strict plan—all these sins which are attributed to the traditional systems, are considered characteristic of the philosophy of history as such. Besides, Croce's saying that 'the philosophy of history has disappeared because historical knowledge has become philosophical' has penetrated the common consciousness. How are this contempt and this assimilation justified?

Psychologically, the distinction between the ambition and ignorance of the philosopher, and the care and learning of the scientist, would be easy to make. But the sociologists who took over the philosopher's claims offered themselves as the only true scholars, as contrasted with the historian, the mere narrator. Let us set aside the antinomy between scientific generalities and historical particularities; let us recognize history, as we have so far studied it, as the knowledge of man's development. How can it be distinguished from philosophy? By the nature, or by the extension, of the results? We shall examine the two hypotheses so as to show the difficulties of the theoretical dissociation, and the impossibility of any practical separation.

* * * *

The doctrines of Hegel or Comte represent the type of what is understood by philosophy of history. Using one single principle—law of the Three States or progress of liberty—periods are organized, their meanings appreciated, and the total evolution is interpreted. But where, logically, is the opposition to science? Does the philosopher have in mind not just the facts, but the *meaning*, that is, values or ends?

Or does he try to take in too wide a field, or to relate diversity to ideas which are too schematic?

The historian knows the goals which such and such individuals have aimed at, but he does not know the goal or goals of history. He retraces events and their consequences, he observes the more or less adequate necessity of a global change, or, on the contrary, the coincidence of relatively independent series. In the realm of understanding he links a phenomenon either with an impulse (capitalism with a certain form of desire for profit), or with a motive (capitalism with an economically rational form of conduct). The further the fact is extended, the less specific is the amount of determination.

Does the philosopher have other pretensions? Despite biases, none. Hegel confines himself to an understanding of what has been accomplished; Comte to a reading of the law of development obeyed by the mind which is inherent in the collective destiny; Marx to deciphering in advance the future implied in the conflicts of today's world. Either the goal becomes one with the temporary phase of the movement, in which case the historian, like the philosopher, interprets it, or the goal is transcendent to reality and assumes a conscious intention, in which case neither of them seeks that finality which would be revealed only to the confidant of Providence.

The difference, if there is one, is tied in with the mode of consideration. Science elaborates a lacunary determinism, philosophy would imagine a continuous one. Instead of a constructed, hypothetical and partial necessity, philosophy would discover in the process itself a total necessity.

We have indeed met with such doctrines expressed as laws, eliminating accidents, suppressing plurality and tracing an evolution or a fatal dialectic. These philosophies, beyond science, transcend positive knowledge, but above all they are ignorant of its nature. Conscious of their particularity and of their uncertainty—the grasp of history's broad outlines is a matter of hypothesis and selection—they would appear either as anticipations of the results at which science finally arrives, or as perspectives into which analytical and objective propositions are inserted.

Spengler's theories are of this type. Scientific dignity will perhaps be denied them because they surpass our knowledge. But they are essentially philosophical only by their dogmatism (biological individuality, solitude and death of cultures, fatality). Stripped of this metaphysics, they come down to schematic interpretations, analogous to those which comparative method, applied to different societies, will in the future make it possible to demonstrate with sufficient probability.

One could, to tell the truth, object that the philosopher tends to approve or condemn the result. Hegel and Comte demonstrate the truth of the end. The human mind realizes itself in positivism, man in freedom. It must still be recalled that the historian specializing in science or philosophy does not escape this retrospective justification, since intellectual evolution owes its unity and direction to the rationality later attributed to it by the historian. The philosopher would extend this interpretation to all of history, whether one universe were given as essential for humanity, or whether in all universes or above them such a necessity were shown.

Does value give us a principle of differentiation? The scientist, it is said, reconstitutes the facts and the philosopher weighs them; the former builds the world of history and the latter criticizes it.

If it is a question of events, the historian, according to the current formula, must be impartial. But he always connects an act with its causes or its consequences; the response is fitting or not, the decision effective or ineffective. In that sense he makes use of the criterion suggested by the ethics of history—success. Would the philosopher, on the contrary, be a moralist? By no means. Kant merges the philosophy of history with the ethics which judges the past and determines the end, but that is a particular philosophy of history, characteristic of an era and an attitude, and not representative of a genre. Private morals and public morals, the morals of intention valid for all or the ethic of action which grants privileges to certain individuals, the antinomy shows up in narratives as in philosophies; it does not mark the frontiers between them.

The distinction is still harder for special histories, since the object is made up of ideas or of monuments. In principle, values realized or asserted by others can be recognized as facts, but the intrinsic understanding must relate the work to its end, show its conformity with the laws of the intellectual universe. Will it suffice to go back to Weber's formula (analysis of values); would the scientist grasp the facts or relations which would become for the critic the material of appreciation? The distinction is more theoretical than practical.

Whether it is a question of art or of philosophy, admiration governs selection, so that history is always a history of monuments (in the Nietzschean sense). Moreover, the interpretation tries to attain that which will in reality justify the claim to agreement. It inevitably contains implicit judgments; in addition, it implies the criteria for those judgments.

The judgments, it is true, limited to the period whose preferences they are supposed to reproduce, leave intact the question of validity in itself and for us. On the other hand, a history of art or philosophy would imply a universally valid theory. It is no more necessary to estimate quality to retrace a series of forms than to understand one among them. But an evolution is composed only by determining the essence, if not the end, of the movement, which involves the transcendence of the retrospective organization over what was lived, the substitution of present or eternal meaning for the historical meaning.

Philosophy, then, would be either the elaboration of implicit judgments or the search for norms applicable to the whole of the past. In order to eliminate all philosophy of the first sort, the historian would have to distort the reality by treating it as a natural phenomenon. It is enough for him to take from each period the principles of organization and hierarchy which he uses to avoid the suspicion of a total philosophy. But if he were to take in a wider development while limiting himself to the juxtaposition of diversities he would inevitably present, instead of a history, a scattering of particulars, which would still be a philosophy, since, according to the old expression, not to philosophize is still a philosophy.

By going back to the conclusions of the preceding chapter, we could have immediately considered a philosophy of history *after* science (especially on the level of the real), a philosophy of history *before* or during science (especially of the order of the mind). One would govern the selection of the facts, the other the synthesis of intellectual worlds or existences; otherwise they would be closely connected. The foregoing discussion has again shown the unity of science and philosophy and the true distinction between them: unity, because science contains at least in part that to which philosophy gives form; distinction because science submits to differences and remains conscious of its particular nature. The philosophy of history is characterized by a dual effort to appreciate the contributions of all times to common knowledge and to confer upon its judgments an unlimited importance.

Thus are explained the two characteristics retained by the current definition: extension of the field and simplicity of the schematic plans.

* * * *

In a collectivity, individuals know approximately what they consider to be historical, the sense they give to their various activities and to their life as a whole. As long as the historian stays inside a closed totality, choice and organization are to a certain extent inscribed in the reality—an immanence which does not guarantee objectivity, since the interpreter is committed and must be so in order to overcome the ambiguities of the conditions of life.

As the historian goes beyond the bounds of a coherent whole, society, period, or civilization, the retrospective interpretation foils the attempt at resurrection or sympathetic understanding. But the opposition is classic: Hegel marks the progression of the narrator from author of memoirs to philosopher as he becomes further removed from events and retraces a development made up of a greater number of individualities. In terms of value Rickert expresses an analogous idea. Science picks out the material according to the values recognized by each collectivity, and philosophy must rise to formal values which are universally admitted. That, in fact, a universal history or a comparative sociology need other means and methods will be easily admitted. But they are different from each other and cannot be confused with a philosophy.

Theoretically, comparative sociology demands the discernment of common problems and differing solutions. Universal history, in addition, demands the orientation of the diversities towards a certain end. The philosophy of history, finally, justifies the interpretation it proposes and the movement it observes.

Sociology needs concepts showing traits common to all societies. Terms such as politics or economics are available, since it is always necessary to subject acts of violence and individual advantages to a permanent authority, to work for the establishment of a temporary and threatened balance between needs and resources. Also, the three terms society, civilization and culture would make it possible, according to A. Weber, to grasp three ever present aspects of collective existences. We have shown elsewhere the ambiguous character of these notions allowing a metaphysical acceptation (soul, mind, body), a sociological meaning (sectors of the reality), a critical meaning (gratuitous or expressive works, knowledge and technique, instincts and desires). The uncertainty is perhaps inevitable, for it marks the necessary return to philosophy of that sociology which tries to get at both the whole of each human nature and human nature as a whole.

A universal history not content with juxtaposing civilizations would have to set itself up as such a system. But to make the transition from an abstract unity, based on the identity of certain fundamental data, to the historical unity of a development, it would also have to discover a convergence of works or of social systems.

Our time, then, would apparently be favourable for such an attempt, since for the first time the whole planet shares a common lot. Cited as one difficulty will be the acquisition of knowledge beyond the capacity of one mind. Scientific strictness condemns these limitless visions; it will be observed that relations between various peoples are still uncertain, their common interests paltry, their unity partial and on the surface. All these propositions are valid, but they do not get to the heart of the matter. If the West still were confident of its mission, a universal history would be written either collectively or individually which would show, starting with isolated adventures, the progressive adhesion of all societies to modern civilization.[67] What makes such a history impossible is the fact that Europe no longer knows whether it prefers what it contributes to what it destroys. It recognizes the special qualities of expressive creations and existences at the moment when it threatens the destruction of unique values. Man fears his conquests, his instruments and his slaves, science, technique, classes, and inferior races.

A comparative sociology, without disqualifying itself, can recognize its particular quality, since like causal relations, it is assured of a hypothetical objectivity. But the grasp of the whole human past, which is directed at an accidental end, would lose all *raison d'être*. So, it calls for a dual justification, that of the ideas it uses to interpret and judge societies and cultures, and that of the condition showing the provisional completion of an evolution. The double justification constitutes the traditional objective of the philosophy of history.

* * * *

Philosophy has appeared as immanent in any global view of the past, and yet, because of the validity it claims, beyond positive knowledge. Is this transcendence legitimate? Actually, it all depends on the mean ing attached to it. It is not given to the philosopher to grasp unity necessity, or totality at the level where the scientist vainly seeks them. Conceived of as a natural object, history must be explored gradually, without the slow progress made by analysis ever reaching the final term. Interpretations which eliminate the plurality of series or the contingency of conjunctures are definitely hypothetical and, at bottom, useless, since they correspond to the intention of the prophet who announces and accepts fatality.

On the other hand, history, as the totality of intellectual developments or of existences, does not lend itself to an impersonal understanding. But the philosophy implying true understanding, far from being ruled out, is demanded by our study. The statement that one must philosophize to appropriate the philosophic past does not con-

[67] Such collections of universal history do exist, but in reality they are only the juxtaposition of the works—often notable—of specialists.

demn philosophy, but it does condemn the refusal to philosophize which hides under the name of positivism. The claim to transcendence of particularity, of periods studied and of current theories, runs the risk of resulting in the alleged universality of philosophies unconscious of their limits; but that risk, since it is inseparable from the effort to reach truth, must be taken. Otherwise we should give up all truth, for the object and subject of philosophy are indistinguishable from those of history. The knowledge of man, also, is knowledge of a history by a historical being.

CONCLUSION

The Relativity of Historical Knowledge

THE PRIMARY relativity is that of individual perception. The same object appears to many observers differently, depending on the situation of each of them. The child, unaware of his egocentricity, experiences his self as an indispensable term of a relationship the other term of which is the whole of the surrounding world.

Science overcomes this relativity by substituting true accounts for sensory impressions. Phenomena retain a particularity inseparable from the finite consciousness, mathematical relations established between them compel recognition by all. But scientific analysis, by origin and by its proofs, does not break away from the world as perceived. It starts with observation and comes back to elucidated and calculated experience, universally valid, but dependent on the human mind. One overcomes perceptive relativity, but not transcendent relativity.

The current meaning of relativity oscillated between these two concepts until science, by its development, recognized and exposed another form of relativity, evolved from the commonplace interpretations of Einstein's theory and of microphysics. It is impossible to locate objects in an absolute time and space as if the container existed before the content, as if the forms of sense perception were independent of fulfilment. All measurement implies an observer who is in the universe; one has no right to neglect the situation and movement of the observer in the calculation of distances or intervals of time. This relativity of each perspective is, however, not science's last word; our consciousness of it makes it possible to pass from one perspective to another, to set up a system of equivalence and to arrive at an objective knowledge of the invariables.

Again, when the physicist comes to microscopic phenomena, he still finds connections, not confirmations. He cannot determine both the position and the energy of the electron at the same time. The interaction of experiment and reality creates a margin of uncertainty. Thus there is introduced the principle that, for science, there are never simple things, but only relationships. The conditions under which we know nature are merged with the characteristics of the object. Moreover, the reality changes according to the level at which we study it; simple laws, established at the mass level, resolve into a statistical result at an elementary level. The various levels assumed by the scientist depend in the first place on the order of greatness of the subject with reference to the object.

Do these ideas have their counterpart in history? At the very point of departure we find perceptive relativity in an aggravated form, partiality and reciprocity of life experiences; actor and spectator, soldier and general, necessarily have patterns, allegedly the same, of different views. History never completely overcomes this relativity, because life experiences constitute the material of the science, and because facts, to the extent that they transcend individuals, exist not in themselves, but by and for consciousnesses. History considers an object which not only has passed (if it is an event), not only has disappeared (if it is a natural or human condition), but which attains existence only in minds, and changes with them.

We have observed, between the inseparable atoms of personalities and the inaccessible whole, the equivalent of the scientific search for laws, the construction of objective facts and of regularities, but these partial, scattered reports cover only part of the field of history, and never compose into a global account. As a result, reduced to understanding, forced to angle for truth by building up the world of history, knowledge seems to gain both particularity and objectivity; it overcomes the relativity of elementary observations only by consenting to the relativity brought about by development of concepts and systems of reference. The historian, a part of the evolution, refers an ever widened and always unfinished past to a condition which is itself variable, so that the science, involved in the development, moves forward to the extent to which the latter progresses in a constant direction, is renewed to the extent that the development, instead of accumulating, contradicts itself in order to advance.

Or again, the historian does not confuse himself with a transcendental self any more than does the soldier or the general. He tends towards and attains impartiality in the criticism of sources and the establishment of facts, but even though he might remain impartial in the organization of classification, he would nevertheless be partial (*biased*) to the very extent that he is partial (*incomplete*).

The fundamental differences, then, would be the following: historical reality cannot be broken up into relationships because it is human and men, actors or victims, are in any event its living centre. One does not rise from perceptive relativity to objective relationships transcendentally relative, but to a historical relativity; the scholar expresses himself and his universe in the past which he chooses.

The relativity is comparable to that in physics. The object, inseparable from the observer, is different depending on the level at which it is grasped; the relativity is also basically original, since, when all is said and done, it is due to the ambiguity of the intellectual development and the incompleteness of the evolution.

Second Part

THE LIMITS OF RELATIVISM IN HISTORY

THE SECOND part of our *Essai sur la théorie de l'histoire* was to deal with historism, the philosophy of historical relativism which developed at the opening of the century, especially after the War, and which followed a time devoted to the analysis of the science. Indeed, it was apparently the continuation, almost the consequence of that period. The critique of historical Reason, in fact, resulted not so much in bringing to light eternal categories as in showing the presence of dialectics in analytics (in the Kantian meaning of the two words). Reflection confirmed the facts of erudition and sanctioned the relativity of human endeavours (including the science of development).

It goes without saying that the failure of the critique was only one ot the sources of historism; in itself it lent itself just as easily to an opposite interpretation (Scheler concluded by *perspectivism* the fictitious character of the supposedly all-powerful evolution). Without studying all the intellectual and social causes of this movement of ideas, let us note two essential elements. Neither the discovery of the primitive, nor of other cultures, aroused scepticism or anarchy so long as the normative, normal so to speak, significance of contemporary society was maintained. The crisis which is shaking the foundations of our civilization is more formidable than the empirical investigation. Evolutionism became historism on the day when the two values on which the confidence of the nineteenth century, positivist science and democracy—that is, basically, rationalism—lost their prestige and authority.

Irrationalism brought on pessimism. History has no goal since man has no destination and since he is always the same and vainly creates ephemeral works. This line of argument, in its turn, expresses an attitude and a situation. The German university teacher, with his claims of aristocracy (biological or intellectual), revolted at our mass civilizations, industrialism, all forms of socialism. Youthful, fertile cultures were considered aggressive and unjust. Historism corresponds not only to a time uncertain of itself, but to a society without a future which rebels against the future it foresees and hesitates between utopian revolt and a self-styled lucid fatalism.

It is not our purpose here to deal with all the problems posed during this period (rhythm of special histories, unity or plurality in history, relations of what is and what ought to be, of knowledge and action, etc.). We should like to demonstrate that the theory of historical knowledge does not necessarily lead to a relativist philosophy; also, we must specify the nature of the hypotheses or decisions which control the science of the past. In the first two chapters we shall expound and discuss the relativist thesis; in the last two, we shall analyse the philosophies of history, concrete interpretations, and modes of consideration.

I. HISTORICAL RELATIVISM

IN THIS first chapter we should like to sum up the argument for relativism in history, an ideal exposition, if one may so call it, not to be found in this form in the work of any author. For relativism is always connected with a certain metaphysics. According to Troeltsch, the development of history is like the gradual revelation, throughout time, of an inaccessible God. In Scheler, relativity, otherwise overcome by the eternally valid hierarchy of values, expresses the necessary collaboration of individual or supra-individual personalities. The world of essences appears fragmentary to everyone, hence the need for the temporal dispersion of ways of life and thought, in order to exhaust the intelligible world. Mannheim conceives a sort of absolute, the historical totality at once both real and meaningful, a pure destiny, neither providential nor demoniac. For French sociologists, societies constitute the principle and origin of changes and ethical imperatives, since they merge with social imperatives, remain valid despite or because of their diversity.

We shall disregard these metaphysics in order to distinguish the different types of arguments used by relativism. Relativism starts with facts; morals, philosophies, religions, vary with collectivities and times. This observation suggests two questions. What is the depth of historical changes? Is the historical diversity of works or of human nature superficial or not? How deep does it go? In addition, logical conclusion is not drawn from fact. Methods may vary with cultures. No one will conclude that the validity of scientific propositions stops at the frontiers of a particular collectivity. In the same way, no system of ethics is admitted or practised everywhere; theoretically, a certain morality could be universally imperative.

In order to pass from observed variability to essential relativity, reliance is placed on two arguments which it is important to distinguish. Either it is shown that ethics, religion, etc., depend on, and derive from a social or historical reality, an irrational principle which brings with it inevitably its intellectual expressions in a lawless development. We shall designate this argument by the term *reduction.* Or, if we consider the successive works inside a universe, we observe, or believe we do, a basic diversity. Relativism recognizes neither an accumulation of truths, nor progress, at most a dialectic without a goal. A philosophy of development, not of evolution, it ends, even if it does not abolish the autonomy of human creations, with an anarchy of values. All these arguments blend, of course, inside systems, but they had to be separated for the sake of the explanation as well as for criticism.

* * * *

We shall skim rapidly over historicism applied to reason and religion. The transformations of reason are in one sense obvious, in another almost imperceptible, since an intelligence without any common dimension with ours would become even more incomprehensible for us than the constructs of the insane.

The problem has been stated by two series of works, two categories of facts. Studies of primitive mentality have shown to what extent ways of thinking, explanatory processes, were susceptible to change. In addition, sociology or the history of cultures showed the plurality of representations of the world, of conceptual resources, of the more formal categories. In this sense, anyone today recognizes the singularity of Chinese or of Indian thought. Neither these historical facts nor the depth of the changes which they reveal are yet decisive, but the interpretation given to them is. Instead of organizing the past along the lines of progress or maturity, instead of contrasting childish fancies with scientific learning, certain philosophers have given up any sort of statement of finality. Even in the realm of learning they have claimed for the West neither privilege nor supremacy.

We shall not discuss this scepticism; it would bring us back either to the historicity of philosophies or to the judgment, not of positive truth, but of its diffusion and importance. Besides, it is not apparent that ethnology necessitates the sacrifice of the unity of the human mind. As much as ontologies differ, it still seems possible to find, if we rise to the level of the deepest tendencies, the most formal rules, an identity of logic. Granted that primitive man is interested in primary rather than secondary causes, that he invokes mysterious forces rather than empirical antecedents; there is nonetheless a demand for explanation and, so to speak, for causal explanation. Participation does not in any sense end in confusing everything, but in identifying and distinguishing things and beings in a different way from ours.

Nor shall we dwell longer on the case of religion, even though it is at the origin of Troeltsch's doctrine. In this case, the argument rests not so much on the depth of the changes as on the connection between the world of religion and the social reality, on the impossibility of discerning in that world any supreme value. Christian revelation must have borrowed too many elements from ancient thought and from eastern beliefs to be separate. The idea of the revelation of a miraculous event, in the strict sense, which would sharply divide man's past in two, would be incompatible with the demands, not of reason, but of the sense of history—that is, of the sense of real and intellectual continuity. Judged by moral or cultural standards it could not be maintained absolutely that the Christian religion is the best. By what right is it superior to Islam or Buddhism? There is no authority for confusing natural religion and Christianity. As a consequence, Troeltsch, imbued with a prolix religiosity, wanting to be and believing he was a Christian, arrived at a paradoxical conciliation of the plurality of religions with the unity of one God, who was perhaps indeterminate, in any case unknowable. All dogmatic representations incarnate truth after their own fashion, they all help to sublimate biological impulses into moral wills; all of them, effective and historically contingent, represent a moment in the education of the human species.

We have put aside the especially difficult problems of the history of religions. We need then, only to recall the fact that there is no direct conflict between the facts of history and theology (with the exception, of course, of cases where criticism and scholarship, by re-establishing texts and events in accord with probability, succeed in contradicting historical interpretations which are still integral parts of the dogma). It is impossible to draw the inference, without a philosophical decision, from a sociology of religion to a sociological theory of religion. Just as there is no philosophy for those who admit no other method than that of positivist science, there is no history of religion—of faith or of communities in touch with God—for the unbeliever who knows only men, their dreams, and their organizations.

It may be that revelation falls under the attack of a rational critique, but it would be hard for a historical critique to attack it. How could a revelation have avoided borrowings from the past? How ought it to have been produced to be probable? How would an entirely human ethics give authority to evaluate religions whose truth is by definition transcendent and perhaps irrational? If Troeltsch insensibly moves from science, which is positivist by postulate, into a historical philosophy of religion, it is because his faith, stripped of all orthodoxy, implies the confusion to begin with.

It is certain that the fact of history sets specific problems, but only for him who admits the originality of the realm of religion.

* * * *

Today it is a commonplace statement that, depending on times, societies, customs, morals, rules of behaviour vary. Everyone is so convinced of this diversity that it seems as useless to emphasize it as to discuss it. But again the fact, which is indisputable, may be variously interpreted. What results do the reality of history infer for the nature of morality, for the validity of imperatives? Historism, in effect, comes to three conclusions which are taken for scepticism: one can neither discover any universally valid laws, nor grasp an ethics which is not the expression or effect of a social structure, nor specify for anyone or everyone what he must do or desire.

The most immediate diversity is that of morals and institutions. Many and changing are the solutions offered for the problem of sexual relations, common to all societies. Innumerable within each of them are the positive or negative commandments. There is no activity, however technical, which does not in one way or another involve the distinction between the permitted or forbidden, which is not subject to traditional prescriptions which are sometimes as sacred as moral principles. Equally indisputable is the variety of types of men representing the ideals in collectivities. Without going outside our Western civilization, the *honnête homme* and the gentleman, the ancient sage and the modern citizen, the bourgeois and the feudal lord, offer proof of the irreducible differences in ways of life, in codes of honour, in the hierarchy of goods.

There are three ways of accepting historical evolution without consenting to reduction. According to a rationalist tradition, history may be held as the material of morality, by the same right as the nature given to each individual. The individual must rise from animality to humanity, from egoism to respect for the law, from blindness to considered behaviour. Thus the historical development is the arena of an indefinite progress, since the ideal remains inaccessible. Whatever the periods distinguished in the past may be, ethics, the norm of history, govern the whole perspective.

Historicism would oppose this universalism, based on the dualism of what is and what ought to be with many arguments. If we attribute absolute value to a determined moral, we run the risk of naïvely assimilating our existence with the essence of humanity and of falling into a relativism of fact. The diversity will seem the more shocking, societies the more degenerate, as the criterion chosen is stricter. Failing to find elsewhere the practices which custom has hallowed, we end in anarchy. An ethics with universal pretentions, as soon as its diffusion is no longer expected, engenders doubt rather than confidence. Men today have neither sufficient faith in their culture, nor enough hope of the future, to hallow their own norms. The definition of progress, *logically*, however independent it may be in theory, needs a certain optimism relatively to *actual* progress.

Moreover, as the irreducible variety of collective organizations is recognized, one comes to the point of opposing ethics and values. The former, ethics, defines individual virtues—sincerity, courage, unselfishness, kindness, etc., secularized residues of the Christian virtues, the humanistic transformation of life conforming to the teachings of religion. But from these formal imperatives (they are general, addressed to the intention, and do not specify the content of actions), it would be impossible to deduce institutions, either domestic, political, or economic. The latter, like religion and culture, change as time passes. They make up a history, that is a development composed of origin totalities linked with each other. The concrete imperatives retain their spiritual quality, their gratuity, their obligatory character, at the same time losing their universality and eternity.

This intermediary solution is doubtless rather weak, for virtues partake of the diversity of the cultures of which they are elements. Since they are not compatible, they call for a choice by the individual, who organizes them into the unity of an attitude. Even if they denote the conditions which any institution must satisfy, they do not suffice to determine the answer prescribed for any one situation, nor do they justify in reason an inevitably historical decision. In short, political conflicts, and consequently the gravest uncertainties, evade the norms which, not strictly applicable as transcendent principles, apply equally well to the most contradictory behaviours.[68]

[68] We shall come back farther on to these statements and try to prove them.

Thus we come to the third solution. Morality considers, not primarily the intention, but the act; it defines the good life and not purity of heart. If we use Scheler's language, we shall say that the philosopher, by phenomenological analysis, reveals a universe of values, but notes that, beyond *mores* and institutions, there is a variety in kinds of *ethos* and *ethics* (that is, the hierarchies of values and the systems of precepts which express those hierarchies).

In addition, each *ethos* (as Scheler uses the word) is linked with a social order. The major argument would cease to be variability within the ideal cosmos, but subordination to an irrational factor (or merely involvement with it). Thus we gradually approach the point of denying the specificity or autonomy of values. The organization of the economy determines, through a series of intermediary terms, the most apparently spiritual imperatives. The latter, in the last analysis, express in strict form the way of life corresponding to the interests of a class or to the needs of a system of government. Shall we say that in this way any society expresses an ethics? Let us admit it—there will still be a sort of psychological adhesion. Directly or indirectly, by justification or dissimulation, ideas go back in the end to the psychological conditions of individuals and groups, to their troubles and their aspirations.

In truth, a frankly sociological interpretation seems to overthrow the force of the arguments. One talks about reduction as long as facts contradict the rational, intellectual, or supra-historical interpretation of morality. On the other hand, the interdependence of morals and societies confirms the validity of our particular imperatives if society is logically as well as in fact the origin and foundation of every obligation. Was not Durkheim's intention to restore morality, which according to him had been shaken by the disappearance of religious beliefs?

Psychologically, it is easy to understand why a new faith was expected from sociological rationalism. French sociologists, democratic, free-thinkers, partisans of individual liberty, justified by their science the values they spontaneously believed in. For them the structure of today's civilization (its density or organic solidarity) demanded a sort of equalitarian ideology, the autonomy of personality, Judgments of value gained rather than lost by becoming collective judgments. In full confidence, society was put in the place of God.

As a matter of fact, the word *society* is not without ambiguity, since in one case it may designate actual collectivities, and in other cases, the idea or ideal of those collectivities. In fact it applies only to particular groups, self contained; but less than the words *fatherland* and *nation*, it suggests to us rivalries and wars (we imagine a society extending to all mankind). It masks the conflicts which rend all human communities.

It makes possible the subordination of class conflict to social unity and the idea of a social ethics which would be scientific without being political. But if this concept, stripped of all sham prestige, defines the partially incoherent pattern of social facts, is it not apparent that *sociologism* adds to a limitless relativity the reduction of values to a reality more natural than spiritual—a sociologism subject to determinism and not open to liberty?

* * * *

There is no need for lengthy comment about philosophical historicism —we need merely to remember Dilthey's concept. There would be no such thing as a philosophy in progress, but conceptions of the world, syntheses of various elements (scientific, social, metaphysical), inevitably involved in an irrational development, since they express the human soul (of small importance is the constancy of certain attitudes towards life, of certain types of doctrines, or of certain antinomies).

Of course Dilthey tried to safeguard an exact philosophy, either previous to, or succeeding conceptions of the world. Previous to them, in the order of methodology or the critique of the sciences, following them in reflection on men and their history. But the positivism to which Dilthey clung rapidly disappeared in Germany, and the phenomenologists have declared that metaphysics always precedes and dominates the theory of knowledge, which is thus deprived of the autonomy which made possible its escape from the relativity of the *Weltanschauungen*. Once the systematic character of philosophy was re-established, either one had to accept historicism, or to oppose a conception of the world to *Philosophie als strenge Wissenschaft*. Hence the decisive significance of Husserl's famous article.

Historicism, a mixture of scepticism and irrationalism, is not so much a philosophy as it is the substitute for a philosophy which is lacking, since one lives neither in the worlds represented by the other *Weltanschauungen*, nor in a *Weltanschauung* of one's own. The attitude is theoretically absurd, but psychologically intelligible. It has been recognized that every philosophy is metaphysical and inseparable from the concrete being who strives for both global understanding and self consciousness. The subject is not the transcendental self, but the social and individual man. The crisis of historicism is due to the conjuncture of these contradictory ideas; they were discovering the impossibility of finding a philosophical truth, and the impossibility of not philosophizing.

Historically, this period marks the end, or rather the disintegration of evolutionism. History gained prestige in proportion as intellectual worlds lost stability and autonomy. It seemed to be the principle of the movement which spans and carries along all man's works, the origin and sum of partial developments. Man reveres, he seeks to penetrate that mysterious power, God, or the demiurge of those who have lost all faith in science and in reason.

II. BEYOND RELATIVISM

HISTORICISM is essentially defined by the substitution of the myth of development for the myth of progress. There is the same resignation to anonymous fate, but instead of the confident optimism that the future will be better than the present, there is a sort of pessimism or agnosticism. The process of history is indifferent to the desires of men, at least to their rational or moral wishes. The future will be different, neither better nor worse. To free oneself from historicism is first of all to overcome fatalism.

The totality of history does not exist in itself, but for us. We compose it of the fragments collected and organized retrospectively by the unity of our interest or the unity we attribute to periods or cultures. Immediate observation shows us multiple activities and, in the object, the gaps in necessity. The discontinuity of the causal web leaves room for action, the incompleteness and diversity of worlds allow for personal decisions.

The power of history, it is true, is not entirely mythological. In social changes, man stakes not merely his comfort or his freedom, he gambles with his very soul. As historians, breaking with factitious divisions, have tried to get another grasp of whole collectivities, they have demonstrated the interdependence of functions, from the construction of tools up to that of metaphysical systems. We are delivered from the tyranny of the common fate by neither the discreetness of the determinism nor by the plurality of the autonomous logical systems.

It would be impossible to fix the limits of the influence exercised by a social regime on ideas. A transformation of institutions is liable to upset men's psychology. (Even though the deepest changes usually occur of themselves, without the voluntary collaboration of individuals.) In spite of everything, the disintegration of the historical totality allows a victory over resignation by revealing the freedom and the duty of choice, and a triumph over nihilism by objective knowledge and philosophical reflection.

* * * *

Philosophies of history obviously fall foul of the relativist argument.

No intellectual construct is more intimately connected with or shares more in the development of the reality. As a consequence does not historicism cast doubt on the legitimacy of our endeavour? If criticism follows ontology, and if the latter expresses an attitude towards life, is not our theory of history, without our knowing it, reduced to an experience or to a private will?

This question does not come from an exaggerated doubt; it points to the necessary doubling back upon itself by reflection. We shall discuss the plurality of philosophies of history in the next two chapters, but even now we can, by use of the results already arrived at, mark out the limits of relativism.

One shows legitimately that historical or sociological researches are connected with extra-scientific intentions. This does not exclude, but on the contrary supposes that, in terms of the testimonies or the documents, the propositions stating facts or relations may be true or false (or more or less probable). The range of experience, organizing concepts, the questions asked, all change and bring on the revision of the perspectives of history. Within contexts which vary with history, there is discerned a sphere of partial or hypothetical truth. We have shown in this book the abstract legitimacy and real difficulties of this dissociation.

The argument is valid for all intellectual constructs falling under the alternative of the true and false. As soon as thought is submitted to the rules of formal logic, of experiment or of probability, the results are *de jure* universally valid. All the social sciences at least partly belong in this category, even though it may be that before or after facts and causal connections there intervene decisions which vary with periods or concrete wills. The separation of the two elements is furthermore, not always practicable, and, above all, the historical character of the total structure is often more interesting than the separation of strictly objective procedures (a separation made still harder by the transformation of the object, and consequently, of the given facts).

Is the same distinction valid for philosophical doctrines? Abstractly, yes, but its importance would be less. The validity of the deduction would matter less than the arbitrary nature of the principles (assuming that the opposition were as clearly apparent). However essential it may be for understanding the system, the analysis of the scientific knowledge integrated into a system would scarcely make it possible to draw from the view of the world and of man (which is bound up with one individual or with one society) the positive truths or the theory of knowledge, partially valid like the state of learning to which it corresponds. In practice, certain problems relative to mathematics and physics are, especially today, almost entirely withdrawn from metaphysics, and hence from the particularity of individuals and groups. They develop, largely, like the sciences with which they are connected. In spite of everything, a philosophy which tries to be radical is inevitably total.

The formal transcendence of historicism no longer consists of reserving the rights of logic within works or systems, but of raising the reflection by which the mind escapes the limits of individuality above the level of thought engaged in existence. Endowed with certain inclinations, members of a society, we are shut into ourselves, bearing all the accidental marks of our heredity and environment. Thought is always, in one sense, a psychological phenomenon, and that is why the possibilities of psychoanalysis and of Marxism are endless. But when we submit ourselves to the rules of truth, the results at which we arrive are universally imperative. In a different but comparable way, reflection, logically, does not express the imprisoned consciousness, and claims universality. For example, reflection on the conditions under which we know history is not essentially relative.

It is historical of course, since it was necessary to discover history and construct the science of the past before understanding the activity of the scientist. It develops in time, following action. Even more, it bears upon a historical action, since it pursues at the same time both the progress of scholarship and the regular rhythm of changing interests.

Thus conceived, philosophy runs the risk of being both retrospective and formal. This is a provisory conclusion, for if the theory of historical knowledge is a logic of all knowledge, then the theory of history would be a philosophy of man. The formalism would show, not the incompetence of reflection, but the inevitable want of eternal verities.

* * * *

Historicism in the moral order is less to be overcome than to be recognized. We shall, indeed, accept as obvious the diversity of kinds of ethos and ethics. Hierarchies of values change with epochs, races, and societies, and consequently, ethics also change (that is, the theoretical formulation of intuitions of values).

The formal morality of good will or purity of heart which would uphold abstract norms above all changes seems to us incompatible with the exact interpretation of the facts of history.

If we leave out of account a transcendent faith, such a morality is a residue. It assumes agreement on a way of life, and it implies a religion from which it derives; the stress on the inner virtues, the subordination of conduct to intention is justified only by the belief in a God, spectator and judge of our secret lives. Since only what we do depends on us, our desires are not so much sins calling for remorse as they are facts to be acknowledged. The ideal of the beautiful is empty unless it is contradictory. One does not ask of the revolutionary the impartiality of the scientist, or of the sage the tragic struggle of the saint, or of the hero the moderation of the judge. In choosing a human model to follow, or a certain activity, one gives up certain merits, and bows to some necessities. Reflection shows man what his decision commits him to.

A subjective morality, it seems, fails doubly. It does not ally itself with the objective morality within a collective order; it appears as bound up with the history from which it claimed to be detached and which it tried to ignore or appraise. The obligations drawn from the universal imperative finally coincide with the concrete imperatives of one time. And if one wishes to keep to principles, one abandons real life to the arbitrary and to development.

Then again, in the category of life, law, as Simmel put it, becomes an individual law. The concrete attitude that the other person expects of one is determined by no general rule. It is singular, like the exchange between two persons. The rational ethic of unselfishness or of justice is useless as soon as the question is one of human communication. People want not only, nor primarily, to be respected, they want to be recognized, valued, loved. Must there be perceived in the other person only an individual subject to law? Or must one exclude from theory the sphere of irrational relations, the most decisive for all? But the philosopher is interested in our whole life.

Of course, it will be asked how far, in fact, moralities differ. But the question, which would require extensive study, does not seem essential from this point of view. It is not so difficult as is generally thought to extract a sort of eternal decalogue from history. As Scheler showed, common relativism invokes the material diversity of behaviours without distinguishing the act from the intention, without taking into account the representations of the world and the degrees of learning, inevitably multiple and contradictory. Neither the priest who sacrifices nor the soldier who kills is a criminal. The fact of ritual killings does not mean that some societies recognize murder as lawful. Every collectivity has imposed respect for the neighbour, however narrow the scope of the category may have been for a long time. The barriers of closed societies had to be broken down to learn to respect humanity in all men.

It is hardly important, basically, whether the reality of such a decalogue is admitted or rejected. It would represent a sort of summary of obligations and prohibitions in force everywhere, because they would be universally indispensable to assure social peace. It would lose prestige because of its very generality. People save the best of themselves for tasks they believe to be original. The most widely accepted rules, such as the injunction not to kill or steal, are also the most obvious, unconsciously obeyed. Of what importance to us is the greater or lesser diffusion of these customs?

Moreover, this series of imperatives does not take form in a human attitude or a concretely defined social system. Universally valid, they are addressed to no one in particular. No one recognizes in them the sign of his calling, they become specific only by being particularized (for example the respect for the property of others becomes, in some societies, respect for the absolute right of ownership). They would answer our uncertainties only when expressed in our language, and hence would be provisory and relative like our lives.

Would not the standard of values stated by Scheler assure the permanence of a fundamental order? Logically, yes. In practice, it is not sure that it would greatly change our situation, since it eliminates neither the uncertainty relative to values of the same calibre, nor the diversity of goods. It makes it possible to condemn errors inspired by resentment (for example, the subordination of culture to civilization or of religion to culture), to fix the level reached by a certain system of ethics (the values considered the highest by a society or by one person), but it does not supply the individual with the means of determining the human type he takes as his ideal, or the sort of life he wishes to lead. Furthermore, everyone lives in a certain world of values. The plan of the total universe which, by definition, eludes us, is of no use to us unless we are, like the philosopher, proof against limitation and the confidant of Divinity.

Outside religion, the grasp by emotional intuitions of an order of values, specifically distinct from reality, remains possible, but not recognition of an eternal hierarchy which would be God's view. In the sight of man alone, the values of knowledge and morality, of utility and culture, are co-ordinate and not subordinate, just as are models of humanity, the artist and the sage, the hero or the saint. All values, all men, appear unique, and that is why everyone is compelled to choose and to make sacrifices. Materialistic ethics implicitly recognizes this choice, without seeing in it the sign of freedom.

Scheler would like to avoid the Kantian formalism which, by obedience to the law determines the rule of conduct, and the total objectivism which would be concerned only with the act. The intentionality would be both concrete and moral at the same time, the will for values would be fixed upon goods without ceasing to be good will. But how does one get at, in self and in others, this *Gesinnung* Scheler speaks of, a sort of final motive which would govern all our actions? Assuming its reality, would we not loose our freedom of will, since it is given and not chosen, like our impulses? Is not the specific quality of the ethical order sacrificed if it is defined as the determination of the will which realizes all values, whatever they may be?

The end of the eternal, however, by no means sanctions the end of morality. We are certainly obliged to recognize the originality of lives. Why should not the same be true of the moralities of history, of which both the particularity and the validity would be accepted, unity being only the final goal set at infinity or the things formally held in common which one manages bit by bit to determine?

Is it necessary to go further and, sacrificing values also, to see in collective imperatives the essence of morals? Ethical obligations would be internalized social commandments, the causes and function of which the individual would have forgotten.

One could specify and shade the idea by discerning the species of moral imperatives in the genus of social imperatives (as opposed to judicial imperatives). In any event, once the distinction was made the problem would still persist: are moral imperatives confirmed or devalued by this explanation of their origin and nature?

If morality logically merges with common opinion, if the right thinking man is the supreme judge, the nonconformist would be essentially immoral. Will it be said that our societies demand and require justice and liberty? Perhaps, but would one be ready to accept collective authority on the day when the system has become totalitarian? And yet, if the collectivity is the supreme resort, by what right is it to be challenged on the day when obedience becomes burdensome?

Shall we say that it is not opinion, but the real structure of the collectivity which is decisive? According to the current expression, each society has the morality it deserves. This is a valid formula, from which however the conclusion would just as well be that men have the society corresponding to their ethos. The concept of social structure has no precise meaning. It designates a multiplicity of different phenomena, incoherent, often contradictory, not existing at the same time. Morality is, like all other sectors of collective life, relatively autonomous and subject to outside influences, with a tradition of its own and threatened by economic changes. Life must have been chrystallized by time for the sociologist to determine the social order and the morality implied by it. As seen by the living individual, there is room for discussion, criticism, an effort at creation. Science shows, at most, the partial fatalities or the fundamental necessities of a certain civilization.

Shall we argue that ethics is social because society is sacred, the source and principle of moral commandments? Psychologically, except in totalitarian systems which worship society because they deify it, men rarely think of their duties in terms of the sociologists' interpretation. They all subject themselves to higher authority, since in the last analysis groups are only collections of individuals, unless one transfigures them by substituting for their tangible nature an ideal one. By the same token, a certain partial and unjust community is no longer adored, but the true community or the everlasting idea of a certain community. Now, in order to determine this idea, one must refer to norms which, logically, do not derive from the existing society, since they are intended to judge it. Sociologists inevitably reintroduce, in order to determine the object and origin of their faith, the values which they claimed to subordinate to the real. The formula, 'collective interest is the supreme law', illustrates this inevitable refuge: there is no collective interest whose definition does not assume a hierarchy of goals.

Society as fact, then, is neither the psychological basis, nor the logical principle, nor the univocal cause of morality. Opinion offers the most faithful image of *mores* and of the common conscience at a certain time. But neither sociology nor the history of ethics leads to rules of action, for they either accept reality and teach submission, or they pass judgment on reality and demand other criteria.

We by no means wish to question the fact that the rules of conduct take on definite content only within a certain social system. Nor do we dream of returning to an ethics of intention, either rationalist or Christian, which seems inevitable to some people as soon as sociologism is cast out. One can admit that values are bound up with history, both in their evolution in fact and in their validity, without confusing *mores* and morality, without emptying the meaning of norms in the opinion of the group. Culture is defined by the universe of values in which one lives; it is for a community the equivalent of destiny for the individual, the totality of existence which is at the same time both suffered and desired.

In fact, there is no other point of departure for reflection than the two realities, mutually connected but irreducible, of a certain society and of certain values, the society being offered to impersonal knowledge, the values to specific intuitions. It is in this dual world that each of us places and creates himself, by determining the order of his preferences and ideal model on the one hand, his place in society and the society he desires on the other. It is vain to demand or hope that all choices should agree.

One and the same act allows of multiple judgments, all of them equally right logically. It is necessary first to go back to the social and moral system of the actor: *sub specie aeternitatis*, there is for man no legitimate valuation. In any case, there are still distinct considerations. Acts are judged directly, objectively, in their perceptible content; the psychological state is measured with increasing certainty by the interpretation of signs. Society rightfully condemns and punishes acts and motives which violate collective prohibitions. But neither acts nor motives are in the last analysis separable for the situation and from the total personality. It is a unique being who is in question, whom we despise or admire, who has our sympathy or friendship. It is no longer a question of conforming with the rules, or of obedience to the laws, but of human quality, an expression which designates approximately what we wish to grasp, beyond conduct, and even beyond merit.

Is this pluralism a form of scepticism? As a matter of fact, we are merely giving expression to universal practice. Who claims to know the secrets of lives? Who assumes the right to impose his attitudes or preferences upon others? Who, on the contrary, does not distinguish the act from the intention, the intention from the person, destiny and virtue?

If any one sees here a form of anarchy, it is because he is the prisoner of a theological representation. Morality, decreed by God, would perhaps divide the realm of things human into two kingdoms, of good and evil. Reflection by the finite mind is not powerless, but it does not attain absolute and universal formulae. The individual discovers in himself imperatives which raise him above the brutes, and outside he finds commandments which oblige him; he elaborates, criticizes, and organizes them. But the decision by which he creates himself is good only for him; the judgment he passes on others is imperfect and relative just as is the knowledge of each individual which he has and others have. Vocations are personal, social standings multiple and irreducible, even though there might be conceived at infinity, a society where the vocations would be reconciled among themselves and with their environment.

The three arguments just sketched, the autonomy of positive and partial truth, the universality of reflection, and the constitution by the person of his spiritual nature, do not claim to refute historicism, or even less to exhaust the problems it states. They do get rid of fatalism and scepticism, and confirm the necessity of decision and of the search for truth.

They leave entirely open the question of what is the depth, the importance, of the changes. We have already met this question in connection with kinds of ethos, and we shall come upon it again in connection with man himself. To answer, it would be necessary to examine in turn the activities of the individual and of the group. Let us merely observe that those who repeat the formula, which they believe to be profound, about the unchangeableness of human nature, are often more concerned with justifying themselves than they are ignorant of diversity. Their resistence then becomes understandable, since it expresses a thought subject to the will and makes it possible to evade the calling into question of personal existence, at the same time as they evade the question of man's self-realization.

III. HISTORY AND IDEOLOGY

WE SHALL not examine all the presuppositions of the science of history, since any judgment of fact and of value, any state of science and of philosophy, can serve as a term of reference for a reconstitution of the past. We shall consider only the theories of real history and of total history, concrete theories on the one hand, modes of consideration on the other.

In this chapter, instead of abstractly analysing the theories, we shall take the example of Marxism and try to dissociate it logically into its component parts in order to specify the nature and modality of each of them.

* * * *

In Marxism we shall first distinguish, as in our former studies, the *theory* and the *perspective*. We call *theory* the dual affirmation relative to the force of the economy among material factors and to the connection between social body and idea. We call *perspective* the orientation of the whole human past towards the present class conflict, the triumph of the proletariat, and the advent of socialism. The theory could logically be universally true, the perspective would be tied to a provisory situation. In fact, this distinction for general history is hard to maintain.

Let us first consider the theory. We discard the over-simplified interpretations, already refuted by our previous discussion. The economy is neither primary nor final cause of historical phenomena. One does not succeed in determining a substructure for the double reason that totalities do not exclude the relative independence of partial movements, and that the comparison of societies shows no one structure. As viewed by causal thought there is no universally privileged term.

In the same way, in so far as the connection of ideas with the real is concerned, one must first recognize the plurality of logically and factually legitimate and indispensable interpretations. Were it only to relate the pattern of a work and of a culture with a human intention, one must proceed by intrinsic understanding and bow to the laws of spiritual worlds.

All these assertions true Marxism, in our opinion, accepts without question since in any case, independent of any philosophy or concrete decision, they are dependent on a description or a formal demonstration. It is beyond or short of this inevitable plurality that Marxism finds unity, the unity of man and his world, or of life and its expressions, anterior to the dissociation of the factors, a unity which would derive from a philosophy or anthropology. We are thus brought back to a larger question, that of the truth of philosophies.

Let us take what we have called the perspective. At first glance it seems that, on the contrary, this is what falls directly under the alternative of true or false. As a matter of fact, the propositions relative to the class struggle, the conflicts of capitalism, the inevitability of depressions and their aggravation—all these propositions lend themselves to proof or scientific refutation. In any case, even admitting the multiplicity of economic theories and of concrete interpretations, they would not be essentially relative; at most, they apply to passing phenomena and are branded with an uncertainty due to the limits of our knowledge and the imperfection of our experimental methods.

The elements of the perspective present this positive character, since they are part and parcel of a partial history (that of our time). The perspective is nonetheless philosophical, because of the fact that it retains these elements in preference to others and because it organizes them in terms of the future. Will it be said that the forecasts of Marxism are no different from the analysis to which it subjects the present? Certain definite forecasts (depressions, concentration), whether true or false, probable or improbable, do not exceed the resources of the positive method. But the global forecast, relative to socialism or individual liberty, will be the condition of universal liberty, the forecast of fatal revolution, of the inevitable triumph of the proletariat (as if the reactions of populations to the crisis of capitalism could be known in advance)—all these distant prophetic anticipations are ideologies, since they transcend the real; they are myths if they exalt faith.

Now, these anticipations are primary. Or at least what is primary is the rejection of capitalism and the desire to destroy it. The image of the future springs from this rejection; it is one, like the perspective of the past. And that is why that perspective, linked with a will, is essentially relative, inseparable from a choice in history. Even more, this choice governs the theory as well as the perspective. The task is at first practical; it is a question for the proletariat, for humanity, of making a revolution which will transform daily life and end with the immanence of ideas in existence. There lies the origin of the subordination of pure thought to action, just as the primacy of the economy, then transposed to all times, is explained by the power of the present economy and by the necessity of acting on the system of production in order to change in depth the social relations (hence the dissociation of the factors, with the economic factor fixing the margin of variation; within capitalism, reforms could not go beyond a certain limit). The Marxist system as a whole expresses an existential attitude.

This real unity of philosophies of history does not compromise the legitimacy of the logical distinctions, but it makes the philosophical problem more urgent. What is the truth which Marxism attributes to itself? A dynamic philosophy, does it consent to particularity, or does it transcend history?

* * * *

We recall to memory the two simplest and weakest answers: that assimilating Marxism with a positivist science, and the one assimilating it with the totality rather than with the various particularities. The translation of Marxism into terms of cause has essentially as its purpose to make possible the first confusion, the use of the Hegelian vocabulary, the second. The impossibility of one, as of the other, is immediately evident from our work. The first would require a determinism of the whole of history. Now the explanation by cause, either before or after the facts, is fragmentary. The series which we extend into the future do not make up real systems; they do not determine the aspects of them which matter most to us. To fill in the gaps there is needed the peculiar optimism on which faith feeds; humanity would always work out the tasks which history sets for it.

As for the truth through the totality, perhaps it is accessible, but only by rising above the level of development. In history, all views are particular, since particularity consists in taking in the whole from a certain point of view. In order to justify his claim, Lukacs substitutes for the individual subject a collective subject, the class, which thinks the truth of history as it creates it. But, without stressing the illegitimacy of this substitution (it is always the individual who thinks), the class itself would not grasp the totality until the society which expressed it were created—that society only, and completely. As long as the plurality of classes persists—and consequently that of visions—the truth of any one of them can be proved only by supra-historical arguments, by the values which each one incarnates or the future it announces.

Will the objection be raised that the question is artificial, that the idea of universal truth is only an ideology? The cult of objectivity expresses certain intentions, psychological or social—the effort to be detached, the claim to be calm. It corresponds to a special scale of values (subjection of action to thought, of existence to meditation), and in this sense, it is an ideology. But these observations do not do away with the difference between a proposition which is true or likely because it agrees with the facts or the rules of logic, and a statement in which the individual is involved, that is, the will at the same time as the mind. Any scientific statement, being involved with changing questions and with a provisory learning is historical in its content. But it would be impossible either to confuse progress toward an increasing approximation to truth with the revision of perspectives, or to assimilate the changes to which a knowledge concerned with still developing material is condemned with the relativity of judgments.

Finally, it is a question not so much of eternity as of choice. Marxism consents to be the truth of one day; it must still prove or justify that truth. Now, in each time, men and groups are opposed, and they give contradictory interpretations of the historical missions. Can Marxism face rival doctrines by invoking the advantage of reality as opposed to ideologies, of real truth as opposed to distortions, evasions or betrayals of the truth?

The antithesis between reality an dideology, although used especially by Marxists, complies with the intention of all historians. All of them would like to distinguish between the true substance of events, the superficial accidents which attract the attention of those living at the time and of the narrator, and finally the consciousness men had of their adventure. In fact, these distinctions are dubious. The accusations of ideologies are as frequent as they are reciprocal, as though, according to a convenient saying, the ideology were the opponent's idea.

We have come across the problem several times without using the term. We have shown the possible difference between the objective deed and the motive the doer cites in justification, between the rational interpretation of others and that of the person concerned.

In addition, historically, the act may be contrasted with the intentions to the extent that it brings about results surpassing or contradicting them; for instance a law increases the unemployment it was supposed to reduce. In this sense, the reality of a historical movement comes under a positive observation, beyond and despite ideologies. Above the elementary dialectics, we have studied in the field of biography the plurality of images. A certain biographer took as his goal to replace the picture which Comte gradually created of himself, by a picture of the actual life of the High Priest of Humanity: in practice, he too, composes one image among others.

In the case of an event, we arrive, through partial or inexact testimony, at reflections of living experience, at reconstitution of the outward fact according to probability. But as the fact gains extension, in proportion as a whole period comes into question, do we not relapse into the biographer's position? Every civilization has built up a representation of what it was or wished to be; the historian records and criticizes the representation, and seeks the reality.

If we place ourselves in a definite sector of history, the law for example, the uncertainty still stands; Kelsen's individual of the norms, as seen by the Marxist, is an ideology, and Kelsen in return holds that the reality of Marxism is alien to the law, and that its concepts are ideological. How would it be possible for the whole of a society to fix the substructure? Both causal and descriptive methods fail. The real in history is not given immediately to simple intuition, it is the object of a determination by philosophy.

But one may ask how such a proposition can be supported. The reality of actions or events is contrasted with the diversity of impressions and the unreality of the intentions, and this antithesis would no longer be valid for a larger whole. Where does the break occur? We could recall that the objectivity of impersonal understanding is dependent on the fact that living experiences be disregarded, an interpretation which becomes more difficult as the object is extended. Also, the extension of the field makes selection more uncertain, or at least more relative to the personality of the interpreter. But this double reservation is not conclusive. Statically, in terms of a theory of society, it would perhaps be possible to succeed in discerning the relations making for a certain collective existence. If such an advantage could not be claimed for Marxism it is because it is a question of choosing between rival doctrines equally concerned with interpreting, beyond the present, what is not yet, but is in the process of becoming.

Non-ideological thought would be that which sticks to reality. Now the philosophy of history is essentially transcendent to what is given, because it situates the past with reference to the future (which is imagined in the image of the past). It is, then, like any committed thought, involved with will. It is the priority of the future in the historical consciousness which condemns concrete philosophies to partiality.

Beyond its psychological or sociological significance, then, ideology has, first, a historical meaning. It points out the anticipations which await the judgment of time. It is objectively possible to measure the gap between ideas and action. The equality of income is not effective in present communist society, but the Soviet system, as one moment in history, is perceptible only within a certain perspective—that of Trotskyism, of Stalinism, or of pessimism (which believes in the permanence of the fundamental phenomena). Retrospectively, one discerns in ideologies what is still Utopian, and what has been made reality.

The objection may be, perhaps, that we have not yet so far proved that in every age there may be several possible responses to the situation. We might merely observe that this plurality is a fact inseparable from the plurality of social groups, and that in any case hesitation persists between the contemporary and future systems. But we shall first of all cite a philosophical reason. Man, Western man especially, is essentially the individual who creates gods, the finite being unsatisfied with his finiteness, who cannot live without faith in an absolute hope. If, then, he no longer conceived an ideology to cast light on his path or to strengthen his will, it is because he would have resigned himself to the world as it is. A logical resignation if his mission were carried out, an inconceivable one as long as man is not reconciled to his environment, his values to the order of society. Here is a dual conflict excluding universal agreement in the order of prerogatives. The final goal as well, if there is one, is gradually determined along with and at the rate of the development, provisory if it is concrete, formal if universally valid.

The absolute validity claimed by Marxism derives from a Hegelianism literally interpreted, but which became contradictory as soon as the truth of the system, which was the basis of truth of a history which had reached its terminus, disappeared. The multiplicity of forces does not compose into a universal dialectic, foreseeable because it is rational. The proletarian revolution, one among many, does not point to a complete break in human development; it does not withdraw the historian from history, and its verification awaits its outcome. In the meantime, like all decisions, it demands double justification—by way of provisory necessities and the ultimate goal, in the real and by the ideal.

* * * *

This discussion does not, any more than the one devoted to causal primacy, constitute either a refutation or confirmation of Marxism. It ends with a logical explanation, a formal, useless conclusion for those more concerned with action than with knowledge.

We had already concluded that Marxism is a philosophy, not a science, because the dialectics of history does not derive from the analysis of cause. Now we conclude that the Marxist doctrine, bound up with a political will and an attitude toward life, is specific as they are, and not universal, like objective knowledge and perhaps reflection. This particularity is legitimate if the concrete interpretations of history are inevitably historical. Only those fanatics and positivists who would condemn the philosophies of others, and bestow upon their own decision the prestige of truth, would have reason to protest.

IV. THE PLURALITY OF MODES OF CONSIDERATION

In the preceding chapter we showed that the concrete interpretations of the past are bound up with wills reaching out to the future. We shall, in this chapter, continue with the same question in respect of the manner of considering and writing history; let us say, in respect of the *modes of consideration.*

We shall observe again the *de facto* plurality, and shall try to see how we can imagine or attain a *de jure* unity.

* * * *

Historiographies are as different as the countries, the times, or the personalities of the historians. A psychology of historians is as conceivable as a history of historiography. Such a history, which would be especially complex, would have to take into account nations and times, social classes and metaphysical systems, aesthetic theories and scientific methods.

The distinctions that have been proposed between the various modes of consideration offer a similar multiplicity. From the logical point of view, we can group them into three categories: those based on the nature of the facts retained (political, economic, social, cultural conceptions of history), those based on the character of the knowledge (narrative, evolutionary, explanatory and psychological histories), and finally those based on the intention of the historian and his relation to the history (monumental, pragmatic, erudite, critical, philosophical history).

The principles of selection vary as the interest in the past is changed. But we have already limited the importance of these modifications, since all applications are logically on the same level unless they are justified by a philosophy. Economic systems, social life, are more important to us today than are accounts of battles or the interplay of politics. We are desirous of grasping whole societies, of interrelating all works and all activities, as though to make real the expression of integral resurrection. Personally, we share these preferences, but there is danger of exaggerating rather than failing to recognize their meaning and novelty.

Ancient historiography, curious mostly about events, is contrasted with the modern method, which is truly scientific since it aims at the general and not the particular, at what is common to all or to many and not at what singularizes a few, at what characterizes daily life rather than at what on the surface stirs the passions or strikes minds. Are not the most important modifications—scientific discoveries or technical progress—which have thrown our civilization into confusion, indifferent to revolutions and wars? Strictly, neither of these two antitheses is valid. The historian of the economy sticks to facts most easily grasped objectively, he takes in wider fields than the historian of politics, but both of them, when all is said and done, recompose a totality or a singular evolution, and the concern with alleged accidents is in itself no more to be despised than the concern with institutions. One would end with forgetting that the destiny of Europe has largely depended in the past, and depends even more today, on conflicts between peoples and classes.

Moreover, the collaboration of specialists, the putting together of partial views, are not enough to solve the problem of a general history. The expression *history of man* specifies neither the place belonging to each activity nor the system of interpretation suitable for intellectual endeavours. The general interaction of forces, the link between ideas and the real and their relative autonomy, all make indispensable a theory which is beyond empirical knowledge and positivist prejudices.

We shall not further insist on the distinctions of the second class. We are tempted to reduce the difference between narrative and evolutionary history, between erudition and explanation. In practice, these concepts will be used to designate types tending to become separate, works of different quality. It is right to note the gap between raw material and elaborated knowledge, between juxtaposition and an understanding of the process. But if our preceding studies are correct, there is no scientific history which does not retain certain characteristics of a narrative, and no narrative which by choice and retrospective reasoning does not tend towards scientific organization. The historian's own intention, not reducible to the establishment of causes and laws, evident both in the establishment of facts and in conceptual expression, remains too ambiguous, too near at one extreme to chronicle, at the other to philosophy, to justify any sharp separations.

Here again it is necessary to link subject with object, the interest of the former with the nature of the latter. Nietzsche's classification (learned, pragmatic, monumental history) starts with this principle, as does Hegel's, which procedes from the witness to the philosopher (from primitive to philosophical history) through reflection (general, pragmatic, critical, particular history). We have explained, in the same way, the different modalities of causal analysis, and the objectives to which understanding aspires, by means of the variations of curiosity.

We shall not stop to discuss the various classifications. Psychologically, the questions asked by the historian have infinite variations. Logically, we have already noted the essential antitheses: comprehensive history and causal history, monumental (history of an isolated work) and evolutive, partial and total history. Philosophically, the decisive antinomies are between the effort to be contemporary and the effort at retrospective interpretation, the psychology of men and the understanding of development, the dispersion of totalities and the reconstitution of one evolution.

One question only need delay us because it is theoretically essential. The question of the truth of a philosophical or reasonable consideration of history. Can it be conceived or justified? How does it overcome the multiplicity of interpretations? Is it reconcilable with the link between the present and the perspectives on the past?

* * * *

No philosophy could do away with either the plurality of considerations or the relativity of perspectives. And, according to the questions asked of it, since the development assumes different aspects, visions of the past must be as different as are men's intentions. Narrative and determinism, pragmatic and monumental history can disappear no more than can the interests they comply with, or the attitudes towards life which they express. It is at another level that philosophy dominates this multiplicity, without eliminating it.

Let us take an example. The witness has the merit of preserving and passing on the memory of those who lived through, if they did not determine, events. Memoirs, then, are true; they throw light on one aspect of reality. But he who sticks only to this aspect neglects the main thing. He subordinates the collective movement to the person who as he sees it, is its centre; actor, victim, *the suffering and active man*, perhaps like himself in his deep impulses. But the philosopher does not need to deny this identity to see, beyond behaviour and individual experience, the social and spiritual development in and through which man attains his human state, supposing that state defined by the mind, and in society.

Consequently, the only problem is to know whether it is given to man to discover the truth about himself while history still continues. A truth which would make possible the answer to the question with which the study of the evolution and of determinism ended: does history, which offers so many marks of contingency and irrationality, reveal, for all that, a necessity which brings a sort of justification to the past as a whole? As a result, we should grasp the totality which was vainly sought. That totality is confused neither with the integral reality, which is inaccessible like any object, nor with the juxtaposition of points of view, which is arbitrary as is any subjective synthesis. It would be the truth which would transcend the particularity of perspectives and the plurality of considerations, by determining the final meaning of the entire process.

But does the expression *truth concerning man* have any sense? The negative answer will be given as obvious. Any truth, it will be said, is a matter of knowledge and implies the possibility of verification. Whether it is a question of goals or of values, man chooses freely, and that liberty of choice excludes universality. The diversity of conceptions of the world is an indisputable fact. Lacking any data which may invalidate or confirm our hypotheses without debate, the diversity calls inevitably for a personal decision by each individual. We do not dream of either denying or questioning this confusion of metaphysical systems or preferences. But if any proposition which does not allow experimental control eludes the alternative of truth or falsehood, philosophy as a whole, including the philosophy of science, will be exempt from the logic of truth. The distinction between what is unverifiable, what is unknowable, and what is arbitrary, remains legitimate.

The negation is not based on observation only. As a matter of fact, it is almost always, explicitly or implicitly, bound up, not with scepticism or agnosticism, but with a form of dogmatism. Man is a beast of prey—he mutilates and degrades himself the moment he sublimates his instincts or represses the impulses which raise him to the position of a master over slaves. Cultures, gratuitously created by a living person or by individualities themselves alive, develop in accordance with a law alien to the mind. This irrationalism, one of the doctrines which emerged from the disintegration of Christianity, consists not so much of recalling the biological origins and nature of man (in that respect it is an integral element of any form of atheism), as of denying the essence or the goal for which he is under obligation to his reason.

This philosophy would be irrefutable if it did not bear within itself a sort of fundamental contradiction. The consciousness of himself acquired by this crude individual becomes a mystery and a disgrace. Why should he philosophize and seek the truth unless he felt capable of defining it? Irrationalism tends to refute itself, since it sets itself up as philosophical truth and denies philosophy's authority. This purely formal discussion will carry no conviction (and does not claim to do so), but at least suggests the basic antinomy between the rational mission of man and brute existence. History exists only because of this contradiction. Either pure mind or blind impulse, it would be equally lost in a continuous progression or in a lawless sequence.

Unable to act like angels without acting like beasts—this same rule applies to individuals and to collectivities. Individuals thinking that either in fact or logically their true self merges with a transcendental personality would not know themselves and would lapse into insincerity. Every individual creates himself by integrating into his personality a part of the character given by heredity or environment. Peoples who, in the name of laws of ethics, would forget the permanent necessities of domestic order and of international rivalry, would condemn themselves to decadence. The fate of states, and consequently of some of the noblest achievements, is still dependent on biological or social factors (such as birth-rates and labour organization). Men's reactions, psychologically understandable, usually follow blind impulses. Social phenomena are properly understood to be subject to a sort of determinism rather than to lucid intentions—and yet men still want a collectivity in which they would know themselves because they would have created it in the image of their ideal.

We do not hark back to the duality of what is and what ought to be. This ideal does not necessarily conform to the moral and humanitarian idealism in which certain illusions about humanity are blended with bourgeois aspirations. Moreover, this ideal is not an extra-historical datum; it is not defined once and for all. From religious doctrines which saw the end from the very beginning, moralists have borrowed an everlasting conception of man, which they set up above changing societies and in the name of which they pass judgment; a double mistake, if the idea is incomplete and if the norms are not separable from the historical material from which they come. It is in the collective development, where horror is compounded with greatness, that humanity rises to consciousness of itself and thus proceeds to contrast its intended purpose with its fate.

* * * *

So far, we have made the distinction between the logic of knowing and the interpretation of the historical process on the one hand, and the theory of a universe and the perspective of that universe, on the other. The example of Marxism has shown that any perspective (for total history) refers us to a materialistic theory, that is, to a definition of humanity claiming validity beyond the present. A philosophically justified will always transcends the immediate objective. Marx saw in communism the reconciliation of ancient antinomies, of essence and existence of men living together and with nature.

His mistake, of course, was the confusion of the immediate goal with the ultimate state, only the concept of which is determinable. But these two elements are inevitably met with in any philosophy of history; a private intention, placed between a known fragment of that past and the foreshadowed future, and an idea which is a provisory representation of the end. The antithesis, then, is entirely relative, or to put it more clearly, dialectic. By means of his ideologies, man always rises above reality, without ever clearly separating his incidental task from his ultimate mission, which he would want to be universal.

In the same way, between the logic of understanding and of cause on the one hand, and a concrete philosophy of history on the other, there seems to be a fundamental break. The first is basically a part of reflection on the object and subject of the evolution; a reflection which in its turn makes progress in time and enriches the consciousness that man acquires of the conditions, either permanent or changing, in which he knows himself. Logic thus unites with theory, as the latter does with the will. The dialectic has three terms, component of existence, indefinite for lack of conciliation, directed at a goal located at infinity.

CONCLUSION

THE EXPRESSION we have used, transcending historicism, is as ambiguous as historicism itself. One finds neither the simplicity of periods absorbed in themselves, nor the fixed point assured by a transcendent faith, nor the naïveté of those believing unreservedly in progress. The primary condition of humanist wisdom is the acceptance of particularity and of development (rather than evolution).

It is true that we have admitted rather than demonstrated the changes, without specifying their depth. As a matter of fact, as we shall show further on, we refuse to admit an antithesis between the permanence of human nature and the affirmation of development. In the order of psychology, one arrives by definition at impulses common to all, whatever influences social environments may have on manifestations of the most primitive tendencies. On the other hand, it is difficult to doubt changes in conceptions of the world, in hierarchies of value, etc. Now, this indisputable diversity is sufficient, since our humanity is not at the level of our drives, but rather of our wills and thoughts. We have, then, limited ourselves to suggesting the formal identity of reason, and to emphasizing the contradictions between the patterns of life and of kinds of ethos, propositions which maintain both the unity and reality of history.

Of course, the diversity of higher cultures poses a problem which we have scarcely faced. We are not competent to deal with it concretely. And, without going outside of our own civilization, we ran into fundamental antinomies: development or evolution, progress or lawless succession, particularity or truth.

We have left aside partial histories since we had shown the subordination of history as science to history as intellectual development. A theory of history of philosophy assumes a theory of philosophy. In truth, the same subordination is again to be found, in a certain sense, in general history. The knowledge man acquires of history depends on the nature he reveals in it, so that we have passed over from reflection about the science to reflection about the subject of the science. The possibility of a philosophy of history finally merges with the possibility of a philosophy in defiance of history, since all philosophy is defined as man's effort to determine himself.

Setting aside the eternal ethic, either transcendent or *a priori*, we have put morality and metaphysics back into time, but thanks to the distinction between committed thought and reflection, between logic and the concrete interpretation, between the immediate intention and the ideal goal, we have suggested the dialectics of life which acts, thinks, and thinks itself (which we shall describe more exactly in the last *Part*). This is a dialectics of history, of course, but one forever struggling to transcend history, and one defined by that act of will, which is always vain and ever renewed. For history disappears just as truly if man has nothing left to learn as if he will never learn anything.

Third Part

MAN AND HISTORY

THE CONSCIOUSNESS of history varies with peoples and times; now it is dominated by nostalgia for the past, now by the feeling of preservation or hope concerning the future. These fluctuations are easily understood. Certain peoples expect greatness, others preserve the memory of it, some feel linked with a tradition they wish to prolong, others are eager for novelty, thirsting for liberty and forgetfulness. Time is at once both the destroying power which sweeps into oblivion monuments and empires, and the principal of life and creation. Neither the optimism of progress nor the pessimism of separation and solitude define properly the historical idea. In this *Part* we should like to rise above these particular philosophies and think about their common origin, the relationship of the two terms: *man* and *history*.

In order to know that *he is in history*, man must discover that he belongs to a collectivity which shares a history common to several collectivities. Society and its history represent the environment in which each realizes himself, an environment inflicted upon him, and which he judges.

If history were nothing but the arena for collective changes, man would not become conscious of his historical nature. Once he has recognized the real development of which he is an atom, he must still, in order to weigh his servitude, perceive within himself that nature he wished to condemn in the name of his ideals. *Man is historical.*

The first two chapters having as their themes these two formulae, pose new problems: if man finds particularity in himself how will he accede to universality? How does he bring his decision under subjection to the law of the true? Thus we come to the antinomy between life and truth; the diversity of conditions of life is faced with the unity of the final purpose of mankind, the contingency of what is given with the essence of the individual.

The solution of this antinomy is suggested by a final formula. *Man is a history* if, as individual duration constitutes the self, so all history becomes one with humanity (if the latter creates itself throughout time and pre-exists neither in the beyond nor in the fixity of a definition) in the adventure in which it is engaged.

Hence the last term of the discussion will be at the same time temporality and liberty (Chapter IV). Time is not a mirror which distorts or a screen hiding the real individual, but the expression of human nature whose finiteness implies an unending progression. History is free because it is not written in advance, or determined as is a sector of nature or a fatality; it is unpredictable, as man is for himself.

I. MAN IN HISTORY: CHOICE AND ACTION

PSYCHOLOGICALLY, the modes of political thought are indefinitely variable. Most people never question their convictions; they have acquired, or rather accepted, ideas and desires simultaneously, without ever looking at their situation in the abstract, without breaking the connection between consciousness and life. We have all known sons of middle-class families who are cynically or peacefully conservative or sons of socialists, as ingenious as their fathers. Those who have made up their minds consciously or more than once—whether because they have moved in contradictory worlds, or whether, lacking spontaneous certainty, they have had to build their world—seem to obey the most varied motives. One becomes a communist by way of Christianity and atheism, discovering the corruption of our society through the intercession of Jesus, not of Marx; another is a royalist because of a love of order not so much the effect of authority as of the concept of Athenian reason. Historically, the statements of the political problem are even more varied (there is no need to emphasize it).

And yet, as we see it, there is logic of political thinking. Not that it is possible to compare and contrast all opinions: between the economist who damns collectivism because it produces at net costs which are too high, and the moralist who condemns a system whose mainspring is the profit motive, there is not and never will be any discussion. At the level of personal preferences, discussions are everlasting because temperaments clash without any mutual assessment or correction. Logic makes it possible, not to decide between ideas, but to think about them and thus to determine the conditions under which the individual, *de facto* and *de jure*, decides, becomes adherent, and active. We shall bring out one of the aspects of this reflection, and shall show the historical nature of political thought and, above all, of the two decisive steps: *choice* and *action.*

* * * *

Three illusions prevent the recognition of the *historicity* of any sort of politics. One is that of the scientists who imagine a science (of society or of morality) which would make it possible to set up a rational art. The second is that of the rationalists who, more dependent than they realize on the Christian ideal, unreservedly admit that practical reason as well as the ideal is the cause of individual conduct and of collective life. The third is the illusion of the pseudo-realists who base their claim on historical experience, on fragmentary regularities or eternal necessities, and pour their contempt on the idealists without realizing that they are subjecting the future to a past which is reconstructed rather than conceived, a shadow of their scepticism and a reflection of their own resignation.

A science of ethics, as we have seen, would bring agreement among all honest people. Strictly, it would confirm common testimonies, but without giving anyone the authority to decide between conflicting sides. If it dropped from sociology into sociologism, set society up as an absolute value, it would still teach only obedience. Submission to the new divinity would be just as sacred as before. Of course, it is possible to reintroduce the plurality of societies or of organizations within a certain society, but by so doing the total unity from which it was claimed rules or goals were deduced is immediately eliminated.

Besides, it is not true that an ethics, or *a fortiori* a system of politics, seem possible without study of the collective reality. We condemn only the claim to apply to the relation between theory and practice (political or moral) the schema of the technical arts (industrial or medical). There is a refusal to admit that the ends here are not indicated by universal agreement. The main point is to know *which* common agreement is desired. The natures of both society and sociology are falsified by imagining society as coherent and univocal, and sociology as total and systematic. Really, the scientist finds in the object the conflicts which disturb other men and himself. Assuming that he casts light on their origins and importance, he at most helps the individual to locate himself in history. If he boasts of any further contribution it is usually because his investigation and conclusions are already governed by the allegedly disinterested desires for knowledge.

The idea of a single mission for all men and peoples is easily justified within a Christian representation of the world. The concrete diversities between temperaments or collectivities do not break up this identity, both original and final which, unperceived by individuals and guaranteed by the presence of God, is free from the danger of formalism; which is both real and efficacious, since it is due to the mystic solidarity of men and to their common sharing in the drama of the species.

On the other hand, the mission, inherent in our spiritual nature and discerned by reflection, becomes necessarily formal if it is to be valid for all times; it reconciles neither individuals nor rival groups. Let us admit with Troeltsch that ethical imperatives survive the deaths of empires and the passage of centuries. Strictly speaking, they suggest an ideal, otherwise rather indefinite, of personal life. But it is a strange illusion, all the more deeprooted because it will not stand up to examination, to suppose that, based on unselfishness, generosity or freedom, one will succeed in setting up the image of a society conforming to the eternal rules.

Let us take the example of the current problems of economics. Schematically, two systems of regulation are possible: one, automatic, by means of the free action of prices in the market, the other in accordance with a plan. In the first case, the capital needed for investment is supplied by personal savings, in the second by capital levies fixed by the administration of the plan. A self-regulated economy implies at the same time as profits, a great inequality. A planned economy undergoes a minimum unevenness, but requires strong authority to determine it in conformity with collective needs (with a political conception of those needs), and the share of the national income assigned each year to the various classes of citizens. The choice between the two systems is decisive: is a reasonable arbitration conceivable? To no degree.

The choice may be made from various points of view: the system assuring greatest production is perhaps the most unjust, the one allowing the least personal independence. Fanatics would try to conceal this plurality—their system would be the most effective, the most harmonious, the most just; it should do away with depressions, the exploitation of man, poverty, etc. Such naïveté does not allow perception of the true facts. A just (or more just) society will, at the beginning, have to sacrifice liberalism to equality and discipline. Even if it is admitted that in the long run all claims, today contradictory, will be satisfied, risks must be run, and the hierarchy of preference governs the order of sacrifices to be made.

Human relations, whether economic or political, present specific problems not reconcilable with the abstract laws of ethics. Let us assume, along with a traditional philosophy, that every man is free because he has a certain capacity for judgment. How is one to specify the liberties to which he has the right, the ones he is ready to give up momentarily in order to reach some goal or other? Concrete definitions are always taken from a historical reality, not from abstract necessity. In other words, as we were saying above, one either dwells in the empyrean of vain principles, or else slips into deduction from precise details valid only for one time.

Let us add that one does not have to choose between two ideal systems—self-regulated and planned—but between two imperfect forms. At a certain moment in the evolution of capitalism, one must decide for or against the system, in favour of some reform or other. In quiet times, when the established system is not questioned, the politics of ideas, dear to certain intellectuals, takes on full significance, it gives form to the ideal conceived by existing society, or expresses and transfigures some concrete claim or other. But during times of crisis political choices show their nature as historical choices. We take sides, side with one class against another, prefer the inconveniences of anarchy to those of tyranny. The rationalist's illusion is not so much not recognizing the reality as it is clinging to the hope that after all he is choosing rationally. In truth, one chooses at and for one moment; one does not give up true liberalism, but a decadent liberalism. One condemns not so much the essence of parliament as a corrupted parliamentarianism. So it is understandable, appearances notwithstanding, that capitalism was overthrown first in the country where it was least developed.

Let us add again that this choice is further idealized by simplifying it to the choice between past and future, by forgetting the plurality of possibilities offered at any one moment, and by confusing the new system with the embodiment of the absolute. The rhythm of progress allows the introduction of a decision, which is always potentially heavy with uncertainty and renunciation, into a global movement preserving some of the prestige borrowed from Providence.

The idea of a political history has a reactionary tone in France. The appeal to experience is a characteristic of conservative thinking. This is because, in reality, the historical nature of any political system is confused with a certain theory of history, the one based on the *lessons of history* or the value of tradition.

The science of history contains no suggestion that what has been must continue to be, or that what endures is better than what passes, or even that what is always found in the past must always be reencountered in the future. With such reasoning the fatality of slavery could long since have been proved. Logically, history leads to politics via observed regularities. The whole problem is to determine the nature of these regularities.

Politically, the historian often brings out *constants*, the relatively stable facts of one situation. Max Weber wrote that in the long run only Russia threatens German's existence. A French historian would say, in the same way, that Germany alone endangers the existence of France. One historian concludes the necessity either to dissolve German unity or to bring together a coalition of small nations, just as the other historian recommended an agreement between southern Slavs or with England.

The inadequacy of these so-called lessons is due to the change of the *constants*, especially in diplomacy; we have, for several years, been able to weigh its weaknesses. Real politics is one which upsets alliances. If there is little change in physical geography, political geography partakes of the development of history. It is an easy matter to talk of experience, but more difficult to make use of it, and even harder to forget it. And yet, effective action, careless of destiny, would grasp opportunities, and would be capable of taking in situations made up of elements already seen, in their novelty.

Will it be said that the antithesis between the effort towards originality and the respect for the past is artificial, that the constants we have taken as an example are too special? Let us try, then, to distinguish the categories of the generalities of history: first, the *elementary regularities*, microscopic, as it were, which have to do with the permanence of certain human impulses; next, the *historical and social regularities* which would designate the characteristics common to all collective organizations (for example, class or group conflicts); finally, all causal relations (analysed above). All these regularities, as we know, are partial and fragmentary. If, then, they are taken as a sole basis to justify politics, it may be said that this politics is historical, but on condition that it is added that this history is the projection into the past of a present intention.

Besides, it is enough for us to return to the results of our previous studies. The science of history comes to three types of conclusions: the pure narrative, the report of causal connections, and a global presentation of the development, a representation which seems to be the last term even though it already inspires conceptual expression and choice of the events. Causal relationships are objective but isolated terms, that is, the questions asked correspond to the historian's problems. The selection of regularities inevitably is political in nature. As for the mental pictures of the total history—the eternity of class conflict, rivalry between governmental authority and citizenry, the basic laws of order, or even, on the contrary, the evolution for the better, the dialectics of totalities—they reflect philosophies, and are dependent on decisions. What makes the idea of a scientific politics absurd, then, is the fact that the science, always biased, is subject to conflicting acts of will. We come again to the dialectics which has been the core of our discussion, the dialectics of the past and of the present straining towards the future, the dialectics of contemplation and action. It is not a question of knowing, as is often thought, whether politics must or must not avail itself of history, but of how it must so do. The history of Maurras is like the world of the Manichees given over to the endless struggle between good and evil, with the good always rejoicing in triumphs which are only doubtful and precarious. The history of Marxism is an over-all movement towards a communal society.

But if all political systems are historical, is it not possible, without leaving out their differences, to force them to a discussion by analysing the logically inevitable content of a doctrine? The historicity of politics (or of morals) condemns scientist pretentions, but sanctions the rights of reflection.

* * * *

The choice so far discussed is logically made up of two distinct steps: the choice of a policy, and the loyalty to a party. These steps, normally confused, can and must be distinguished.

The first one requires us to recognize, within society as it is, the attainable and desirable objectives, or, again, the system of government which could succeed the present one. The second step assumes that we accept the members of a party or class, that we commit ourselves fully, rather than that we express a wish or preference. Now, one does not always proceed from anticipation or from desire to an act of will.

How, unless one is blinded by fanaticism, can this dualism be denied? What recourse, except abstention or resignation, is there, for those who face a detestable, but seemingly inevitable future—like the pagan during the centuries in which the triumph of Christianity was already being consummated—or for those who approve the end without consenting to the means, or to the discipline prescribed—like the modern liberal or the humanitarian communist? Of course, there will be defeats, defeats are perhaps inevitable if man is the being who recognizes the possible and reaches out for the impossible, who is subject to history and wishes to choose it.

Between adhesion and action there is no obstacle. The man who is integrated into a group has accepted service. If we separate the two steps, it is because action, by the leader, by the soldier, poses different problems for the conscience and for the intelligence, problems not confused either with those of choice, or with those of adhesion.

Psychologically, as we have said, the content of political choice varies indefinitely, even within a given society, or in a given period of time. Logically, it is important first of all to accept or not the existing order: the first alternative would be pro or con what exists. Reformers and conservatives oppose revolutionaries, those who would like, not to improve capitalism, but to do away with it altogether. The revolutionary tries, by destroying the environment, to become reconciled with himself since man is in accord with himself only if he agrees with the social relations of which he is, willy-nilly, the captive.

He who places himself within the framework of the given system varies in a thousand ways his acceptance of principle. The conservative, depending on his intelligence, is always more or less a reformer; he sets himself up as the defender of a certain value or of certain interests. The revolutionary however, has no programme, unless it is a demagogic one. Let us say that he has an *ideology*, that is, the idea of another system, surpassing the present one and probably unrealizable; but only the outcome of the revolution will make it possible to distinguish between the anticipation and the Utopia.

If, then, one were to stick to ideologies, one would spontaneously join the revolutionaries who normally promise more than the others. The resources of imagination necessarily win out over reality, even when distorted or transfigured by falsity. Thus is explained the prejudice of intellectuals for so-called advance parties. There is no need to invoke faith in progress. Without any question, the societies known until now have been unjust (measured by present concepts of justice). It still remains to be seen what a just society would be, if it is definable and realizable.

From the standpoint of reason it would be important, as we pointed out above for the economy, to compare the present with the future organization. This comparison would give conclusions which would be at least likely and positive, but these abstract considerations are of less importance than one is tempted to believe. One would have to compare capitalism as it has developed with communism as it will be, given the men who historically are given the opportunity and responsibility of bringing it about. But the second term of the proposition eludes us. The revolutionaries will be changed by their own victory. Between the fragmentary preconceptions and the future totality there is still a vast margin, the margin of ignorance, and perhaps of freedom.

Supposing that fewer drawbacks are found in the declining than in the incoming system, assuming that the antinomies of capitalism seem less objectionable with reference to sacred values than does collectivist despotism, will one be ready for that reason to take one's stand with capitalism, to become its defender? The revolt of the masses is a reality also, which proves at the least the possibility of another system. One does not share all the hopes of the fanatics, but there is no denying the meaning of the cataclysm. And the uncertainty of the future forbids scepticism and surrender.

It would be too simple to say that the choice is the better of two evils, or that one chooses the unknown: let us say that a choice always implies sacrifices and that one chooses *against* some thing when one chooses revolution.

There are two separate problems of action: first that of obtaining or preserving power, then that of utilizing it for an end.

There is no need for us to study political conditions by systems and countries. It is for political sociology to analyse the technique of propaganda or dictatorship. Only one thing concerns us, because it has to do with our main theme: the gap between the reality and consciousness. Action aimed at power inevitably makes use, as does any action, of the means suited to the proposed end. It is a matter of fact that the masses are more effectively influenced by demagogy than by appeal to truth which is usually distasteful. To submit to what is practical would be to consider other men as instruments, to force oneself to lie, even for the sake of honesty. Ideology and myth are a permanent part of social life, because men never recognize and are never willing to recognize the history they are making.

One bias, then, is just as much to be feared as the idealist's, and leads to disappointments just as great: the technician's (who is today the economist or financier), who compares the acts of government with what, according to the science, would have been desirable. Pareto's treatise systematizing the resentments of a disappointed liberal illustrates this absurdity of human behaviour, if rationality is confused with economic rationality. Let us add that Weber's realism is scarcely less illusory. Even though he analysed without pity the conditions of modern politics (party, prebends, spoils, etc.), he refused to commit himself; he wanted to oblige everyone to fight with flags flying, as though no party was capable of distinguishing between existing and desired conditions, or of foreseeing the results of measures recommended or put into effect.

The only way to avoid Pareto's pessimism is to restore its historical dimension to reality. Conflicts between factions and classes, revolutions and despotic regimes represent a series of absurd disasters unless one catches at least a glimpse of the pattern leading societies and minds toward a different future. The contemporary man legitimately compares acts and intentions, principles and behaviour: a certain socialist government accelerates the concentration of capital, and in the name of prosperity prolongs the crisis. But he must not be unaware of the transient quality of his criticism, however necessary that criticism may be. In the last analysis, it is history that passes judgment on the man of action—not the economy or ethics.

The grasp of power is the supreme reward of the demagogue, but the leader's measure is still to be taken.

Is the ideal, then, that of Max Weber? To take in situations, to discern the complexity of the determinism, and to fit into reality the new fact which gives the greatest chance of attaining the goal which has been set? To tell the truth, here we come upon a fundamental antinomy between a *politics of compromise* and a *politics of reason*, which corresponds to the antinomy between chance and evolution. In the one case, strategy is made up only of tactics indefinitely revised; in the other tactics are subordinate to a strategy which is in its turn adjusted to an image of the development.

The *politician of compromise*, such as Max Weber, or Alain tries to preserve certain goods—peace, or liberty,—or to attain a single objective,—national greatness—in ever new situations which succeed each other without organization. He is like the pilot who would navigate without knowing the port. A dualism of means and ends, of reality and values. There is no present totality or fatal future; each moment is new for him.

The *politician of reason*, on the other hand, foresees at least the immediate phase of the evolution. The Marxist is certain of the inevitable disappearance of capitalism, and the only problem is to adapt the tactics to the strategy, the compromise with the present regime in preparation for the future one. Means and ends, change and goal, reform and revolution—these classical antitheses recall the conflicts, in which those who act in the present, without ignoring the future they desire, become involved.

These two types are, it goes without saying, ideal types, they mark the extreme attitudes. One runs the risk of degenerating into resignation, the other into blindness, the one becomes impotent by dint of trusting itself to history, and the other by forgetting it; the one is wiser, the other more heroic. This is to say that any politics is at the same time both one and the other. There is no momentary action which does not obey a remote concern, no confidant of Providence who does not watch for special opportunities. The qualities of prophet and empiricist should not be too different. Politics is at one and the same time both the art of irrevocable choice and of long term plan. The man of action, though ready to take advantage of accidental incidents, would aim inflexibly at his goal. It more frequently happens, though, that we see wisdom serving some foolish enterprise, or the contempt for technique jeopardizing a reasonable plan.

* * * *

Choice and action are historical in three ways. They answer a situation of which the individual assumes the burden without bearing the responsibility. One does not go back on what is accomplished: one restores the monarchy, but not feudal rights. A mistake is not righted by a mistake in the opposite direction. Hitler's Germany needs a policy different from that of the Weimar Republic. One must avoid regrets and remorse, which are useless and dangerous.

In the second place, action consents to the uncertainty of the future. Whether one adheres to a social system or resorts to a financial measure, there are risks to be run, because it is never possible to predict human reactions, because only part of reality is known, and all of it is effective.

Finally, action begins by accepting the conditions fundamental to all politics, and the conditions peculiar to a given time. One needs to be capable of lucidity and faith; to believe in a historical purpose without believing either in myths or in mobs. In terms of human psychology, no group, no party could ethically claim superiority or privilege.

This triple historicity answers a triple need: to claim a heritage, to look forward to an unknown future, and to find one's place in a movement which transcends the individual.

II. HISTORICAL MAN: THE DECISION

THE CHOICE appeared historical, because it becomes clearer and firmer in proportion as we discover, in a backward and forward motion, the situation we are living in and the policy to which we adhere. Our discussion, purposefully limited, overlooked one aspect of the given.

The choice is historical also because the values in the name of which we judge the present come from history; they are deposited in us by the objective mind, which we have assimilated in acquiring personal consciousness. And on the other hand, the choice is not an act external to our true being; it is the decisive action by which we commit ourselves and fix the social environment which we recognize as ours. Really, choice in history merges with a decision about ourselves, since its origin and object are our own lives.

* * * *

During the rare periods of peace, when private life developed on the fringe of public affairs, when one's occupation had nothing (or almost nothing) to expect or fear from authority, politics appeared to be a speciality, given over to a few professionals, one trade among others, more fascinating than serious. It took war to reawaken men to the fact that they are citizens before they are private individuals; the collectivity, whether class or country, rightly requires of everyone that he sacrifice himself to a cause. Whether it is national defence or revolution, the individual belonging to history is obliged to assume the supreme risk.

These two choices are rarely put on the same plane. Moralists and doctrinarians dream of a pacified and pacifist mankind. However it may be for those hopes, there has been no State so far which has not used force to stand against its enemies, both domestic and foreign. In today's world, it is absurd or naïve to preach non-violence as long as social and colonial regimes rely on an authority which has less need of consent than of police.

Will it be said that revolutionary violence has precisely the aim of triumphing over the violence which is crystallized in institutions? Let us admit it temporarily. In any case, the revolutionary could invoke no sort of conscientious objection. The minute he consents to kill in certain cases, he chooses one war rather than another. The choice is political, not moral.

It will be said that this is the final violence to put an end to all violence. Pacifists and idealists aim at this self-justification. It is conceived that a war may appear provisionally as the last one for Europe, and that it will set up between certain nations an agreement which will for a time exclude further conflict. Such a peace, though limited, would be one stage of the historical development, would sanction a certain redistribution of possessions, a certain state of institutions. In other words, the result would still be political, and would have characteristics of the instability, and of the partial injustice, of any policy. In the same way it can be hoped that some future regime will be better than the present one, but not that with a planned economy bureaucracy will vanish, and that each will receive recompense in proportion to merit.

In advanced parties three types of men are found: idealists, anarchists, and true revolutionaries. The revolutionaries say no to the existing order and want another; anarchists say no to any sort of social order; the idealists judge, or imagine they do, in terms of an eternal ideal, without troubling to confront their demands with the permanent conditions of collective life. Without realizing it, they take the most futile attitude—that of revolt which does not end in revolution. It is normal that a young man who measures the distance between the principles he has been taught and existing society should be a rebel. Perhaps man should put his dignity to the pursuit of an ideal which he will never reach. But rebellion, however attractive it may be aesthetically or, in some cases, humanly, is childish, for it puts desire in the place of volition and substitutes claims for action. It is not nobility—it is folly to say no to both present and future in order to assent to a dream. Besides, rebellion against the social order also implies, in the end, the sacrifice of life. The conscientious objector cannot be refuted if he consents to anything rather than to obey an obligation unacceptable to him. The liberty of concrete choice is limited by the nature of communities and the historical conditions. But liberty of the individual is still total, for he judges history at the same time that he judges in history.

Again he must, if he wishes to be lucid, face the consequences of his decision. The objector who becomes indignant at the penalties inflicted on him has no more understood the world than he has understood himself. A collectivity which would consent that the laws should not be obligatory for all, that citizens, in case of need, should not be obliged to defend it, though it is not inconceivable, is still unheard of. So, he who prefers the salvation of his soul to that of the state should not be surprised if the latter answers his refusal with a reprisal. Common will and personal conscience are bound to clash, and the latter is wrong unless it is based on a divine law, since it opposes the universal imperative and fails to recognize human destiny, which is achieved only in the community.

No doubt this extreme conflict is historical, since the obligation to serve, in its present form, is of recent date. Even today he who does not recognize himself as part of either the present regime, or of the one being prepared for, still has the moral right to shun society; stoic, sage, or resigned, he consents to live alone. But no one ever wants solitude; one prefers it sometimes to a determined collectivity. If political choice at times is liable to involve the choice of certain death, it is always because it means the choice of a certain life.

Here again, the present-day movement of politics is apt to hide from us the extent of our commitments. It is clear today that public life determines all private life, that by wishing for a certain social order, one is wishing for a mode of life. Everything would not be overwhelmed by a revolution. There would still be more continuity than fanatics imagine. The mind is not entirely possessed by the common destiny. Relations between men, commercial practice, the nature of authority, the family even, would be transformed. The lives of each and every one would be different, there would be other convictions, other ideologies. He who wants a new society wishes for another self, since he belongs to society as it is, the one which has formed him and which he denies.

He usually invokes transcendent imperatives or calls for an ideal future. But, as we have seen, the latter is only the transfiguration, authorized by ignorance, of an imperfect system, the imperatives are the hypostasis of realized values, affirmed or dreamed of by present society. Thus it is explicable that the revolutionary often invokes principles borrowed from the heritage he rejects. It is in the name of democracy that communists work for a social order radically different from the form of democracy in which we are living. And again, socialism, itself the denial of capitalism, bears more marks than it thinks of the society which created it and which it now hates. The ideas of the future system accumulate within the declining system. Social contradictions are doubled by contradictions of men in themselves. Individuals no longer accept their environment, their consciences condemn their existence. Revolution seems one solution, although it reconciles certain persons with themselves and their environment, but not the ideal with reality.

* * * *

The life of an individual in time involves the three dialectics of past and future, of knowledge and desire, of self and others. These three elementary dialectics are subordinate to that of the world and the person. We discover the situation in which we exist, but we recognize it as ours only by accepting or refusing it, that is, by determining the one in which we are willing to live. The choice of an environment is a decision about ourselves, but this decision, like the choice, emerges from what we are (so that there are repeated here the dialectics of knowledge and will, of values and the given); the decision is as deeply historical as is the choice. Now, it creates our spiritual universe at the same time that it settles the place to which we lay claim in collective life. Can we still stick to our decision if we become conscious of the particularity of our own being and of our preferences?

Psychologically, the question has little significance. Fanaticism will be only too quick to exalt a passing need or to assimilate an immediate goal to the final human goal. Most men make no distinction between the God whom they adopt and the one who might be. Marxists demonstrate daily that the absolute in history is easily discovered.

The real question is not psychological (even though perhaps faith is all the more intolerant and blind as it feels more incapable of proof).

Is a historical decision philosophically conceivable? If such a decision is compared with the one made by the believer or the moralist, the difference may be measured. The believer does not have to will, but to be. Good and evil are pre-existent to him, beyond the world of living beings; it is for each one, all through life and at each moment of it, to work out his salvation, and to play his eternal part in time. The Christian moves towards or away from God who, unchangeable, inaccessible, suffers and triumphs with him. The moralist, although the discernment of values is human and not divine, hears a word addressed to all. The command not to kill, to control one's passions, or to obey the categorical imperative, is a command neither for one time nor for one day. Its validity is as wide as the humanity whose vocation it expresses and whom it reconciles in respect for itself. On the contrary, the concrete decision of the communist, the National Socialist, the republican, the Frenchman, integrates the individual into collectivities closed into themselves; it obeys no universal law, it responds to a singular contingency which it does not outlive. It seems relative, like everything connected with perishable things.

In our day of blind beliefs, one hopes rather that individuals may remember that the concrete object of their attachment is not revealed, but worked out according to probability, and that it should not, like the transcendent religions, divide the world into opposing camps. One is tempted to emphasize the uncertainty of opinions rather than the absoluteness of commitments. As long as there remains room for discussion, it is better, indeed, to remember that no humanity is possible without tolerance, and that the possession of total truth is granted to no one. But it is enough that there should come extreme situations, wars or revolutions, for wisdom to become powerless and for the fundamental disagreement again to arise. As his historical task, man must assume the risk which for him carries everything with it.

Philosophically, contradiction disappears as soon as the decision is no longer judged by the religious standard. The man who is conscious of his finiteness, who knows his one and limited existence, must, if he does not renounce life, dedicate himself to ends whose value he consecrates by subordinating his own personality to them. Without this, all things would be wasted in indifference, and men would debase themselves in nature, since they would be what they are by accident of birth or of environment. Besides, these formulae express a truth so commonplace that the opposite thesis, dishonour rather than death, has offended those very ones who implicitly accepted it by unconditionally refusing violence.

So, without yielding to a pathetic mode of philosophy, and without taking the anguish of a disordered era as an eternal datum, nor yet allowing oneself to sink into nihilism, one can recall that man determines both himself, and his mission, by measuring himself against nothingness. This is, indeed, only to affirm the power of man, who creates himself by judging his environment, and by choosing himself. Only in this way does the individual overcome the relativity of history by the absolute of decision, and make the history he bears within, and which becomes his history, truly a part of himself.

* * * *

If the decision imparts to the choice its unconditional quality, the latter in return gives the decision its particularity. We are not above the social life we lead; we are identical with our destiny; we are shut into the contingency of the psychological and historical bases given which we have collected and assimilated. Can we escape this particularity, or must we accommodate ourselves to it?

In a sense, we escape it the moment we recognize it. Now, the science of history is by definition a reflective branch of knowledge, since it shows us what we are in history, we among others. Are we to say, agreeing with Dilthey's concept, that it is history itself which frees us from history?

We have elsewhere developed and specified the idea, which may be understood in three different ways. Either objective knowledge of the past raises us above ourselves; or retrospection has the privilege of grasping truth; or, finally, reflection alone sets us free from our limitations.

In his writings, Dilthey juxtaposed rather than united the two contradictory ideas that one understands what one has experienced or might have experienced in life, and that one understands the other person. Thence at the same time the sameness of mankind and the achievement of humanity by development. We have tried to define exactly and to bring together these themes, but we have had to reject the basic hypothesis upon which the objectivity of the science is founded. Dilthey grants that the historian becomes completely detached from himself, that he coincides with the various epochs, because he is not bound up with the present. According to our study, this would be error and illusion. It would be an error in the sense that the historian, in so far as he lives historically, has a tendency to action and seeks the past pertaining to his future. It would be an illusion in the sense that as a spectator, he would be unable to understand with exactitude. Like the principle of all life, as the subject itself never appears to the onlooker, the latter organizes human worlds by reconstructing them.

The origin of that reconstruction is in the personality of the student, whose historicity entails that of understanding.

Consequently, the question of universal validity which occurred to Dilthey for any history of philosophy, the philosophy emerging from history or the totality which would reconcile partial conceptions—that question occurs for any knowledge of the past. Partial histories are dependent on theories and perspectives, which historian and historical being alike seek.

The significance of a period is fixed only on two conditions: either that it dwell within itself or that it be related to a definitive term. We have shown the impossibility of a truth of equivalence, and the future reveals only bit by bit, never definitively, the truth about the past.

As for reflection, it shields us from particularity because it is linked neither with the commitment nor with the limitation of our personality; but if the object of the reflection remains formal, if we know in accordance with truth the necessity of the decision, we then meet with the impossibility of a truth about history in history.

* * * *

We have met one after the other all the significations of the traditional saying that man is a historical being; a mortal being who thinks his death, a social being who wishes to be individual, a conscious being who reflects upon his particularity. History is the dialectic in which these contradictions become creative, the infinite in and through which he recognizes his finite being.

III. THE HISTORY OF MAN: THE SEARCH FOR TRUTH

THE FIRST formula, 'man is in history', opposed the individual and his social environment. The second, 'man is historical', re-established the unity, but sanctioned the particularity of personalities and the relativity of wills. The last formula, that 'man is history', confirms this limitation, since it merges the personality and humanity with the unfolding of their temporal existence. And yet, perhaps man succeeds if he defines himself even as he creates himself, in overcoming history by recognizing and determining it.

* * * *

History is the development of spiritual worlds simultaneously with collective unities, the development of culture if by that term is meant the works which man builds and by which he transcends himself. It signifies that the worlds are always connected with a partially irrational origin and that they develop in time. How are these two qualities combined?

The Parthenon, having become existent, has nothing to expect from time but destruction. Graven in matter, the mind is subject to the fragility of things; the centuries offer it no other enrichment than that of an ever new admiration. Masterpieces give to one moment of a life an assurance of a sort of endlessness; they offer others a possibility of escape, since he who contemplates is, like the object, freed from the flight of time. The posthumous history of art is made up of separate moments, in the image of the monuments which have been handed down and of the successive individuals who transfigure them.

It is of small importance that styles develop together or in opposition, and that each artist prolongs or denies a tradition. The theory we are outlining is not that of history, external or intrinsic, inherent in the evolution of society; we are thinking solely of the essence of aesthetic creation and enjoyment. Nor does it matter whether beauty obeys eternal norms or whether on the contrary its forms are irreducibly various. We claim neither that it is separable from lives nor that it is defined once and for all. The everlastingness is that of the finished work, with no other end than itself, irreplaceable, accessible to conscious minds in the fullness of separate moments.

The idea appears quite clearly if we refer to the contrary type of activity, that is, science. The contrast has less to do with the fact that the validity of a judgment is indifferent to its origins than with the subordination of each discovery to the one preceding or following it in the continuity of progress. Again, it is not a question of the real development which, exposed to all influences, shares the vicissitudes of the movement of history. Just as the perfection of the beautiful decomposes duration into a scattered plurality, so the imperfection of all scientific truth makes up the continuation of an unending conquest. The artist is alone and measures himself by God, the scientist locates himself in humanity in progress and knows his own finiteness.

Yet it is the scientist, not the artist, who transcends history. The finished work is sufficient for itself, but is to be understood only through the life it expresses, in the same way as is the amateur's enjoyment only through a certain affinity with the creator. Material destruction, then, is not the only sort of death that threatens it. Barbarians, or a new race, cheerfully sacrifice values which have been sacred. Of course, a truth which is established and definitely valid (by unanimity of judgment or, to a given degree of approximation, by the agreement of reckoning and experience) requires a consciousness to think it. But in the order of knowledge, the future preserves the past. The rules of truth are not legitimately variable as are aesthetic norms. Knowledge is by its nature incomplete, but it is endlessly accumulated.

It is true that within this history there recurs a sort of dialectic. Is the system built up, or does it, so to speak, exist before the mind? Observing the contingency of men and of circumstances one inclines toward the first hypothesis; retrospectively, there is the tendency to hypostasize the mathematical entities into an ideal cosmos, to project into the real the equations by means of which we grasp it. And yet, is there anything harder to conceive of than the objectivity of our ideas, previous to our thinking? This is a dialectic of scientific development and logical expression, of creation and elaboration, which doubtless constitutes our intelligence.

Whatever the case may be, the approximate and partial truth of a time is preserved at the same that it is surpassed. Whoever devotes himself to positive research, strong in the permanence of his goal, feels his own involvement with an enterprise which is common to humanity and universally valid. He takes part in a progress which, as it moves onward, seems to wipe out the traces of its accidental realization.

Applied to general history, this opposition suggests two questions. How are the singular value of each instant and the supreme value of the whole combined? Is it by science or by art that philosophy is to be inspired?

If the exploration of nature and the creation of masterpieces were the sole end of man, there would be no further interest in social history for itself. It would deserve study only for the influence it exerts on the only essentially historical activities. Such a conclusion would be as fragile as the anthropology upon which it is based. Man is not only a scientist; he is satisfied by no fragmentary function; now, as soon as he asks himself why he wants to live, he sees the whole movement on which both the life he actually leads, and the mission he assigns himself, depend.

* * * *

Each human being is unique, irreplaceable in himself and for a few others, sometimes for humanity itself. And yet history consumes individuals at a frightful rate, a consumption we see no means of avoiding as long as violence is necessary for social changes. Men are sacrificed as means to historical ends, and yet the latter are not above the men; history's goals are necessarily here on earth.

Behaviour ought to be subject to the moral judgment that relates the act to the agent. And this judgment is revealed as ludicrous in face of the monstrous sublimity of history, entirely condemned if measured by the law of love or by the imperative of good will. Must the leader or the master be subject to the common rule? Since he is one among others, how are we to evade the affirmative answer? Since he is accountable for his accomplishment rather than for his conduct, the negative answer is imposed.

This plurality could not be reduced without sacrificing one of the aspects of reality. The quality of souls is not reducible to that of ideas, nor does one judge causes by the devotion of their partisans; all of them, in that case would be sacred. Each personality, each society, is valuable in and by itself in so far as it realizes one of the forms of humanity, but none is entirely closed, none realizes itself totally, all seem to be in search of a final terminus. Is this a collective illusion? Has humanity no other end than the vain creation or achievement of a few individualities?

Thus we come back to the question with which our book closes. Pure historism defeats itself; it dissolves all truth and, finally, history. But moralism would lead to an opposite anarchy, since it would sacrifice action to ethical imperatives and, as it were, societies to justice. There is an antithesis between abstract morality and history, between the moments and the goal. Reflection shows the necessity for it and suggests the ideal solution.

* * * *

There are two ways of denying that man has a history; one is the way of the psychologist, the other that of the moralist. They come together in popular humanism.

The director of a bank or a business is no more greedy than the Chinese merchant or the Jewish usurer. The longing for power would not disappear from a classless society. In all revolutions, the keen observer would see a similar mixture of devotion and meanness, of betrayals of trust and of sacrifices, of cowardliness and enthusiasm. Individuals, freed from the limits imposed by collective discipline, abandoned to their contradictory impulses and their weaknesses, must appear partly the same. Soviet bureaucracy is probably in certain ways comparable to all bureaucracies, as the entourage of dictators is to all courts. The chronicler and the moralist are always right, but they are also always wrong.

The protestant-minded capitalist, never sated with temporal successes but indifferent to pleasures, has nothing in common with the eternal idea of the miser. Love-matches or marriages of convenience characterize a society. Each people has its preferred ideologies, its own way of obeying or rebelling; romanticism and organization, transformation of souls and overthrow of authority, are differently compounded. The communist industrial chief, the union secretary, the member of a political committee, represent original types, not for the characterologist who will place them in his categories or analyse them into already observed elements, but for the historian who is interested in actual life.

Impulses are inseparable from beliefs and social relations, which determine their mode of expression and fixation. The subordination of *mobiles* to *motifs*, going back to the terms we used above, establishes the originality of the historical order and the irreducibility of individual lives to analysis, or to generalities.

He who insists that man has only one way of feeling and acting, then, is wrong because he fails to recognize the diversity of conduct, the depth of sentimental and intellectual differences, the influence of institutions on psychical balance, the changing connections between psychological types and social situations, the presence of historical categories even in the intimacy of the individual. Whatever importance these remarks may be held to have, the constancy of human nature will be justly upheld. The affirmation is frequent in the writings of historians, and valid as long as the main interest is in ways of reacting rather than in systems of knowledge, of values, and of ends. It is certain (as we showed above) that one can see impulses common to all individuals, and laws or mechanisms occurring everywhere which are the mark of specific unity.

But in reality the moralist is not content with this constancy alien to all ethics, more akin to physiology than to mind. He attributes to this schematic being more precise qualities, suggested to him by a certain philosophy. Alain, for example, makes no distinction between the universality of the passions of the soul and that of Cartesian magnanimity. The confusion is necessary in order to give the concept of man the richness and prestige of which it would be stripped if it appeared as the ideal type of an anatomic and instinctive constitution. The confusion is nonetheless inadmissible. Whether it is a question of collective organization, of conception of the world or even of the categories of reason, simple observation proves the changes. Let us admit that the categories are gradually organized into a definitely valid system, that man's situation, with regard to metaphysics, is basically the same at all times; the fact still remains that the answers given to the one question vary with the evolution of the sciences, of religions, and of societies. Would, then, this change be external to man who, indifferent and unchangeable, would witness the procession of his ephemeral works? In truth, eternal man would be either above or below humanized man, an animal, or a god.

Why is so much energy spent in maintaining this unchangeableness of mankind, an expression which takes, on the lips of unbelievers, a solemn and almost sacred tone? Doubtless they wish to preserve one of the elements of the Christian heritage, the foundation of modern democracy, the absolute value of the soul, the presence in all men of an identical reason. By the same token they hope to devalue the particularities of class, nation, and race, in order to arrive at a total reconciliation of men, in themselves and with each other.

Does rationalism, in the absence of religious dogma, give a sufficient justification? Does it resist the criticism of the biologist and the sociologist, who show races, and perhaps classes and individuals, unequally gifted, nations definitely singularized by their histories? Is it still, today, an object of living faith? In any case, it does not authorize withdrawing man from history. The capacity for judgment is formed gradually; it has been gradually recognized in each individual.

Absolute universality can only be final or entirely abstract (based on the determination of rules or of formal tendencies). Reason is not pre-existent to the exploration of nature, nor beauty to the conscious minds which realize or experience it, nor man to the creation of States, to the elaboration of the spiritual universes, to the increase of knowledge and the conscious awareness of all his works. In this sense, the formula 'man is an unfinished history', far from being provocative or paradoxical, is rather vulgar because of its banality.

Thus understood, the formula restores reasonable meaning to the optimism which the ideologies of progress threatened to disqualify. The hope of improvement becomes intelligible. The proportion of goodness and wickedness, of unselfishness and egoism, in each and in all is hardly likely to change, but individuals will show unequal qualities or faults, according to the hierarchy of classes, standards of life or modes of authority. They will accumulate fewer resentments if they consent more to their fates, if they free themselves from complexes arising from prejudices or from collective interdictions. Without being different in his innermost soul, man in a changed environment might reveal a new face.

Yet this would be a result and not the goal, which the psychologist is unable to determine. What should this changed environment be? What different existence? We come back once again to the question we regard as inevitable, without answering it (a thing which would be impossible in a study limited as is this one). The discussion between systems of metaphysics and ideologies proves, at least within a certain culture, a community which calls for a search for truth.

This truth ought to be above the plurality of activities and values, otherwise it would drop back to the level of particular and contradictory wills. It should be concrete, otherwise, like ethical norms, it would remain on the threshold of action. It should be both theoretical and practical, in the image of the goal conceived by Marxism. By means of the power gained over nature, man would arrive at an equal control of the social order. Thanks to participation in the two collective works, the State which makes each individual a citizen, the culture which makes the common heritage accessible to all, he would realize his mission: the conciliation of mankind and nature, of essence and existence. The ideal is of course indefinite, since participation and reconciliation are variously conceived, but at least it would be neither angelic nor abstract. Animality, both individual and social, is still, in history, a condition and an integral part of the decision. And in the final state, the living man, animal and spiritual, should be made one in himself and integrated with the community.

* * * *

This final state would be tantamount to a Utopia if it were not linked with the consciousness of the present and with reflection on the development, if it were not indispensable for any philosophy. Conceptions of the world, at first sight, express a human attitude, but historical anthropology undergoes in its turn the interpretation which it inflicts on systems by relinking them with their psychological and historical origins. Inevitably, free reflection is re-established, above committed thinking. But reflection, to reach beyond the experience of life, to the essence, must either limit itself to the eternal condition and thus still be impoverished and formal, or show the truth of the evolution—that is, determine an end. Once more, philosophy and history, philosophy of history and total philosophy, are inseparable. Philosophy, also, is in history to begin with since it is contained within the bounds of a particular being. It is historical, since it is the soul or expression of a time; it is history since it is the conscious grasp of an unfinished creation. Philosophy is the radical question which man, in search of truth, addresses to himself.

IV. HISTORICAL TIME AND FREEDOM

THERE IS nothing either below or beyond the development; humanity merges with its history, the individual with his duration. Such in a few words is the conclusion of the foregoing studies, which are completed and summed up by the description of temporal existence. This description we shall reduce to two essential features: the relations of temporal dimensions, and freedom in time.

* * * *

The experience of duration is both that of the continuous and that of the present. Actuality embraces a field wide enough for the passage of time to be experienced, and for the past to be extended into the future without going beyond the limits of the fullness of experience. The qualitative diversity composes into an unending progression.

These immediate data could be the origin and model of a whole philosophy. The type of the free act is the artist's creation. Sincerity requires that one remain at each moment contemporary with oneself. True morality arises from the depths of the being, beyond the limits of intelligence. Spirituality retains the character of the vital impulse, mysticism seems to prolong the primary intuition, consciousness grows wider until it coincides with the divine principle.

We should like to note briefly the contrasting features of a historical philosophy. Life's essence and goal is not total reconciliation, but an ever renewed action, an unending struggle. The novelty of the development is only the elementary form, the condition so to speak of freedom properly human, which unfolds throughout the contradictions and struggles. The contrast is connected with the fundamental antinomy between duration and historical time, defined not by the actuality, but by the tension between a double futurity.

Historical meaning is often confused with the cult of tradition or the taste for the past. In fact, for the individual as for collectivities, the future is the primary category. The old man with nothing but memories is as alien to history as the child absorbed in a present without memory. To know oneself, just as to know the collective development, the decisive act is the one which transcends the real, which restores to what no longer is a sort of reality by giving it a continuation and a goal.

The historical present, then, does not possess the richness of contemplation or of total accord, but neither is it reduced to the elusive point of an abstract representation. It at first merges with experience, with what is not consciously thought and remains by nature inaccessible to all thought. For reflection it is an intermediary, the last phase of what no longer is, an approach to what will be. The time we are living is defined for us by the trends we discern in it. Formerly, perhaps, for peoples without any historical consciousness, it was a closed totality, today it is the moment of an evolution, the means of a conquest, the origin of a will. To live historically is to locate oneself with reference to a double transcendency.

Each of the temporal dimensions is the object of the most varied feelings. Our past is still an integral part of ourselves, not only because it has formed us, but because it is transfigured by feelings we have with regard to it. Now it reminds us of another being whom we scarcely recognize, now it awakens feelings we had thought dead, or revives buried sufferings. Whether impoverished, since we are no longer what we have been, or enriched by our experiences, we learn, from the memory of times past, neither the flight, nor the permanence of things, nor the fruitfulness of duration; or at least those contradictory values depend on present life.

Each dimension is on this account no less characterized and as it were defined by a human attitude. The past is dependent on knowing, the future on will, it is not to be observed but created. One single affection is essentially linked with our temporal career, the remorse which shows us our act at the same time as a fact, that is definitely real, and as a duty, that is free. In tragic helplessness we still feel the obligation we evaded. The fault belongs to what no longer is, since it is the object of knowledge, and we continue to deny it as if it did not yet exist.

The example is instructive: the characteristic attitude of one temporal dimension can be assumed with regard to any fragment of history. Thus one strives to restore to ancient events the uncertainty of action. Or, on the other hand, one views the whole movement as predetermined. The vain and implacable law of the eternal return would denote the conclusion of this fatalistic consideration. As for the pure narrative, it would rob time of depth and quality, to reduce it to the indefinite line upon which are strung, spatially, the memories told like beads by those who have given up volition.

True history retains simultaneously the two terms, regularities and accidents, and looks not for a synthesis of them, but for their interweaving, as expressed in the developing determinism. All dogmatists, prophets or scientists, look upon the development as if it were already accomplished, as if they themselves were above it. But the historian is a man, and man always lives as though he were free, even when he speaks as though he considered himself bound.

The historian, like each one of us, transfigures the past by the way he looks at it. But does not the metaphysical question, which we set aside in order to analyse fragmentary necessity, again come up? Is not one of the contradictory images the true one?

We have shown, in knowledge of self and of history, the gap separating duration from the later reconstruction. Those who deny freedom always manage to neglect this opposition, to confuse the motives with the forces which should inevitably cause the decision to be arrived at, the causes conceptually elaborated with a preceding determination. In this sense, our criticism is inspired by the Bergsonian analysis, since we have returned to the antithesis of the event and the retrospective illusions, of what is being done and what has been done. The contemporary impression of contingency is the immediate datum.

But it is not yet a proof. The determinism is built up gradually, always retrospective and partial, but the forecasts, limited or abstract, of the behaviours of others as social events, are verified. Does not this success lend a certain likelihood to the hypothesis of the whole determinism, a hypothesis which transcends our knowledge by reason of the qualitative diversity of the connected terms and of the fragmentary quality of the causal relations? Moreover, does not the spontaneous and organic evolution, of persons and of collectivities, sanction the fatality of character, of heredity, or of circumstances, rather than the power of novelty? Is not our innermost being principally our given being? If we are our development, we are not slaves of a past which, as we retrace its course, escapes us more and more?

Freedom, according to Bergson's doctrine, is based on the perpetual diversity of successive experiences. It remains to change the possibility into reality, or at least to describe concretely the freedom to which man is to aspire and can attain. Between the nothingness of what is already past and that of the not-yet, how are the contradictory demands of permanence and change to be met?

* * * *

In opposition to the fluctuations of caprice, the will represents stability, which differentiates the engagement of the impulses or of blind feelings. But how can I commit myself without perhaps condemning myself to insincerity? I do not know whether I shall still feel tomorrow what I feel today. The right to change denotes first of all the claim of life against thought or decision, which claim absolute immutability.

But it would be dangerous to confuse assent to the past with the triumph of personal strength. The formation of the psychological nature, psychoanalysis has definitely shown, is a history in which first impressions often exercise an unconscious tyranny. Allegedly considered actions often express directly or indirectly, by transference or by compensation, a rejected tendency. All neurotics cling to their neuroses; deliverance comes with the consciousness which breaks with childish illusions, recognizes the world for what it is and not as children dream it or parents describe it.

Finally, even more in the order of the mind, freedom is inconceivable without conversion. We have received from others or from our heredity what we believe we think. To justify during one's whole life one's rages or youthful convictions is to enslave oneself to outer accidents or to one's temperament. Here again one must renew oneself in order to choose.

In moral order, remorse calls for conversion, commitment for fidelity. People often imagine a gradual healing of the bad conscience which little by little assimilates, as it were, the fault and finally finds serenity again. Suffering is appeased in forgiveness. But, in this change an essential virtue is lacking; the material fact perhaps still persists. The conscience reconciled with itself, as long as the results of the evil continue, would resemble a Pharisaical conscience. The transfiguration of the past in and through memories must follow the redemption by action which wipes out or compensates. Generally, liberation changes either the reality which comes from old decisions, or the individuals themselves.

Fidelity could not consist of feigning sentiments which no longer exist. Even lasting love is not fixed. One follows its inevitable development as soon as one has the courage to observe the true experiences instead of clinging to words or to a complacent representation of oneself. Not that it is reduced to the rare moments when one experiences its reality (between these moments there still exists the receptivity to joy or pain), but it would decompose into attitudes and contradictory impressions unless the will upheld the actual unity of it. When the affections have died out, one can still show by one's conduct that one has neither forgotten nor repudiated. Between the sincerity which desires instability and the constancy of obstinacy or blindness, there is still room for the double effort of sincerity and genuineness.

This solution will doubtless seem insufficient and vague, since it limits itself at bottom to pointing out the contradictions of life. But faced with these contradictions, common to all, each finds himself alone, and each one works out his solution. Total fidelity would be pledged only to a superior being whom one could not abandon without betraying oneself, for faithfulness to self is either short of decisions in the psycho-physiological individuality, or else it admits of renewal.

Historically there is no revolution which, like any conversion, does not at the same time change the environment and the individuals. There is a dual liberation; from the real, which is a continuation of the past, and from the past itself, different since it leads to another future and because it appears to a new point of view. In the same way, there would be room to study the meaning and value of historical fidelity, equally unrecognized by revolutionaries until, certain of victory, they re-adopt tradition, and by conservatives who confuse it with immobility. Fidelity is as hard to specify abstractly for nations as for individuals, and is even more indispensable for nations since peoples, in depth, seem to stay like themselves, definitely stamped, by their history, or by nature, for a unique destiny.

Neither permanence of will nor the change in life characterizes or defines freedom. This is a foregone conclusion if it is true that freedom is not demonstrable and that it belongs to the order of the mind. The theories which deny it are refuted, their uncertainty and their contradiction with the internal evidence are demonstrated. Beyond is the action in which alone it is experienced. Now properly human and intellectual action implies that the individual sticks consciously to his line of conduct. The dialectic time of history rises above duration (collectivities also obscurely live out their development). The essential thing is still the double detachment of reflection and of choice, which divides the person from itself, but frees it, through thought, for the search for the truth.

Above, we contrasted continuity with discontinuity, as we did the accumulation of vital experiences with the momentariness of the voluntary regrasp. In fact, we met several times with the opposition of the evolution and the breaks. In a formal sense, the opposition corresponds to that of events and regularities. Concretely, the evolution appears successively as the erosion of institutions, the impoverishment of races and peoples, or, on the contrary, the progress of technical means. As for the breaks, they are military disasters or social upsets which suddenly reveal a latent crisis, or again great works, apparently solitary, which rise up from the nameless crowds and reveal to men their unexpressed feelings. The antithesis is valid for all movements, at all the levels of reality.

It nonetheless retains an essential meaning for life. Because he is at once both brute and spirit, man must be capable of overcoming minor fatalities, those of the passions by will power, that of blind impulse by consciousness, that of vague thought by decision. In this way, freedom, at each instant, puts everything at stake again, and asserts itself in action in which man is reunited with himself.

* * * *

Liberty, possible in theory, effective in and through practice, is never complete. The past of the individual limits the margin in which personal initiative is effective, the historical situation fixes the possibilities of political action. Choice and decision do not rise from obscurity; perhaps they are subject to the most elementary drives, in any case partially determined if they are referred to their antecedents.

Only thought would rightfully escape the causal explanation, to the extent to which it confirms its independence by verifying its judgments. But learning, ever devoted to the exploration of objects and by essential nature incomplete, is always surpassed. Now, for man to be in entire harmony with himself, he would have to live according to the truth, he would have to recognize himself as autonomous both in his creation and in his consciousness of it. This would be an ideal reconciliation, incompatible with the destiny of those who do not set up an idol in the place of God.

Human life is dialectic, that is, dramatic, since it is active in an incoherent world, is committed despite duration, and seeks a fleeting truth, with no other certainty but a fragmentary science and a formal reflection.[69]

[69] A philosophical inquiry, partial as this one is, allows no conclusion. So, this Section ends with this chapter. The omission is inevitable and intentional. The whole of this final *Part* transposes into anthropological terms the results already obtained and in itself represents a sort of conclusion, since it shows the meaning for life of the abstract propositions previously demonstrated. Moreover, in the three *Parts* of the last Section, we have again met with the same fundamental antinomy between historical perspectives, and philosophical considerations of history, ideologies and the progressive truth of retrospection, particularity of decisions and universality of vocation. We could not go further than this without concretely interpreting the present situation of man and philosophy. Surely this book is explained by this situation; its purpose is to make possible the understanding of it. But that would be the object of another book.

INDEX